THE LIFE TABLE
AND
ITS APPLICATIONS

THE LIFE TABLE
AND
ITS APPLICATIONS

CHIN LONG CHIANG

Professor of Biostatistics
University of California, Berkeley

ROBERT E. KRIEGER PUBLISHING COMPANY
MALABAR, FLORIDA
1984

Original Edition **1984**

Printed and Published by
ROBERT E. KRIEGER PUBLISHING COMPANY, INC.
KRIEGER DRIVE
MALABAR, FL 32950

Printed in the United States of America

**Library of Congress Cataloging in
Publication Data**

Chiang, Chin Long
  The life table and its applications.

  Bibliography: p.
  Includes index.
  1. Biostatistics
  2. Demography
  3. Health Statistics
  4. Actuarial sciences. I. Title.
HB1322.C47 1983 312'.2   82-20331
ISBN 0-89874-570-5

To

J. Yerushalmy

Development of this manuscript was made possible with the
support of
United Nations Fund for Population Activities
and World Health Organization

Foreword

In the mid-1970's, the World Health Organization, with the support of the United Nations Fund for Population Activities, initiated a new series of teaching aids which addressed themselves to a wide spectrum of professionals in public health, medical research, statistics and demography. The first publication in this series, the Manual of Mortality Analysis, focused on basic methods which are commonly used in national offices of vital statistics. At the same time, the World Health Organization was fortunate to secure the assistance of Professor Chin Long Chiang, an outstanding authority in the application of the stochastic approach to the studying of death processes, to contribute a complementary book on more sophisticated methods of mortality analysis. Like the first one, this book, Life Tables and Mortality Analysis, soon was out of print. In view of this encouraging reception, the World Health Organization asked Professor Chiang to update his book for a second edition. However, in the course of the work, it was soon discovered that a mere updating would not be sufficient to meet the growing demand for a publication which combined mathematical elegance with the lucid exposition of the fundamentals of mathematical reasoning in a way which appeals also to readers who are less familiar with higher mathematics. The outcome of this effort has been what constitutes an essentially new book "The Life Table and its Applications". Not only have certain defects been corrected which have been brought to light by experience in its application to instruction but also account has been taken of new developments in this rapidly expanding area. Professor Chiang has drawn on his vast experience to demonstrate the applicability of the life table technique to the study of a wide range of problems in the social and medical sciences. The new textbook thus constitutes a fortunate combination of solid theoretical foundation with "down to earth" application in practice. It should be of use not only as a teaching aid but also for self-instruction particularly to those who want to keep abreast of new developments and apply them in their everyday work.

August 5, 1982
Dr. Harald Hansluwka
Chief Statistician
Global Epidemiological Surveillance and
    Health Situation Assessment
World Health Organization, Geneva

Preface

Traditionally, the life table was used primarily in the actuarial science for analysis of life contingencies and in demography to study population changes. Adequate mathematics had been provided in line with activities in these fields. Gompertz (1825) and Makeham (1867) derived "mortality laws" to ease computation of annuities and premiums. Euler (1760) introduced the concept of stationary population which has been used as the basis for population projections. And Lotka (1922) proposed the intrinsic rate of natural increase for the measurement of population growth. At the turn of the century, U.S. Government agencies began to apply life table methodology to vital statistics and census data for the purpose of summarizing the mortality experience of the current population. These activities continued but they remained outside the domain of statistics proper, and the potential of the life table as an analytic tool was not recognized for the next 50 years.

Due primarily to the work of health statisticians in medical follow-up studies in the early 1950's, the life table has begun to attract the attention of biostatisticians. But it was advances in probability and statistical theory that made it possible to address the life table from a purely stochastic point of view and to provide the subject with a theoretical foundation. We can now use the life table for survival analysis and make statistical inference about the elements in the table and about other parameters underlying the mortality pattern of a study population. "Life table analysis" has emerged as a rigorous and exact statistical method. In fact, life table analysis is unique in the statistical field in that given the survival experience of a sample of individuals, there is a sequence of sample means in the expectations of life $(\hat{e}_0, \hat{e}_1, \ldots)$, and sequences of sample proportions in $(\hat{q}_0, \hat{q}_1, \ldots)$ and $(\hat{p}_{01}, \hat{p}_{02}, \ldots)$. These sample values are maximum likelihood estimators of the corresponding mathematical expectations and probabilities with optimum properties.

A recent development in survival analysis takes into account the fact that many chronic conditions advance in stages from mild through intermediate stages to severe to death. The force of mortality varies with the stage of the disease. The morbid process is often irreversible but a patient may die while being in any one of the stages. When the concept of the staging process is introduced to the life table framework, we find a new life table where age intervals are not predetermined and are subject to variation; indeed they are random variables. The new life table has applications in many fields of research where the concept of staging can be defined and the end result need not be death. The new table is presented in the last chapter of this book. Its application is illustrated with a fertility table for the analysis of human reproduction.

The purpose of this book is to present both the theory and application of life table methodology from a statistical perspective. The theoretical treatment of the subject by necessity involves some mathematics, while the remainder of the book is presented in a way that needs no prerequisite in statistics. To provide some background knowledge and for easy reference, three chapters are devoted to preliminaries: Chapter 1 on elements of probability, Chapter 2 on fundamental concepts of statistics, and Chapter 3 on the normal distribution and statistical inference. Since usually the sample size in a life table is large, one can invoke the central limit theorem and use the normal distribution and the chi-square test for statistical estimation and hypothesis testing for the biometric functions in the life table.

Mortality rates and adjustment of rates are akin to the life table; they are presented in Chapters 4 and 5, respectively. The complete life table and the abridged life table are described separately in Chapter 6 and Chapter 7 merely for convenience and completeness, but a certain amount of repetition has occurred as a result. Statistical inference regarding the life table functions illustrated in Chapter 8 is based essentially on the statistical methods described in Chapter 3. Chapter 9 covers two separate topics: a description of the cohort life table and some applications of the life table. The latter is not entirely within the domain of the cohort life table, in particular the antenatal life table in Section 5 and the family life cycle in Section 7.

The theory of the life table in Chapter 10 should be of interest to mathematical statisticians for exercise in statistical theory and to actuaries and demographers whose work is closely related to the life table, but it may be omitted at first reading for those readers who use the life table mainly for applications. In Chapter 11, which concerns medical follow-up studies, a number of formulas for the estimate of the survival probabilities are given. Regrettably, appropriate data to demonstrate the use of every one of these formulas were not available. However, the data on the survival experience of certain cancer patients in a frequency form were kindly furnished by the Resource for Cancer Epidemiology of the California State Department of Health Services. The final chapter is devoted to the aforementioned new life table. Some theoretical background and an application of the table for the analysis of human reproduction are given.

This book may be used as a text for a semester or a quarter course in health statistics using the following chapters:

Chapters 1, 2, 3, 4, 5, 7, 8, 9, 11, 12 (section 6).

It may also be used as a reference book for courses in epidemiology, demography, biostatistics, or actuarial science.

I wish to acknowledge my indebtedness to a number of friends whose encouragement and help have made the publication of this book possible: to H. Hansluwka of the World Health Organization who initiated the idea of a manual on the life table and mortality analysis; to B. J. van den Berg for consultation on fetal and infant mortality, and for her permission to use our joint work on fertility analysis as an illustrative example in Chapter 12; to C. Langhauser for her help in preparing all the statistical tables and computations; to J. Hughes who has read an early version of the book; to my son Robert who wrote the computer programs; and to my students at the University of California, Berkeley, who "proofread" the manuscript. Finally, my deep appreciation is due to B. Hutchings who has carried out every administrative aspect of the preparation of the manuscript with efficiency and proficiency.

University of California, Berkeley   Chin Long Chiang
March, 1983

Table of Contents

CHAPTER *1*

Elements of Probability

1. Introduction

A good understanding of the basic concept of probability is fundamental to proper analysis of mortality data. Because of its potential as an analytic tool, probability theory has been increasingly used in analyses of vital statistics and life tables. Studies of vital data are no longer limited to a mere description of tables or interpretation of numerical values; statistical inference can be made regarding mortality and survival patterns of an entire population. Although it is a mathematical concept, probability has an interesting intuitive appeal. Many natural phenomena can be described by means of the laws of probability; occurrences of daily events also seem to follow a definite pattern. Even such spontaneous events as accidents can be predicted in advance with a certain degree of accuracy. Probabilistic mortality laws were proposed by B. Gompertz in 1825 and revised by W. M. Makeham in 1867, and have been used ever since in studies of human survival and death in the field of public health, in demography, and in the actuarial sciences. We begin this volume by introducing the fundamental concept of probability, some related formulas, and illustrative examples.

2. Fundamental Concept

2.1. Components of a probability. The concept of probability involves three components: (a) a random experiment, (b) possible outcomes of that experiment, and (c) an event of interest. A random experiment is an experiment that has a number of possible outcomes, any one of which *may* occur when the experiment is performed, although precisely which one *will* occur is not known. Thus, when discussing probability, one must have in mind a random experiment under consideration and an event of interest.

2.2.   Definition of probability.   The probability of the occurrence of event A in an experiment ("the probability of A" for short) is defined as the ratio of the number of outcomes where event A occurs to the total number of possible outcomes.

Suppose that a random experiment may result in a number n of possible (and equally likely) outcomes, and in $n(A)$ of these outcomes event A occurs. Then the probability of event A is defined as follows:

$$\Pr\{A\} = \frac{n(A)}{n}. \tag{2.1}$$

Thus, the probability of event A in a random experiment is a measure of the likelihood of the occurrence in event A.

2.3.   Illustrative examples.   The following examples elucidate the concept of probability.

Example 1.   In tossing a fair coin once, what is the probability of a head turning up? Here the random experiment is *tossing a fair coin once*; the possible outcomes are a head and a tail; the event A is "the coin lands heads up". The number of possible outcomes is $n = 2$, and the number of outcomes where a head occurs is $n(A) = 1$. Therefore, the probability is

$$\Pr\{A\} = \frac{n(A)}{n} = \frac{1}{2}.$$

Example 2.   In rolling a fair die once, there are six possible outcomes. Let event A be "3 dots show". Here $n = 6$ and $n(A) = 1$; therefore

$$\Pr\{A\} = \frac{n(A)}{n} = \frac{1}{6}.$$

Let event B be "an even number of dots appear"; then $n(B) = 3$, since event B occurs when the die shows a two, a four, or a six. The probability of B is:

$$\Pr\{B\} = \frac{n(B)}{n} = \frac{3}{6} = \frac{1}{2}.$$

Example 3.   The names of 39 women and 81 men appear on a list. One name is picked at random from this list of 120. Let event F

be "a female name is chosen", and event M be "a male name is chosen". The corresponding probabilities are

$$\Pr\{F\} = \frac{n(F)}{n} = \frac{39}{120} = \frac{13}{40} \quad \text{and} \quad \Pr\{M\} = \frac{n(M)}{n} = \frac{81}{120} = \frac{27}{40}$$

and their sum

$$\Pr\{F\} + \Pr\{M\} = \frac{13}{40} + \frac{27}{40} = 1.$$

Example 4. A list of $n = 100$ names consists of $n(s) = 98$ names of survivors and $n(d) = 2$ of those who have died. A name is drawn at random from the list. The probability that the name drawn will be that of a survivor is

$$\Pr\{s\} = \frac{n(s)}{n} = \frac{98}{100} = .98,$$

and that it will be the name of one who has died is

$$\Pr\{d\} = \frac{n(d)}{n} = \frac{2}{100} = .02.$$

Clearly, the sum of the two probabilities is unity:

$$\Pr\{s\} + \Pr\{d\} = .98 + .02 = 1.$$

2.4. Values of a probability. We see from the definition that the probability of an event is an idealized proportion (or relative frequency) of the occurrence of that event. Thus, a probability can only take on values between zero and one, i.e.,

$$0 \leqslant \Pr\{A\} \leqslant 1, \tag{2.2}$$

for any event A.

2.5. Sure event and impossible event. A sure event is an event that always occurs in an experiment. If I is a sure event, then

$$\Pr\{I\} = 1. \tag{2.3}$$

An impossible event is an event that never occurs in an experiment. If $\emptyset$ is an impossible event, then

$$\Pr\{\emptyset\} = 0. \tag{2.4}$$

2.6. Complement (or negation) of an event. In Example 3, event F (female name) is the complement of event M (male name) in the sense

Table 1. Examples of an event and its complement

Experiment	A	$\overline{A}$
Sex of a baby	baby is a boy	baby is a girl
Toss of a coin	heads	tails
Toss of a die	3 dots	anything but 3 dots
Toss of a die	even no. of dots	odd no. of dots
Survival analysis	survival	death

that event F occurs when and only when event M does not occur. By the same token, in Example 4, event s (survival) is the complement of event d (death). The notion of the complement of an event can be further illustrated by a few more examples in Table 1. The symbol $\overline{A}$ denotes the complement of event A.

When event $\overline{A}$ is the complement of event A, then event A is the complement of event $\overline{A}$. The two events are said to be complementary to each other.

In a random experiment the total number of outcomes can be divided into two groups according to the occurrence of A or of $\overline{A}$,

$$n = n(A) + n(\overline{A}).$$

The probability of $\overline{A}$ in a random experiment is, by definition,

$$\Pr\{\overline{A}\} = \frac{n(\overline{A})}{n}.$$

So it is clear that, whatever event A may be,

$$\Pr\{A\} + \Pr\{\overline{A}\} = \frac{n(A)}{n} + \frac{n(\overline{A})}{n} = 1, \tag{2.5}$$

or

$$\Pr\{\overline{A}\} = 1 - \Pr\{A\}. \tag{2.5a}$$

In words, the probability of the complement of A is equal to the complement of the probability of A. In Example 3, the probability of event F and the probability of event M have the relationship

$$\Pr\{F\} = 1 - \Pr\{M\} \quad \text{or} \quad \frac{13}{40} = 1 - \frac{27}{40}.$$

3. Two or More Events—Multiplication Theorem

For simplicity we have introduced the basic concept of probability in terms of a single event. We now discuss the probability of two or more events.

3.1.   Composite event (A and B).   Given event A and event B, we define a composite event, "A and B" (or $A \times B$, or $A \cap B$, or AB for short), by saying that the event AB occurs if both event A and event B occur.

Example 5.   Consider a group of 800 children divided according to sex and congenital abnormality. Let A = abnormal, $\overline{A}$ = normal, B = boy, and $\overline{B}$ = girl. The composition of the children with respect to sex and abnormality is shown in Table 2:

Table 2. Distribution of 800 children by sex and by a congenital abnormality (hypothetical data)

Congenital Abnormality	Boy B	Girl $\overline{B}$	Marginal Row Total
Abnormal	70	50	120
A	$n(AB)$	$n(A\overline{B})$	$n(A)$
Normal	330	350	680
$\overline{A}$	$n(\overline{A}B)$	$n(\overline{A}\,\overline{B})$	$n(\overline{A})$
Marginal Column Total	400	400	800
	$n(B)$	$n(\overline{B})$	n

Suppose that a child is picked at random from the group. What is the probability that the child picked is a congenitally abnormal boy? Here the composite event is AB and the probability is

$$\Pr\{AB\} = \frac{n(AB)}{n}$$

$$= \frac{70}{800}. \tag{3.1}$$

Other possible composite events are:

$$A\overline{B} = \text{a congenitally abnormal girl,}$$

$$\overline{A}B = \text{a normal boy,}$$

$$\overline{A}\overline{B} = \text{a normal girl.}$$

The probabilities $\Pr\{A\overline{B}\}$, $\Pr\{\overline{A}B\}$, and $\Pr\{\overline{A}\overline{B}\}$ can be computed similarly from the above table.

3.2.   Conditional Probability.   The probability of B occurring given that A has occurred is called "the conditional probability of B given A", and is written as $\Pr\{B \mid A\}$, where the vertical line "$\mid$" between B and A means "given" while the event to the right of "$\mid$" is the condition. (See §6.1 for comments on when this notion is meaningful.) It is given by

$$\Pr\{B|A\} = \frac{\Pr\{AB\}}{\Pr\{A\}}. \tag{3.2}$$

Since

$$\Pr\{AB\} = \frac{n(AB)}{n} \quad \text{and} \quad \Pr\{A\} = \frac{n(A)}{n},$$

we have

$$\Pr\{B|A\} = \frac{n(AB)/n}{n(A)/n} = \frac{n(AB)}{n(A)}. \tag{3.3}$$

Continuing the previous example, $\Pr\{B|A\}$ is the probability that a child chosen at random *from the abnormal children* will be a boy. Since there are $n(A) = 120$ abnormal children, and among them $n(AB) = 70$ are boys, we have

$$\Pr\{B|A\} = \frac{n(AB)}{n(A)} = \frac{70}{120},$$

or, using

$$\Pr\{AB\} = \frac{n(AB)}{n} = \frac{70}{800} \quad \text{and} \quad \Pr\{A\} = \frac{n(A)}{n} = \frac{120}{800}$$

and

$$\Pr\{B|A\} = \frac{\Pr\{AB\}}{\Pr\{A\}} = \frac{70/800}{120/800} = \frac{70}{120},$$

we obtain the same value.

Exercise. Use the above example to compute and interpret the following conditional probabilities: $\Pr\{A|B\}$, $\Pr\{B|\overline{A}\}$, $\Pr\{\overline{A}|B\}$, $\Pr\{\overline{B}|A\}$, $\Pr\{A|\overline{B}\}$, $\Pr\{\overline{A}|\overline{B}\}$, and $\Pr\{\overline{B}|\overline{A}\}$.

3.3. Independence. Event A is said to be independent of event B if the conditional probability of A given B is equal to the (absolute) probability of A. In symbols,

$$\Pr\{A|B\} = \Pr\{A\}. \tag{3.4}$$

This means that the likelihood of the occurrence of A is not influenced by the occurrence of B. Clearly, if A is independent of B, then A is also independent of $\overline{B}$, i.e.,

$$\Pr\{A|B\} = \Pr\{A\} = \Pr\{A|\overline{B}\}. \tag{3.5}$$

To ascertain whether an event A is independent of an event B in a particular problem, we compute separately

$$\Pr\{A \mid B\} \quad \text{and} \quad \Pr\{A\}.$$

If the two numerical values are equal, we say that A is independent of B.

Let A = congenital abnormality, B = boy. If it were true that

$$\Pr\{\text{abnormal child} \mid \text{boy}\} = \Pr\{\text{abnormal child}\},$$

then it would follow that

$$\Pr\{\text{abnormal child} \mid \text{girl}\} = \Pr\{\text{abnormal child}\}$$

and we would say that congenital abnormality is independent of the sex of the child.

In Example 5, section 3.1,

$$\Pr\{A \mid B\} = \frac{70}{400} \quad \text{and} \quad \Pr\{A\} = \frac{120}{800}$$

Since $70/400$ is *not* equal to $120/800$, congenital abnormality is dependent on the sex of the child according to the information given in this example.*

3.4.   Multiplication Theorem.   *The probability of the event AB is equal to the product of the probability of A and the conditional probability of B given A, or*

$$\Pr\{AB\} = \Pr\{A\} \times \Pr\{B \mid A\}. \tag{3.6}$$

Proof.

$$\Pr\{AB\} = \frac{n(AB)}{n} = \frac{n(A)}{n} \times \frac{n(AB)}{n(A)}$$

$$= \Pr\{A\} \times \Pr\{B \mid A\}.$$

For example, in Table 2 of Example 5, we see that

$$\Pr\{AB\} = \frac{70}{800}$$

and

$$\Pr\{A\} \times \Pr\{B \mid A\} = \frac{120}{800} \times \frac{70}{120} = \frac{70}{800};$$

therefore

$$\Pr\{AB\} = \Pr\{A\} \times \Pr\{B \mid A\}.$$

---

*See the Chi-square test for the significance of the difference (Chapter 3, section 4, page 65).

Since the event AB is the same as the event BA, the multiplication theorem has an alternative formula:

$$\Pr\{AB\} = \Pr\{B\} \times \Pr\{A\,|\,B\}. \tag{3.7}$$

The formulas of the multiplication theorem for three and four events are

$$\Pr\{ABC\} = \Pr\{A\} \times \Pr\{B\,|\,A\} \times \Pr\{C\,|\,AB\} \tag{3.8}$$

and

$$\Pr\{ABCD\} = \Pr\{A\} \times \Pr\{B\,|\,A\} \times \Pr\{C\,|\,AB\} \times \Pr\{D\,|\,ABC\}. \tag{3.9}$$

The proof is by repeated substitution of (3.6). For example

$$\Pr\{ABC\} = \Pr\{A\}\Pr\{BC\,|\,A\}$$
$$= \Pr\{A\}\Pr\{B\,|\,A\}\Pr\{C\,|\,AB\}.$$

3.5. Multiplication theorem when events are independent. If the events are independent, then the formulas of the multiplication theorem become

$$\Pr\{AB\} = \Pr\{A\} \times \Pr\{B\}, \tag{3.10}$$

$$\Pr\{ABC\} = \Pr\{A\} \times \Pr\{B\} \times \Pr\{C\}, \tag{3.11}$$

$$\Pr\{ABCD\} = \Pr\{A\} \times \Pr\{B\} \times \Pr\{C\} \times \Pr\{D\}. \tag{3.12}$$

For example, if B is independent of A, then $\Pr\{B\,|\,A\} = \Pr\{B\}$; formula (3.6) reduces to (3.10).

3.6. Multiplication theorem concerning a sure event or an impossible event. If I is a sure event and A is any event, then

$$\Pr\{AI\} = \Pr\{A\}. \tag{3.13}$$

If $\varnothing$ is an impossible event, then

$$\Pr\{A\varnothing\} = 0. \tag{3.14}$$

3.7. A theorem of (pairwise) independence. *If B is independent of A, then A is independent of B, and A and B are said to be independent events.* Symbolically, the theorem may be stated as follows:

$$\text{If}\quad \Pr\{B\,|\,A\} = \Pr\{B\}\quad \text{then}\quad \Pr\{A\,|\,B\} = \Pr\{A\}.$$

Proof. If $\Pr(B) = 0$ or $\Pr(A) = 0$, then the theorem is evident, since an impossible event is independent of any other event. If not, then according to (3.6) and (3.7) in the multiplication theorem,

$$\Pr\{AB\} = \Pr\{A\} \times \Pr\{B \,|\, A\} \text{ and } \Pr\{AB\} = \Pr\{B\} \times \Pr\{A \,|\, B\}.$$

It follows that

$$\Pr\{A\} \times \Pr\{B \,|\, A\} = \Pr\{B\} \times \Pr\{A \,|\, B\}. \qquad (3.15)$$

If B is independent of A, then $\Pr\{B \,|\, A\} = \Pr\{B\}; (3.15)$ now becomes

$$\Pr\{A\} \times \Pr\{B\} = \Pr\{B\} \times \Pr\{A \,|\, B\},$$

and consequently, dividing by $\Pr\{B\}$,

$$\Pr\{A\} = \Pr\{A \,|\, B\}.$$

Conversely, if B is dependent on A, then A is dependent on B. In Example 5, Section 3.1,

$$\Pr\{B \,|\, A\} = \frac{70}{120}, \quad \Pr\{B\} = \frac{400}{800} \quad \text{and} \quad \Pr\{B \,|\, A\} \neq \Pr\{B\},$$

so that B is dependent on A, while

$$\Pr\{A \,|\, B\} = \frac{70}{400}, \quad \Pr\{A\} = \frac{120}{800} \quad \text{and} \quad \Pr\{A \,|\, B\} \neq \Pr\{A\},$$

so that A is dependent on B.

4.   Two or More Events—Addition Theorem

4.1.   Composite event (A or B).   By a composite event (A or B) we mean either A, or B, or both. Thus event (A or B) occurs if either A occurs, or B occurs, or AB occurs.

4.2.   Mutual exclusion.   Two events are said to be mutually exclusive if the occurrence of one implies the non-occurrence of the other; in other words, they cannot occur simultaneously in a single experiment. If A and B are mutually exclusive events, then $n(AB) = 0$ and $\Pr\{AB\} = 0$. Clearly, any event and its complement are mutually exclusive events, since $n(A\overline{A}) = 0$.

4.3.   Addition theorem.   *The probability of the event (A or B) may be expressed in terms of the probabilities* $\Pr\{A\}$, $\Pr\{B\}$ *and* $\Pr\{AB\}$ *as follows:*

$$\Pr\{A \text{ or } B\} = \Pr\{A\} + \Pr\{B\} - \Pr\{AB\}. \qquad (4.1)$$

Proof. When does the event $(A$ or $B)$ occur? We divide the possible outcomes of the corresponding experiment into four categories: (1) AB, both A and B occur; (2) $A\bar{B}$, A occurs and B does not; (3) $\bar{A}B$, B occurs and A does not; and (4) $\bar{A}\bar{B}$, neither A nor B occurs. Thus event $(A$ or $B)$ occurs in the first of three categories (cf. Table 3):

Table 3. A 2 by 2 Contingency Table

	B	$\bar{B}$	Marginal Row Total
A	$n(AB)$	$n(A\bar{B})$	$n(A)$
$\bar{A}$	$n(\bar{A}B)$	$n(\bar{A}\bar{B})$	$n(\bar{A})$
Marginal Column Total	$n(B)$	$n(\bar{B})$	n

The probability of $(A$ or $B)$ is

$$\Pr\{A \text{ or } B\} = \frac{n(AB) + n(A\bar{B}) + n(\bar{A}B)}{n}. \qquad (4.2)$$

We see from Table 3

$$n(A\bar{B}) = n(A) - n(AB) \quad \text{and} \quad n(\bar{A}B) = n(B) - n(AB),$$

therefore,

$$\Pr\{A \text{ or } B\} = \frac{n(A) + n(B) - n(AB)}{n}.$$

Splitting the fraction we have

$$\Pr\{A \text{ or } B\} = \frac{n(A)}{n} + \frac{n(B)}{n} - \frac{n(AB)}{n}$$

or

$$\Pr\{A \text{ or } B\} = \Pr\{A\} + \Pr\{B\} - \Pr\{AB\}. \qquad (4.3)$$

Example 6. Let A = abnormal, B = boy. $\Pr\{A$ or $B\}$ is the probability of an abnormal girl, a normal boy, or an abnormal boy. Using Example 5, we find

$$\Pr\{A \text{ or } B\} = \Pr\{A\} + \Pr\{B\} - \Pr\{AB\}$$

$$= \frac{120}{800} + \frac{400}{800} - \frac{70}{800} = \frac{450}{800}.$$

The formulas of the addition theorem for three and four events are:

$$\Pr\{A \text{ or } B \text{ or } C\} = \Pr\{A\} + \Pr\{B\} + \Pr\{C\}$$
$$- \Pr\{AB\} - \Pr\{BC\} - \Pr\{AC\} + \Pr\{ABC\}, \quad (4.4)$$

and

$$\Pr\{A \text{ or } B \text{ or } C \text{ or } D\} = \Pr\{A\} + \Pr\{B\} + \Pr\{C\} + \Pr\{D\}$$
$$- \Pr\{AB\} - \Pr\{AC\} - \Pr\{AD\}$$
$$- \Pr\{BC\} - \Pr\{BD\} - \Pr\{CD\}$$
$$+ \Pr\{ABC\} + \Pr\{ABD\} + \Pr\{ACD\}$$
$$+ \Pr\{BCD\} - \Pr\{ABCD\}. \quad (4.5)$$

These are sometimes called *inclusion-exclusion* formulas.

4.4   Addition theorem when events are mutually exclusive.   When events are mutually exclusive, the formulas of the addition theorem become

$$\Pr\{A \text{ or } B\} = \Pr\{A\} + \Pr\{B\} \quad (4.6)$$

$$\Pr\{A \text{ or } B \text{ or } C\} = \Pr\{A\} + \Pr\{B\} + \Pr\{C\} \quad (4.7)$$

$$\Pr\{A \text{ or } B \text{ or } C \text{ or } D\} = \Pr\{A\} + \Pr\{B\} + \Pr\{C\} + \Pr\{D\} \quad (4.8)$$

For example, if events A and B are mutually exclusive, then $\Pr\{AB\} = 0$, and formula (4.3) reduces to (4.6).

5.   Remarks on Addition and Multiplication Theorems

5.1.   Summary of the addition and multiplication theorems.   Simple as they may appear to be, the addition and multiplication theorems are indispensible in computing probabilities. Table 4 facilitates applications of these two theorems.

Table 4. Use of addition and multiplication theorems

Which theorem	Multiplication theorem	Addition theorem
When to use	A AND B	A OR B
Formula	$\Pr\{AB\}$	$\Pr\{A \text{ or } B\}$
	$\quad = \Pr\{A\} \times \Pr\{B \mid A\}$	$\quad = \Pr\{A\} + \Pr\{B\} - \Pr\{AB\}$
Are the events	independent?	mutually exclusive?
Particular form	If independent, then	If mutually exclusive, then
of formula	$\Pr\{AB\} = \Pr\{A\} \times \Pr\{B\}$	$\Pr\{A \text{ or } B\} = \Pr\{A\} + \Pr\{B\}$

5.2. The distributive law. When the computation of a probability requires both the addition and multiplication theorems, rules like those of arithmetic can be applied where "*A and B*" converts to multiplication and "*A or B*" converts to addition. The most useful rule of operation in arithmetic is the distributive law: $a(b + c) = (a \times b) + (a \times c)$. For example:

$$2(3 + 4) = (2 \times 3) + (2 \times 4).$$

In a probability problem, this becomes:

$$\Pr\{A(B \text{ or } C)\} = \Pr\{AB \text{ or } AC\}. \tag{5.1}$$

A more complex example is

$$(2 + 3)(4 + 5) = (2 \times 4) + (2 \times 5) + (3 \times 4) + (3 \times 5)$$

and

$$\Pr\{(A \text{ or } B)(C \text{ or } D)\} = \Pr\{AC \text{ or } AD \text{ or } BC \text{ or } BD\}. \tag{5.2}$$

Using Example 5 once again, we have

$$\Pr\{A(B \text{ or } \overline{B})\} = \Pr\{AB \text{ or } A\overline{B}\}$$

$$= \Pr\{AB\} + \Pr\{A\overline{B}\}$$

$$= \frac{70}{800} + \frac{50}{800} = \frac{120}{800}. \tag{5.3}$$

In this case, $(B \text{ or } \overline{B}) = I$ is a sure event, so that

$$\Pr\{A(B \text{ or } \overline{B})\} = \Pr\{AI\} = \Pr\{A\} = \frac{120}{800},$$

and the rule is verified.

5.3. The product of complements vs. the complement of the product. Composite events such as AB, ABC, etc. ($A \times B$, $A \times B \times C$, etc.) are also called products of events. However, the complement of the product of events is different from the product of the complements of the events. In the case of two events, for example, the complement of the product is $\overline{A \times B}$, while the product of complements is $(\overline{A} \times \overline{B})$. The event $\overline{A \times B}$ occurs exactly when the event $A \times B$ does not occur, while the event $\overline{A} \times \overline{B}$ occurs when both $\overline{A}$ and

$\overline{B}$ occur. Their respective probabilities are:

$$\Pr\{\overline{A \times B}\} = 1 - \Pr\{A \times B\}$$

$$= 1 - \frac{n(AB)}{n}, \qquad (5.4)$$

and

$$\Pr\{\overline{A} \times \overline{B}\} = \frac{n(\overline{A}\,\overline{B})}{n}. \qquad (5.5)$$

Incidentally, the first equation in (5.4) shows that the probability of the complement of a product is equal to the complement of the probability of the product.

In Example 5, we have

$$\Pr\{\overline{A \times B}\} = \Pr\{\text{not an abnormal boy}\}$$

$$= 1 - \Pr\{\text{an abnormal boy}\} = 1 - \Pr\{A \times B\}$$

$$= 1 - \frac{70}{800} = \frac{730}{800}$$

and

$$\Pr\{\overline{A} \times \overline{B}\} = \Pr\{\text{a normal girl}\} = \frac{350}{800}.$$

The distinction between the two events $\overline{A \times B}$ and $\overline{A} \times \overline{B}$ is clear.

6.   Misuses of Probability—Some Examples

6.1.   Order of events in a conditional probability. In applying conditional probability to a practical problem, one should note the order that exists in the occurrence of events. If event B occurs before event D, then the conditional probability $\Pr\{D\,|\,B\}$ is meaningful, but the conditional probability $\Pr\{B\,|\,D\}$ may not be meaningful. For example, in a study of sex differential infant mortality, the sex of a live born infant, boy (B) or girl ($\overline{B}$), is known before survival (S) or death (D) in the first year of life is determined. The conditional probabilities

$$\Pr\{D\,|\,B\} = \Pr\{\text{a boy baby will die in the first year of life}\}$$

$$\Pr\{S\,|\,\overline{B}\} = \Pr\{\text{a girl baby will survive the first year of life}\}$$

and $\Pr\{S\,|\,B\}$ and $\Pr\{D\,|\,\overline{B}\}$ are all meaningful and useful measures. But the conditional probabilities $\Pr\{B\,|\,D\}$ or $\Pr\{\overline{B}\,|\,D\}$ may not be meaningful. The following example is such a case.

Example 7. A certain county hospital in the United States registered 1950 births during a calendar year; among them 1000 were males and 950 were females. During the first year of life, 18 of the male babies died and 13 of the female babies died. The survival experience of these infants is summarized in Table 5:

Table 5. Distribution of infants by sex and survival in the first year of life (hypothetical data)

Sex	Survival in the first year of life Survived (S)	Died (D)	Total
Boys (B)	982 $n(BS)$	18 $n(BD)$	1000 $n(B)$
Girls ($\overline{B}$)	937 $n(\overline{B}S)$	13 $n(\overline{B}D)$	950 $n(\overline{B})$
Total	1919 $n(S)$	31 $n(D)$	1950 n

If a newborn baby is subject to the survival experience of this group of infants, then the probability that a boy baby will survive the first year of life is

$$\Pr\{S\,|\,B\} = \frac{n(BS)}{n(B)} = \frac{982}{1000} \text{ or } 982.0 \text{ per } 1000$$

and the probability that a girl baby will survive the first year of life is

$$\Pr\{S\,|\,\overline{B}\} = \frac{n(\overline{B}S)}{n(\overline{B})} = \frac{937}{950} \text{ or } 986.3 \text{ per } 1000.$$

The probability a boy baby will die in the first year of life is

$$\Pr\{D\,|\,B\} = \frac{18}{1000} \text{ or } 18.0 \text{ per } 1000$$

and the probability a girl baby will die in the first year of life is

$$\Pr\{D\,|\,\overline{B}\} = \frac{13}{950} \text{ or } 13.7 \text{ per } 1000.$$

Thus the chance of dying in the first year of life is greater for a boy baby than for a girl baby. On the other hand, the conditional probabilities $\Pr\{B\,|\,D\}$, $\Pr\{\overline{B}\,|\,D\}$, $\Pr\{B\,|\,S\}$ and $\Pr\{\overline{B}\,|\,S\}$ are all meaningless.

The following section on prospective and retrospective studies further discusses the conditional probability when occurrence of events is ordered.

6.2. Prospective study vs. retrospective study.

Example 8. Cigarette smoking and lung cancer. To ascertain the extent of the association between cigarette smoking and incidence of lung cancer, a (retrospective) study of the smoking habits of 1465 cancer patients and 1465 controls (non-cancer patients) was conducted with the findings shown in Table 6.

Table 6. Distribution of 2930 patients by illness status and by smoking habit

Disease Group	Smokers (S)	Non-Smokers ($\bar{S}$)	Total
Cancer patients (C)	$n(CS)$ 1418 a	$n(C\bar{S})$ 47 b	$1465 = n(C)$
Non-cancer patients ($\bar{C}$)	$n(\bar{C}S)$ 1345 c	$n(\bar{C}\bar{S})$ 120 d	$1465 = n(\bar{C})$
Total	2763	167	2930

Source: Adapted from Doll, R., and Hill, A. B.: "A study of the etiology of carcinoma of the lung," *Brit. Med. J. 2*, p. 1271 (1952).

Based on the above information, we compute the conditional probabilities

$$\Pr\{S\,|\,C\} = \Pr\{\text{a cancer patient is a smoker}\}$$

$$= \frac{n(CS)}{n(C)} = \frac{1418}{1465} = .97$$

$$\Pr\{S\,|\,\bar{C}\} = \Pr\{\text{a non-cancer patient is a smoker}\}$$

$$= \frac{n(\bar{C}S)}{n(\bar{C})} = \frac{1345}{1465} = .92$$

so that a cancer patient is more likely to be a smoker than a non-cancer patient. However, it is incorrect to compute directly from the above data the following probabilities:

$$\Pr\{C\,|\,S\} = \Pr\{\text{a smoker will develop cancer}\}$$

and

$$\Pr\{C\,|\,\bar{S}\} = \Pr\{\text{a non-smoker will develop cancer}\}.$$

Through carelessness, one would find in this example $\Pr\{C\,|\,S\}$ $= 1418/2763 = .51$ and $\Pr\{C\,|\,\bar{S}\} = 47/167 = .28$. These figures are obviously absurd. The probabilities $\Pr\{C\,|\,S\}$ and $\Pr\{C\,|\,\bar{S}\}$ should be derived from cancer incidence among smokers and non-smokers in a prospective study. This approach, however, is impractical because of the length of time needed for the development of cancer. An alternative method is often used (cf., Cornfield, 1951).

From equation (3.15) we see that the two conditional probabilities $\Pr\{S\,|\,C\}$ and $\Pr\{C\,|\,S\}$ are related as follows:

$$\Pr\{C\}\Pr\{S\,|\,C\} = \Pr\{S\}\Pr\{C\,|\,S\}$$

and similarly

$$\Pr\{C\}\Pr\{\bar{S}\,|\,C\} = \Pr\{\bar{S}\}\Pr\{C\,|\,\bar{S}\}.$$

From these formulas we find the required probabilities to evaluate the effect of smoking on the development of lung cancer:

$$\Pr\{C\,|\,S\} = \frac{\Pr\{C\}\Pr\{S\,|\,C\}}{\Pr\{S\}} \quad \text{and} \quad \Pr\{C\,|\,\bar{S}\} = \frac{\Pr\{C\}\Pr\{\bar{S}\,|\,C\}}{\Pr\{\bar{S}\}}$$

$$(6.1)$$

We still need the probability $\Pr\{C\}$ to compute the probabilities in (6.1).

6.3.   Relative risk and odds ratio.   In epidemiological studies of the effect of a factor (such as smoking) on the incidence of a disease (such as lung cancer), a quantity known as the relative risk is often used. Relative risk compares the probability of getting a disease when exposed to a factor to the probability when not exposed. Using smoking and lung cancer as an example, the relative risk is

$$\text{Relative risk} = \frac{\Pr\{C\,|\,S\}}{\Pr\{C\,|\,\bar{S}\}}. \qquad (6.2)$$

Thus relative risk is a measure of the effect of the factor on the chance of contracting the disease.

Relative risk is quite useful in retrospective studies. We have seen in the above example of smoking and lung cancer the conditional probabilities $\Pr\{C\,|\,S\}$ and $\Pr\{C\,|\,\bar{S}\}$ cannot be obtained in a retrospective study without the additional knowledge of the prevalence of cancer in the general population. Relative risk, however, needs no such additional information. The probability $\Pr\{C\}$, which appears in both formulas in (6.1), will be cancelled out when (6.1) is substituted in (6.2),

$$\text{Relative risk} = \frac{\Pr\{S\,|\,C\,\}\Pr\{\bar{S}\,\}}{\Pr\{S\,\}\Pr\{\bar{S}\,|\,C\,\}}.\tag{6.3}$$

Assuming that the controls (non-cancer patients) are representative of the general population and the cases (cancer patients) are representative of all cases, the probabilities on the right-hand side of (6.3) can be estimated from a retrospective study; namely,

$$\Pr\{S\,\} = \Pr\{S\,|\,\bar{C}\,\} = \frac{n(\bar{C}S)}{n(\bar{C})}, \quad \Pr\{\bar{S}\,\} = \Pr\{\bar{S}\,|\,\bar{C}\,\} = \frac{n(\bar{C}\bar{S})}{n(\bar{C})}$$

$$\Pr\{S\,|\,C\,\} = \frac{n(CS)}{n(C)} \quad \text{and} \quad \Pr\{\bar{S}\,|\,C\,\} = \frac{n(C\bar{S})}{n(C)}\tag{6.4}$$

Substituting the above probabilities in (6.3) yields a formula which is known as the odds ratio:

$$\text{Odds ratio} = \frac{n(CS) \times n(\bar{C}\bar{S})}{n(C\bar{S}) \times n(\bar{C}S)}.\tag{6.5}$$

If we identify these numbers by $n(CS) = a$, $n(C\bar{S}) = b$, $n(\bar{C}S) = c$ and $n(\bar{C}\bar{S}) = d$, as in Table 6, then we can rewrite the odds ratio in (6.5) as

$$\text{Odds ratio} = (a \times d)/(b \times c),\tag{6.6}$$

a formula which frequently appears in the literature. It should be noted that validity of using the odds ratio for the relative risk is based on the assumption in (6.4) that the controls are representative of the general population. If this assumption is false, formulas (6.5) and (6.6) are no longer a valid substitute for the relative risk in (6.3).

The odds ratio in the above example is

$$\text{Odds ratio} = \frac{1418 \times 120}{47 \times 1345} = 2.7.$$

6.4.   Probability of A given B vs. probability of B given A.   It is clear that the conditional probability $\Pr\{B\,|\,A\}$ is different from the conditional probability $\Pr\{A\,|\,B\}$. In Example 5, section 3.1, the probability that a congenitally abnormal child will be a boy is computed from

$$\Pr\{B\,|\,A\} = \frac{n(AB)}{n(A)} = \frac{70}{120},$$

while the probability that a boy will be congenitally abnormal is computed from

$$\Pr\{A\,|\,B\} = \frac{n(AB)}{n(B)} = \frac{70}{400}.$$

Although the distinction between the two conditional probabilities is clear, it often escapes the attention of an inexperienced researcher.

Example 9. In an article reporting a study of 400 suicides in San Mateo County, California, U.S.A., during the years 1961 through 1965, the author writes:

> " . . . sixty-six percent of the group were males . . . In both sexes approximately 50 percent of the suicides were married . . . widows constituted 15 percent of the (female) suicides, but the comparable figures in widowers was only 5 percent, suggesting that males better tolerate the loss of their marital partners . . . "

In other words, the author claims that

Pr{a widower commits suicide} < Pr{a widow commits suicide}.

Here a widower is a widowed male, while a widow is a widowed female.

On the basis of $n = 400$ suicides, we find 264 ($= 400 \times .66$) male suicides and 136 ($= 400 \times .34$) female suicides. Among the male suicides, 13 ($= .05 \times 264$) were widowed, while among the female suicides, 20 ($= .15 \times 136$) were widowed. Using these calculations, we have reconstructed the information in Table 7:

Table 7. Suicides in San Mateo County, California, U.S.A. by sex and widowhood

Sex of suicides	Widowed (W)	Not Widowed* $(\overline{W})$	Total
Male	13 $n(MW)$	251 $n(M\overline{W})$	264 $n(M)$
Female	20 $n(FW)$	116 $n(F\overline{W})$	136 $n(F)$
	33 $n(W)$	367 $n(\overline{W})$	400 n

*"not widowed" category includes individuals who are either married, or single, or divorced.
Source: George Krieger, "Suicides in San Mateo County," *California Medicine*, August, 1967, Vol. 107, pp. 153–155.

In order to substantiate his conclusion, the author should have computed the required probabilities from the following formulas:

$$\text{Pr}\{\text{a widower commits suicide}\}$$

$$= \frac{\text{Number of widowers who commit suicide}}{\text{Number of widowers}}$$

and

$$\text{Pr}\{\text{a widow commits suicide}\}$$

$$= \frac{\text{Number of widows who commit suicide}}{\text{Number of widows}}$$

According to the 1960 census, there were 15,166 widows and 3227 widowers in San Mateo County. Thus, there were almost five times as many widows as widowers in the county, and yet the widows contributed only 20 suicides while the widowers contributed 13 suicides. Therefore, in San Mateo County, the ratio of the two required probabilities is

$$\text{Pr}\{\text{a widower commits suicide}\} : \text{Pr}\{\text{a widow commits suicide}\}$$

$$= \frac{13}{3227} : \frac{20}{15116} = 3 : 1.$$

Thus, the probability that a widower commits suicide is about three times as large as the probability that a widow commits suicide. This finding contradicts the author's contention, " . . . males better tolerate the loss of their marital partners."

7.   An Example from Life Table

Table 8 is adapted from a life table for the 1975 United States population. Column (1) shows the age intervals in years. Column (2) is the number of (life table) people living at the beginning of each age interval. Thus, the column shows that there are 100,000 (life table) people alive at the exact age 0 (that is, the population size at birth); of these 98,400 survived to the exact age of 1 year (the first birthday), 98,100 survived to the exact age of 5 years, etc., and finally 25,000 survived to the exact age of 85 years. Each figure in column (3) is the number of (life table) people dying within the corresponding age interval. Among the 100,000 living at age 0, 1600 died during the age interval (0, 1), 300 died between ages 1 and 5, etc., and 25,000 died beyond 85 years of age.

For the purpose of illustration, we consider a newborn who is subject to the mortality experience of the 1975 United States population. What is the probability that a newborn baby will survive to its

Table 8. The number of survivors and the number died out of 100,000 live births (adapted from the 1975 United States Life Table)

Age Interval (in years)	Number living at age x_i	Number dying in interval (x_i, x_{i+1})
x_i to x_{i+1} (1)	l_i (2)	d_i (3)
0–1	100000	1600
1–5	98400	300
5–10	98100	200
10–15	97900	200
15–20	97700	500
20–25	97200	700
25–30	96500	600
30–35	95900	700
35–40	95200	1000
40–45	94200	1500
45–50	92700	2300
50–55	90400	3500
55–60	86900	5000
60–65	81900	7200
65–70	74700	9000
70–75	65700	12000
75–80	53700	14300
80–85	39400	14400
85 +	25000	25000

first birthday? Here the "random experiment" is the baby's first year of life; possible outcomes are survival and death of the infant; the event of interest is the newborn's survival to its first birthday. Since of the $l_0 = 100,000$ newborns, $l_1 = 98,400$ actually survived, the probability that a newborn survives to its first birthday is

$$\frac{\text{No. living at age 1}}{\text{No. living at age 0}} = \frac{l_1}{l_0} = \frac{98,400}{100,000} = .9840 \text{ or } 984 \text{ per } 1000.$$

Similarly, the probability that a newborn survives to its fifth birthday is $98,100/100,000 = .981$, to the 10th birthday is $97,900/100,000 = .979$.

For the probability of death, we use the corresponding number of deaths in the numerator of the formula. Thus we have

Pr{a newborn dies during the first year of life}

$$= \frac{1600}{100,000} = .016 \text{ or } 16 \text{ per } 1000$$

and

$$\text{Pr}\{\text{a newborn dies in age interval } (1,5)\}$$

$$= \frac{300}{100.000} = .003 \text{ or } 3 \text{ per } 1000.$$

Remark. The event in the last example is a composite event. Since a newborn must first survive to age 1 before it is subject to the risk of dying in the interval $(1,5)$, we may interpret the event as follows:

$$\{\text{a newborn dies in age interval } (1,5)\}$$

$$= \{\text{a newborn survives to age 1 } and \text{ dies in interval } (1,5)\}.$$

Using the multiplication formula in (3.6),

$$\text{Pr}\{\text{a newborn dies in age interval } (1,5)\}$$

$$= \text{Pr}\{\text{a newborn survives to age 1}\}$$

$$\times \text{Pr}\{\text{a child of age 1 will die in age interval } (1,5)\}$$

$$= \frac{l_1}{l_0} \times \frac{d_1}{l_1} = \frac{98,400}{100,000} \frac{300}{98,400}$$

$$= \frac{300}{100.000},$$

which is the same numerical value as before.

7.1. Conditional probability. The probability

$$\text{Pr}\{\text{a child of age 1 dies in age interval } (1,5)\}$$

discussed above is a conditional probability, the condition being "the child is alive at age 1," or more explicitly,

$$\text{Pr}\{\text{a child dies in age interval } (1,5) \,|\, \text{child is alive at age 1}\}$$

$$= \frac{\text{number dying in age interval } (1,5)}{\text{number living at age 1}}$$

$$= \frac{300}{98,400} = .00305 \text{ or } 3.05 \text{ per } 1000.$$

The probability a child of age 5 dies in interval $(5,10)$ is also a conditional probability:

$$\text{Pr}\{\text{a child dies in age interval } (5,10) \,|\, \text{child is alive at age 5}\}$$

$$= \frac{\text{number dying in age interval } (5,10)}{\text{number living at age 5}}$$

$$= \frac{200}{98,100} = .00204 \text{ or } 2.04 \text{ per } 1000.$$

These conditional probabilities, which are based on the number of individuals living at the beginning of the corresponding age intervals, are known as the age-specific probabilities of dying. Other conditional probabilities are possible, depending upon the given condition and the event of interest. Here are a few examples:

$$\text{Pr}\{\text{an individual of age 25 survives to age 50}\}$$

$$= \frac{\text{number living at age 50}}{\text{number living at age 25}} = \frac{90,400}{96,500} = .93679,$$

and

$$\text{Pr}\{\text{an individual of age 25 dies before age 50}\}$$

$$= \frac{\text{number dying between ages 25 and 50}}{\text{number living at age 25}}$$

$$= \frac{96,500 - 90,400}{96,500}$$

$$= \frac{6,100}{96,500} = .06321.$$

Here the number 6,100 can be determined also from the number of deaths in all the intervals from 25 to 50:

$$6,100 = 600 + 700 + 1000 + 1500 + 2300.$$

Since an individual alive at age 25 either survives to age 50 or dies before age 50, the corresponding probabilities must add to unity:

$$.93679 + .06321 = 1.00000$$

For an individual alive at age 20, the corresponding probabilities are:

$$\text{Pr}\{\text{an individual of age 20 survives to age 45}\} = \frac{92,700}{97,200} = .95370,$$

and

$$\text{Pr}\{\text{an individual of age 20 dies before age 45}\} = 1 - .95370 = .04630.$$

7.2. Probability of composite events involving two or more people. Let M be an event that a male of age 25 survives to age 50 and $\overline{M}$ that he dies before age 50; let F be an event that a female of age 20 survives to age 45 and $\overline{F}$ she dies before age 45. If they are subject to the probabilities of surviving or dying given in Table 8, and if their survivals are independent events, then we can use the multiplication theorem to compute the following probabilities:

Pr{both the male and the female live for 25 years}

$$= \Pr\{M \times F\} = \Pr\{M\} \times \Pr\{F\}$$
$$= .93679 \times .95370 = .89342,$$

Pr{both die within 25 years}

$$= \Pr\{\overline{M} \times \overline{F}\} = \Pr\{\overline{M}\} \times \Pr\{\overline{F}\}$$
$$= .06321 \times .04630 = .00293,$$

Pr{the male lives and the female dies in 25 years}

$$= \Pr\{M \times \overline{F}\} = \Pr\{M\} \times \Pr\{\overline{F}\}$$
$$= .93679 \times .04630 = .04337$$

and

Pr{the male dies and the female lives for 25 years}

$$= \Pr\{\overline{M} \times F\} = \Pr\{\overline{M}\} \times \Pr\{F\}$$
$$= .06321 \times .95370 = .06028.$$

Since either (1) both the male and female will survive a period of 25 years, or (2) one of them dies, or (3) both die, the sum of the above probabilities is equal to one:

$$.89342 + .00293 + .04337 + .06028 = 1.00000.$$

Suppose the couple has a newborn baby who is also subject to the survival and dealth probabilities in the above life table. Let B be the event that the baby survives to age 25. What is the probability that all three will be alive on the child's 25th birthday? Using the multiplication theorem and assuming independence, we find the desired probability:

$$\Pr\{M \times F \times B\} = \Pr\{M\} \times \Pr\{F\} \times \Pr\{B\}$$
$$= .93679 \times .95370 \times .96500 = .86215.$$

Exercise.   Interpret and compute the probabilities: $\Pr\{\overline{M} \times F \times B\}$, $\Pr\{M \times \overline{F} \times B\}$, $\Pr\{(M \text{ or } F) \times B\}$, $\Pr\{(\overline{M \times F}) \times B\}$. The reader is urged to compute similar probabilities for other ages or for a different time period in order to become familiar with the use of the formulas.

7.3.   Probability of Dissolution of Marriage.   The above probabilities can be used to compute joint life insurance premiums or the chance of dissolution of marriages. For example, if a husband is of age 25 and his wife is of age 20, the probability that their marriage will be dissolved in 25 years because of death may be computed as follows:

Pr{dissolution of marriage in 25 years due to death}

$$= \text{Pr}\{\text{one or both of them die in 25 years}\}$$

$$= \text{Pr}\{(M \times \bar{F}) \text{ or } (\bar{M} \times F) \text{ or } (\bar{M} \times \bar{F})\}.$$

Here the three events $(M \times \bar{F})$, $(\bar{M} \times F)$, and $(\bar{M} \times \bar{F})$ are mutually exclusive. Applying the addition theorem gives the probability

$$\text{Pr}\{(M \times \bar{F})\} + \text{Pr}\{(\bar{M} \times F)\} + \text{Pr}\{(\bar{M} \times \bar{F})\}$$

$$= .04337 + .06028 + .00293 = .10658.$$

The probability of the dissolution of their marriage, therefore, is

Table 9. French Annuitants of French
Companies (1895)

Age Interval (in years)	Number living at age x_i	Number dying in interval (x_i, x_{i+1})
x_i to x_{i+1} (1)	l_i (2)	d_i (3)
0–1	100000	3602
1–5	96398	7122
5–10	89276	2608
10–15	86668	1723
15–20	84945	2529
20–25	82416	2737
25–30	79679	2511
30–35	77168	2617
35–40	74551	2817
40–45	71734	3156
45–50	68578	3696
50–55	64882	4519
55–60	60363	5703
60–65	54660	7275
65–70	47385	9093
70–75	38292	10660
75–80	27632	11016
80–85	16616	9168
85 +	7448	7448

Source: Émile Borel (1934), *Les Probabilités et la Vie*. Presses Universitaires de France.

better than 10 percent. On the other hand,

$$\Pr\{\text{their marriage will not be dissolved in 25 years}\}$$
$$= \Pr\{\text{both live for 25 years}\}$$
$$= \Pr\{M \times F\} = .89342.$$

Obviously, the two probabilities are complementary to each other, and

$$.10658 + .89342 = 1.00000.$$

7.4.   A mortality table of French insurance companies. In his book, *Les Probabilités et la Vie*, Émile Borel discusses probabilities of life, death, diseases and accidents. He has also reproduced from the *Annuaire du Bureau des Longitudes* several tables to illustrate the computation of probabilities for the use of insurance companies. The figures in Table 9 are derived from one of these tables. The reader is advised to compute all the probabilities in Section 7.3 using the information in Table 9.

8.   Problems for Solution

1.   Compute and interpret the probabilities $\Pr\{A\bar{B}\}$, $\Pr\{\bar{A}B\}$, and $\Pr\{\bar{A}\bar{B}\}$, using the numerical data in Table 2, page 5.

2.   Compute and interpret the conditional probabilities $\Pr\{A\,|\,B\}$, $\Pr\{B\,|\,\bar{A}\}$, $\Pr\{\bar{A}\,|\,B\}$, $\Pr\{\bar{B}\,|\,A\}$, $\Pr\{A\,|\,\bar{B}\}$, $\Pr\{\bar{A}\,|\,\bar{B}\}$, and $\Pr\{\bar{B}\,|\,\bar{A}\}$, using the numerical data in Table 2, page 5.

3.   Show that if $\bar{B}$ is independent of A, then A is independent of $\bar{B}$.

4.   The multiplication theorem for the event AB has been proven in Section 3.4, page 7. Use a similar approach to prove the following formulas:

$$\Pr\{ABC\} = \Pr\{A\}\Pr\{B\,|\,A\}\Pr\{C\,|\,AB\} \tag{3.8}$$

$$\Pr\{ABCD\} = \Pr\{A\}\Pr\{B\,|\,A\} \times \Pr\{C\,|\,AB\}\Pr\{D\,|\,ABC\} \tag{3.9}$$

5.   Prove the formulae (4.4) and (4.5) in section 4.3, page 11 for the addition theorem for three and four events, respectively.

6.   Use the data in Table 8, section 7, page 20, to compute and interpret the following probabilities: $\Pr\{\bar{M} \times F \times B\}$, $\Pr\{M \times \bar{F} \times B\}$, $\Pr\{(M \text{ or } F) \times B\}$, and $\Pr\{(\overline{M \times F}) \times B\}$.

7.   *Continuation.* For a husband of age 30 and his wife of age 25, find the probability that their marriage will be dissolved due to death in 25 years. In 30 years.

8. Use the information in Table 9, page 24, to compute the probability that:

    (1) A child of age 1 will survive to age 10.
    (2) An individual of age 20 will survive to age 45.
    (3) A woman of age 20 either will die in interval (40, 45) or will die in interval (50, 55).

9. Use the definitions of M, F, B in Section 7.2 and the information in Table 9 to compute and interpret the following probabilities:

    (1) $\Pr\{(M \times \bar{F}) \text{ or } (\bar{M} \times F) \text{ or } (\bar{M} \times \bar{F})\}$

    (2) $\Pr\{\bar{M} \times F \times B\}$, $\Pr\{M \times \bar{F} \times B\}$, $\Pr\{(M \text{ or } F) \times B\}$,

    $\Pr\{(\overline{M \times F}) \times B\}$, $\Pr\{\overline{M \times F \times B}\}$, and $\Pr\{M \text{ or } \overline{F \times B}\}$.

10. A club has 90 members. Fifty are lawyers and 50 are liars and everyone is in at least one of the two classes. What is the probability that a randomly selected member is both a lawyer and a liar? What is the probability that the member is a lawyer but not a liar? What is the probability that a lawyer will not be a liar?

11. A hotel has 10 rooms in a row on one floor. The rooms are all empty and the clerk assigns two guests to two rooms at random. What is the probability that they will have adjoining rooms?

12. An experiment consists of tossing a fair coin followed by drawing a ball from one of two urns. There are 3 white balls and 2 black balls in the first urn, and 4 white balls and 3 black balls in the second urn.

    (1) If the coin lands heads up, draw a ball from the first urn; if tails up, draw a ball from the second urn. Find the probability that the ball drawn will be a white ball.
    (2) If all the balls are merged in one urn and then a ball is drawn, what is the probability of getting a white ball.
    (3) Are the two probabilities equal? Explain.

13. When event A is independent of event B and event A is independent of event C, it does not necessarily follow that event A is independent of the composite event BC. Prove this by a counterexample.

14. Repeated multiplications of n positive integers from 1 to n (written as $n!$) is called "n factorial".

    (1) Show that the number of permutations (arrangements) of n distinct objects is equal to $n!$
    (2) Arrange the three letters DNA. The four letters TGIF. Count the number of arrangements in each case.

(3)   Show that the number of permutations of k out of n distinct
        objects is equal to $n!/(n-k)!$

15.   Show that the number of combinations (groupings) of k out of n
        distinct objects is

$$\binom{n}{k} = \frac{n!}{k!\,(n-k)!} \ .$$

16.   A family has five children, three girls and two boys. A sample of three
        children is called at random. Find the probability that there will be no
        girls in the sample. One girl; two girls; three girls.

17.   In problem 16, suppose three children are called one at a time, and a
        child is returned to the family before the next child is called (sampling
        with replacement). Find the probability that there will be k girls in the
        sample, for $k = 0, 1, 2, 3$.

18.   Balls are drawn from three urns in succession. Urn i contains a
        proportion of p_i white balls and q_i black balls, for $i = 1, 2, 3$. A ball is
        drawn from urn 1. If the ball drawn is a white ball, a ball is drawn
        from urn 2. If the ball drawn from urn 2 is a white ball, a ball is
        drawn from urn 3. What is the probability that all three balls drawn
        are white balls? First two balls are white and the third ball is black?

19.   The public health building on the University of California Berkeley
        campus has five floors. Suppose that one morning the elevator in the
        building starts at the ground floor with three passengers and that each
        passenger is equally likely to get off at any one of the next five floors.
        Compute:

(1)   Pr{the three passengers get off at the same floor}
(2)   Pr{exactly two of the three passengers get off at the same floor}
(3)   Pr{the three passengers all get off at different floors}

20.   Mr. A has four fair coins and Mr. B has three fair coins, and they toss
        their coins simultaneously.

(1)   Find the probability that A will get k heads, for $k = 0, 1, 2, 3, 4$.
(2)   Find the probability that B will get k heads, for $k = 0, 1, 2, 3$.
(3)   Find the probability that A will get more heads than B; fewer
        heads than B; A and B will get the same number of heads.

CHAPTER *2*

Basic Concepts of Statistics

1. Introduction

Every statistical study deals with measurements of some variables associated with subjects under consideration. In a mortality analysis of a human population, for example, the sex, age and cause of death of each person in the study population are observed, recorded, tabulated and analyzed. Here *sex*, *age* and *cause of death* are variables, as they assume different values for different persons. Age is a continuous variable, as it can assume any of a continuum of values; cause of death, which can assume any of several values, is called a categorical variable; sex, which can assume only two values, male and female, is called a dichotomous variable. Thus a dichotomous variable is a special case of a categorical variable when there are only two categories. If a variable is ranked or ordered, it is called an ordinal variable. For example, wine is often ranked according to quality, students ranked according to their scholastic performance, cities ranked by the size of the population, and countries ranked on the basis of their life expectancy.

Generally, we consider only two kinds of variables: Continuous variables and discrete variables. A continuous variable assumes an infinite number of values within a defined interval, while a discrete variable takes on a finite number of values. Clearly, discrete variables include dichotomous and categorical variables. Continuous variables are ordinal automatically, while a discrete variable may or may not be. Due to the limitation of measuring scales, every continuous variable is *expressed* in discrete units; weight is expressed in kilograms, height in centimeters, age in years, or in age intervals. The most beautiful example and one that greatly enriches human life is music where the sound wave length within each octave is expressed by only twelve notes. To avoid distraction, it suffices to consider only discrete variables in understanding statistical methods of analysis.

Observed values of variables are often expressed numerically so that the information derived from the study can be subject to a statistical analysis. If the values of a variable are not implicitly numerical, such as those of a categorical variable, we can record the number of observations falling in each category of the variable. For example, sex of a person is not numerical. But the number of females in a group of one person is numerical. It takes on value one if the person is female and value zero if the person is male.

2. Random Variable

A variable, discrete or continuous, takes on different values with unequal frequencies. A person is more likely to survive a calendar year than die during the year; a death is more attributable to heart disease than to influenza. When the frequencies, or probabilities, are taken into account in conjunction with the values of a variable, we have a random variable. Specifically, a random variable is a variable with the following two properties:

(1)   It takes on a number of numerical values, and
(2)   For each value it takes on, there is a corresponding probability.

This is only the first instance of the concept of probability formally relating to statistics. The uses of probability are evident in every aspect of statistics.

Example 1. In tossing a coin once, let p be the probability that it lands heads up, and q, tails up. Then $p + q = 1$. Let X be the number of times it lands heads up. Here X can take on two values

$$X = 0 \quad \text{when it lands tails up;}$$
$$X = 1 \quad \text{when it lands heads up.}$$

The corresponding probabilities are

$$\Pr\{X = 0\} = q \quad \text{and} \quad \Pr\{X = 1\} = p$$

with

$$\Pr\{X = 0\} + \Pr\{X = 1\} = q + p = 1.$$

If the coin is a fair one, then $p = q = 1/2$ and

$$\Pr\{X = 0\} = 1/2 \quad \text{and} \quad \Pr\{X = 1\} = 1/2.$$

Example 2. In tossing a coin twice, the possible outcomes are:
$$TT, TH, HT, HH.$$
Let Y be the number of times the coin lands heads up, which takes on values 0, 1, and 2 with probabilities

$$\Pr\{Y = 0\} = \Pr\{TT\} = q^2$$
$$\Pr\{Y = 1\} = \Pr\{TH \text{ or } HT\} = 2pq$$
$$\Pr\{Y = 2\} = \Pr\{HH\} = p^2.$$

Their sum is also equal to one:

$$q^2 + 2pq + p^2 = 1.$$

Example 3. A sample of $n = 3$ people is taken with replacement* from a population consisting of 60 males and 40 females. Let Z be the number of females in the sample. The random variable Z assumes values 0, 1, 2, and 3 with the probabilities

$$\Pr\{Z = 0\} = (.6)^3 = .216$$
$$\Pr\{Z = 1\} = 3(.4)(.6)^2 = .432$$
$$\Pr\{Z = 2\} = 3(.4)^2(.6) = .288$$
$$\Pr\{Z = 3\} = (.4)^3 = .064.$$

The sum of the probabilities is again equal to one.

The set of probabilities taken together with the corresponding values of a random variable is called *the probability distribution* of the random variable. The probability distributions of the three random variables X, Y and Z are exhibited in Table 1.

The significance of the concept of random variables is that probability distribution provides precise measures of uncertainties associated with the random variable. In Example 3, for instance,

Table 1. Examples of Probability Distributions

Random Variable	Values	Probability Distribution
X	$(0, 1)$	(q, p)
Y	$(0, 1, 2)$	$(q^2, 2pq, p^2)$
Z	$(0, 1, 2, 3)$	$(.216, .432, .288, .064)$

---

*There are two sampling procedures in general use: *Sampling with replacement* and *sampling without replacement*. In sampling with replacement, each item in the sample is returned to the population before the next item is taken, while in sampling without replacement, items are not returned in the process of sampling. The difference between the two procedures is insignificant when the population size is large.

although the number of women in a particular sample is uncertain, the probabilities of various numbers of females in a sample are known. The probability that there will be no females in a sample is .216; one female, .432; two females, .288; and three females, .064. Using the probability distribution we can also determine the average value of a random variable. In Example 3, if many samples were taken, each of size $n = 3$, the proportion of samples having 0, 1, 2, or 3 females will be approximately equal to the corresponding probabilities. About 21.6% of the samples will have no females; 43.2% of the samples will have one female; 28.8%, two females; and 6.4%, three females. The average number of females in a sample is

$$0 \times (.216) + 1 \times (.432) + 2 \times (.288) + 3 \times (.064) = 1.2. \quad (2.1)$$

This number, 1.2, a weighted mean of the numbers 0, 1, 2, and 3, is called the expectation of the random variable Z. A formal definition follows.

2.1. Expectation (mean, expected value) of a random variable. The expectation of a random variable X, written as $E(X)$, is the weighted mean of the values that X assumes with the corresponding probabilities used as weights. In formula,

$$E(X) = \sum_k k \Pr\{X = k\}, \quad (2.2)$$

where the summation is taken over all possible values of k. Therefore, the expectation of a random variable is merely the mean (average) value of the random variable.

The expectation of a constant is equal to the constant itself: If c is a constant, then $E(c) = c$.

In Example 1, the expectation of X is

$$E[X] = 0 \times \Pr\{X = 0\} + 1 \times \Pr\{X = 1\} = 0 \times q + 1 \times p = p.$$

In Example 2, the expectation of Y is

$$E[Y] = 0 \times \Pr\{Y = 0\} + 1 \times \Pr\{Y = 1\} + 2 \times \Pr\{Y = 2\}$$
$$= 0 \times q^2 + 1 \times 2pq + 2 \times p^2 = 2p.$$

For the expectation of random variable Z in Example 3, see equation (2.1).

Theorem 1 (rule of expectation): *The expectation (mean) of a linear combination of random variables is equal to the linear combination of the expectations of the random variables. Let a, b, c be constants and X and Y be random variables. Then*

$$E[a + bX + cY] = a + bE(X) + cE(Y). \quad (2.3)$$

The formula in (2.3) can be extended to any number of random variables.

Let X and Y be the random variables in Examples 1 and 2, respectively. According to Theorem 1, the expectation of the sum $X + Y$ is given by

$$E[X + Y] = E(X) + E(Y). \qquad (2.4)$$

Substituting $E(X) = p$ and $E(Y) = 2p$ in (2.4) yields

$$E[X + Y] = p + 2p = 3p.$$

Since $X + Y$ is the (total) number of times heads come up in tossing a coin three times, $E[X + Y] = 3p$ is what one may have anticipated.

2.1.1. Expectations of sample proportion and of sample mean. A sample proportion is generally used as an estimate of the population proportion, and a sample mean is used as an estimate of the population mean. They have an important optimum property as discussed below.

Expectation of a sample proportion. A sample of n people is taken with replacement from a population consisting of a proportion p of females and $q(= 1 - p)$ of males. Let X_i be the number of females in the ith individual in the sample, for $i = 1, \ldots, n$. Clearly X_i takes on value 0 if the ith individual is a male and value 1 if the ith individual is a female, with the expectation $E(X_i) = p$ (cf. Example 1). The sum $(X_1 + \cdots + X_n)$ is the total number of females in the sample, and

$$\hat{p} = \frac{1}{n}(X_1 + \cdots + X_n) \qquad (2.5)$$

is the proportion of females in the sample. Using the rule in (2.3), we find the expectation of the sum

$$E(X_1 + \cdots + X_n) = np, \qquad (2.6)$$

and the expectation of the sample proportion

$$E(\hat{p}) = p. \qquad (2.7)$$

Thus, the expectation of a sample proportion is equal to the population proportion. For this reason, the sample proportion is said to be an *unbiased estimate* of the population proportion.

Using the rule in (2.3) once again, we can show that the expectation of the difference between two sample proportions is equal to the difference between the two population proportions,

$$E(\hat{p}_1 - \hat{p}_2) = p_1 - p_2. \qquad (2.8)$$

Expectation of a sample mean.   A sample of n observations $(X_1, \ldots, X_n)$ is taken of a random variable X, which has an expectation (population mean) $E(X) = \mu$. The sample mean of the n observations is

$$\overline{X} = \frac{1}{n} X_1 + \frac{1}{n} X_2 + \cdots + \frac{1}{n} X_n. \qquad (2.9)$$

Using formula (2.3), we compute the expectation of $\overline{X}$,

$$E(\overline{X}) = \frac{1}{n} \mu + \frac{1}{n} \mu + \cdots + \frac{1}{n} \mu = \mu. \qquad (2.10)$$

This shows that the expectation of a sample mean is equal to the population mean. For this reason, the sample mean is said to be an unbiased estimate of the population mean.

It follows from the rule in (2.3) that the expectation of the difference between two sample means is equal to the difference between the two population means,

$$E(\overline{X}_1 - \overline{X}_2) = \mu_1 - \mu_2. \qquad (2.11)$$

2.2.   Variance and standard deviation of a random variable.   The expectation (the mean) of the random variable is a measure of the central tendency of the probability distribution of a random variable. The variance of a random variable is a measure of the spread of the distribution, or of the variation of the random variable. Both the expectation and the variance of a random variable are essential in the description of a probability distribution. For example, the normal distribution is completely determined by its expectation and variance. Furthermore, in making a statistical inference about a population value, knowledge of the variance of the random variable is indispensable.

The *variance* of a random variable X, denoted by σ_X^2 or Var(X), is the weighted mean of the squares of deviations of the values of X from the mean of X. In formula,

$$\sigma_X^2 = \sum_k [k - E(X)]^2 \Pr\{X = k\}. \qquad (2.12)$$

The *standard deviation* of a random variable is the square root of the variance, that is, σ_X.

The variance of a constant is equal to zero since a constant is subject to no variation. If c is constant, then

$$\sigma_c^2 = 0.$$

In Example 1, the random variable X takes on values 0 and 1

Table 2. Calculation of the variance of a random variable

Value of Z k	Pr{Z = k}	$[k - E(Z)]^2$	$[k - E(Z)]^2 \times \text{Pr}\{Z = k\}$
0	.216	1.44	.31104
1	.432	.04	.01728
2	.288	.64	.18432
3	.064	3.24	.20736
Total	1.000	–	.72000

and $E(X) = p$. According to formula (2.12), the variance of X is

$$\sigma_X^2 = (0 - p)^2 \text{Pr}\{X = 0\} + (1 - p)^2 \text{Pr}\{X = 1\}$$
$$= (0 - p)^2 q + (1 - p)^2 p = pq, \tag{2.13}$$

and the standard deviation is $\sigma_X = \sqrt{pq}$.

In Example 2, the random variable Y takes on values 0, 1 and 2 with $E(Y) = 2p$. Using formula (2.12), we compute the variance of Y,

$$\sigma_Y^2 = (0 - 2p)^2 q^2 + (1 - 2p)^2 2pq + (2 - 2p)^2 p^2.$$

Since

$$(1 - 2p)^2 = (q - p)^2 = q^2 - 2pq + p^2,$$

and

$$(2 - 2p)^2 = 4q^2,$$

the variance is

$$\sigma_Y^2 = 4p^2q^2 + (q^2 - 2pq + p^2)2pq + 4p^2q^2$$
$$= (p^2 + 2pq + q^2)2pq = 2pq,$$

and the standard deviation is $\sigma_Y = \sqrt{2pq}$.

In Example 3, the expectation of Z is $E(Z) = 1.2$. Table 2 shows the calculation of the variance of Z. According to the formula in (2.12), $\sigma_Z^2 = .72$ and therefore the standard deviation of Z is $\sigma_Z = \sqrt{.72} = .849$.

Exercise. Let W be the number of times a fair coin lands heads up when it is tossed four times. Find (1) the values W takes on, (2) the corresponding probabilities, (3) the expectation, $E[W]$, (4) the variance, σ_W^2, and (5) the standard deviation, σ_W.

Definition. Independence of two random variables. Two random variables X and Y are said to be independently distributed random variables if, for every i and j,

$$\Pr\{X = i \text{ and } Y = j\} = \Pr\{X = i\} \times \Pr\{Y = j\}$$

(Note the similarity between this and the definition of independent events in Chapter 1, section 3.3.)

Let X be the number of times a coin lands heads up when tossed once, and Y be the number of times it lands heads up when tossed twice. Then X and Y are independent random variables. For example, the probability

$$\Pr\{X = 0 \text{ and } Y = 0\} = \Pr\{X = 0\} \times \Pr\{Y = 0\} = qq^2 = q^3.$$

Exercise. Find the probabilities for the above example, $\Pr\{X = i \text{ and } Y = j\}$, for $i = 0, 1$; $j = 0, 1, 2$. Use these probabilities to compute the expectation and the variance of the sum $X + Y$.

Theorem 2 (rule of variance). *The variance of a linear function of independent random variables, X and Y, is*

$$\text{Var}[a + bX + cY] = b^2\text{Var}(X) + c^2\text{Var}(Y). \qquad (2.14)$$

For example, when $a = 0$, $b = c = 1$, we have the variance of the sum of the random variables,

$$\text{Var}[X + Y] = \text{Var}(X) + \text{Var}(Y). \qquad (2.15)$$

When $a = 0$, $b = 1$, $c = -1$, we have the variance of the difference of two random variables,

$$\text{Var}[X - Y] = \text{Var}(X) + \text{Var}(Y). \qquad (2.16)$$

Equations (2.15) and (2.16) show that the variance of $X + Y$ is equal to the variance of $X - Y$. This seemingly unreasonable result is, in fact, true. The difference $X - Y$ is subject to the same amount of

Table 3. Computation of the variance of $X + Y$, where $E(X + Y) = 3p$

Value of $X + Y$ k	Values of X and values of Y	$\Pr\{X + Y = k\}$	$[k - E(X + Y)]^2$ $\times \Pr\{X + Y = k\}$
0	($X = 0$ and $Y = 0$)	q^3	$(0 - 3p)^2 q^3$
1	($X = 0$ and $Y = 1$) or ($X = 1$ and $Y = 0$)	$q(2pq)$ $+ pq^2$	$(1 - 3p)^2 3pq^2$
2	($X = 0$ and $Y = 2$) or ($X = 1$ and $Y = 1$)	qp^2 $+ p(2pq)$	$(2 - 3p)^2 3p^2q$
3	($X = 1$ and $Y = 2$)	p^3	$(3 - 3p)^2 p^3$
Total		1	$\sigma^2_{X+Y} = 3pq$

Table 4. Computation of the variance of $X - Y$, where $E[X - Y] = -p$

Value of $X - Y$ k	Value of X and value of Y	$\Pr\{X - Y = k\}$	$[k - E(X - Y)]^2$ $\times \Pr\{X - Y = k\}$
-2	$(X = 0 \text{ and } Y = 2)$	qp^2	$(-2 + p)^2 qp^2$
-1	$(X = 0 \text{ and } Y = 1)$ or $(X = 1 \text{ and } Y = 2)$	$q(2pq)$ $+ p^3$	$(-1 + p)^2(2pq^2 + p^3)$
0	$(X = 0 \text{ and } Y = 0)$ or $(X = 1 \text{ and } Y = 1)$	q^3 $+ p(2pq)$	$(0 + p)^2(q^3 + 2p^2 q)$
1	$(X = 1 \text{ and } Y = 0)$	pq^2	$(1 + p)^2 pq^2$
Total		1	$\sigma_{X-Y}^2 = 3pq$

variation as the sum $X + Y$. The following example makes this point clear.

Let X be the number of heads which occur after tossing a coin once as in Example 1, and let Y be the number of heads that occur after tossing a coin twice as in Example 2. The sum $X + Y$ assumes values 0, 1, 2 and 3 with an expectation $E(X + Y) = 3p$; while the difference $X - Y$ assumes values -2, -1, 0 and 1 with the expectation $E(X - Y) = -p$. Tables 3 and 4 show that the variances of $X + Y$ and $X - Y$ are both equal to $3pq$.

Exercise. Let X and Y be the random variables discussed above. Compute the expectation and the variance of each of the following linear functions of X and Y: (1) $Y - X$; (2) $2X + Y$; (3) $2X - Y$; (4) $Y - 2X$; (5) $X + 2Y$; (6) $X - 2Y$; (7) $2Y - X$. Which of these variances are equal? Explain. Try to convince yourself that these equalities are reasonable.

2.2.1. Variances of sample proportion and of sample mean. In the discussion of expectation of random variables in Section 2.1, we alluded to the fact that a sample proportion is an "unbiased" estimate of the population proportion, and a sample mean is an "unbiased" estimate of the population mean. The "goodness" of an estimate is also judged by the variance (or the standard deviation) of the estimate. We now derive the formulas for the variances of these estimates.

Variance of a sample proportion. Let X_i be a dichotomous random variable as in Example 1, whose variance is equal to pq (cf. Equation (2.13)), for $i = 1, \ldots, n$. Using the rule in (2.14), we find the variance of the sum $(X_1 + \cdots + X_n)$

$$\text{Var}(X_1 + \cdots + X_n) = npq, \tag{2.17}$$

and the variance of the sample proportion $\hat{p} = (1/n)(X_1 + \cdots + X_n)$,

$$\text{Var}(\hat{p}) = \left(\frac{1}{n}\right)^2 npq = \frac{1}{n}\,pq. \tag{2.18}$$

It follows that the standard deviation of the sample proportion is

$$\sigma_{\hat{p}} = \sqrt{pq/n}\ . \tag{2.19}$$

Note: The standard deviation of an estimate, such as the sample proportion and the sample mean, is also called the standard error of the estimate. We shall use the two terms alternately in this book. In this case,

$$\text{S.E.}\,(\hat{p}) = \sqrt{pq/n}\ .$$

Variance of a sample mean. Suppose a random variable X has a variance σ^2. Writing the sample mean $\overline{X}$ as

$$\overline{X} = \frac{1}{n}X_1 + \cdots + \frac{1}{n}X_n,$$

we apply the rule in (2.14) to find the variance of the sample mean $\overline{X}$;

$$\sigma_{\overline{X}}^2 = \left(\frac{1}{n}\right)^2\sigma^2 + \cdots + \left(\frac{1}{n}\right)^2\sigma^2 = \sigma^2/n. \tag{2.20}$$

It follows that the standard error (standard deviation) of the sample mean is

$$\text{S.E.}\,(\overline{X}) = \sigma/\sqrt{n}\ . \tag{2.21}$$

Formulas (2.18) and (2.20) show that the variance of a sample proportion (or a sample mean) is equal to the variance of any individual X divided by the sample size, n. As the sample size n increases, the variance of the sample proportion (or sample mean) decreases. Thus the proportion (or the mean) of a large sample is subject to less variation than the proportion (or the mean) of a small sample. Consequently, the larger the sample, the more accurate is the sample proportion (or sample mean) as an estimate of the population proportion (or population mean).

Variance of the difference between two sample proportions, $\hat{p}_1 - \hat{p}_2$. Consider now two proportions, $\hat{p}_1$ and $\hat{p}_2$, in two samples of sizes n_1 and n_2 taken from two populations, respectively. According to the formula in (2.16), the variance of the difference $\hat{p}_1 - \hat{p}_2$ is

$$\text{Var}(\hat{p}_1 - \hat{p}_2) = \text{Var}(\hat{p}_1) + \text{Var}(\hat{p}_2). \tag{2.22}$$

Introducing formula (2.18) in (2.22) yields the variance of the difference,

$$\text{Var}(\hat{p}_1 - \hat{p}_2) = \frac{p_1 q_1}{n_1} + \frac{p_2 q_2}{n_2}, \tag{2.23}$$

and the standard error of the difference is

$$\text{S.E.}(\hat{p}_1 - \hat{p}_2) = \sqrt{\frac{p_1 q_1}{n_1} + \frac{p_2 q_2}{n_2}}. \tag{2.24}$$

Variance of the difference between two sample means, $\overline{X}_1 - \overline{X}_2$. Let $\overline{X}_1$ and $\overline{X}_2$ be means of two samples of sizes n_1 and n_2 taken from population 1 and population 2, which have the variances σ_1^2 and σ_2^2, respectively. According to the formula in (2.16), the variance of the difference is

$$\text{Var}(\overline{X}_1 - \overline{X}_2) = \text{Var}(\overline{X}_1) + \text{Var}(\overline{X}_2). \tag{2.25}$$

Introducing (2.20) in (2.25) yields

$$\text{Var}(\overline{X}_1 - \overline{X}_2) = \frac{\sigma_1^2}{n_1} + \frac{\sigma_2^2}{n_2}, \tag{2.26}$$

and hence the standard error of the difference,

$$\text{S.E.}(\overline{X}_1 - \overline{X}_2) = \sqrt{\frac{\sigma_1^2}{n_1} + \frac{\sigma_2^2}{n_2}} \tag{2.27}$$

When the two population variances are equal, $\sigma_1^2 = \sigma_2^2 = \sigma^2$, then

$$\text{Var}(\overline{X}_1 - \overline{X}_2) = \sigma^2 \left(\frac{1}{n_1} + \frac{1}{n_2} \right) \tag{2.28}$$

and

$$\text{S.E.}(\overline{X}_1 - \overline{X}_2) = \sigma \sqrt{\frac{1}{n_1} + \frac{1}{n_2}}. \tag{2.29}$$

Formulas (2.18) through (2.29) will be used frequently in later chapters.

3.   The Binomial Distribution

The simplest variables in statistical analysis are dichotomous variables. Sex of a person, survival or death during a year, death from cancer or from other causes, etc., are prominent examples. The corresponding random variable is the binomial random variable. Because of its importance in the discussion of mortality and life tables in this book, we will discuss the binomial distribution in some detail.

Definition.   A binomial random variable is the number of "successes" in a number (n) of independent and identical "trials". Each trial is an experiment which can result in one of two ways, called "success" and "failure"; the probability of "success" in each trial is a constant.

In Example 1 in the preceding section, X is the number of successes (heads) in $n = 1$ trial (toss of a coin), while in Example 2, Y is the number of successes (heads) in $n = 2$ trials (tosses of a coin). The probability that heads turn up in each trial, p, is constant; therefore X and Y are examples of binomial random variables.

In Example 3, the number of females in a sample of $n = 3$ is also a binomial random variable. The corresponding probability distribution, as we have seen, is

$$\Pr\{Z = 0\} = (.6)^3$$
$$\Pr\{Z = 1\} = 3(.4)(.6)^2$$
$$\Pr\{Z = 2\} = 3(.4)^2(.6)$$
$$\Pr\{Z = 3\} = (.4)^3.$$

The coefficients $(1, 3, 3, 1)$ are the numbers of ways the corresponding events (zero, one, two or three females in a sample) can occur.

3.1.   The probability distribution.   Let X be a binomial random variable in n independent trials with the probability of success p. Then X takes on values $0, 1, \ldots, n$, and the corresponding probabilities are:

$$\Pr\{X = k\} = \frac{n!}{k!(n-k)!}\, p^k q^{n-k}, \qquad k = 0, 1, \ldots, n, \quad (3.1)$$

where $n!$ (n factorial) represents repeated multiplications from 1 to n, or $n! = 1 \cdot 2 \cdot \ldots \cdot (n-1) \cdot (n)$. The product $p^k q^{n-k}$ is the probability that k specified trials result in success and the remaining $n - k$ trials result in failure. For example, the first k trials may be successes, and the last $n - k$ trials failures, as represented by the sequence $(S \ldots SFF \ldots F)$. The combinatorial factor (or binomial coefficient)

$$\frac{n!}{k!(n-k)!} \qquad (3.2)$$

is the number of ways in which k successes and $n - k$ failures can occur in n trials. Using the expansion of the binomial function $(p + q)^n$, we find the sum

$$\sum_{k=0}^{n} \frac{n!}{k!(n-k)!}\, p^k q^{n-k} = (p + q)^n = 1, \qquad (3.3)$$

or, the sum of the probabilities equals one

$$\sum_{k=0}^{n} \Pr\{X = k\} = 1,$$

as is expected with a probability distribution.

The expectation and the variance of a binomial random variable have been computed in Section 2, namely

$$E(X) = np \qquad (2.6)$$

and

$$\mathrm{Var}(X) = npq. \qquad (2.17)$$

Exercise. Find the expectation $E(X)$ and the variance $\mathrm{Var}(X)$ of X using the probabilities in (3.1).

Pascal pyramid. We have seen the binomial coefficients (1, 1), (1, 2, 1), and (1, 3, 3, 1) in Examples 1, 2, and 3, respectively. For example, when $n = 3$, for $k = 0, 1, 2$ and 3, the respective coefficients are

$$\frac{3!}{0!3!} = 1, \qquad \frac{3!}{1!2!} = 3, \qquad \frac{3!}{2!1!} = 3, \qquad \frac{3!}{3!0!} = 1.$$

For different values of n, the binomial coefficients are related in an elegant way which is displayed in the following pyramid.

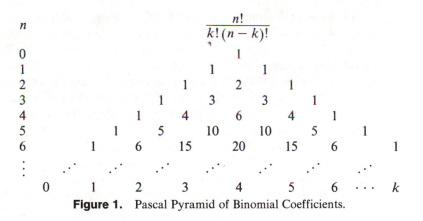

Figure 1.   Pascal Pyramid of Binomial Coefficients.

The label on the horizontal axis (k) is read diagonally, as indicated. Each number in the pyramid is the sum of the two numbers immediately above it. For each n, the $(n + 1)$ numbers in row n are the corresponding binomial coefficients. The sum of these $(n + 1)$ numbers is equal to 2^n. For example $1 + 3 + 3 + 1 = 2^3$. The pyramid is attributed to the French mathematician, Blaise Pascal (1623–1662), who, in his work *Traité du triangle arithmétique*, laid the foundations for the calculus of probabilities.

3.2.   The binomial probability p (or q).   The importance of the study of the binomial distribution lies not in the computation of the probabilities in equation (3.1), or the expectation, or the variance based on a known probability, but rather in making inference about an *unknown probability* based on the observed value of the binomial random variable. We may use this information to estimate the probability or to compare proportions of two or more populations.

There are two distinct situations where a binomial random variable is generated: The first situation is experimentation. Coin tossing is the most cited example of experimentation [cf. Examples 1 and 2 in Section 2]. Life experience of individuals during a year also is a binomial "experiment", in which each individual's life experience during a year constitutes a trial; survival and death are the two possible outcomes. In order to use the binomial theory to study mortality, we need to comply with the conditions in the definition and require the individuals in a group to be alike with respect to the probability of surviving the year. For this reason, usually people are grouped by age, sex and possibly other demographic variables. The mortality experience of the people within a group can then be used for making statistical inference about the survival probabilities or the unknown mortality rates.

The second situation is sampling—taking a sample from a dichotomous population consisting of a proportion (p) of individuals who have a certain characteristic [cf. Example 3 in Section 2]. When the population size is large, the number of individuals in the sample having the characteristic is a binomial random variable, even if the sample is taken without replacement. The characteristic in question may be sex, congenital anomalies in infants, death from a particular cause, etc. In each case, statistical inference about the corresponding proportion can be made by using the binomial theory.

While the concept of a binomial distribution is simple, the formula for the probability distribution is a little complex. When the binomial theory is used for making inference concerning a probability p, we need to deal with, at a minimum, such cumulative probabilities as

$$\Pr\{X \geqslant k\} = \sum_{j=k}^{n} \frac{n!}{j!(n-j)!} p^j q^{n-j},$$

which involves a large number of terms when n is large. When inference is about two or more probabilities, the corresponding formulas are even more involved and their meaning is far less clear. In order to devote our attention to the understanding of statistical inference without having to unravel the meaning of complex formulas, we will explore an *approximation* to the binomial distribution which is relatively simple. The most commonly used approximation is the normal approximation. When the purpose of a mortality analysis is to make statistical inference about probabilities of death, or for the comparison of mortality rates, a study population is in effect a sample. Since a study population usually is large, the normal distribution is a close approximation to the binomial distribution. The basic theorem that justifies the approximation is the central limit theorem, which is presented in the next section. The formulas derived there are simple and explicit, and the statistical reasoning straightforward. Therefore, whenever appropriate, we will use the normal distribution for making statistical inference in this volume.

4. Problems for Solution

1. Show that the sum of the probabilities in the last column in Table 4, page 37, is equal to $3pq$.

2. Find the expectations $E(X + Y)$ from the probability distribution in Table 3, page 36, and the expectation $E(X - Y)$ from the probability distribution in Table 4, page 37.

3. Let X be the number of heads that occur in tossing a coin once and Y be the number of heads that occur in tossing a coin twice. Compute the expectation and the variance of each of the following linear functions of X and Y: (1) $Y - X$; (2) $2X + Y$; (3) $2X - Y$; (4) $Y - 2X$; (5) $X + 2Y$; (6) $X - 2Y$; and (7) $2Y - X$.

4. Verify the equation (3.3), page 40, for $n = 4$.

5. Find the expectation $E(X)$ and the variance $\mathrm{Var}(X)$ from the probability distribution in (3.1), page 40.

6. A class has 10 students, 6 males and 4 females. A sample of $n = 5$ students is drawn from the class with replacement. Let X be the number of female students in the sample.

(1) Find the probability $\Pr\{X = k\}$, for $k = 0, 1, \ldots, 5$.
(2) Compute from the probability distribution in (1) the expectation $E(X)$ and variance $\mathrm{Var}(X)$.

7. *Continuation.* In problem 6, if the class has 100 students with 60 males and 40 females, and a sample $n = 5$ students is taken with replacement, find the probabilities $\Pr\{X = k\}$ for $k, = 0, 1, \ldots, 5$, $E(X)$ and $\mathrm{Var}(X)$.

8. *Continuation.* Do all parts in problem 6 if a sample $n = 5$ students is taken from the class *without* replacement.

9. *Continuation.* Do all parts in problem 7 if a sample is taken *without* replacement.

10. *Continuation.*   Discuss the effect of population size on the probability distribution of X, $E(X)$ and $\text{Var}(X)$ on the basis of your results in problems 6, 7, 8 and 9.

11. Verify that the sum of the four terms in the last column in Table 3, page 36, is equal to $3pq$.

12. A population consists of N individuals with m males and $N - m$ females. A sample of n individuals is taken with replacement from the population and let a random variable X be the number of males in the sample.

   (1)   Find the probability $\Pr\{X = k\}$.
   (2)   Show that

$$\sum_{k=0}^{n} \Pr\{X = k\} = 1.$$

   (3)   Find the expectation and the variance of X.

13. Do problem 12 when the sample is taken *without* replacement.

14. The variance of a random variable is often computed from the formula

$$\sigma_Z^2 = E[Z^2] - [E(Z)]^2 \tag{A}$$

instead of the formula

$$\sigma_Z^2 = E[Z - E(Z)]^2 \tag{B}$$

or

$$\sigma_Z^2 = \sum_k [k - E(Z)]^2 \Pr\{Z = k\}. \tag{C}$$

   (1)   Show that the above three formulas are identical.
   (2)   Use formula (A) to compute the variance of Z in Table 2, p. 35.

15. Let a random variable Z have the probability distribution in Table 2, p. 35. Compute the expectation and variance of the random variable $W = 2Z$.

16. Let Z_1 and Z_2 be two independently distributed random variables and have the identical distribution given in Table 2. Compute the expectation and the variance of the random variable

$$V = Z_1 + Z_2.$$

Are the expectation and the variance of V equal to the expectation and the variance of W in problem 15? Explain.

CHAPTER *3*

The Normal Distribution and Statistical Inference

1. The Normal Distribution

The normal distribution is a probability distribution of a continuous random variable symmetrical with respect to the mean. Its values extend from minus infinity to plus infinity. The distribution can be described by a bell-shaped curve as shown in the next page. The area between the curve and the horizontal line is equal to unity. Since a continuous variable assumes an infinite number of values, the probability that it will take on a particular value is extremely small; equal to zero, to be exact. Therefore, in dealing with a normal random variable, we speak only of the probability that it will assume values less than a particular number or greater than a particular number or in some interval. The probability that a normal random variable X will take on values less than or equal to a number x_1, for example, is represented by the area under the curve, above the line, and to the left of the point x_1. The probability that X will take on values greater than x_2 is represented by the area under the curve to the right of x_2. Finally, the probability that X will assume values greater than x_1 and less than x_2 is represented by the area under the curve between the two points x_1 and x_2 in Figure 1.

The exact shape of a normal distribution depends on the values of the mean and the standard deviation of the distribution. The normal distribution which has mean zero (0) and standard deviation one (1) is called the *standard normal distribution*. Since any normally

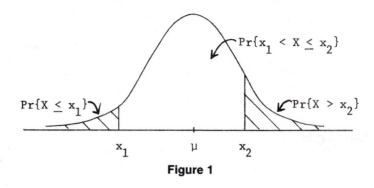

Figure 1

distributed variable can be converted to a standard normal variable by moving the origin and changing the scale, the standard normal distribution is the most important distribution in making statistical inferences. Suppose X is a normal random variable with a mean $E(X) = \mu$ and the standard deviation σ; then

$$Z = \frac{X - \mu}{\sigma} \tag{1.1}$$

is a standard normal random variable with a mean zero and a standard deviation one.

Exercise.   Use the rules of expectation and variance in Chapter 2 to show that the standard normal random variable Z in (1.1) has a mean zero and a variance one.

The values of the standard normal random variable and the corresponding probabilities have been tabulated and reproduced at the end of this chapter. The table gives the area to the left of each value of Z. For $Z = 1.96$, for example, one finds the probability

$$\Pr\{Z < 1.96\} = .975.$$

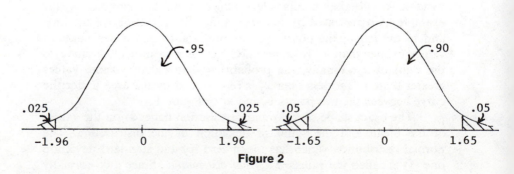

Figure 2

For a given probability, say .95, the corresponding value is $Z = 1.65$

$$\Pr\{Z < 1.65\} = .95.$$

The diagrams in Figure 2 show the relationships between the values of Z and the corresponding probabilities.

Example 1. Suppose the weights of a group of boys are normally distributed, with a mean weight $\mu = 40$ kilograms (kg) and a standard deviation $\sigma = 4$ kg.

(1)   What percent of the boys weigh less than 46.6 kg? Less than 46.84 kg? Less than 36 kg? More than 37.6 kg? More than 32.16 kg? More than 44 kg?

(2)   If a boy is picked at random from the group, what is the probability that his weight is between 33.4 kg and 46.6 kg? Between 36 kg and 44 kg? Between 33.4 kg and 47.84 kg? Between 32.16 kg and 46.6 kg?

(3)   Find the weight so that 10% of the boys weigh more than this value. Less than this value. 15% of the boys weigh more. Weigh less.

(4)   Find two weights equally distant from 40 kg so that 90% of the boys have weights between these two. 80% of the boys have weights between these two. 95% of the boys have weights between these two.

Solution: Let X be the weight of a boy. The first part of (1) calls for the probability

$$\Pr\{X < 46.6\}. \tag{a}$$

Converting X to a standard normal random variable,

$$\Pr\left\{ \frac{X - \mu}{\sigma} < \frac{46.6 - 40}{4} \right\} \tag{b}$$

or

$$\Pr\{Z < 1.65\} = .95. \tag{c}$$

The last probability was obtained by consulting the normal distribution table. Thus, 95 percent of the children weigh less than 46.6 kg.

For the first part of (2), we need to find the probability

$$\Pr\{33.4 < X < 46.6\}. \tag{a}$$

Converting X to a standard normal random variable

$$\Pr\left\{ \frac{33.4 - 40}{4} < \frac{X - \mu}{\sigma} < \frac{46.6 - 40}{4} \right\} \tag{b}$$

and consulting the normal distribution table, we find

$$\Pr\{-1.65 < Z < 1.65\} = .90. \qquad (c)$$

Thus the probability that the boy selected will weigh between 33.4 kg and 46.6 kg is .90.

In (3), the probability is given. What needs to be determined is the corresponding weight x. That is,

$$\Pr\{X > x\} = .10. \qquad (a)$$

Standardizing X yields

$$\Pr\left\{\frac{X - \mu}{\sigma} > \frac{x - 40}{4}\right\} = .10$$

or

$$\Pr\left\{Z > \frac{x - 40}{4}\right\} = .10. \qquad (b)$$

From the normal distribution table, we find

$$\Pr\{Z > 1.28\} = .10 \qquad (c)$$

and, by comparing equations in (b) and (c), the equation

$$\frac{x - 40}{4} = 1.28.$$

Solving the equation for x gives the desired value

$$x = 45.1 \text{ kg}.$$

The first part of (4) also requires that we determine the values of X for a given probability i.e.,

$$\Pr\{40 - c < X < 40 + c\} = .90. \qquad (a)$$

Converting X to the standard normal random variables gives

$$\Pr\left\{\frac{-c}{4} < \frac{X - \mu}{\sigma} < \frac{c}{4}\right\} = .90 \qquad (b)$$

or

$$\Pr\left\{-\frac{c}{4} < Z < \frac{c}{4}\right\} = .90.$$

From the normal distribution table, we have

$$\Pr\{-1.65 < Z < 1.65\} = .90. \qquad (c)$$

Therefore

$$\frac{c}{4} = 1.65$$

or

$$c = 6.6 \text{ kg},$$

and the desired weights are $40 - 6.6 = 33.4$ kg and $40 + 6.6 = 46.6$ kg.

The above example shows two types of problems. The first type of problem is to find the probability for a given value, or values, of the random variable, while the second type of problem is to determine the value, or values, of the random variable X for a given probability. The two types of problems cover a large percentage of the problems involving the normal distribution. The solution to each of these problems consists of three steps: (a) stating the problem in terms of a probability; (b) standardizing the random variable X; and (c) consulting the table of the standard normal distribution.

1.1.   The Central Limit Theorem.   The Central Limit Theorem has had a far reaching effect on the development of statistical theory. It is also the basis for the application of statistical methods to many fields of scientific research. We state the theorem below.

Theorem 1.   Let $X_1, \ldots, X_n$ be a sample of n independent observations of a random variable X, which has a mean $E(X) = \mu$ and a variance σ^2. Let

$$\overline{X} = \frac{X_1 + \cdots + X_n}{n} \tag{1.2}$$

be the sample mean. For large sample size n, the standardized random variable

$$Z = \frac{\overline{X} - \mu}{\sigma/\sqrt{n}} \tag{1.3}$$

is approximately normally distributed with mean zero and variance one.

Since the standard deviation of the sample mean is [cf. Chapter 2, equation (2.21)]

$$\sigma_{\overline{X}} = \sigma/\sqrt{n}$$

the standard random variable Z in (1.3) may be written as

$$Z = \frac{\overline{X} - \mu}{\sigma_{\overline{X}}} . \tag{1.4}$$

Example 2.   A group of recruits has the mean height $\mu = 170$ cm and a standard deviation of $\sigma = 20$ cm. (a) What is the probability that the mean height of a sample of $n = 16$ recruits will exceed 175 cm? (b) Under 162.5 cm? (c) Between 165 and 177.5 cm?

Solution to (a):   Let $\bar{X}$ be the sample mean; its standard deviation is $\sigma_{\bar{X}} = \sigma/\sqrt{n} = 20/\sqrt{16} = 5$. We need to determine the probability

$$\Pr\{\bar{X} > 175\}.$$

Standardizing $\bar{X}$ gives

$$\Pr\left\{\frac{\bar{X} - \mu}{\sigma_{\bar{X}}} > \frac{175 - 170}{5}\right\}$$

or

$$\Pr\{Z > 1\}.$$

From the normal distribution table we find that $\Pr\{Z > 1\} = .16$. Therefore, the probability is .16 that the sample mean height will exceed 175 cm.

Example 3.   In Example 2, find two points equally distant from the mean such that the sample mean of $n = 16$ recruits will fall between the two values with a probability (a) .95, (b) .90, (c) .80.

Solution to (a):   Let the two values be $170 - c$ and $170 + c$ and determine the number c from the probability

$$\Pr\{170 - c < \bar{X} < 170 + c\} = .95. \tag{a}$$

Standardizing $\bar{X}$ yields

$$\Pr\left\{-\frac{c}{20/\sqrt{16}} < \frac{\bar{X} - \mu}{\sigma/\sqrt{n}} < \frac{c}{20/\sqrt{16}}\right\} = .95. \tag{b}$$

From the normal distribution table, we find

$$\Pr\{-1.96 < Z < 1.96\} = .95. \tag{c}$$

Comparing (b) with (c) gives the equation

$$\frac{c}{20/\sqrt{16}} = 1.96, \quad \text{or} \quad c = 9.8.$$

Therefore, the two values are $170 - 9.8 = 160.2$ cm and $170 + 9.8 = 179.8$ cm.

Example 4.   In the above example, if you were told the probability is .95 that the sample mean will be between 165 to 175 cm, how large is the sample size? Here the unknown quantity to be determined is the sample size n. Writing first

$$\Pr\{165 < \bar{X} < 175\} = .95 \tag{a}$$

and standardizing $\bar{X}$ yields

$$\Pr\left\{\frac{165-170}{20/\sqrt{n}} < \frac{\bar{X}-\mu}{\sigma/\sqrt{n}} < \frac{175-170}{20/\sqrt{n}}\right\} = .95. \qquad \text{(b)}$$

Consulting the normal distribution

$$\Pr\{-1.96 < Z < 1.96\} = .95$$

we find the equation

$$\frac{175-170}{20/\sqrt{n}} = 1.96$$

and the value n,

$$n = 62.$$

The significance of the Central Limit Theorem is that the theory holds regardless of the original distribution of X. If X is a dichotomous random variable taking on values 0 and 1, then, according to the theory, for large n, the standardized sample proportion

$$Z = \frac{\hat{p}-p}{\sqrt{pq/n}} \qquad (1.5)$$

is approximately normally distributed with mean zero and variance one.

Example 5. A sample of $n = 100$ death certificates is taken from a vital statistics office where the proportion of death from chronic heart diseases is $p = 20$ percent. Find the probability that there will be more than 25% deaths from chronic heart diseases in the sample, or

$$\Pr\{\hat{p} > .25\}.$$

Standardized $\hat{p}$ gives the probability

$$\Pr\left\{\frac{\hat{p}-p}{\sqrt{pq/n}} > \frac{.25-.20}{\sqrt{.20\times.80/100}}\right\}$$

or

$$\Pr\{Z > 1.25\} = .106.$$

The Central Limit Theorem applies also to the difference between two sample means and to the difference between two proportions. The standardized variable of $(\bar{X}_1 - \bar{X}_2)$,

$$Z = \frac{(\bar{X}_1 - \bar{X}_2) - (\mu_1 - \mu_2)}{\text{S.E.}(\bar{X}_1 - \bar{X}_2)}, \qquad (1.6)$$

has an approximately normal distribution with mean zero and standard deviation one, when the sample sizes n_1 and n_2 are moderately large. The denominator is the standard error of the difference $\overline{X}_1 - \overline{X}_2$. If the variances σ_1^2 and σ_2^2 are equal, $\sigma_1^2 = \sigma_2^2 = \sigma^2$, then

$$\text{S.E.}(\overline{X}_1 - \overline{X}_2) = \sigma\sqrt{\frac{1}{n_1} + \frac{1}{n_2}} \ . \tag{1.7}$$

The standardized variable of $(\hat{p}_1 - \hat{p}_2)$,

$$Z = \frac{(\hat{p}_1 - \hat{p}_2) - (p_1 - p_2)}{\text{S.E.}(\hat{p}_1 - \hat{p}_2)} , \tag{1.8}$$

also has an approximately normal distribution with mean zero and standard deviation one, when the sample sizes n_1 and n_2 are sufficiently large. The denominator is the standard error of the difference $\hat{p}_1 - \hat{p}_2$ as given in (2.24) in Chapter 2,

$$\text{S.E.}(\hat{p}_1 - \hat{p}_2) = \sqrt{\frac{p_1 q_1}{n_1} + \frac{p_2 q_2}{n_2}} \ . \tag{1.9}$$

Note that each of the standardized random variables in (1.3), (1.5), (1.6), and (1.8) is the deviation of the random variable from its mean expressed in terms of its standard error. The right-hand side of (1.8), for example, is the deviation of $(\hat{p}_1 - \hat{p}_2)$ from its expectation $(p_1 - p_2)$ in the units of the standard error $\text{S.E.}(\hat{p}_1 - \hat{p}_2)$. These standardized random variables are the basic component used in making statistical inferences about population means or about population proportions.

2.   Statistical Inference—Interval Estimation

Statistical inference about population means and about population proportions fall into two major categories: estimation and hypothesis testing. The underlying theory is somewhat complex, but its application to practical problems is relatively simple.

2.1.   Interval estimation—confidence interval.   We have seen in Chapter 2 that the sample mean $\overline{X}$ is an unbiased estimate of the population mean, μ. Since it assumes a single value, it is called a single-valued estimate, or a point estimate. Obviously, a sample mean is unlikely to be exactly equal to the population mean, and it varies from one sample to another. Furthermore, $\overline{X}$ is subject to variation as measured by its standard error, $\text{S.E.}(\overline{X})$. From this perspective, the sample mean is not as intuitively appealing an estimate as it first

seemed. Neither is any other point estimate. To resolve the predicament, the concept of interval estimation was developed. The *confidence* interval incorporates both the point estimate and its standard error in the estimation. Specifically, we establish an interval $(\bar{X} - c, \bar{X} + c)$ around $\bar{X}$ and claim that it contains the population mean μ. Since the population mean is unknown we cannot be *entirely* confident that the interval $(\bar{X} - c, \bar{X} + c)$ will contain μ. But we do have a certain degree of confidence that the interval $(\bar{X} - c, \bar{X} + c)$ will contain μ. Our confidence increases as the length of the interval increases. The exact relationship between the degree of confidence and the length of an interval can be established by using the Central Limit Theorem.

Consider a sample of size n with the sample mean $\bar{X}$ and the sample standard deviation S as point estimates of the population mean μ and the population standard deviation σ, respectively. We wish to find the 95% confidence interval for the population mean based on the sample information. That is to say, we wish to find an interval $(\bar{X} - c, \bar{X} + c)$ such that $\Pr\{\bar{X} - c < \mu < \bar{X} + c\} = .95$. From the normal distribution table, we find two numbers -1.96 and $+1.96$ for which

$$\Pr\{-1.96 < Z < 1.96\} = .95. \tag{2.1}$$

Recalling the standardized random variable of the sample mean $\bar{X}$ in (1.3) and using the Central Limit Theorem, we can write the inequalities inside the curly brackets as

$$-1.96 < \frac{\bar{X} - \mu}{S/\sqrt{n}} < 1.96, \tag{2.2}$$

where the sample standard deviation,

$$S = \sqrt{\frac{1}{n-1} \sum_{i=1}^{n} (X_i - \bar{X})^2} \, ,$$

is used in place of the unknown population standard deviation. This is almost always done, and the fact that the sample standard deviation is different from the population standard deviation subtracts slightly from our confidence. On the other hand, it is as good a substitution as one can hope for, since the sample standard deviation is an unbiased estimator of the population standard deviation. Formula (2.2) rearranges to yield the desired interval,

$$\bar{X} - 1.96S/\sqrt{n} < \mu < \bar{X} + 1.96S/\sqrt{n} \, . \tag{2.3}$$

The two limits $\bar{X} - 1.96S/\sqrt{n}$ and $\bar{X} + 1.96S/\sqrt{n}$ are called the lower confidence limit and the upper confidence limit, respectively. The interval from the lower limit to the upper limit is the desired confidence interval. The initial probability .95 is called the confidence coefficient, which measures the confidence that we have in the statement, "the interval $(\bar{X} - 1.96S/\sqrt{n}, \bar{X} + 1.96S\sqrt{n})$ contains μ."

For a given sample, the statement "the interval $(\bar{X} - 1.96\ S/\sqrt{n}, \bar{X} + 1.96S/\sqrt{n})$ contains μ" may be true or it may be false. However, if a large number of samples was taken, each of size n, and such a statement was made for each sample, then 95 percent of the statements would be true. In reality, we take only one sample and make only one statement. Therefore, we have some confidence in the truth of the statement, with .95 as a measure of our confidence.

The confidence coefficient is usually denoted by $1 - \alpha$, and the corresponding percentiles of the normal variable by $Z_{\alpha/2}$ and $Z_{1-\alpha/2}$. When $1 - \alpha = .95$, then $Z_{\alpha/2} = -1.96$ and $Z_{1-\alpha/2} = 1.96$. When $1 - \alpha = .90$, then $Z_{\alpha/2} = -1.65$ and $Z_{1-\alpha/2} = 1.65$. The 90 percent confidence interval for the population mean is

$$\bar{X} - 1.65S/\sqrt{n} < \mu < \bar{X} + 1.65S/\sqrt{n} . \tag{2.4}$$

Example 6.   Find the 95% confidence interval for the population mean μ of the "height of army recruits," when the sample mean height of $n = 400$ recruits is 173 cms.; the sample standard deviation is $S = 20$ cms.

Substituting the observed sample values in (2.3) gives the limits:

$$\bar{X} - 1.96S/\sqrt{n} = 173 - 1.96\frac{20}{\sqrt{400}} = 171 \text{ cm.}$$

and

$$\bar{X} + 1.96S/\sqrt{n} = 173 + 1.96\frac{20}{\sqrt{400}} = 175 \text{ cm.}$$

Thus we have a 95% confidence that the interval from 171 cm to 175 cm contains the population mean height μ.

All this applies equally well to the interval estimation of a population proportion, a difference between two population means, or a difference between two population proportions.

The 95% confidence interval for the population proportion p is

$$\hat{p} - 1.96\sqrt{\frac{\hat{p}\hat{q}}{n}} < p < \hat{p} + 1.96\sqrt{\frac{\hat{p}\hat{q}}{n}} ; \tag{2.5}$$

for the difference between means, it is

$$\left(\overline{X}_1 - \overline{X}_2\right) - 1.96 S_p \sqrt{\frac{1}{n_1} + \frac{1}{n_2}}$$

$$< \mu_1 - \mu_2 < \left(\overline{X}_1 - \overline{X}_2\right) + 1.96 S_p \sqrt{\frac{1}{n_1} + \frac{1}{n_2}} \; , \qquad (2.6)$$

where the pooled sample standard deviation of samples 1 and 2,

$$S_p = \sqrt{\frac{(n_1 - 1)S_1^2 + (n_2 - 1)S_2^2}{n_1 + n_2 - 2}} \; ,$$

is an estimate of the common standard deviation σ of X_1 and X_2 in (1.7). Finally, the 95% confidence interval for the difference between two population proportions is

$$\left(\hat{p}_1 - \hat{p}_2\right) - 1.96 \sqrt{\frac{\hat{p}_1 \hat{q}_1}{n_1} + \frac{\hat{p}_2 \hat{q}_2}{n_2}}$$

$$< p_1 - p_2 < \left(\hat{p}_1 - \hat{p}_2\right) + 1.96 \sqrt{\frac{\hat{p}_1 \hat{q}_1}{n_1} + \frac{\hat{p}_2 \hat{q}_2}{n_2}} \; . \qquad (2.7)$$

3. Statistical Inference—Hypothesis Testing

   Hypothesis testing—Many scientific investigations are performed for the purpose of verifying some theory (or hypothesis) under consideration. A biochemist may wish to determine the sensitivity of a new test for the diagnosis of cancer; a demographer may want to compare the longevity of people in different countries. In a mortality analysis, one may be interested in the trend of survivorship over a period of time. Statistical hypothesis testing is a procedure designed for such purposes.

3.1. Testing hypotheses of two proportions (probabilities).

Suppose a study is conducted in order to evaluate the effectiveness of a new drug (D_1) compared to an old drug (D_2) for relieving hay fever symptoms. A group of n_1 patients receives the new drug (D_1) and a group of n_2 patients receives the old drug (D_2). Proportions of patients in the two groups, $\hat{p}_1$ and $\hat{p}_2$, respectively, find the drug effective. What can we say about the effectiveness of the new drug? Is the new drug an improvement over the old drug? These questions can be answered by the test of a statistical hypothesis concerning two probabilities. Let p_1 be the probability that a patient who receives the new drug will find it effective, and p_2 be the probability that a patient who received the old drug will find it effective. The hypothesis being tested, or the null hypothesis, is $H_0: p_1 = p_2$ that the two drugs are equally effective; it is tested against the alternative hypothesis $H_1: p_1 > p_2$, that the new drug is better.

   To test the hypothesis using the sample information we compare the sample difference $\hat{p}_1 - \hat{p}_2$ with its expectation $E(\hat{p}_1 - \hat{p}_2) = p_1 - p_2$. If the hypothesis $H_0: p_1 = p_2$ (or $p_1 - p_2 = 0$) is true, then the sample difference $\hat{p}_1 - \hat{p}_2$ should not be too much greater than zero. If the difference $\hat{p}_1 - \hat{p}_2$ is significantly greater than zero, then the hypothesis H_0 is probably false and should be rejected. The significance of a given $\hat{p}_1 - \hat{p}_2$ is determined as follows: We express the deviation $(\hat{p}_1 - \hat{p}_2) - 0$ in units of the standard error,

$$\frac{(\hat{p}_1 - \hat{p}_2) - 0}{\text{S.E.}(\hat{p}_1 - \hat{p}_2)}, \tag{3.1}$$

and compute the probability

$$\Pr\left\{ Z > \frac{(\hat{p}_1 - \hat{p}_2) - 0}{\text{S.E.}(\hat{p}_1 - \hat{p}_2)} \right\}. \tag{3.2}$$

This is the probability that the difference of any two sample proportions will exceed the observed differences $\hat{p}_1 - \hat{p}_2$ if H_0 is true. If this probability is small, say

$$\Pr\left\{ Z > \frac{(\hat{p}_1 - \hat{p}_2) - 0}{\text{S.E.}(\hat{p}_1 - \hat{p}_2)} \right\} \leqslant .05, \tag{3.3}$$

then the observed difference $\hat{p}_1 - \hat{p}_2$ is significant and H_0 is rejected.

   In a practical problem where both the difference $\hat{p}_1 - \hat{p}_2$ and the standard error are known, the probability in (3.2) can be computed and appropriate action can be taken regarding rejection or acceptance of H_0. The observed value of the probability in (3.2) is often known as "the P value", so H_0 is rejected if "the P value" is small, smaller than .05, for example. The typical value of the probability, such as .05, is called the level of significance.

   The formula for the standard error in (3.1) has a slightly different form from that given in (1.9) and (2.7) and needs some explanation. Under the hypothesis $H_0: p_1 = p_2 = p$, the common p can be estimated with the pooled information of the two samples. The sum $n_1\hat{p}_1 + n_2\hat{p}_2$ is the total number of patients in the entire group of $(n_1 + n_2)$ who have found the drugs effective, and

$$\hat{p} = \frac{n_1\hat{p}_1 + n_2\hat{p}_2}{n_1 + n_2} \tag{3.4}$$

is the corresponding sample proportion. Using $\hat{p}$ as an estimate of the common value of p_1 and p_2, the standard error of the difference becomes

$$\text{S.E.}(\hat{p}_1 - \hat{p}_2) = \sqrt{\frac{\hat{p}\hat{q}}{n_1} + \frac{\hat{p}\hat{q}}{n_2}} = \sqrt{\hat{p}\hat{q}\left(\frac{1}{n_1} + \frac{1}{n_2}\right)}. \qquad (3.5)$$

This formula of the standard error is preferred since the estimate $\hat{p}$ in (3.4) is based on a larger sample (namely, $n_1 + n_2$), and thus subject to less variation.

Suppose in the hay fever example, $n_1 = 200$, $n_2 = 200$ and $\hat{p}_1 = .85$ and $\hat{p}_2 = .75$. We find $\hat{p}_1 - \hat{p}_2 = .85 - .75 = .10$,

$$\hat{p} = \frac{200 \times .85 + 200 \times .75}{200 + 200} = .80$$

and the standard error

$$\text{S.E.}(\hat{p}_1 - \hat{p}_2) = \sqrt{.80 \times .20\left(\frac{1}{200} + \frac{1}{200}\right)} = .04.$$

Substituting these values in (3.2) yields the probability

$$\Pr\left\{Z > \frac{.10}{.04}\right\}$$

or

$$\Pr\{Z > 2.5\} = .006.$$

Since the probability .006 is much smaller than .05 or .01, we reject the hypothesis $H_0: p_1 = p_2$ and conclude that $p_1 > p_2$, the new drug is better.

Remark 1. The quantity in (3.1) is known as the test statistic, or the Z-score. The value of the test statistic can be used directly in testing a hypothesis. Since

$$\Pr\{Z > 1.65\} = .05,$$

formula (3.3) is equivalent to the statement

$$\frac{\hat{p}_1 - \hat{p}_2}{\text{S.E.}(\hat{p}_1 - \hat{p}_2)} > 1.65.$$

Therefore, if the test statistic in (3.1) exceeds 1.65, H_0 is rejected. Thus, in testing a statistical hypothesis, the action of rejecting or accepting a null hypothesis H_0 may be taken on the basis of either the probability in (3.2) or the value of the statistic in (3.1). The results are the same.

Remark 2. *The level of significance and the critical value of the statistic.*
The typical value, such as .05, with which one compares the probability in (3.2) are known as the level of significance and is denoted by α.
The level of significance is the probability of rejecting the null
hypothesis H_0 when H_0 is in fact true, or the probability of "the first
kind" of error. The more serious the consequence of rejecting a true
hypothesis (making the first kind of error), the smaller should be the
corresponding probability, α. The recommended values for common
use are $\alpha = .05, .01, .001$.

The statistic in (3.1) is the basic instrument for testing a statistical hypothesis. The value of this statistic is what determines our
action. The relationship between the critical values of the statistic and
the level of significance is demonstrated in formula (3.3). For each
level of significance, there is a corresponding value of the statistic.
For $\alpha = .05, .01$, and .001, the critical values are $Z_{1-\alpha} = 1.65, 2.33$
and 3.09, respectively.

Remark 3. *Rejection of a hypothesis and the level of significance.*   It is not
uncommon in practice that the null hypothesis H_0 is rejected at one
level of significance but not rejected at another. For example, if the
value of the statistic is 1.75 (or the probability in (3.2) is .04), H_0 is
rejected at the 5% level of significance but not at the 1% level.
Therefore, in rejecting or accepting a null hypothesis, the level of
significance should be stated or the probability in (3.2) should be
given. A statement such as "H_0 is rejected at the 5% level of
significance" is meaningful while "H_0 is rejected" is useless.

Remark 4. *One-sided test vs. two-sided test.*   In the above example, the
hypothesis $H_0 : p_1 = p_2$ was tested against the alternative hypothesis
$H_1 : p_1 > p_2$. The test is to reject H_0 if the observed difference $\hat{p}_1 - \hat{p}_2$
is too large, or if the probability

$$\Pr\left\{ Z > \frac{\hat{p}_1 - \hat{p}_2}{\text{S.E.}(\hat{p}_1 - \hat{p}_2)} \right\} \qquad (3.2)$$

is too small. This test is called a one-sided test, as we use the one-side
(upper side) of the normal curve for our action. The alternative
hypothesis $H_1 : p_1 > p_2$ is called a one-sided alternative. If the null
hypothesis H_0 is tested against the alternative $H_2 : p_1 < p_2$, H_0 is
rejected if the difference $\hat{p}_1 - \hat{p}_2$ is too small, or the probability

$$\Pr\left\{ Z < \frac{\hat{p}_1 - \hat{p}_2}{\text{S.E.}(\hat{p}_1 - \hat{p}_2)} \right\} \qquad (3.6)$$

is too small. The alternative hypothesis H_2 also is a one-sided alternative and the test is a one-sided test, using the lower side of the normal
curve.

If the null hypothesis $H_0: p_1 = p_2$ is tested against the alternative hypothesis $H_3: p_1 \neq p_2$, then H_0 is rejected if the difference $\hat{p}_1 - \hat{p}_2$ is either too large or too small, or the probability,

$$\Pr\left\{ Z < \frac{\hat{p}_1 - \hat{p}_2}{\text{S.E.}(\hat{p}_1 - \hat{p}_2)} \text{ or } Z > \frac{\hat{p}_1 - \hat{p}_2}{\text{S.E.}(\hat{p}_1 - \hat{p}_2)} \right\} \quad (3.7)$$

is too small. Here the test is a two-sided test, the statistic has two critical values. For the level of significance $\alpha = .05$, for example, the critical values of the statistic are -1.96 and $+1.96$.

The choice of an alternative hypothesis, $H_1: p_1 > p_2$, $H_2: p_1 < p_2$, or $H_3: p_1 \neq p_2$, in a practical situation depends on the nature of the problem. The rule of thumb is that the alternative hypothesis could contain a statement that one wishes to prove. If one wishes to prove that the new drug is better than the old drug in relieving hay fever symptoms, the alternative hypothesis should be $H_1: p_1 > p_2$.

3.1.1.   Summary.   The above procedure for testing hypotheses is summarized below:

(1)   *Type of hypothesis*: Hypotheses concerning two probabilities.
(2)   *Hypothesis tested* (or null hypothesis): $H_0: p_1 = p_2$.
(3)   *Alternative hypothesis*: $H_1: p_1 > p_2$.
(4)   *Test statistic*:

$$Z = \frac{(\hat{p}_1 - \hat{p}_2) - 0}{\text{S.E.}(\hat{p}_1 - \hat{p}_2)}.$$

(5)   *Rule of action*: Reject H_0 if the value of the statistic is too large, larger than $Z_{1-\alpha} = 1.65$, for example. *or*, reject H_0 if the probability in (3.2) is too small, smaller than $\alpha = 0.5$, for example.

3.2.   Testing hypotheses of population proportions, and of population means—A summary.   We have presented in the preceding section the basic ideas of hypothesis testing. They apply to testing hypotheses concerning a single proportion, a single population mean, two population means, and others, with minor changes of the test statistic. For example, in testing the hypothesis concerning a single

Table 1. Levels of significance and critical values

Level of Significance α	Critical Values of Z			
	$Z_{\alpha/2}$	Z_{α}	$Z_{1-\alpha}$	$Z_{1-\alpha/2}$
.05	-1.96	-1.65	1.65	1.96
.01	-2.58	-2.33	2.33	2.58
.001	-3.30	-3.09	3.09	3.30

Table 2. Test of Hypothesis-Summary

Type of Hypothesis	Hypothesis tested (null hypothesis)	Alternative Hypothesis	Test Statistic	Rule of action: Reject H_0 if: the value of the test statistic is:
(I) Concerning a single population mean	$H_0 : \mu = \mu_0$	$H_1 : \mu > \mu_0$ $H_2 : \mu < \mu_0$ $H_3 : \mu \neq \mu_0$	$Z = \dfrac{\bar{X} - \mu_0}{S/\sqrt{n}}$	$Z > Z_{1-\alpha}$ $Z < Z_\alpha$ $Z < Z_{\alpha/2}$ or $Z > Z_{1-\alpha/2}$
(II) Concerning the means of two populations where S_p is the pooled sample standard deviation	$H_0 : \mu_1 = \mu_2$	$H_1 : \mu_1 > \mu_2$	$Z = \dfrac{(\bar{X}_1 - \bar{X}_2) - 0}{S_p\sqrt{1/n_1 + 1/n_2}}$	$Z > Z_{1-\alpha}$
(III) Concerning a single population	$H_0 : p = p_0$	$H_1 : p > p_0$	$Z = \dfrac{\hat{p} - p_0}{\sqrt{p_0 q_0/n}}$	$Z > Z_{1-\alpha}$
(IV) Concerning proportions of two populations where $\hat{p}$ is the pooled sample proportion	$H_0 : p_1 = p_2$	$H_1 : p_1 > p_2$	$Z = \dfrac{(\hat{p}_1 - \hat{p}_2) - 0}{\sqrt{\hat{p}\hat{q}(1/n_1 + 1/n_2)}}$	$Z > Z_{1-\alpha}$

population mean μ, the null hypothesis specifies the value of μ, $H_0: \mu = \mu_0$. The corresponding test statistic is

$$Z = \frac{\overline{X} - \mu_0}{\text{S.E.}_{\overline{X}}} . \qquad (3.8)$$

The other steps in the test of $H_0: \mu = \mu_0$ follow line by line the procedure given in the preceding section. To avoid repetition and for the convenience of the reader, critical values of Z corresponding to the level of significance $\alpha = .05, .01, .001$ are given in Table 1 and a summary of tests of each of the four hypotheses is given in Table 2.

4. The Chi-Square Test

The chi-square test is one of the most commonly used tests in statistics. Generally, it is for testing hypotheses concerning the distribution of a random variable rather than the parameter (μ or σ) of the distribution. The hypothesis may be regarding:

(a) the distribution of a discrete variable—the number of children in a family who have measles has a binomial distribution, or
(b) the distribution of a continuous variable—the heights of army recruits have a normal distribution, or
(c) the independence of two or more random variables—the blood type distribution in a population is independent of national origin.

In each case the data are in the form of a frequency distribution. The hypothesis tested provides direction for the computation of expected frequencies. The test statistic is based on the comparison of the expected frequencies with the corresponding observed frequencies. We shall illustrate the use of the chi-square for testing the hypothesis concerning the *independence of two variables*.

The usual layout of the frequency distribution of two categorical variables, say X and Y, is a two-way contingency table as in Table 3, where the n_{ij}'s are the frequencies. Each expected frequency is the product of the two corresponding marginal totals divided by the total sample size N. For example, the expected frequency E_{12} is computed from $E_{12} = m_1 n_2 / N$ or generally

$$E_{ij} = \frac{m_i n_j}{N}, \qquad i = 1, \ldots, r; \quad j = 1, \ldots, c, \qquad (4.1)$$

where r (for "rows") is the number of categories of X and c (for "columns") is the number of categories of Y. The test statistic is

$$\chi^2 = \frac{(n_{11} - E_{11})^2}{E_{11}} + \cdots + \frac{(n_{rc} - E_{rc})^2}{E_{rc}}, \qquad (4.2)$$

Table 3. Joint Frequency Distribution of Variables X and Y

Categories of Variable X	Categories of Variable Y 1	2	$\cdots$	c	Marginal Row Totals
1	n_{11} (E_{11})	n_{12} (E_{12})	$\cdots$	n_{1c} (E_{1c})	m_1
2	n_{21} (E_{21})	n_{22} (E_{22})	$\cdots$	n_{2c} (E_{2c})	m_2
$\vdots$	$\vdots$	$\vdots$		$\vdots$	$\vdots$
	n_{r1} (E_{r1})	n_{r2} (E_{r2})	$\cdots$	n_{rc} (E_{rc})	m_r
Marginal Column Totals	n_1	n_2	$\cdots$	n_c	N

which has the chi-square distribution with $(r - 1) \times (c - 1)$ degrees of freedom, if the hypothesis of independence is true. The chi-square distribution is actually a set of distributions, one for each number of degrees of freedom. Just as $(\overline{X} - \mu)/\text{S.E.}(\overline{X})$ has a normal distribution in the previous section, χ^2 has a chi-square distribution. Using the χ^2 test is exactly analogous to using the test in the previous section. The magnitude of the chi-square depends primarily on the difference $(n_{ij} - E_{ij})$. If the chi-square value is too large, the null hypothesis is rejected.

Example 7.   The blood type distribution of the human population is known to vary with national origin. For example, blood type B seems to be more prevalent among Chinese than among Europeans, while blood type A is more prominent among Americans than Chinese. In his book *Immunology and Serology*, P. L. Carpenter discusses this problem in some detail. The data in Table 4 are adapted from this book. The null hypothesis is that the blood type distribution is independent of national origin. Under this hypothesis, the proportions

Table 4. Distribution of Blood Type in Three Populations— American, Chinese, and Norwegian

Blood Type	U.S.	Chinese	Norwegian	Marginal Row Totals
O	450(376)	300(376)	190(188)	940
A	410(364)	250(364)	250(182)	910
B	100(196)	350(196)	40(98)	490
AB	40(64)	100(64)	20(32)	160
Marginal Column Totals	1000	1000	500	2500

Adapted from: Philip L. Carpenter, *Immunology and Serology*, Saunders: Philadelphia, 1956.

of people having blood type (O, A, B, AB) in each of the three populations are expected to be

$$\left(\frac{940}{2500}, \frac{910}{2500}, \frac{490}{2500}, \frac{160}{2500} \right).$$

Applying these proportions to each group gives the corresponding expected frequencies. These are the numbers in parentheses in the table. The expected number of Americans in a group of 1000 that will have blood type O, for example, is

$$1000\left(\frac{940}{2500} \right) = 376.$$

The chi-square value is

$$\chi^2 = \frac{(450 - 376)^2}{376} + \cdots + \frac{(20 - 32)^2}{32} = 333.$$

In this case, the chi-square has $(3 - 1) \times (4 - 1) = 6$ degrees of freedom. The critical value at $\alpha = .01$ level of significance is $\chi^2_{.99} = 16.81$. The observed chi-square value is highly significant. Therefore, the blood type distributions of the three national origins are different. A casual inspection of the table confirms the impression that blood type B is more common among Chinese, blood type A is more common among Americans and Norwegians, and blood type O is more prevalent in the U.S. than in either China or Norway.

An important special case of the two-way contingency table is when both variables are dichotomous, $r = 2$ and $c = 2$. The resulting table is a 2 by 2 table, or a four-fold table. The chi-square test for four-fold data has been used to study the effect of the exposure to an antecedent factor (smoking) to the presence of a condition (lung cancer), to the study of the response to a treatment in a case-control study, and many others. Table 5 is a typical four-fold table. The formula for the chi-square is usually written as

$$\chi^2 = \frac{(n_{11}n_{22} - n_{12}n_{21})^2 N}{m_1 m_2 n_1 n_2}, \tag{4.3}$$

which is the same as (4.2) when $r = 2$ and $c = 2$.

Table 5. A Four-fold Table

Categories of X	Categories of Y 1	2	Row Totals
1	n_{11}	n_{12}	m_1
2	n_{21}	n_{22}	m_2
Column Totals	n_1	n_2	N

Remark 5.   *Relation of the chi-square test with the normal test.*   When the two variables X and Y are dichotomous variables, the hypothesis that the distribution of variable X is independent of variable Y is the same as the hypothesis that the proportions (of $X = 1$) in the two populations $(Y = 1)$ and $(Y = 2)$ are equal. That is, $H_0: p_1 = p_2$. The estimates of the two proportions (of $X = 1$) are

$$\hat{p}_1 = \frac{n_{11}}{n_1} \quad \text{and} \quad \hat{p}_2 = \frac{n_{12}}{n_2} . \tag{4.4}$$

Under the hypothesis $H_0: p_1 = p_2 = p$ the estimate of the common proportion p is

$$\hat{p} = \frac{m_1}{N} . \tag{4.5}$$

The test statistic, as we have seen in (3.1), is

$$Z = \frac{(\hat{p}_1 - \hat{p}_2) - 0}{\sqrt{\hat{p}\hat{q}\left(\dfrac{1}{n_1} + \dfrac{1}{n_2}\right)}} . \tag{4.6}$$

Obviously, there is a definite relationship between the χ^2 statistic in (4.3) and the Z statistic in (4.6). The relationship is

$$Z^2 = \chi^2, \tag{4.7}$$

the square of the standard normal random variable has a chi-square distribution with one degree of freedom.

The following example shows the equivalence of the two tests in numerical values.

Example 8.   We have discussed in Section 3.1 an example of responses to two drugs, D_1 and D_2, for relief of hay fever symptoms. The null hypothesis was that the drugs were equally effective, or $H_0: p_1 = p_2$. On the basis of the observed values $\hat{p}_1 = .85$, $\hat{p}_2 = .75$, S.E.$(\hat{p}_1 - \hat{p}_2) = .04$. The value of the test statistic was

$$Z = \frac{(\hat{p}_1 - \hat{p}_2) - 0}{\text{S.E.}(\hat{p}_1 - \hat{p}_2)} = \frac{.10}{.04} = 2.5,$$

which exceeds the critical $Z = 1.96$. The two drugs are not equally effective.

We now use the chi-square test to study the problem. The data are produced in a four-fold table in Table 6. The null hypothesis that the responses to the treatment are independent of the drugs is tested against the alternative hypothesis that the responses vary with the

Table 6. Response to Drugs D_1 and D_2

Responses	Drugs D_1	D_2	Row Totals
Effective	170	150	320
	(160)	(160)	
Not Effective	30	50	80
	(40)	(40)	
Column Totals	200	200	400

drugs. Using formula (4.3) we find

$$\chi^2 = \frac{(170 \times 50 - 150 \times 30)^2 400}{320 \times 80 \times 200 \times 200} = 6.25$$

which is equal to the square of $Z = 2.5$, as anticipated from the relation in (4.7). Since 6.25 exceeds the critical $\chi^2_{.95} = 3.84$, the null hypothesis is rejected. The two drugs are not equally effective.

Remark 6. *The chi-square test and one-sided alternative.* Generally, the chi-square test is used to test the hypothesis of independence against the alternative that the independence hypothesis is not true, or $p_1 \neq p_2$, a two-sided alternative. The chi-square value is compared with the critical value $\chi^2_{1-\alpha}$. For example, at the $\alpha = .05$ level of significance, the critical value is $\chi^2_{.95} = 3.84$. Here $3.84 = (\pm 1.96)^2$ and -1.96 and $+1.96$ are the critical values of Z for the two-sided alternative $H_1 : p_1 \neq p_2$. If the hypothesis of independence is tested against a one-sided alternative $H_2 : p_1 > p_2$, then the computed chi-square value should be compared with the critical value $\chi^2_{1-2\alpha}$: for $\alpha = .05$, the critical value is $\chi^2_{.90} = 2.71$. Here $2.71 = (1.65)^2$, and 1.65 is the critical value of Z for the one-sided alternative $H_2 : p_1 > p_2$. Although the chi-square value detects only the significance of a test and not the direction of significance, it is easy to check with the data whether a significant chi-square value is due to $\hat{p}_1 > \hat{p}_2$ or due to $\hat{p}_2 > \hat{p}_1$. In reality, when one wishes to prove $p_1 > p_2$, it is unlikely that the observed value $\hat{p}_2$ will be significantly greater than $\hat{p}_1$.

Example 9. *Congenital abnormality and sex of infant.* This example appeared in Chapter 1, Section 3. We computed two conditional probabilities of congenital abnormality,

$$\Pr\{\text{a boy is abnormal}\} = \Pr\{A \mid B\} = \frac{n(AB)}{n(B)} = \frac{70}{400} = .175$$

$$\Pr\{\text{a girl is abnormal}\} = \Pr\{A \mid \overline{B}\} = \frac{n(A\overline{B})}{n(\overline{B})} = \frac{50}{400} = .125.$$

Table 7. Distribution of 800 children by sex and by congenital abnormality (hypothetical data)

Congenital Abnormality	Sex Boy B	Sex Girl $\overline{B}$	Marginal Row Total
Abnormal	70	50	120
A	$n(AB)$	$n(A\overline{B})$	$n(A)$
Normal	330	350	680
$\overline{A}$	$n(\overline{A}B)$	$n(\overline{A}\overline{B})$	$n(\overline{A})$
Marginal	400	400	800
Column Total	$n(B)$	$n(\overline{B})$	n

The difference between the two probabilities may be due to chance. We can now ascertain the significance of the difference by means of the chi-square test. The null hypothesis that congenital abnormality is independent of the sex of a child is tested against the alternative hypothesis that the abnormality is dependent upon the sex of a child. We reproduced the data in Table 7 and compute the chi-square value

$$\chi^2 = \frac{(70 \times 350 - 330 \times 50)^2 800}{400 \times 400 \times 120 \times 680} = 3.92,$$

which is highly significant. Therefore, the difference of the two probabilities is not due to chance. Congenital abnormality is dependent upon the sex of a child.

This example illustrates the importance of statistical hypothesis testing; the fact that the two sample proportions differ does not imply an underlying dependence of distributions. The chi-square test determines if the difference is statistically significant.

Epilogue. The material presented in Chapter 2 and in this chapter is a brief resumé of the fundamental concepts of statistics and is included for the convenience of the reader of this book. The fine points of statistical theory have been omitted. Since studies of mortality and life tables usually are based on the experience of a large population, the normal distribution is a good approximation to the distribution of the standardized sample means or sample proportions. Readers interested in a more detailed discussion on statistical principles and methods should consult a textbook on statistics.

5.   Problems for Solution

1.   Use the rules of expectation and variance to show that the standardized random variable

$$Z = \frac{X - \mu}{\sigma}$$

Table 8. Standard Cumulative Normal Distribution

Area	z	Area	z	Area	z	Area	z
.0006	-3.25	.1587	-1.00	.8531	1.05	.00001	-4.265
.0007	-3.20	.1711	$-.95$	.8643	1.10	.0001	-3.719
.0008	-3.15	.1841	$-.90$	.8749	1.15	.001	-3.090
.0010	-3.10	.1977	$-.85$	.8849	1.20	.005	-2.576
.0011	-3.05	.2119	$-.80$	.8944	1.25	.01	-2.326
.0013	-3.00	.2266	$-.75$	.9032	1.30	.02	-2.054
.0016	-2.95	.2420	$-.70$	.9115	1.35	.025	-1.960
.0019	-2.90	.2578	$-.65$	.9192	1.40	.03	-1.881
.0022	-2.85	.2743	$-.60$	.9265	1.45	.04	-1.751
.0026	-2.80	.2912	$-.55$	.9332	1.50	.05	-1.645
.0030	-2.75	.3085	$-.50$	.9394	1.55	.06	-1.555
.0035	-2.70	.3264	$-.45$	.9452	1.60	.07	-1.476
.0040	-2.65	.3446	$-.40$	.9505	1.65	.08	-1.405
.0047	-2.60	.3632	$-.35$	.9554	1.70	.09	-1.341
.0054	-2.55	.3821	$-.30$	.9599	1.75	.10	-1.282
.0062	-2.50	.4013	$-.25$	.9641	1.80	.15	-1.036
.0071	-2.45	.4207	$-.20$	.9678	1.85	.20	$-.842$
.0082	-2.40	.4404	$-.15$	.9713	1.90	.25	$-.674$
.0094	-2.35	.4602	$-.10$	.9744	1.95	.30	$-.524$
.0107	-2.30	.4801	$-.05$	.9772	2.00	.35	$-.385$
.0122	-2.25			.9798	2.05	.40	$-.253$
.0139	-2.20			.9821	2.10	.45	$-.126$
.0158	-2.15	.5000	.00	.9842	2.15	.50	.000
.0179	-2.10			.9861	2.20	.55	.126
.0202	-2.05			.9878	2.25	.60	.253
.0228	-2.00	.5199	.05	.9893	2.30	.65	.385
.0256	-1.95	.5398	.10	.9906	2.35	.70	.524
.0287	-1.90	.5596	.15	.9918	2.40	.75	.674
.0322	-1.85	.5793	.20	.9929	2.45	.80	.842
.0359	-1.80	.5987	.25	.9938	2.50	.85	1.036
.0401	-1.75	.6179	.30	.9946	2.55	.90	1.282
.0446	-1.70	.6368	.35	.9953	2.60	.91	1.341
.0495	-1.65	.6554	.40	.9960	2.65	.92	1.405
.0548	-1.60	.6736	.45	.9965	2.70	.93	1.476
.0606	-1.55	.6915	.50	.9970	2.75	.94	1.555
.0668	-1.50	.7088	.55	.9974	2.80	.95	1.645
.0735	-1.45	.7257	.60	.9978	2.85	.96	1.751
.0808	-1.40	.7422	.65	.9981	2.90	.97	1.881
.0885	-1.35	.7580	.70	.9984	2.95	.975	1.960
.0968	-1.30	.7734	.75	.9987	3.00	.98	2.054
.1056	-1.25	.7881	.80	.9989	3.05	.99	2.326
.1151	-1.20	.8023	.85	.9990	3.10	.995	2.576
.1251	-1.15	.8159	.90	.9992	3.15	.999	3.090
.1357	-1.10	.8289	.95	.9993	3.20	.9999	3.719
.1469	-1.05	.8413	1.00	.9994	3.25	.99999	4.265

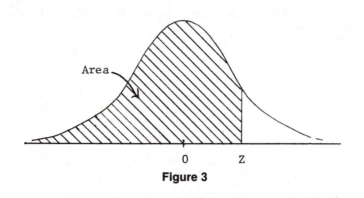

Figure 3

Note: The reader should consult the above diagram in using the normal distribution table on page 67.

---

has a mean zero and a variance one. Does X have to be a normal random variable?

2. Suppose the weights of a group of boys are normally distributed with a mean weight $\mu = 40$ kilograms (kg) and a standard deviation $\sigma = 4$ kg. What percent of the children weigh less than 47.84 kg? Less than 36 kg? More than 37.6 kg? More than 32.16 kg? More than 44 kg?

3. *Continuation.* If a boy is picked at random from the group in problem 2, what is the probability that his weight is between 36 kg and 44 kg? Between 33.4 kg and 47.84 kg? Between 32.16 kg and 46.4 kg?

4. *Continuation.* Find the weight so that 10% of the boys weigh less than this value. 15% of the boys weigh more. Weigh less.

5. *Continuation.* Find two weights equally distant from 40 kg so that 80% of the boys weigh between these two weights. 95% of the boys weigh between these two weights?

6. A group of recruits has the mean height $\mu = 170$ cm and a standard deviation $\sigma = 20$ cm. What is the probability that the mean weight of a sample of n recruits will be under 162.5 cm if $n = 16$? If $n = 4$?

7. *Continuation.* What is the probability that the mean height of a sample of n recruits will be above 162.5 cm if $n = 4$? If $n = 16$? If $n = 36$? If $n = 64$?

8. *Continuation.* What is the probability that the mean height of a sample of n recruits will be between 165 and 177.5 cm if $n = 4$? If $n = 16$? If $n = 36$? If $n = 64$?

9. *Continuation.* Find two points equally distant from the mean $\mu = 170$ cm such that a sample mean of n recruits will fall between the two values with a probability .95 if $n = 4$? If $n = 36$? If $n = 64$?

10. *Continuation.* Find the two points in Problem 9 for the probability .90. For the probability .80.

11. *Continuation.* In the above example, if you were told the probability was .90 that the sample mean will be between 165 to 175 cm, how large is the sample size? Between 162 and 178 cm? Between 160 and 180 cm?

12. A sample of n death certificates is taken from a vital statistics office where the proportion of deaths from chronic heart disease is $p = 20$ percent. Find the probability that there will be more than 25% deaths from chronic heart disease in the sample if $n = 100$. If $n = 144$. If $n = 225$. If $n = 400$.

13. *Continuation.* Find the probability that the proportion of deaths from chronic heart disease in a sample of $n = 100$ certificates is less than 15%. Between 15% and 25%. In a sample of $n = 144$ certificates. $n = 225$ certificates. $n = 400$ certificates. $n = 400$ certificates.

14. *Continuation.* In the above example, if you were told the probability is .95 that the proportion of deaths from chronic heart disease in the sample of n certificates is between 15% and 25%, how large is n? Between 18% and 22%? Between 15% and 22%?

15. Find the 90% confidence interval for the mean weight of a group of school children when the sample mean weight of $n = 100$ children is $\bar{X} = 38$ kg and the sample standard deviation is $S = 4$ kg. Find the 95% confidence interval.

16. *Continuation.* If the population standard deviation is $\sigma = 4$ kg, how large should a sample size n be so that the length of the 95% confidence interval for the population mean is at most 2 kg? For a 90% confidence interval?

17. It was pointed out in Remark 5, page 64 that the standard normal random variable Z (with a zero mean and unit variance) and the χ^2 statistic with one degree of freedom have the following relationship

$$Z^2 = \chi^2. \tag{4.7}$$

In the case of testing hypotheses concerning two proportions $p_1 = p_2$ with the observed data shown in Table 5, page 63, we have

$$\chi^2 = \frac{(n_{11}n_{22} - n_{12}n_{21})^2 N}{m_1 m_2 n_1 n_2} \tag{4.3}$$

and

$$Z = \frac{(\hat{p}_1 - \hat{p}_2) - 0}{\sqrt{\hat{p}\hat{q}\left(\dfrac{1}{n_1} + \dfrac{1}{n_2}\right)}}$$

(4.6)

where $\hat{p}_1$, $\hat{p}_2$ and $\hat{p}(\hat{q} = 1 - \hat{p})$ are given in (4.4) and (4.5), respectively. Show that algebraically the relationship in (4.7) holds true in this case.

18. The sample variance of n observations, $X_1, \ldots, X_n$, is commonly given in the formula

$$S^2 = \frac{1}{n - 1} \sum_{i=1}^{n} (X_i - \bar{X})^2.$$

(A)

Alternately it can be expressed as

$$S^2 = \frac{1}{2n(n - 1)} \sum_i \sum_j (X_i - X_j)^2.$$

(B)

Prove the equality of these two expressions.

CHAPTER *4*

Age-Specific Death Rate and Other Measures of Mortality

1. Introduction

The age-specific probability of death and the age-specific death rate are two distinct measures of the risk of death among individuals in the population. The probability of death for an age interval is defined as the number of deaths in the interval divided by the number of individuals living at the beginning of the interval. However, there are several definitions of the age-specific death rate; some do not reflect the true meaning of the rate. For a review of different definitions, refer to Linder and Grove (1959). We will give the exact formula of the age-specific death rate and its relationship with the probability of death in Section 2.

Age-specific probability of death is the basic quantity in the construction of life tables. It is also the ultimate measure in studies of the mortality pattern of a population, in determining mortality trend, in comparing survival experience of different communities, in computing insurance premiums, and in many other situations. The definition of the probability is simple and clear; statistical inference concerning the probability, as outlined in Chapter 3, can be easily made. Therefore, the age-specific probability of death has all the ingredients of an optimum measure of mortality. The analytic meaning of the age-specific death rate, however, is not fully recognized. The age-specific death rate is either regarded as an ill-defined statistical quantity, or else it is treated as if it were another name for the probability. These misconceptions require correction. The age-specific death rate is an important measure of human mortality itself and exists in its own right. The death rate is also a meaningful analytic concept, but it is not another name for the probability.

2. Age-Specific Death Rate

The death rate for age interval (x_i, x_{i+1}) is defined by

$$M_i = \frac{\text{No. of individuals dying in the age interval } (x_i, x_{i+1})}{\text{No. of years lived in } (x_i, x_{i+1}) \text{ by those alive at } x_i}. \quad (2.1)$$

Suppose that of l_i individuals alive at exact age x_i, d_i die between age x_i and x_{i+1}, and each of d_i individuals live on the average a fraction a_i of the interval (x_i, x_{i+1}). Then the death rate M_i defined in (2.1) may be expressed in the formula

$$M_i = \frac{d_i}{n_i(l_i - d_i) + a_i n_i d_i}, \quad (2.2)$$

where $n_i = x_{i+1} - x_i$ is the length of the interval (x_i, x_{i+1}), $n_i(l_i - d_i)$ is the number of years lived in (x_i, x_{i+1}) by the $(l_i - d_i)$ survivors and $a_i n_i d_i$ is the number of years lived by the d_i people who die in the interval. The units of the death rate are deaths per person-year.

Graphically, the death rate M_i is demonstrated in Figure 1. The curve in the figure is a survival curve, showing the number of people living at each age beginning with age 0. The heights of the two vertical lines at x_i and x_{i+1} are the numbers living at the two ages, respectively. Their difference $(l_i - l_{i+1}) = d_i$ is the number of people dying during the interval (x_i, x_{i+1}). The shaded area under the curve between the two lines is the total number of years lived in the interval (x_i, x_{i+1}) by the l_i people. The single-hatched rectangle represents the number of years lived by the $l_{i+1} = l_i - d_i$ survivors; that is, the first term in the denominator in formula (2.2). The double-hatched area represents the number of years lived by those who died in (x_i, x_{i+1}); that is, the second term in the denominator in (2.2). The graph shows that the death rate M_i is the linear segment d_i divided by the shaded area.*

---

*The shaded area can be represented by an integral so that the death rate M_i is also given in formula:

$$M_i = \frac{d_i}{\int_{x_i}^{x_{i+1}} l_x \, dx}.$$

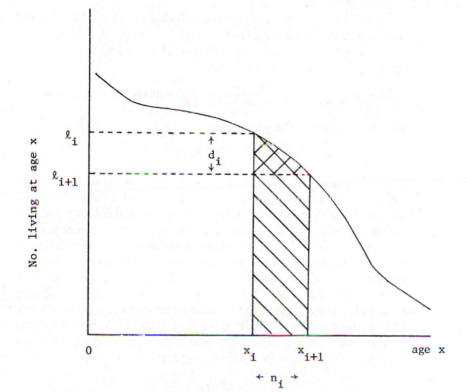

Figure 1. A Survival Curve

The formula for the estimate of the probability of dying in age interval (x_i, x_{i+1}) is

$$\hat{q}_i = \frac{d_i}{l_i} . \qquad (2.3)$$

According to the concept of probability introduced in Chapter 1, l_i is the number of people exposed to the risk of dying in the interval (x_i, x_{i+1}), and d_i, the number of people who have died. Clearly, the numerator d_i is a part of the denominator and $\hat{q}_i$ is a pure number, as are all probabilities. While the two formulas differ, the death rate and the estimate of the probability have a formal relationship. From (2.2) and (2.3), we find

$$\hat{q}_i = \frac{n_i M_i}{1 + (1 - a_i) n_i M_i} . \qquad (2.4)$$

The numerical values of the two quantities, of course, are also different; $\hat{q}_i$ is nearly n_i times as large as the death rate M_i.

Consider as an example age interval $(5, 10)$ and the 1975 United States life table population from Chapter 1, page 20. Here $x_i = 5$, $x_{i+1} = 10$, and $n_i = 5$ years; $l_i = 98100$, $d_i = 200$, and $a_i = .46$ [cf. Appendix I].** The death rate is

$$M_i = \frac{200}{5(98100 - 200) + .46 \times 5 \times 200} = .0004 \text{ per person-year.}$$

while the estimate of the probability

$$\hat{q}_i = \frac{200}{98100} = .002.$$

In formula (2.2), the age-specific death rate is expressed in terms of a life table framework, in which the lives of l_i individuals are followed for n_i years to determine the number dead (d_i) and the number surviving $(l_i - d_i)$ at the end of n_i years. In a current population, such as the 1975 United States population, age specific death rates are computed from the mortality and population data during a calendar year (1975). Instead of d_i defined as in a life table, we have D_i, the observed number of deaths in the age group (x_i, x_{i+1}) during the calendar year. To establish a relationship between the death rate and the estimate of the probability as in (2.4), we let N_i be the number of people alive at age x_i, among whom D_i deaths occur. Then the estimate of the probability of death is expressed by

$$\hat{q}_i = \frac{D_i}{N_i}, \tag{2.5}$$

and the death rate by

$$M_i = \frac{D_i}{n_i(N_i - D_i) + a_i n_i D_i}, \tag{2.6}$$

which is the same as formula (2.2) when the corresponding symbols are identified. Eliminating the unknown N_i from (2.5) and (2.6) yields the relationship

$$\hat{q}_i = \frac{n_i M_i}{1 + (1 - a_i) n_i M_i}. \tag{2.4}$$

Since N_i is unknown, the death rate for a current population cannot be computed from (2.6). It is customary to estimate the denominator of (2.6) by the midyear (calendar year) population P_i for

------

** a_i is known as the fraction of the last age interval of life for interval (x_i, x_{i+1}). Numerical values of a_i for different countries are given in the tables in Appendix I.

age group (x_i, x_{i+1}), and to compute the age-specific death rate from

$$M_i = \frac{D_i}{P_i}.$$ (2.7)

Although this is a well known and widely accepted definition of the age-specific death rate, formula (2.7) is not very meaningful. As it stands, the right-hand side is a pure number; it is inconsistent with the definition of the age-specific death rate in (2.1). As a pure number, it is not a probability, since those of D_i who died before the midyear will not be counted in P_i and hence the numerator is not a part of the denominator. But, formula (2.7) can be salvaged as a definition of the age-specific death rate if it is interpreted correctly. The denominator is in fact a product of two factors: (i) P_i and (ii) one year. The product "P_i years" is the total length of time that the individuals in age group (x_i, x_{i+1}) have lived during the current year. Under this interpretation, the age-specific death rate becomes

$$M_i = \frac{D_i}{P_i} \quad \text{per person-year,}$$ (2.8)

which is in agreement with the definition in (2.1).

In the United States during 1975, there were $D_1 = 9060$ deaths occurring in age interval $(1, 5)$, $P_1 = 12,804,000$ people of ages 1 to 5 years at midyear and $a_1 = .4$ [cf. Appendix I]. Therefore, the corresponding death rate was

$$M_1 = \frac{9060}{12,804,000} = .000707 \quad \text{per person-year,}$$

and the estimate of the probability is

$$\hat{q}_1 = \frac{4 \times .000707}{1 + (1 - .4)4 \times .000707} = .002823.$$

A death rate is usually a small number; its significance is not easily comprehended. The compensate for this, the numerical value of a death rate is multiplied by a large number, typically 1000, which is called the base. The formula for a death rate often appears as

$$M_i = \frac{D_i}{P_i} \times 1000 \quad \text{per 1000 person-years.}$$ (2.9)

Thus, instead of $M_1 = .000707$ per person-year, we have $M_1 = .707$ per 1000 person-years. The number of deaths D_i and the midyear population P_i in formula (2.8) and (2.9) refer to the same population, such as the 1975 United States population between ages 1 and 5 years. The population and the base must be clearly stated in a death rate. For example, the death rate for age group 1 to 5 years in the 1975 United States population is .707 per 1000 person-years.

Table 1 shows the age-specific death rates for selected groups in several countries. The 1975 rates are the most recently available for most countries; for France and Central and South American countries, the 1974 rates used are the most recent.

Table 1. Age-specific death rates per 1000 person-years for selected age intervals and for sample countries.

Country	Age Interval (in exact years)							
	< 1	1–5	5–15	15–25	· · ·	55–65	65–75	All ages
Costa Rica* (1974)	37.57	1.97	0.54	1.19	· · ·	12.03	31.07	4.95
Chile* (1974)	63.26	2.60	0.73	1.32	· · ·	16.51	38.55	7.77
Venezuela* (1974)	45.76	3.95	0.79	1.45	· · ·	18.41	39.89	6.34
U.S.A.** (1975)	16.41	0.71	0.36	1.19	· · ·	14.96	31.89	8.89
Hongkong* (1975)	15.00	0.78	0.34	0.57	· · ·	13.95	29.78	4.85
Japan* (1975)	10.05	0.85	0.31	0.72	· · ·	10.43	29.60	6.31
Thailand* (1975)	26.26	3.74	1.35	22.89	· · ·	16.97	33.27	5.94
Austria* (1975)	20.54	8.37	3.87	1.16	· · ·	14.27	36.90	12.77
France* (1974)	12.22	0.75	0.35	1.03	· · ·	13.51	30.39	10.49
G.D.R.* (1975)	15.87	0.74	0.38	0.91	· · ·	14.41	40.06	14.27
Hungary* (1975)	32.89	0.74	0.35	0.89	· · ·	16.38	40.82	12.44
Netherlands* (1975)	10.65	0.69	0.31	0.61	· · ·	11.94	30.96	8.32
Poland* (1975)	24.85	0.91	0.39	0.93	· · ·	14.80	35.90	8.69
Portugal* (1975)	39.29	1.90	0.62	1.22	· · ·	14.02	34.73	10.37
Sweden* (1975)	8.90	0.44	0.29	0.75	· · ·	10.74	28.63	10.77
Switzerland* (1975)	10.74	0.66	0.34	0.92	· · ·	11.01	28.48	8.80
Scotland* (1975)	17.19	0.71	0.34	0.72	· · ·	17.49	40.71	12.13

Source: *World Health Organization: *World Health Statistics Annual*, 1977, Table 7, pp. 160–623, Geneva, Switzerland.
**National Center for Health Statistics: *United States Vital Statistics*, 1975, Vol. II, Part A, Table 1–4, p. 1–26, Government Printing Office, Washington, D.C., U.S.A.

2.1.   Other specific death rates.   Death rates may be computed for any specific category of people in a population. Examples are sex-specific death rates, occupation-specific death rates, age-sex-specific death rates. In each case, the specific rate is given as the number of deaths in the stated category during the calendar year divided by the midyear population of the same category.

Cause-specific death rate.   Another type of death rate is the cause-specific death rate, defined as the number of deaths from a specific cause divided by the midyear population. In this case, it is deaths that are categorized rather than members of the population. If D_{tb} is the number of deaths due to tuberculosis in a calendar year and P is the mid-year population, we have the death rate from tuberculosis:

$$M_{tb} = \frac{D_{tb}}{P} \times 100{,}000 \text{ per } 100{,}000 \text{ person-years.} \qquad (2.10)$$

Here we use 100,000 as a base because of the small magnitude of the rate.

Age-cause-specific death rate.   Prevalence of disease varies with age. Death from cardiovascular disease, for example, is more prevalent among the aged than among the young; the opposite is true for death by infectious diseases. Therefore, age-cause-specific death rates are in common use. For the age interval (x_i, x_{i+1}) and cause R_δ, the specific death rate is given by

$$M_{i\delta} = \frac{D_{i\delta}}{P_i} \times 100{,}000, \qquad (2.11)$$

where $D_{i\delta}$ is the number of deaths from cause R_δ occurring in age group (x_i, x_{i+1}) during a calendar year, and P_i is the midyear population of the same age group. Again 100,000 is used as base. For example, the cancer death rate for age group $(40, 45)$ is

$$\frac{\text{No. of cancer deaths in age group } (40, 45)}{\text{Midyear population for age group } (40, 45)} \times 100{,}000. \quad (2.12)$$

In the specific rates discussed so far, the reference number is the base population. There are measures which relate the number of deaths from a specific cause to some other numbers. The following are examples.

Case fatality rate for disease R.

$$\frac{\text{No. of deaths due to disease } R}{\text{No. of individuals affected with disease } R} \times 100. \qquad (2.13)$$

This is a measure of the severity of the disease, and is often used for acute illness such as pneumonia, whooping cough, and others. However, it is not an effective index for chronic disease: an individual with a chronic disease may live several years after the time of diagnosis and may eventually die from some cause other than the disease in question.

Proportionate mortality from a specific cause R.

$$\frac{\text{No. of deaths from cause } R}{\text{No. of deaths from all causes}} \times 100. \qquad (2.14)$$

Unlike all the other rates, this is not a measure of risk of death. (The denominator is not the number of people exposed to the risk of death from the specific cause.) It is merely a measure of mortality of a specific cause relative to other causes. However, it shows the relative importance of the disease and thus provides public health planners with direction for emphasis in health care and medical services.

3.   Standard Error of the Age-Specific Death Rate

An age-specific death rate, as all observable statistical quantities, is subject to variation. The measure of variation is the standard deviation, or standard error, of the rate. We use the standard error in estimation, testing hypotheses, and in making other statistical inferences concerning the mortality of a population. With the standard error one can assess the degree of confidence that may be placed in the findings and conclusions based on the death rate [cf. Chapter 3].

Since a death rate is often determined from the mortality experience of an entire population rather than from a sample, it is sometimes argued that there is no sampling error; and therefore the standard deviation, if it exists, can be disregarded. This point of view, however, is static. Statistically speaking, human life is a random experiment and its outcome, survival or death, is subject to chance. If two people were subjected to the same risk of dying (force of mortality) during a calendar year, one might die during the year and the other survive. If a person were allowed to relive the year he survived the first time, he might not survive the second time. Similarly, if a population were allowed to live the same year over again, the total number of deaths occurring during the second time would assume a different value and so, of course, would the corresponding death rate. It is in this sense that a death rate is subject to random variation even though it is based on the total number of deaths and the entire population.

The formula for the standard error, or the variance, of an age-specific death rate of a current population may be derived directly from the formula

$$M_i = \frac{D_i}{P_i} . \tag{2.7}$$

According to the rule of variance in Chapter 2, the sample variance of M_i is

$$S_{M_i}^2 = \frac{1}{P_i^2} S_{D_i}^2 . \tag{3.1}$$

The number D_i is a binomial random variable in N_i trials with the probability of dying q_i. From Chapter 2, page 41, we have the formulas for the expected value

$$E(D_i) = N_i q_i , \tag{3.2}$$

and the variance

$$\sigma_{D_i}^2 = N_i q_i (1 - q_i). \tag{3.3}$$

Here N_i is unknown in a current population. We estimate the product $N_i q_i$ with the observed number of deaths D_i and estimate the variance in (3.3) with the sample value

$$S_{D_i}^2 = D_i (1 - \hat{q}_i). \tag{3.4}$$

Substituting (3.4) for the variance of D_i in (3.1) and simplifying, we obtain the desired formula for the sample variance of the age specific death rate:

$$S_{M_i}^2 = \frac{1}{P_i} M_i (1 - \hat{q}_i), \tag{3.5}$$

and the standard error of M_i:

$$\text{S.E.}(M_i) = \sqrt{\frac{1}{P_i} M_i (1 - \hat{q}_i)} . \tag{3.6}$$

The variance of the estimate of the probability $\hat{q}_i$ is

$$\sigma_{\hat{q}_i}^2 = \frac{1}{N_i} q_i (1 - q_i). \tag{3.7}$$

Estimating N_i with $D_i / \hat{q}_i$ and q_i with $\hat{q}_i$ gives the formula for the sample variance of $\hat{q}_i$,

$$S_{\hat{q}_i}^2 = \frac{1}{D_i} \hat{q}_i^2 (1 - \hat{q}_i) \tag{3.8}$$

and the standard error of $\hat{q}_i$,

$$\text{S.E.}(\hat{q}_i) = \hat{q}_i \sqrt{\frac{1}{D_i} (1 - \hat{q}_i)} . \tag{3.9}$$

When $\hat{q}_i$ is so small that $1 - \hat{q}_i$ is close to one, the standard error of M_i is approximately

$$\text{S.E.}(M_i) = \sqrt{\frac{1}{P_i} M_i} \, , \tag{3.10}$$

and the standard error of $\hat{q}_i$ is approximately

$$\text{S.E.}(\hat{q}_i) = \hat{q}_i / \sqrt{D_i} \, . \tag{3.11}$$

Using the age group $(1, 5)$ in the United States 1975 population as an example again, we find the standard error of the death rate M_1:

$$\text{S.E.}(M_1) = \sqrt{\frac{1}{12,804,000} \, .000707(1 - .002823)}$$

$$= .00000742,$$

and the standard error of $\hat{q}_1$:

$$\text{S.E.}(\hat{q}_1) = .002823 \sqrt{\frac{1}{9060} (1 - .002823)}$$

$$= .00002962.$$

The small values of the standard errors are due to the large population size P_i and the small rate M_i.

The formulas for the standard error of the sex-specific rate, cause-specific rate, and age-cause-specific rate mentioned in Section 2.1, are similar to the formula in (3.6), except that the rate, the estimate of probability, and the midyear population in the formula should be replaced with those relevant to the rate in question.

3.1. Age specific death rates determined from a sample of deaths.

For the purpose of publishing life tables and other vital statistics of a population on a more current basis, a sample of death certificates is frequently taken; age, sex and cause of death of each case in the sample are ascertained. The number of deaths for age interval (x_i, x_{i+1}) determined from the sample is then used to estimate the corresponding number of deaths in the population and to compute the age specific death rate for the age interval. The death rate so determined is subject to sampling variation in addition to the random variation associated with occurrence of each death.

Suppose that a sample of δ death certificates is taken without replacement from a total of D certificates. The ratio

$$\frac{\delta}{D} = f \tag{3.12}$$

is called the sampling fraction. If $f = .10$, we have a 10 percent sample; if $f = .20$, 20 percent sample. When the age at death in each of the δ certificates is ascertained, there will be δ_i death certificates belonging to the age group (x_i, x_{i+1}). The sum of δ_i over all age groups is the sample size, or

$$\Sigma \delta_i = \delta. \tag{3.13}$$

The number of deaths (D_i) occurring in the age group (x_i, x_{i+1}) in the current population is estimated from

$$\frac{\delta_i}{D_i} = f \quad \text{or} \quad D_i = \frac{\delta_i}{f}, \tag{3.14}$$

and the corresponding death rate from

$$M_i = \frac{D_i}{P_i} = \frac{\delta_i}{fP_i}. \tag{3.15}$$

The estimate of the probability q_i is determined from

$$\hat{q}_i = \frac{n_i M_i}{1 + (1 - a_i) n_i M_i}. \tag{3.16}$$

Formulas for the variances of M_i in (3.15) and $\hat{q}_i$ in (3.16) were derived in Chiang (1967). When the total number of deaths (D) is large, the approximate formula for the sample variance of M_i is

$$S_{M_i}^2 = \frac{1}{P_i} M_i \left[(1 - \hat{q}_i) + \left(\frac{1}{f} - 1 \right) \left(1 - \frac{D_i}{D} \right) \right], \tag{3.17}$$

and for the sample standard error of M_i is

$$\text{S.E.}(M_i) = \sqrt{ \frac{1}{P_i} M_i \left[(1 - \hat{q}_i) + \left(\frac{1}{f} - 1 \right) \left(1 - \frac{D_i}{D} \right) \right] }. \tag{3.18}$$

The second term on the right hand side in (3.17) (and in (3.18)) is due to sampling. The larger the sampling fraction, the smaller the sample variation and the smaller the second term. When all the D deaths are observed, $f = 1$, there is no sampling variation and the second term vanishes.

The sample variance and the sample standard error for the estimated probability $\hat{q}_i$ are

$$S_{\hat{q}_i}^2 = \frac{1}{D_i} \hat{q}_i^2 \left[(1 - \hat{q}_i) + \left(\frac{1}{f} - 1 \right) \left(1 - \frac{D_i}{D} \right) \right], \tag{3.19}$$

and

$$\text{S.E.}(\hat{q}_i) = \hat{q}_i \sqrt{ \frac{1}{D_i} \left[(1 - \hat{q}_i) + \left(\frac{1}{f} - 1 \right) \left(1 - \frac{D_i}{D} \right) \right] }, \tag{3.20}$$

respectively.

When the number of deaths for each age interval is determined from a sample of death certificates, the age-specific death rates for any two different age intervals are correlated. For age intervals (x_i, x_{i+1}) and (x_j, x_{j+1}), the sample covariance of the two specific rates M_i and M_j is*

$$S_{M_i, M_j} = -\left(\frac{1}{f} - 1\right)\frac{M_i M_j}{D} \tag{3.21}$$

and the covariance of the two estimates of probabilities is

$$S_{\hat{q}_i, \hat{q}_j} = -\left(\frac{1}{f} - 1\right)\frac{\hat{q}_i \hat{q}_j}{D} . \tag{3.22}$$

The two covariances vanish when $f = 1$.

4.   Infant Mortality and Maternal Mortality

In the human population, mortality is the highest among newborns and the elderly. Infant mortality is dependent upon the medical and health care provided to the mother and child in a community; it also has a great impact on the age distribution of the population. Various efforts have been made in different countries to reduce infant deaths, and many of these efforts have resulted in considerable success, especially in more developed countries. Since different causes effect mortality between the time of conception and the end of the first year after birth, this period has been divided into sub-intervals designated by special names. For example, a fetal death is classified as an early fetal death, an intermediate fetal death, or a late fetal death, according to the length of gestation. Because of incompleteness of reporting or registration, several states in the U.S. and some

Table 2. Fetal death and infant mortality.

Designation	Interval
Early fetal death	Under 20 weeks of gestation
Intermediate fetal death	20–27 weeks of gestation
Late fetal death	28 or more weeks of gestation
Perinatal death	(1) 28 weeks of gestation to 7th day after birth
	(2) 20 weeks of gestation to 28th day after birth
Neonatal death	Under 28 days of life
Post neonatal death	28 days to end of first year of life
Infant death	Under one year of age

---

*Generally, the covariance of two random variables X and Y from a sample of n paired observations $(X_1, Y_1)(X_2, Y_2), \ldots, (X_n, Y_n)$ is defined as

$$S_{X,Y} = \sum_{i=1}^{n} (X_i - \bar{X})(Y_i - \bar{Y})/(n - 1).$$

countries require registration only of intermediate and late fetal deaths. There are also two definitions of perinatal period: (1) from 28 weeks of gestation to the 7th day after birth, and (2) from 20 weeks of gestation to the 28th day after birth. The second definition covers a longer period both in gestation and after birth. Table 2 shows the intervals and the corresponding designations. The definitions of the death rates for these intervals differ somewhat from the definition of the age-specific death rate discussed in Section 2. The following rates are for a population during a calendar year.

Fetal death rate ("stillbirth rate"). Two definitions are currently used:

$$\frac{\text{Number of fetal deaths of 28 or more weeks of gestation}}{\text{Number of live births} + \text{fetal deaths of 28 or more weeks of gestation}} \times 1000 \qquad (4.1)$$

$$\frac{\text{Number of fetal deaths of 20 or more weeks of gestation}}{\text{Number of live births} + \text{fetal deaths of 20 or more weeks of gestation}} \times 1000 \qquad (4.2)$$

Neonatal mortality rate.

$$\frac{\text{Number of deaths under 28 days of life}}{\text{Number of live births}} \times 1000 \qquad (4.3)$$

Perinatal mortality rate. There are two definitions in common use:

$$\frac{\text{Number of deaths under 7 days of life} + \text{fetal deaths of 28 or more weeks of gestation}}{\text{Number of live births} + \text{fetal deaths of 28 or more weeks of gestation}} \times 1000 \qquad (4.4)$$

$$\frac{\text{Number of deaths under 28 days of life} + \text{fetal deaths of 20 or more weeks of gestation}}{\text{Number of live births} + \text{fetal deaths of 20 or more weeks of gestation}} \times 1000 \qquad (4.5)$$

Post neonatal mortality rate.

$$\frac{\text{Number of deaths between 28 days and one year of life}}{\text{Number of live births} - \text{neonatal deaths}} \times 1000 \qquad (4.6)$$

One must subtract neonatal deaths from live births in the denominator to render the rate a meaningful measure of risk.

Infant mortality rate.

$$\frac{\text{Number of deaths under one year of age}}{\text{Number of live births}} \times 1000. \qquad (4.7)$$

The mortality rates defined above resemble probabilities more than age-specific death rates. The fetal death rate, for example, is an estimate of the probability that a fetus of 20 (or 28) weeks of gestation will die before birth. The neonatal death rate is an estimate of the probability that a live born child will die in 28 days. Therefore, each of these rates may be treated as a binomial proportion and its standard error may be obtained from Chapter 2. For example, the standard error of the infant mortality rate (IMR) as defined in (4.7) is

$$\text{S.E.} (IMR) = \sqrt{\frac{1}{\text{No. of live births}} IMR(1 - IMR)} . \qquad (4.8)$$

There are measures of mortality which resemble neither probabilities nor age-specific death rates, but which are quite useful in mortality analysis nevertheless. Some examples follow.

Fetal death ratio.

$$\frac{\text{Number of fetal deaths of 20 or more weeks of gestation}}{\text{Number of live births}} \times 1000$$
$$(4.9)$$

Abortion ratio.

$$\frac{\text{Number of legal abortions}}{\text{Number of live births}} \times 1000 \qquad (4.10)$$

Maternal mortality rate.

$$\frac{\text{Number of maternal deaths}}{\text{Number of live births}} \times 1000. \qquad (4.11)$$

A maternal death is a death occurring to a woman due to complications during pregnancy, childbirth and the peurperium (period after delivery). While not strictly a measure of risk, the maternal mortality rate indicates the "price" (in terms of mothers' lives) that a human population pays for each infant brought into the world. When the number of fetal deaths is added, the denominator becomes an estimate of the number of pregnancies and the ratio,

$$\frac{\text{No. of maternal deaths}}{\text{No. of live births} + \text{No. of fetal deaths}},$$

is an estimate of the probability that a conception will result in the loss of the mother's life.

Table 3 shows the number of deaths in each of the four categories per 1000 live births for the years 1965 and 1974 and for sample countries. The numbers in columns (2), (3) and (4) are the neonatal mortality rates, infant mortality rates, and maternal mortality rates as defined in this section, respectively. However, the numbers in column (1) are not perinatal mortality rates as given in formula (4.5), since they do not include fetal deaths in the denominator.

Table 3. Infant mortality and maternal mortality rates per 1000 live-births for sample countries, 1965 and 1974.

Country	Perinatal Mortality* (1)	Neonatal Mortality (2)	Infant Mortality (3)	Maternal Mortality (4)
Mauritius				
1965	82.0	31.5	64.1	83.7
1974	55.5	24.1	45.6	89.1
Mexico				
1965	35.6	22.9	60.7	164.7
1974	29.8	20.1	52.0	107.6
Philippines				
1966	42.9	35.9	72.9	207.8
1974	31.5	29.5	58.9	137.8
Singapore				
1965	25.8	17.9	26.3	39.5
1974	16.7	10.2	14.0	11.6
England & Wales				
1965	27.3	13.0	19.0	25.6
1974	20.6	11.0	16.3	10.7
Netherlands				
1965	23.4	11.4	14.4	26.9
1974	16.9	8.0	11.3	13.4
Norway				
1965	21.6	11.9	16.8	18.1
1974	15.7	7.4	10.5	3.3
Portugal				
1965	48.0	25.4	64.9	84.6
1974	32.7	20.9	37.9	40.1
Romania				
1966	20.8	13.7	44.1	85.9
1974	19.4	12.8	35.0	30.9
U.S.A.				
1965	27.6	17.7	24.7	31.6
1974	18.9	12.3	16.7	13.8

*Fetal deaths $\geqslant$ 28 weeks of gestation and deaths under one week of age. The figures in this column are not perinatal mortality rates as defined in formula (4.4) since they do not include fetal deaths in the denominator.
SOURCE: World Health Organization: *World Health Statistics Annual*, 1965 and 1977. Geneva, Switzerland.

5.   Problems for Solution

1.   Derive the formula

$$\hat{q}_i = \frac{n_i M_i}{1 + (1 - a_i)n_i M_i} \tag{2.4}$$

from equations (2.2) and (2.3) in Section 2, pages 72, 73.

2.   In reference to the infant mortality and maternal mortality rates in Table 3, page 85, compute for each country the percent decrease in the death rate for each of the four categories.

3.   The following data were taken from the 1970 California population. For each age interval compute: (1) age-specific death rate M_i; (2) the probability of death $\hat{q}_i$; (3) standard errors of M_i and $\hat{q}_i$, respectively.

Table A. Midyear population, number of deaths and the fraction of last age interval of life for 1970 total population of California, U.S.A.

Age Interval (in years)	Midyear population in interval (x_i, x_{i+1})	Number of deaths in interval (x_i, x_{i+1})	Fraction of last age interval of life
x_i to x_{i+1} (1)	P_i (2)	D_i (3)	a_i (4)
0–1	340,483	6234	.09
1–5	1,302,198	1049	.41
5–10	1,918,117	723	.44
10–15	1,963,681	735	.54
15–20	1,817,379	2054	.59
⋮	⋮	⋮	⋮

4.   *Continuation.*   Use the above data to compute:

(1)   The probability $\hat{p}_i$.
(2)   The probability of surviving from age x_0 to x_i, $\hat{p}_{0i}$, for each possible i in the table.
(3)   The formula for the sample variance of $\hat{p}_{0i}$ is

$$S^2_{\hat{p}_{0i}} = \hat{p}^2_{0i} \sum_{h=0}^{i-1} \hat{p}_h^{-2} S^2_{\hat{p}_h}.$$

Compute the sample variance of $\hat{p}_{0i}$ for each survival probability in part (2).

5.   *Continuation.*   For each i, plot the point $\hat{p}_{0i}$ and join these points with line segments to form a survival curve from age 0 to age 20 years.

Table B. Vital statistics data, 1976, San Francisco Department of Public Health

Variable	All ages	Under 5	5–14	15–24	25–44	45–64	65 +
Population, midyear est.[2]	665,000	33,200	77,800	127,000	169,700	156,900	100,400
Live births, recorded	12,020						
Live births, resident	7,867						
Deaths, resident	7,902[1]	132	19	156	517	1,776	5,294
Disease of heart	2,600						
Cirrhosis of liver	313						
Accidents	429						
Suicide	192[3]	—	—	18	72	62	39
Tuberculosis	17						
Fetal deaths[2]	73						
Infant deaths[2]	110						
Neonatal deaths[2]	76						
Maternal deaths[2]	2						
New cases of tuberculosis[2]	331						

[1]Includes 8 deaths; ages unknown   [2]by place of residence   [3]includes 1 death; age unknown

6. *Continuation.* Compare the probability of surviving the interval $(0, 5)$ and the interval $(5, 10)$. What percent is the probability of surviving $(5, 10)$ greater than the probability of surviving $(0, 5)$?

7. *Continuation.* Test the hypothesis that the probability of surviving the age interval $(5, 10)$ is equal to the probability of surviving the age interval $(10, 15)$ against the alternative that it is smaller.

8. The data in Table B are taken from the Statistical Report for 1976 by the San Francisco Department of Public Health.

    (1) Compute the following:
    (a) birth rate by place of residence   (g) infant mortality rate
    (b) birth rate by place of occurrence (h) maternal mortality rate
    (c) crude death rate   (i) incidence rate for tuberculosis

    (d) fetal death rate   (j) tuberculosis case fatality rate

    (e) neonatal mortality rate   (k) death rate from cirrhosis of the liver

    (f) postneonatal mortality rate   (l) the highest age-specific death rate for suicide

    (2) In which age group is the proportionate mortality highest for suicide?

9. Use the data in Table C to compute the following quantities for the United States population and for each race:

    (1) Fetal death rate
    (2) Neonatal death rate
    (3) Perinatal mortality rate
    (4) Post neonatal mortality rate
    (5) Infant mortality rate
    (6) Fetal death ratio
    (7) Maternal death rate and
    (8) Birth-death ratio, or "vital index",

$$\text{Birth-death ratio} = \frac{\text{Number of births}}{\text{Number of deaths}} \times 100.$$

10. *Continuation.* Determine the standard errors of the infant mortality rates for whites and for blacks in Problem 9 (5).

11. *Continuation.* Test the hypothesis that the two infant mortality rates are equal against the alternative that the rate for blacks is greater than the rate for whites at the .1% level of significance.

Table C. Live births, total deaths, infant and neonatal deaths and fetal deaths, by race, United States population, 1977.

	Number of live births	Number of Deaths				
		All ages	Under 1 year	Under 28 days	Fetal deaths[1]	Maternal deaths
United States	3,326,632	1,899,597	46,975	32,860	33,053	373
White	2,691,070	1,664,100	33,199	23,540	23,628	208
All other	635,562	235,497	13,776	9,320	9,425	165
Black	544,221	220,076	12,863	8,749	8,643	—

Source: National Center for Health Statistics, U.S. Department of Health and Human Services, *Vital Statistics of the United States*, 1977, Vol. I. Natality, p. 1–6, Table 1–2; Vol. II. Mortality, Part B, p. 7–3, Table 7–1; Part A, p. 1–73, Table 1–15.

Age Specific Death Rates Determined From A Sample of Deaths

For the purpose of publishing vital statistics on a more current schedule, a sample of death certificates, instead of all deaths occurring in a calendar year, is often used to determine age specific death rates. Let D be the total number of deaths and let d be the number of deaths in the sample, so that

$$\frac{d}{D} = f$$

is a preassigned sampling fraction. Let d_i and D_i be the numbers of deaths of individuals belonging to the age interval (x_i, x_{i+1}) in the sample and in the current population, respectively, so that

$$d_0 + d_1 + \cdots + d_w = d$$

and

$$D_0 + D_1 + \cdots + D_w = D$$

where d_w and D_w are the number of deaths in the highest age interval, e.g., 85 years and over. The number d_i is determined in the sample while D_i is estimated from

$$\hat{D}_i = \frac{d_i}{f}.$$

Solve the following problems under the sampling scheme described above.

12. Given D_i, D and the sample size d (or the sampling fraction f), find the conditional expected value of d_i and the conditional variance of d_i,

$$E(d_i \mid D_i, D, f) \quad \text{and} \quad V(d_i \mid D_i, D, f).$$

13. *Continuation.*   The conditional expectation $E(d_i \mid D_i, D, f)$, a function of D_i and D, is a random variable and therefore has a variance. Find its variance $V[E(d_i \mid D_i, D, f)]$.

14. *Continuation.*   The conditional variance $V(d_i \mid D_i, D, f)$, a function of D_i and D, is a random variable and therefore has an expectation. Find its expectation $E[V(d_i \mid D_i, D, f)]$.

15. *Continuation.*   The variance of the conditional expectation in problem 13 and the expectation of the conditional variance in problem 14 are related as follows:

$$V[d_i] = V[E(d_i \mid D_i, D, f)] + E[V(d_i \mid D_i, D, f)].$$

Use the above relationship to find the variance of d_i.

CHAPTER 5

Adjustment of Rates

1. Introduction

The specific death rates presented in Chapter 4 are essential in mortality analysis. Individually, these rates describe mortality experience in various categories of people. Collectively, they represent the overall mortality pattern of a population. One of the central tasks in the statistical analysis of mortality data is to make comparisons of the experiences of various communities or countries. For comparisons and other purposes, summarizing a group of specific rates in a single number is extremely important. Since age-sex distribution varies from one community to another, and from one country to another, adjustment for such variation must be made in summarizing specific rates. The resulting number is called an adjusted rate. Adjustment can be made with respect to age, sex, occupation and other demographic variables. For simplicity, we consider only age-adjusted rates. Others, such as sex-adjusted rates, age-sex-adjusted rates, etc., are computed similarly. Various methods of adjustment have been proposed; some of these are listed in Table 1. An extensive literature review by T. D. Woolsey may be found in Linder and Grove (1943). The purpose of this chapter is to present the methods of adjustment in Table 1 and the standard errors of these adjusted rates. First we introduce some notation.

In the adjustment of rates, two populations are usually involved: A community, u, during a calendar year (the population of interest) and a standard population, s. For each age interval (x_i, x_{i+1}) in the community, u, let D_{ui} be the number of deaths; P_{ui}, the midyear

Table 1. Age-adjusted death rates and mortality indices.

Section	Title	Formula*	Reference
(2.1)	Crude death rate (C.D.R.)	$\dfrac{\sum P_{ui} M_{ui}}{P_u}$	Linder, F. E. and Grove, R. D. (1943)
(2.2)	Direct method of adjustment (D.M.D.R.)	$\dfrac{\sum P_{si} M_{ui}}{P_s}$	"The Registrar General's Statistical Review of England & Wales for the Year 1934"
(2.3)	Comparative mortality rate (C.M.R.)	$\dfrac{1}{2} \sum \left(\dfrac{P_{ui}}{P_u} + \dfrac{P_{si}}{P_s} \right) M_{ui}$	Ibid.
(2.4)	Indirect method of adjustment (I.M.D.R.)	$\dfrac{(D_s/P_s)(D_u/P_u)}{\sum P_{ui} M_{si}/P_u}$	"The Registrar General's Decennial Supplement, England & Wales, 1921, Part III"
(2.5)	Standardized mortality ratio (S.M.R.)	$\dfrac{\sum P_{ui} M_{ui}}{\sum P_{ui} M_{si}}$	"The Registrar General's Statistical Review of England & Wales, 1958"
(2.6)	Life table death rate (L.T.D.R.)	$\dfrac{\sum L_i M_{ui}}{\sum L_i}$	Brownlee, J. (1913)(1922)
(2.7)	Equivalent average death rate (E.A.D.R.)	$\dfrac{\sum n_i M_{ui}}{\sum n_i}$	Yule, G. U. (1934)
(2.8)	Relative mortality index (R.M.I.)	$\dfrac{\sum P_{ui}(M_{ui}/M_{si})}{P_u}$	Linder, F. E. and Grove, R. D. (1943)
(2.9)	Mortality index (M.I.)	$\dfrac{\sum n_i(M_{ui}/M_{si})}{\sum n_i}$	Yerushalmy, J. (1951)

*The summations are taken over all age groups.

population; M_{ui}, the specific death rate; and let $n_i = x_{i+1} - x_i$ be the length of the interval. The sum

$$\sum_i D_{ui} = D_u \tag{1.1}$$

is the total number of deaths occurring in the community during the calendar year. The sum

$$\sum_i P_{ui} = P_u \tag{1.2}$$

is the total midyear population. For the standard population, the symbols D_{si}, P_{si}, M_{si}, D_s and P_s are defined similarly. (These symbols are identical to those used in Chapter 4 except for the addition of the subscripts u and s.)

2.   Adjusted Rates

The methods of adjustment discussed in this section have been developed since the early 1900's. Although each method was introduced on the basis of a specific philosophic argument and designed to serve a definite purpose, they all assume the general form of a linear function of the age-specific death rates. We begin with the crude death rate.

2.1.   The Crude Death Rate (C.D.R.).   The crude death rate is the death rate for people of all ages in a community. In formula,

$$\text{C.D.R.} = D_u/P_u . \tag{2.1}$$

The crude death rate is the most commonly used and conveniently computed single value, and is closely related to age-specific death rates. The numerator in (2.1) is the number of deaths occurring in all age categories in the community:

$$D_u = \sum_i D_{ui} . \tag{2.2}$$

By definition, the age-specific death rate for age interval (x_i, x_{i+1}) is given by

$$M_{ui} = D_{ui}/P_{ui} , \tag{2.3}$$

so that the number of deaths (D_{ui}) is the product of the age-specific death rate (M_{ui}) and the corresponding midyear population (P_{ui}):

$$D_{ui} = P_{ui} M_{ui} , \tag{2.4}$$

and the total number of deaths in (2.2) may be rewritten as

$$D_u = \sum_i P_{ui} M_{ui} .$$

(2.5)

Substituting (2.5) in (2.1) yields

$$\text{C.D.R.} = \sum_i \frac{P_{ui}}{P_u} M_{ui} ,$$

(2.6)

where the summation is taken over all ages. Thus the C.D.R. is the weighted mean of the age-specific death rates, with the actual population proportions P_{ui}/P_u which experience the mortality being used as weights. From this viewpoint, the C.D.R. is the most meaningful single figure summarizing the mortality experience of a given population.

The C.D.R., however, is not without deficiencies. The quantity on the right-hand side of (2.6) is a function of both the age-specific death rates and the age-specific population proportions. As a weighted mean of age-specific death rates, the C.D.R. is affected by the population composition of the community in question. This disadvantage becomes apparent when the C.D.R. is used to compare the mortality experience of several communities. The example in Table 2 illustrates this point.

Although the age-specific death rate for each age group in Community A is lower than that for the corresponding age group in Community B, the crude death rate for Community A (12.40 per 1000), is higher than that for Community B (11.80 per 1000). This apparent inconsistency is explained by differences in the population composition of the two communities. Community A has a larger proportion of older people, who are subject to a higher mortality and contribute more deaths. As a result, Community A's overall crude death rate is higher than that of the more youthful Community B.

Table 2 Age-specific death rates and crude death rates for communities A and B.

| | Community A | | | Community B | | |
	Popu-lation	Deaths	Rate per 1000	Popu-lation	Deaths	Rate per 1000
Children	10,000	80	8.00	25,000	250	10.00
Adults	15,000	165	11.00	15,000	180	12.00
Senior Citizens	25,000	375	15.00	10,000	160	16.00
Total	50,000	620	12.40	50,000	590	11.80

2.2. Direct Method Death Rate (D.M.D.R.). One way of adjusting for peculiarities of population composition is to introduce a standard population. When the age-specific death rates of a community are applied to this standard population, we obtain a death rate "adjusted by the direct method":

$$D.M.D.R. = \sum_i \frac{P_{si}}{P_s} M_{ui}. \qquad (2.7)$$

The D.M.D.R. is thus a weighted mean of the age-specific death rates of a community with standard population proportions, P_{si}/P_s, applied as weights. If formula (2.7) is rewritten as

$$D.M.D.R. = \frac{\sum_i P_{si} M_{ui}}{P_s}, \qquad (2.8)$$

the numerator becomes the number of deaths that would occur in the standard population if it were subject to the age-specific death rates of the given community. The ratio of the "expected number of deaths" to the entire standard population yields the D.M.D.R. The logic involved is straightforward and the formula is easy to understand; therefore, the direct method of adjustment is the most popular among all the methods of adjustment. However, the D.M.D.R. (not to mention other age-adjusted rates that follow) is not designed to measure the mortality experience of a community. It is simply a means for evaluating the mortality experience of one community relative to another. Any consideration of an age-adjusted rate should take this into account.

Computation of the D.M.D.R. based on the example in Table 2 is given in Table 3. In this illustration, the combined population of the two communities is used as the standard population shown in column (1). The age-specific rates in the two communities are recorded in

Table 3 Computation of the age-adjusted rates for Communities A and B.

| Population | Community A | | Community B | |
	Rate per 1000	Expected No. of deaths	Rate per 1000	Expected No. of deaths
(1)	(2)	(3)	(4)	(5)
35,000	8.0	280	10.0	350
30,000	11.0	330	12.0	360
35,000	15.0	525	16.0	560
100,000		1,135		1,270

Adjusted Rate: Community A = 11.35/1,000
              Community B = 12.70/1,000

columns (2) and (4), respectively. Each of the specific rates is then applied to the standard population in the same age group to obtain the number of deaths expected in the standard population shown in columns (3) and (5). Summing these expected numbers of deaths over all age groups yields the total number of deaths, 1,135 and 1,270, respectively. Dividing this by the total standard population, we obtain the D.M.D.R.

By using a single standard population, the direct method of adjustment eliminates the effect of differences in age-composition of the communities under study, but the result still depends upon the composition of the population selected as a standard. When communities with very different mortality patterns are compared, different standard populations may even produce contradictory results. In computing the age-adjusted rate for the 1940 white male population of Louisiana and New Mexico, Yerushalmy (1951) found that the age-adjusted rate for Louisiana (13.06 per 1,000) was slightly higher than the rate for New Mexico (13.05 per 1,000) when the 1940 U.S. population was used as the standard; but the rate for Louisiana (10.14 per 1,000) was lower than the rate for New Mexico (11.68 per 1,000) when the 1901 population of England and Wales was used as the standard. This kind of dilemma has led to the development of other methods of adjustment.

2.3. Comparative Mortality Rate (C.M.R.).   In this method of adjustment, the age composition of both the community and the standard population are taken into account. The formula is

$$\text{C.M.R.} = \frac{1}{2} \sum_i \left(\frac{P_{ui}}{P_u} + \frac{P_{si}}{P_s} \right) M_{ui}. \tag{2.9}$$

Easy computations show that the first sum is the crude death rate of the community,

$$\sum_i \frac{P_{ui}}{P_u} M_{ui} = \sum_i \frac{D_{ui}}{P_u} = \frac{D_u}{P_u}, \tag{2.10}$$

while the second sum is the direct method death rate. Thus the C.M.R. is simply the mean of the C.D.R. and D.M.D.R. Using the previous example once again, we find

$$\text{C.M.R.(Community A)} = \frac{1}{2}(12.4 + 11.35) = 11.87 \text{ per } 1000,$$

$$\text{C.M.R.(Community B)} = \frac{1}{2}(11.8 + 12.70) = 12.25 \text{ per } 1000.$$

2.4.   Indirect Method Death Rate (I.M.D.R.).   The age-adjusted death
rate by the direct method requires the age-specific death rates for all
age groups of a population in question. This requirement limits the
use of the rate in practice. Frequently, the required information either
is unavailable or else it is unreliable because of the small number of
people in individual age groups in a community. The adjusted rate by
the indirect method does not need these specific rates. Instead, it
requires the specific rates in the standard population (M_{si}). The
specific rates in the standard population are always available and are
more stable, since they are based on a larger population.

To compute the I.M.D.R., we multiply the crude death rate of
the community by the ratio of the crude death rate of a standard
population to the death rate that would be expected in the standard
population if it had its own mortality rates (M_{si}) but a population
composition like that of the community (P_{ui}). The formula is

$$\text{I.M.D.R.} = \frac{D_s/P_s}{\sum_i P_{ui} M_{si}/P_u} \left(\frac{D_u}{P_u} \right). \tag{2.11}$$

The ratio in the denominator of the adjusting factor

$$\frac{\sum_i P_{ui} M_{si}}{P_u} \tag{2.12}$$

is a D.M.D.R. in which the positions of the community and the
standard population are interchanged. The age-specific death rates of
a standard population (M_{si}) are applied to a community population
(P_{ui}). The Registrar-General's office in England recognizes that this
ratio "is dependent solely on the age constitution of the (community)
population" and hence it is "an indication of the mortality proneness
of the population in question." They have thus found the indirect
method useful for adjustment and published the I.M.D.R. in the early
volumes of the *Registrar-General's Statistical Review of England and
Wales*.

When the population composition of a community and a standard population are the same so that

$$\frac{P_{ui}}{P_u} = \frac{P_{si}}{P_s}$$

for every interval (x_i, x_{i+1}), then the first factor in (2.11) becomes
unity

$$\frac{D_s/P_s}{\sum_i P_{ui} M_{si}/P_u} = \frac{\sum_i P_{si} M_{si}/P_s}{\sum_i P_{ui} M_{si}/P_u} = 1.$$

In this case, the I.M.D.R. is equal to the C.D.R. of the community. If

Table 4. Age-specific death rates of a standard population and the populations of Communities A and B.

| | Standard Population | | | Community A | Community B |
| Age Group | Population | Death | Rate per 1000 | Population | Population |
(1)	P_{si} (2)	D_{si} (3)	M_{si} (4)	P_{ui} (5)	P_{ui} (6)
Children	35,000	330	9.43	10,000	25,000
Adults	30,000	345	11.50	15,000	15,000
Senior Citizens	35,000	535	15.29	25,000	10,000
Total	100,000	1210	12.10	50,000	50,000

a community has a higher proportion of young people than the standard population, and for the young age groups,

$$\frac{P_{ui} M_{si}}{P_u} > \frac{P_{si} M_{si}}{P_s},$$

then the crude rate of the community is smaller than the I.M.D.R.

A computation of the I.M.D.R. is demonstrated with the hypothetical data used for the D.M.D.R. in Section 2.2. The basic data for the standard population and the population compositions of communities A and B are shown in Table 4. The crude death rates for the two communities are C.D.R.(A) = 12.40 per 1000 and C.D.R.(B) = 11.80 per 1000 as given in Table 2. Table 5 shows the computation of the expected number of deaths in each age group of community A and community B, when they are subject to the age-specific death rates of the standard population. The ratio of the expected total

Table 5. Computation of age-adjusted death rates by the indirect method for Communities A and B.

| | | Community A | | Community B | |
| Standard Population Rate per 1000 | Population | Expected No. of deaths | Population | Expected No. of deaths |
M_{si} (1)	P_{ui} (2)	$P_{ui} M_{si}$ (3)	P_{ui} (4)	$P_{ui} M_{si}$ (5)
9.43	10,000	94.3	25,000	235.8
11.50	15,000	172.5	15,000	172.5
15.29	25,000	382.2	10,000	152.9
12.10	50,000	649.0	50,000	561.2

number of deaths to the total population [cf. (2.12)] is

$$\frac{649.0}{50,000} = 12.98 \text{ per } 1000 \text{ for community A}$$

and

$$\frac{561.2}{50,000} = 11.22 \text{ per } 1000 \text{ for community B.}$$

Substituting these figures together with the crude death rates of the standard population and the two communities in formula (2.11) yields

$$\text{I.M.D.R.}(A) = \frac{12.10 \times 12.40}{12.98} = 11.56 \text{ per } 1000$$

$$\text{I.M.D.R.}(B) = \frac{12.10 \times 11.80}{11.22} = 12.72 \text{ per } 1000.$$

Note that for Community B, which has a slightly higher proportion of young people than the standard population, the crude death rate (11.80 per 1000) is smaller than the I.M.D.R. (12.72 per 1000), and the converse is true for community A.

2.5. Standardized Mortality Ratio (S.M.R.).   While the I.M.D.R. has the advantage over the D.M.D.R. in requiring less information from the community, interpretation of the rate is difficult. The complexity of the formula further discourages users from applying this method of adjustment to practical problems. However, inspection of the formula in (2.11) reveals that the only quantity in the I.M.D.R. that is dependent upon the community in question is the ratio

$$\text{S.M.R.} = \frac{D_u}{\sum_i P_{ui} M_{si}} ; \qquad (2.13)$$

the other factors in the rate play no role in the comparison of the mortality experience of different communities. The quantity in (2.13), known as the Standardized Mortality Ratio (S.M.R.), is the ratio of the observed number of deaths in a community to the expected number of deaths if the community population is subject to the specific death rates of the standard population. Since it is as effective as the I.M.D.R. in differentiating mortality levels among several populations, the simplicity of the interpretation and the formula make the S.M.R. a logical substitute for the I.M.D.R. The Registrar-General's Office of Great Britain began to use the S.M.R. in the *Statistical Review of England and Wales* in 1958.

Using the data in Table 5 we find the S.M.R. for the two communities:

$$\text{S.M.R.}(A) = \frac{620}{649.0} = .955$$

and

$$\text{S.M.R.}(B) = \frac{590}{561.2} = 1.051.$$

The ratio of these two values is equal to the ratio of the two corresponding I.M.D.R.'s in Section 2.3. That is,

$$\frac{\text{S.M.R.}(A)}{\text{S.M.R.}(B)} = \frac{.955}{1.051} = .909$$

and

$$\frac{\text{I.M.D.R.}(A)}{\text{I.M.D.R.}(B)} = \frac{11.56}{12.72} = .909,$$

as anticipated in the formulas.

2.6. Life Table Death Rate (L.T.D.R.). Most of the methods of adjustment rely on a standard population or its rates. One exception is the L.T.D.R. which is defined as

$$\text{L.T.D.R.} = \sum_i \frac{L_i}{T_0} M_{ui}, \qquad (2.14)$$

where L_i is the number of years spent in ages (x_i, x_{i+1}) by a life table population and

$$T_0 = L_0 + L_1 + \cdots \qquad (2.15)$$

is the total number of years lived by the life table population during the year of compilation of the table. A full appreciation of this method of adjustment requires a thorough knowledge of life tables. These are discussed in detail in Chapter 6. In the meantime, here is a brief discussion on formula (2.14).

Given l_0 people alive at age 0 who are subject to the age-specific death rates of the community, L_i/T_0 is the proportion of their life time spent in the age interval (x_i, x_{i+1}). In other words, the L.T.D.R. as shown in formula (2.14) is a weighted mean of the age-specific death rates (M_{ui}) with the proportion of life time spent in (x_i, x_{i+1}) being used as weights. Since the weights L_i/T_0 depend solely on the age-specific death rates, the L.T.D.R. is independent of the population composition of either a community or a standard population.

As we will see in Chapter 6, the age-specific death rate M_{ui} is equal to the ratio d_i/L_i, where d_i is the number of life table deaths in the age interval (x_i, x_{i+1}). Hence

$$L_i M_{ui} = d_i, \qquad (2.16)$$

and the sum

$$d_0 + d_1 + \cdots = l_0, \qquad (2.17)$$

is the total number of individuals living at age 0. Substituting (2.16) in (2.14) and using (2.17) we get

$$\text{L.T.D.R.} = l_0/T_0. \qquad (2.18)$$

The inverse

$$T_0/l_0 = \hat{e}_0 \qquad (2.19)$$

is known as the (observed) expectation of life at age 0; therefore

$$\text{L.T.D.R.} = \frac{1}{\hat{e}_0}. \qquad (2.20)$$

2.7.   Equivalent Average Death Rate (E.A.D.R.).   In this method of adjustment each age-specific rate is weighted with the corresponding interval length rather than the number of people for whom the rate is computed. In formula, it is:

$$\text{E.A.D.R.} = \sum_i \frac{n_i}{\sum_i n_i} M_{ui}, \qquad (2.21)$$

where $n_i = x_{i+1} - x_i$. The last age interval is an open interval, such as "60 and over", and the corresponding death rate is usually high. An upper limit must be set for this interval in order to prevent the high death rate of the elderly from asserting an undue effect on the resulting adjusted rate. G. U. Yule, the original author of the index, suggested that the upper limit of the last age interval be set at 65 years. Note that since there are fewer people in the old age group, the E.A.D.R. places more emphasis on old ages than the C.D.R. or the D.M.D.R.

2.8.   Relative Mortality Index (R.M.I.).   The basic quantities used in the relative mortality index are the ratios of the specific rates of a given community to the corresponding rates of a standard population. The index is a weighted mean of these ratios, obtained by using the community age-specific population proportions as weights. The formula for the R.M.I. is

$$\text{R.M.I.} = \sum_i \frac{P_{ui}}{P_u} \frac{M_{ui}}{M_{si}}. \tag{2.22}$$

Since $P_{ui} M_{ui} = D_{ui}$, the index can be computed without the knowledge of the community's population by age.

2.9. Mortality Index (M.I.). This index is also a weighted average of the ratios of community age-specific death rates to the corresponding rates of a standard population. It differs from the relative mortality index by using the lengths of the age intervals as weights. The formula for the index is

$$\text{M.I.} = \frac{\sum n_i (M_{ui}/M_{si})}{\sum n_i}. \tag{2.23}$$

Generally, the R.M.I. reflects the mortality pattern in young age groups more than the M.I. does. Consider, for example, age groups $(0, 15)$ and $(65, 80)$. The population proportion P_{ui}/P_u in the young age group is much greater than the old age group. Therefore, the corresponding ratio M_{ui}/M_{si} for the young is weighted more heavily than the ratio M_{ui}/M_{si} for the old. However, since the two age intervals are of equal length, $n_i = 15$ years, the ratios M_{ui}/M_{si} for the two age groups receive the same weight in the Mortality Index.

In his introduction of the index, Yerushalmy (1951) emphasizes the point that the M.I. reflects the "*proportionate* and not the *absolute* differences in the individual age-specific rates." For age intervals of the same length, a constant change of the *ratio* M_{ui}/M_{si} will have an equal effect on the values of the index. We illustrate this point with an example.

In Tables 6 and 7 are the computations of the Mortality Index for a community for two time periods: year 1 and year 2. Table 7

Table 6. Computation of mortality index for a community in year 1.

Age Interval	Interval length (in years)	Death Rate per 1000		Ratio
		Community	Standard Population	
(x_i, x_{i+1})	n_i	M_{ui}	M_{si}	M_{ui}/M_{si}
(1)	(2)	(3)	(4)	(5)
0–15	15	8.00	9.43	.848
15–65	50	11.00	11.50	.957
65–80	15	15.00	15.29	.981

M.I. $= .941$

Table 7. Computation of mortality index for a community in year 2.

Age Interval	Interval length (in years)	Death Rate per 1000		Ratio	Remark
		Community	Standard Population		
(x_i, x_{i+1})	n_i	M_{ui}	M_{si}	M_{ui}/M_{si}	
(1)	(2)	(3)	(4)	(5)	(6)
0–15	15	8.94	9.43	.948	$= .848 + .100$
15–65	50	11.00	11.50	.957	no change
65–80	15	13.47	15.29	.881	$= .981 - .100$

M.I. $= .941$

shows that the ratio M_{ui}/M_{si} for the young in year 2 has increased over year 1 by .100, while the ratio for the old in year 2 has decreased from year 1 by the same amount [col. (6)]. The value of the M.I. for year 2, nevertheless, remains the same as the M.I. for year 1.

3. Standard Error of the Adjusted Rates

The age-adjusted death rates presented in Section 2 all assume the general form of a weighted mean of the age-specific death rates. With the exception of the indirect method adjusted rate, the weights add to unity. The sum of the weights in the I.M.D.R. can be greater or less than unity, depending upon the difference between the age composition of the community and that of the standard population. Because of this, the indirect method death rate is not strictly comparable with any other adjusted rate, nor is its standard error.

The inclusion of the crude death rate in the list of adjusted rates is significant. Since it is usually expressed as a ratio of all deaths to the total midyear population, the crude death rate is occasionally treated as a binomial proportion, which leads to an incorrect formula for its standard deviation. Individuals differing in age and sex obviously do not have the same probability of dying, and the notion of an average probability is senseless; a direct application of the binomial theory is therefore inappropriate. If, however, it is viewed as the weighted mean of the specific death rates, as shown in Section 2.1, then the correct formula for the standard error of the rate can be obtained.

In all the adjusted rates, the weights applied to specific rates are based on: (1) the population proportions, and (2) the relative interval lengths of specific age groups. For the crude rate, the weights are the community proportions in specific age groups (P_{ui}/P_u); for the direct method of adjustment, the standard population proportions in specific age groups (P_{si}/P_s); for the comparative mortality rate, the

Table 8. Formulas and weights used to compute the crude death rate, age-adjusted rates and mortality indices.

Title (1)	Formula (2)	Weight (w_i) (3)
Crude Death Rate (C.D.R.)	$\dfrac{\sum P_{ui} M_{ui}}{P_u}$	$\dfrac{P_{ui}}{P_u}$
Direct Method Death Rate (D.M.D.R.)	$\dfrac{\sum P_{si} M_{ui}}{P_s}$	$\dfrac{P_{si}}{P_s}$
Comparative Mortality Rate (C.M.R.)	$\dfrac{1}{2}\sum\left(\dfrac{P_{ui}}{P_u}+\dfrac{P_{si}}{P_s}\right)M_{ui}$	$\dfrac{1}{2}\left(\dfrac{P_{ui}}{P_u}+\dfrac{P_{si}}{P_s}\right)$
Indirect Method Death Rate (I.M.D.R.)	$\dfrac{(D_s/P_s)(D_u/P_u)}{\sum P_{ui} M_{si}/P_u}$	$\dfrac{D_s/P_s}{\sum P_{ui} M_{si}}P_{ui}$
Standardized Mortality Ratio (S.M.R.)	$\dfrac{\sum P_{ui}}{\sum P_{ui} M_{si}}M_{ui}$	$\dfrac{P_{ui}}{\sum P_{ui} M_{si}}$
Life Table Death Rate (L.T.D.R.)	$\dfrac{\sum L_i M_{ui}}{\sum L_i}$	$\dfrac{L_i}{\sum L_i}$
Equivalent Average Death Rate (E.A.D.R.)	$\dfrac{\sum n_i M_{ui}}{\sum n_i}$	$\dfrac{n_i}{\sum n_i}$
Relative Mortality Index (R.M.I.)	$\dfrac{\sum P_{ui}(M_{ui}/M_{si})}{P_u}$	$\dfrac{P_{ui}}{P_u M_{si}}$
Mortality Index (M.I.)	$\dfrac{\sum n_i(M_{ui}/M_{si})}{\sum n_i}$	$\dfrac{n_i}{(\sum n_i)M_{si}}$

average of the two population proportions; for the life table death rate, the life table population proportions for specific age groups (L_i/T_0); and for the equivalent average death rate, the relative interval lengths of the age groups $(n_i/\sum n_i)$. The weights used in the indirect method of adjustment are functions of the age-specific rates for the standard population, community population proportions, and standard population proportions.

The methods of adjustment listed in Table 8 include the standardized mortality ratio as well as two indices, the relative mortality index and the mortality index. As seen in the second column of Table 8, the two indices are weighted means of the ratios of a community's specific death rates to the corresponding specific rates for the standard population. The difference is that the relative mortality index uses the population proportions of the community for specific age groups as weights, while the mortality index uses the relative lengths of the age intervals. In the present discussion, we shall consider them as linear functions of the age-specific death rates with coefficients as listed in column 3.

3.1.   A general formula for the variance of an adjusted rate.   To derive the formula for the sample variance of an adjusted death rate, it is first essential to identify the random variables involved. Clearly, the age-specific death rates for a community are random variables, while the interval lengths for age groups are constants. Community and standard population proportions for specific age groups will not be treated as random variables because the random event under study is death, not population change. The age-specific death rates of the standard population are random variables, as are those of the commu- nity. But since adjusted death rates are derived for the purpose of making inference concerning the mortality experience of communi- ties, only that part of the random variation associated with the communities in question should be taken into consideration. Random variations attributable to the age-specific rates for the standard popu- lation should not be included in the variance of the adjusted rates. To summarize, we shall consider only the community age-specific death rates for specific age groups as random variables in the derivation of the sample variance. The variance of the life table death rate will be treated separately in Section 5.

With this understanding, the adjusted rates and the mortality indices are linear functions of the basic random variables, the age- specific death rates of the community. The general formula is

$$R = \sum_i w_i M_{ui} , \qquad (3.1)$$

where the summation is taken over all age groups. The coefficients w_i are those given in Table 8.

Since the death rates of any two different age intervals are uncorrelated, according to the rule for the variance of a linear function of random variables in Chapter 2, page 36, the variance of the adjusted rate in (3.1) is simply

$$S_R^2 = \sum_i w_i^2 S_{M_{ui}}^2 . \qquad (3.2)$$

The variance of M_{ui} was derived in Chapter 4, equation (3.5). It is

$$S_{M_{ui}}^2 = \frac{M_{ui}}{P_{ui}} (1 - \hat{q}_{ui}). \qquad (3.3)$$

Substituting (3.3) in (3.2) yields the general formula for the sample variance of an age-adjusted death rate:

$$S_R^2 = \sum_i w_i^2 \frac{M_{ui}}{P_{ui}} (1 - \hat{q}_{ui}). \tag{3.4}$$

When the estimate of the probability $\hat{q}_{ui}$ is small so that $(1 - \hat{q}_{ui})$ is close to unity, we have an approximate formula:

$$S_R^2 = \sum_i w_i^2 \frac{M_{ui}}{P_{ui}}. \tag{3.5}$$

Remark.   When the age-specific death rates are determined from a sample of deaths, the formula for the sample variance of a death rate is different from (3.3) and there is a covariance of any two death rates. The formulas for the variance and covariance are given in Chapter 4, equations (3.17) and (3.21), on pages 81 and 82, respectively.

4.   Computation of the Sample Variance of the Direct Method Age-Adjusted Death Rate

Computation of the sample variance of the age-specific death rate is the essential part common to all the methods of adjustment except for the life table death rate. Therefore, it suffices to use the direct method of adjustment (D.M.D.R.) as an example. The formula for the sample variance of D.M.D.R. is obtained from (3.3) with $w_i = P_{si}/P_s$:

$$S_R^2 = \sum_i \left(\frac{P_{si}}{P_s}\right)^2 \frac{M_{ui}}{P_{ui}} (1 - \hat{q}_{ui}) \tag{4.1}$$

For this illustration, we will use the death rates of the total California population of 1970, and the United States 1970 population as the standard population. The steps involved in the computation are shown in Table 9.

The variance of the specific rate for the last age interval, "85 and over", is equal to zero, as the probability $\hat{q}_{85} = 1$. For each of the remaining age groups we use formula (3.3) to compute the sample variance of the death rate M_{ui}

$$S_{M_{ui}}^2 = \frac{M_{ui}}{P_{ui}} (1 - \hat{q}_{ui}) \tag{3.3}$$

as shown in column (7) in Table 9. Multiplying each variance by the corresponding weight squared $(P_{si}/P_s)^2$ as in column (8) gives the product

$$\left(\frac{P_{si}}{P_s}\right)^2 S_{M_{ui}}^2 = \left(\frac{P_{si}}{P_s}\right)^2 \frac{M_{ui}}{P_{ui}} (1 - \hat{q}_{ui}); \tag{4.2}$$

Table 9. Computation of sample standard error of the age-adjusted death rate for total population, California, 1970. (Adjustment is made by the direct method. The standard population is the total population of the United States, 1970)

Age Interval (in years)	Length of Interval	Mid-year Population in Interval (x_i, x_{i+1})	Death Rate	Fraction of Last Age Interval of Life	Probability of Dying in Interval	Sample Variance of Age Specific Death Rate	Square of Standard Population Proportion (U.S., 1970)
x_i to x_{i+1}	n_i	P_{ui}	M_{ui}	a_i	$\hat{q}_{ui}$	$10^{12} S^2_{M_{ui}}$	$10^8 (P_{si}/P_s)^2$
(1)	(2)	(3)	(4)	(5)	(6)	(7)	(8)
0–1	1	340483	.018309	.09	.01801	52806	29416
1–5	4	1302198	.000806	.41	.00322	617	452459
5–10	5	1918117	.000377	.44	.00188	196	964405
10–15	5	1963681	.000374	.54	.00187	190	1046618
15–20	5	1817379	.001130	.59	.00564	618	880681
20–25	5	1740966	.001552	.49	.00773	885	649013
25–30	5	1457614	.001421	.51	.00708	968	439833
30–35	5	1219389	.001611	.52	.00802	1311	316393
35–40	5	1149999	.002250	.53	.01119	1935	298733
40–45	5	1208550	.003404	.54	.01689	2769	347604
45–50	5	1245903	.005395	.53	.02664	4215	355480
50–55	5	1083852	.008256	.53	.04049	7309	298581
55–60	5	933244	.012796	.52	.06207	12860	240855
60–65	5	770770	.018565	.52	.08886	21946	179801
65–70	5	620805	.027526	.51	.12893	38623	118374
70–75	5	484431	.039529	.52	.18052	66869	71765
75–80	5	342097	.062336	.51	.27039	132948	35612
80–85	5	210953	.095419	.50	.38521	278084	12636
85 +	–	142691	.157564	–	1.00000	0	5528

adding the products in (4.2) over all age groups yields the sample variance of R in formula (4.1).

For the California 1970 population the age-adjusted death rate is

$$R = \sum \frac{P_{si}}{P_s} M_{ui}$$

$$= \frac{1{,}787{,}768}{203{,}211{,}926}$$

$$= .0087976 \text{ or } 8.7976 \text{ per } 1000 \text{ person-years.}$$

The computation in Table 9 shows that the sample variance is

$$S^2_R = 340.631 \times 10^{-12}$$

and the standard deviation is

$$S_R = \sqrt{340.631 \times 10^{-12}} = .018456 \text{ per } 1000.$$

By comparison, the standard deviation S_R is much smaller than the age-adjusted death rate.

The age-adjusted death rate of 8.7976 per 1000 for the California 1970 population may be compared with the total United States 1970 population death rate, 9.453 per 1000, since both are based on the same population distribution. Because of the small standard deviation ($S_R = .018456$ per 1000), we conclude that in 1970 the California population had a significantly lower mortality than the United States as a whole.

If one wishes to formally test the hypothesis that in 1970 the California mortality is the same as that of the general population of the United States: H_0: $R = 9.453$ per 1000, one may use the procedure described in Chapter 3 and compute the standardized random variable of R,

$$Z = \frac{R - .009453}{\text{S.E.}(R)},$$

to find

$$Z = \frac{.0087976 - .009453}{.000018456} = -35.51,$$

which is highly significant, and one arrives at the same conclusion.

5.   Sample Variance of the Life Table Death Rate

The life table death rate is a special case, since the weights $L_x / \sum_x L_x$, (which are functions of the age-specific death rates), are themselves random variables and are correlated with each other and with the specific death rates. Obviously, a derivation of the sample variance of the life table death rate based on the approach presented in the previous sections would involve a series of complicated and difficult computations. The life table death rate, however, has a simple inverse relationship with the observed expectation of life at birth, $\hat{e}_0$ [cf., Equation (2.20), page 101],

$$R = \frac{1}{\hat{e}_0}. \tag{5.1}$$

Employing the general rule for the variance of the inverse of a random variable, we have

$$S_R^2 = \frac{1}{\hat{e}_0^4} S_{\hat{e}_0}^2. \tag{5.2}$$

Here the sample variance of $\hat{e}_0$, which may be found in Chapter 8, is

$$S_{\hat{e}_0}^2 = \sum_{x \geqslant 0} \hat{p}_{0x}^2 \left[(1 - a_x)n_x + \hat{e}_{x+n_x} \right]^2 S_{\hat{q}_x}^2. \tag{5.3}$$

Substituting this in (5.2) gives the required formula

$$S_R^2 = \frac{1}{\hat{e}_0^4} \sum_{x \geq 0} \hat{p}_{0x}^2 \left[(1 - a_x)n_x + \hat{e}_{x+n_x} \right]^2 S_{\hat{q}_x}^2 , \qquad (5.4)$$

where

$$S_{\hat{q}_x}^2 = \frac{\hat{q}_x^2 [1 - \hat{q}_x]}{D_x}$$

which is from Chapter 4, page 79.

6. Problems for Solution

1. Use the population in Table A as the standard population to compute the Direct Method Death Rates and the Comparative Mortality Rates for Community A and Community B in Table 2, page 94.

Table A. Population and the number of deaths for each age group of a standard population.

	Population, P_{si}	Number of deaths, D_{si}
Children	37,000	54
Adults	50,000	210
Senior Citizens	13,000	576
	100,000	840

2. Use the standard population in Table A, problem 1, to compute the Indirect Method Death Rates and the Standardized Mortality Ratios for Community A and Community B.

3. Suppose the interval lengths of the three age groups for Community A and Community B are $n_1 = 20$, $n_2 = 40$, and $n_3 = 20$ years. Compute the Equivalent Average Death Rate for Community A and Community B.

4. Compute the Relative Mortality Index and the Mortality Index for Community A and Community B, assuming $n_1 = 20$, $n_2 = 40$, and $n_3 = 20$ years.

5. Compute the standard error of each of the five age specific death rates for the United States Population in Table B, page 110.

6. *Continuation.* Express the crude death rate of the U.S. population (878.1 per 100,000) as a weighted mean of the five age specific death rates and compute the standard error of the weighted mean.

Table B. Deaths and Death Rates by Age: United States, Each Division and State, 1977
(rates per 100,000 population specific group in each area)

Geographic Division	Number							Rate					
	Total	Under 5 years	5–19 years	20–44 years	45–64 years	65 years and over	Not Stated	Total	Under 5 years	5–19 years	20–44 years	45–64 years	65 years and over
United States	1,899,597	55,282	34,022	129,585	437,795	1,242,344	569	878.1	362.9	59.2	169.7	1,000.0	5,288.1
Geographic Divisions													
New England	108,067	2,093	1,442	5,447	23,267	75,802	16	882.8	287.1	44.6	127.1	905.3	5,330.7
Middle Atlantic	353,803	8,068	4,731	20,376	82,743	237,748	137	955.2	352.3	49.9	161.1	998.0	5,500.9
East North Central	361,122	10,608	6,383	23,068	83,203	237,834	26	879.6	365.3	56.9	159.2	1,014.9	5,606.6
West North Central	155,142	4,047	2,686	8,299	28,701	111,390	19	918.9	348.0	59.6	143.1	869.2	5,286.7
South Atlantic	308,785	9,420	5,564	22,862	78,762	192,061	116	900.1	392.2	61.9	187.1	1,146.8	5,010.7
East South Central	130,479	4,409	2,662	9,667	30,538	83,168	35	943.0	415.2	70.7	201.0	1,134.4	5,504.2
West South Central	183,033	6,907	3,958	14,642	42,010	115,419	97	843.2	393.3	66.6	190.7	1,023.1	5,187.4
Mountain	72,404	2,963	2,061	6,771	16,355	44,210	44	721.9	337.1	74.0	189.2	874.1	4,810.7
Pacific	226,762	6,767	4,535	18,453	52,216	144,712	79	775.7	329.5	60.2	170.1	888.3	4,961.0

Source: National Center for Health Statistics, U.S. Department of Health and Human Services. Vital Statistics of the United States, 1977, Vol. II—Mortality, Part A, p. 1–47, Table 1–12.

Compute the standard error of the crude death rate directly using formula (3.1) on page 79 for total population. Compare the two standard errors and explain their difference.

7. *Continuation.* Express the crude death rates of the Pacific and New England regions in terms of the corresponding age specific death rates and determine the standard errors.

Test the hypothesis that the Pacific and New England regions have the same crude death rates.

8. *Continuation.* Use the U.S. population as the standard population to determine the direct method death rates for the Pacific and New England regions.

Compare the direct method death rate with the crude death rate and explain the difference for each of the two regions.

9. *Continuation.* Determine the standard error for each of the two direct method death rates in problem 8. Are the two rates significantly different?

10. *Continuation.* Use the U.S. population as the standard population to compute:

(1)   the indirect method death rates and
(2)   the standardized mortality ratios

for the Pacific and New England regions. Compare the results.

11. *Continuation.* Use the U.S. age specific death rates as the standard to compute the relative mortality index and mortality index for the Pacific and New England regions (assuming $n_i = 20$ for age interval 65 years and over). Compare the results.

12. *Continuation.* For a region of your choice and using the U.S. as the standard population, compute:

(1)   crude death rate
(2)   direct method death rate
(3)   comparative mortality rate
(4)   indirect method death rate
(5)   standard mortality ratio
(6)   equivalent average death rate
(7)   relative mortality index, and
(8)   mortality index

(assuming $n_i = 20$ years for age interval 65 and over). Discuss the relative merit of these rates.

CHAPTER 6

The Life Table and Its Construction— the Complete Life Table

An Historical Note

Long before the development of modern probability and statistics, people were concerned with the length of life and constructed tables to measure longevity. The longevity of famous persons and individuals who were reported to have died at extremely old ages have attracted particular interest. A crude table, constructed in the middle of the third century and credited to the Roman Praetorian Praefect Ulpianus, indicates a life expectancy of thirty years. But since its purpose was to serve as a basis for determining annuity grants, it seems unlikely that it reflects mortality in the general population. Nevertheless, it continued in official use in northern Italy until the end of the eighteenth century.

John Graunt's *Bills of Mortality*, published in 1662, and Edmund Halley's famous table for the city of Breslau, published in 1693, mark the beginning of modern life tables. In *Bills of Mortality*, Graunt introduced the proportions of people surviving to various ages. Halley's table already contained most of the columns in use today. A rough calculation of the average length of life from Graunt's data for seventeenth century London yields a figure of 18.2 years; Halley's estimate for Breslau near the end of the century was 33.5 years. During the next hundred years several life tables were constructed, including the French tables of Deparcieux (1746), of Buffon (1749), of Mourgue and of Duvillard (both published in the 1790's), the Northampton table of Richard Price (1783), and Wigglesworth's table for Massachusetts and New Hampshire (1793) in the United States. The first official English life table was published in 1843 during William Farr's term as Compiler of Abstracts in the General Records Office. Several countries in Continental Europe have published series of life tables dating back almost two centuries. Sweden, for example, began a series in 1755, Netherlands in 1816, France in 1817, Norway in 1821, Germany in 1871 and Switzerland in 1876. Reliable mortality statistics for the construction of United States life tables were not available until 1900; at that time, J. W. Glover of the Bureau of the Census determined that the expectation of life at birth was 46.07 years for males and 49.42 for females.

1. Introduction

The life table is primarily a product of actuarial science, but the computation of insurance premiums is not its only application. Recent advances in theoretical statistics and stochastic processes have made it possible to study longevity from a purely statistical viewpoint, making the life table a valuable analytical tool for demographers, epidemiologists, biologists, and research workers in other fields.

There are two principal forms of the life table: the cohort (or generation) life table and the current life table. In its strictest form, the *cohort life table* records the actual mortality experience of a particular group of individuals (the cohort) from the birth of the first to the death of the last member of the group. The difficulties involved in constructing such a table for a human population are self-evident. Individuals in a given cohort may emigrate or die unrecorded, and the life expectancy of a group of people already dead is of little more than historical interest. However, cohort life tables do have practical applications in the study of animal populations and have even been extended to assess the durability of inanimate objects such as engines, electric light bulbs, and other mechanical objects. Modified or adapted cohort tables have been useful in epidemiological, sociological, medical and paramedical studies of human subjects. The analysis of chance and duration of patient-survival in studies of treatment effectiveness has made extensive use of life table methods. These will be discussed in more detail in Chapter 11.

The current life table, as the name implies, gives a cross-sectional view of the mortality and survival experience of a population during a current year (e.g., the California population of 1970). It is entirely dependent on the age-specific death rates prevailing in the year for which it is constructed. Such tables project the life span of each individual in a hypothetical cohort on the basis of the actual

death rates in a given population. When we speak of the life expectancy of an infant born in the current year, for example, we mean the
life expectancy that would be obtained if that infant were subjected
throughout his life to the same age-specific mortalities prevailing in the
current year. The current life table is then a reflection of the mortality
experience of a real population during a calendar year. It is also the
most effective means of summarizing the mortality and survival
experience of a population, and forms a sound basis for statistical
inferences about the population under study. The reader can confirm
that the current life table is a useful tool for comparing international
mortality data and for assessing mortality trends on the national level.

Cohort and current life tables may be either complete or
abridged. In a *complete life table* the functions are computed for each
year of life; an *abridged life table* deals with age intervals greater than
one year, except the first years of life. A typical set of intervals is 0–1,
1–5, 5–10, 10–15, etc.

A current life table may be based on the deaths occurring over
several (typically three) calendar years instead of one, e.g., the years
1969, 1970 and 1971. For each age group the average number of
deaths per year is determined and is then divided by the corresponding population size of the middle year (1970, in this example) to
obtain an age-specific death rate. Usually, the middle year is a census
year, so that population figures are available and more accurate. The
purpose of such a procedure is to reduce the effect of abnormalities in
the mortality pattern which may exist in a single calendar year.

Techniques for refinement of life table data were developed by
actuarial scientists. These include graduation and other methods for
reducing the effect of extreme values. But it is difficult to make
proper statistical inference about life table functions based on such
information.

This chapter will describe a general form of the life table with
interpretations of its various functions and present a method of
constructing a current life table. Theoretical aspects of life table
functions will be discussed in detail in Chapter 10.

2. Description of the Life Table

Cohort and current life tables are identical in appearance but
different in construction. The following discussion refers to the complete current life table. Each column is defined and its relation to the
other columns explained; conventional symbols have been modified
for the sake of simplicity. The complete current life table for the
California total population in 1970, presented in Table 2, will serve as
an example.

Column 1.   Age interval $(x, x + 1)$—Each interval in this column is defined by the two exact ages stated except for the final age interval, which is open-ended (e.g., "85 and over"). The starting point for the final age interval is denoted by w.

Column 2.   Proportion of those alive at age x dying in the interval $(x, x + 1)$, $\hat{q}_x$—Each $\hat{q}_x$ is an estimate of the probability that an individual alive at the exact age x will die during the year. These proportions are the basic quantities from which the figures in other columns of the table are computed. They are derived from the corresponding age-specific death rates of the current population, using formulas that will be presented in the next section. To avoid decimals, the proportions are sometimes expressed as the number of deaths per 1,000 population, and the column is correspondingly labeled "1000 $\hat{q}_x$".

Column 3.   Number alive at age x, l_x—The first number in this column, l_0, is an arbitrary figure called the "radix," while each successive figure represents the number of survivors at the exact age x from a group of size l_0. Thus, the figures in this column have meaning only in conjunction with the radix l_0, and do not describe any observed population. The radix is usually assigned a convenient number, such as 100,000. Table 2 shows that l_1 or 98,199 of every 100,000 persons born alive will survive to their first birthday, provided they are subject to the same mortality experience as that of the 1970 California population.

Column 4.   Number dying in interval $(x, x + 1)$, d_x—The figures in this column are the product of l_x and $\hat{q}_x$ and thus also depend upon the radix l_0. Again using the 1970 California experience, we see that out of $l_0 = 100,000$ born alive, $d_0 = 1801$ will die in the first year of life. But the number 1801 is meaningless by itself, and is certainly not the number of infant deaths occurring in California in 1970. For each age interval $(x, x + 1)$, d_x is merely the number of life table deaths.

Summarizing in formulas, the figures in the columns l_x and d_x are related to the values $\hat{q}_0, \hat{q}_1, \ldots, \hat{q}_w$, and the radix l_0 by

$$d_x = l_x \hat{q}_x, \qquad x = 0, 1, \ldots, w, \tag{2.1}$$

and

$$l_{x+1} = l_x - d_x, \qquad x = 0, 1, \ldots, w - 1. \tag{2.2}$$

Starting with the first age interval, we use equation (2.1) for $x = 0$ to obtain the number d_0 dying in the interval $(0, 1)$ and equation (2.2) for

$x = 0$ to obtain the number l_1 who survive to the end of the interval. With l_1 persons alive at the exact age 1, we again use the relations (2.1) and (2.2) for $x = 1$ to obtain the corresponding figures for the second interval. Similarly, we recursively compute all the figures in columns 3 and 4.

Column 5. Fraction of last year of life for age x, a'_x—Each of the d_x people who have died during the interval $(x, x + 1)$ has lived x complete years plus some fraction of the year $(x, x + 1)$. The average of these fractions, denoted by a'_x, plays an important role in the construction of life tables, and in the theoretical studies of life table functions as presented in Chapter 10. This is explained more fully in the next section.

Column 6. Number of years lived by the total cohort in interval $(x, x + 1)$, L_x—Each member of the cohort who survives the interval $(x, x + 1)$ contributes one year to L_x, while each member who dies during the year $(x, x + 1)$ contributes, on the average, a fraction a'_x of a year, so that

$$L_x = (l_x - d_x) + a'_x d_x, \qquad x = 0, 1, \ldots, w - 1. \qquad (2.3)$$

The first term on the right side is the number of years lived in the interval $(x, x + 1)$ by the $(l_x - d_x)$ survivors, and the second term is the number of years lived in $(x, x + 1)$ by the d_x persons who died during the interval. When a'_x is assumed to be $1/2$ (which is usually the case for ages greater than 5), this becomes

$$L_x = l_x - \tfrac{1}{2} d_x. \qquad (2.4)$$

Note that L_x is closely related to the notion of "person-years" introduced in Chapter 4.

Column 7. Total number of years lived beyond age x, T_x—This total is essential for computation of the life expectancy. It is equal to the sum of the number of years lived in each age interval beginning with age x, or

$$T_x = L_x + L_{x+1} + \cdots + L_w, \qquad x = 0, 1, \ldots, w. \qquad (2.5)$$

There is an obvious relationship between T_x and T_{x+1}; namely:

$$T_x = L_x + T_{x+1}. \qquad (2.6)$$

Column 8. Expectation of life at age x, $\hat{e}_x$—This is the number of years, on the average, yet to be lived by a person of age x. Since the total number of years of life remaining to the l_x individuals is T_x, the expectation is

$$\hat{e}_x = \frac{T_x}{l_x}, \qquad x = 0, 1, \ldots, w. \tag{2.7}$$

Each $\hat{e}_x$ summarizes the mortality experience of persons beyond age x in the population under consideration, making this column the most important in the life table. Furthermore, this is the only column in the table other than $\hat{q}_x$ and a'_x that is meaningful without reference to the radix l_0. As a rule, the expectation of life $\hat{e}_x$ decreases as the age x increases, with the exception of the first year of life where the reverse is true because of the high mortality during the first year. In the 1970 California population, for example, the expectation of life at birth is $\hat{e}_0 = 71.90$ years whereas the expectation at age one is $\hat{e}_1 = 72.22$.

Remark 1.   Some useful quantities which are not listed in the conventional life table are:

$$\hat{p}_x = 1 - \hat{q}_x, \tag{2.8}$$

the proportion of survivors over the age interval $(x, x + 1)$, and

$$\hat{p}_{xy} = \hat{p}_x \hat{p}_{x+1} \cdots \hat{p}_{y-1} = \frac{l_y}{l_x}, \tag{2.9}$$

the proportion of those living at age x who will survive to age y. When $x = 0$, $\hat{p}_{0y}$ becomes the proportion of the total born alive who survive to age y; clearly,

$$\hat{p}_{0y} = l_y / l_0.$$

3.   Construction of the Complete Current Life Table

In constructing a current life table, one is mainly concerned with the computation of the estimate of the probability of death in the age interval $(x, x + 1)$ from the corresponding age-specific death rate. The remaining quantities in the table are then computed from the formulas described in Section 2.

The most important element in converting the age-specific death rate to the estimate of probability of death is the fraction of the last year of life lived by those who have died at each age. For example, a man who dies at age 30 has lived 30 complete years plus a fraction of the 31st year. The average value of this fraction is denoted by a'_x where x refers to the age at the last birthday. It might seem reasonable to expect that the average value of this fraction is one-half on the assumption that there are as many deaths at 30 years plus one month as at 30 years plus two months, and at each month thereafter through the 11th; or, in other words, on the assumption that deaths occur uniformly throughout each year of age. Extensive studies (Chiang, et al. [1961]) of this fraction have been made using the 1960 California mortality data collected by the State of California Department of Health Services, and the 1963 U.S. data collected by the National Vital Statistics Division of the National Center for Health Statistics. The results obtained so far show that after age 4 the fractions a'_x are invariant with respect to race, sex, and age, and that the assumed value of .5 is valid. However, because of the large proportion of infant deaths occurring in the first weeks of life, a much smaller value has been observed for the first year of life. The data suggest values: $a'_0 = .09$, $a'_1 = .43$, $a'_2 = .45$, $a'_3 = .47$, $a'_4 = .49$ for the first five years of life and $a'_x = .50$ for $x \geqslant 5$.

Returning to the computation of the estimate of the probability of death, we need a relationship between the estimate of probability $\hat{q}_x$ and age specific death rate M_x so that the probability of dying can be computed from the death rate for each age x. This relationship has been established in equation (2.4) in Chapter 4, page 73, for age intervals greater than one year. For age interval $(x, x + 1)$, the relationship is

$$\hat{q}_x = \frac{M_x}{1 + (1 - a'_x)M_x}, \qquad \text{for} \quad x = 0, 1, \ldots, w - 1. \qquad (3.1)$$

When the age-specific death rate M_x is determined from the number of deaths D_x and the midyear (calendar year) population P_x during the calendar year,

$$M_x = \frac{D_x}{P_x}, \qquad \text{for} \quad x = 0, 1, \ldots, w - 1, \qquad (3.2)$$

the estimate of the probability $\hat{q}_x$ can be computed from (3.1).

To illustrate the computation, let us consider the 1970 California population as shown in Table 1. For the first year of life, the population size is $P_0 = 340,483$ and the number of infant deaths is $D_0 = 6,234$, as shown in columns 2 and 3, respectively. The age-specific death rate for $x = 0$ shown in column 4 is

$$M_0 = \frac{D_0}{P_0} = \frac{6,234}{340,483} = .018309 \text{ or } 18.309 \text{ per } 1000 \text{ person-years.}$$

The average fraction of the year lived by an infant who dies in his first year of life is $a'_0 = .09$. Therefore, the estimate of the probability of dying (computed from (3.1)) is

$$\hat{q}_0 = \frac{.018309}{1 + (1 - .09).018309} = .01801.$$

Table 1. Construction of the complete life table for total California population, U.S.A., 1970.

Age interval (in years)	Midyear population in interval $(x, x+1)$	Number of deaths in interval $(x, x+1)$	Death rate in interval $(x, x+1)$	Fraction of last year of life	Probability of dying in interval $(x, x+1)$
x to $x+1$	P_x	D_x	M_x	a'_x	$\hat{q}_x$
(1)	(2)	(3)	(4)	(5)	(6)
0–1	340483	6234	.018309	.09	.01801
1–2	326154	368	.001128	.43	.00113
2–3	313699	269	.000858	.45	.00086
3–4	323441	237	.000733	.47	.00073
4–5	338904	175	.000516	.49	.00052
5–6	362161	179	.000494	.50	.00049
6–7	379642	171	.000450	.50	.00045
7–8	386980	131	.000339	.50	.00034
8–9	391610	121	.000309	.50	.00031
9–10	397724	121	.000304	.50	.00030
10–11	406118	126	.000310	.50	.00031
11–12	388927	127	.000327	.50	.00033
12–13	395025	138	.000349	.50	.00035
13–14	388526	158	.000407	.50	.00041
14–15	385085	186	.000483	.50	.00048
15–16	377127	235	.000623	.50	.00062
16–17	368156	344	.000934	.50	.00093
17–18	366198	385	.001051	.50	.00105
18–19	354932	506	.001426	.50	.00142
19–20	350966	584	.001664	.50	.00166
20–21	359833	583	.001620	.50	.00162
21–22	349557	562	.001608	.50	.00161
22–23	365839	572	.001564	.50	.00156
23–24	370548	564	.001522	.50	.00152
24–25	295189	421	.001426	.50	.00143
25–26	304013	416	.001368	.50	.00137
26–27	305558	391	.001280	.50	.00128
27–28	310554	461	.001484	.50	.00148
28–29	275897	411	.001490	.50	.00149
29–30	261592	392	.001499	.50	.00150
30–31	264083	399	.001511	.50	.00151
31–32	247777	378	.001526	.50	.00152
32–33	241726	388	.001605	.50	.00160
33–34	232025	365	.001573	.50	.00157
34–35	233778	434	.001856	.50	.00185
35–36	234338	439	.001873	.50	.00187
36–37	224302	475	.002118	.50	.00212
37–38	228652	519	.002270	.50	.00227
38–39	226727	549	.002421	.50	.00242
39–40	235980	606	.002568	.50	.00256

Table 1. (continued)

x to $x + 1$	P_x	D_x	M_x	a'_x	$\hat{q}_x$
(1)	(2)	(3)	(4)	(5)	(6)
40–41	249027	665	.002670	.50	.00267
41–42	232893	719	.003087	.50	.00308
42–43	239747	863	.003600	.50	.00359
43–44	238783	874	.003660	.50	.00365
44–45	248100	993	.004002	.50	.00399
45–46	253828	1140	.004491	.50	.00448
46–47	249857	1268	.005075	.50	.00506
47–48	247955	1362	.005493	.50	.00548
48–49	252137	1422	.005640	.50	.00562
49–50	242126	1530	.006319	.50	.00630
50–51	243799	1594	.006538	.50	.00652
51–52	220599	1710	.007752	.50	.00772
52–53	213448	1793	.008400	.50	.00837
53–54	203618	1870	.009184	.50	.00914
54–55	202388	1981	.009788	.50	.00974
55–56	201750	2217	.010989	.50	.01093
56–57	193828	2333	.012036	.50	.01196
57–58	187257	2483	.013260	.50	.01317
58–59	178602	2392	.013393	.50	.01330
59–60	171807	2517	.014650	.50	.01454
60–61	174613	2733	.015652	.50	.01553
61–62	157734	2743	.017390	.50	.01724
62–63	154174	2911	.018881	.50	.01870
63–64	144149	2968	.020590	.50	.02038
64–65	140100	2954	.021085	.50	.02086
65–66	135857	3391	.024960	.50	.02465
66–67	129386	3278	.025335	.50	.02502
67–68	123925	3352	.027049	.50	.02669
68–69	112574	3331	.029589	.50	.02916
69–70	119063	3736	.031378	.50	.03089
70–71	114066	3846	.033717	.50	.03316
71–72	100781	3704	.036753	.50	.03609
72–73	93031	3706	.039836	.50	.03906
73–74	89992	3830	.042559	.50	.04167
74–75	86561	4063	.046938	.50	.04586
75–76	81003	4275	.052776	.50	.05142
76–77	73552	4383	.059590	.50	.05787
77–78	70516	4259	.060398	.50	.05863
78–79	60616	4181	.068975	.50	.06668
79–80	56410	4227	.074934	.50	.07223
80–81	57646	4424	.076744	.50	.07391
81–82	48299	4288	.088780	.50	.08501
82–83	39560	3995	.100986	.50	.09613
83–84	34439	3753	.108975	.50	.10334
84–85	31009	3669	.118320	.50	.11171
85 +	142691	22483	.157564		1.00000

Table 2. Complete life table for total California population, U.S.A., 1970.

Age interval (in years)	Probability of dying in interval $(x, x+1)$	Number living at age x	Number dying in interval $(x, x+1)$	Fraction of last year of life	Number of years lived in interval $(x, x+1)$	Total number of years lived beyond age x	Expectation of life at age x
x to $x+1$	$\hat{q}_x$	l_x	d_x	a'_x	L_x	T_x	$\hat{e}_x$
(1)	(2)	(3)	(4)	(5)	(6)	(7)	(8)
0–1	.01801	100000	1801	.09	98631	7190390	71.90
1–2	.00113	98199	111	.43	98136	7092029	72.22
2–3	.00086	98088	84	.45	98042	6993893	71.30
3–4	.00073	98004	72	.47	97966	6895851	70.36
4–5	.00052	97932	51	.49	97906	6797885	69.41
5–6	.00049	97881	48	.50	97857	6699979	68.45
6–7	.00045	97833	44	.50	97811	6602122	67.48
7–8	.00034	97789	33	.50	97772	6504311	66.51
8–9	.00031	97756	30	.50	97741	6406539	65.54
9–10	.00030	97726	29	.50	97711	6308798	64.56
10–11	.00031	97697	30	.50	97682	6211087	63.58
11–12	.00033	97667	32	.50	97651	6113405	62.59
12–13	.00035	97635	34	.50	97618	6015754	61.61
13–14	.00041	97601	40	.50	97581	5918136	60.64
14–15	.00048	96561	47	.50	97538	5820555	59.66
15–16	.00062	97514	60	.50	97484	5723017	58.69
16–17	.00093	97454	91	.50	97408	5625533	57.73
17–18	.00105	97363	102	.50	97312	5528125	56.78
18–19	.00142	97261	138	.50	97192	5430813	55.84
19–20	.00156	97123	161	.50	97043	5333621	54.92
20–21	.00162	96962	157	.50	96884	5236578	54.01
21–22	.00161	96805	156	.50	96727	5139694	53.09
22–23	.00156	96649	151	.50	96574	5042967	52.18
23–24	.00152	96498	147	.50	96424	4946393	51.26
24–25	.00143	96351	138	.50	96282	4849969	50.34
25–26	.00137	96213	132	.50	96147	4753687	49.41
26–27	.00128	96081	123	.50	96020	4657540	48.48
27–28	.00148	95958	142	.50	95887	4561520	47.54
28–29	.00149	95816	143	.50	95745	4465633	46.61
29–30	.00150	95673	144	.50	95601	4369888	45.68
30–31	.00151	95529	144	.50	95457	4274287	44.74
31–32	.00152	95385	145	.50	95312	4178830	43.81
32–33	.00160	95240	152	.50	95164	4083518	42.88
33–34	.00157	95088	149	.50	95014	3988354	41.94
34–35	.00185	94939	176	.50	94851	3893340	41.01
35–36	.00187	94763	177	.50	94674	3798489	40.08
36–37	.00212	94586	201	.50	94486	3703815	39.16
37–38	.00227	94385	214	.50	94278	3609329	38.24
38–39	.00242	94171	228	.50	94057	3515051	37.33
39–40	.00256	93943	240	.50	93823	3520994	36.42

Table 2. (continued)

x to $x+1$	$\hat{q}_x$	l_x	d_x	a'_x	L_x	T_x	$\hat{e}_x$
(1)	(2)	(3)	(4)	(5)	(6)	(7)	(8)
40–41	.00267	93703	250	.50	93578	3327171	35.51
41–42	.00308	93453	288	.50	93309	3233593	34.60
42–43	.00359	93165	334	.50	92998	3140284	33.71
43–44	.00365	92831	339	.50	92661	3047286	32.83
44–45	.00399	92492	369	.50	92307	2954625	31.94
45–46	.00448	92123	413	.50	91916	2862318	31.07
46–47	.00506	91710	464	.50	91478	2770402	30.21
47–48	.00548	91246	500	.50	90996	2678924	29.36
48–49	.00562	90746	510	.50	90491	2587928	28.52
49–50	.00630	90236	568	.50	89952	2497437	27.68
50–51	.00652	89668	585	.50	89376	2407485	26.85
51–52	.00772	89083	688	.50	88739	2318109	26.02
52–53	.00837	88395	740	.50	88025	2229370	25.22
53–54	.00914	87655	801	.50	87255	2141345	24.43
54–55	.00974	86854	846	.50	86431	2054090	23.65
55–56	.01093	86008	940	.50	85538	1967659	22.88
56–57	.01196	85068	1017	.50	84559	1882121	22.12
57–58	.01317	84051	1107	.50	83497	1797562	21.39
58–59	.01330	82944	1103	.50	82393	1714065	20.67
59–60	.01454	81841	1190	.50	81246	1631672	19.94
60–61	.01553	80651	1253	.50	80025	1550426	19.22
61–62	.01724	79398	1369	.50	78713	1470401	18.52
62–63	.01870	78029	1459	.50	77299	1391688	17.84
63–64	.02038	76570	1560	.50	75790	1314389	17.17
64–65	.02086	75010	1565	.50	74228	1238599	16.51
65–66	.02465	73445	1810	.50	72540	1164371	15.85
66–67	.02502	71635	1792	.50	70739	1091831	15.24
67–68	.02669	69843	1864	.50	68911	1021092	14.62
68–69	.02916	67979	1982	.50	66988	952181	14.01
69–70	.03089	65997	2039	.50	64978	885193	13.41
70–71	.03316	63958	2121	.50	62897	820215	12.82
71–72	.03609	61837	2232	.50	60721	757318	12.25
72–73	.03906	59605	2328	.50	58441	696597	11.69
73–74	.04167	57277	2387	.50	56083	638156	11.14
74–75	.04586	54890	2517	.50	53632	582073	10.60
75–76	.05142	52373	2693	.50	51026	528441	10.09
76–77	.05787	49680	2875	.50	48243	477415	9.61
77–78	.05863	46805	2744	.50	45433	429172	9.17
78–79	.06668	44061	2938	.50	42592	383739	8.71
79–80	.07223	41123	2970	.50	39638	341147	8.30
80–81	.07391	38153	2820	.50	36743	301509	7.90
81–82	.08501	35333	3004	.50	33831	264766	7.49
82–83	.09613	32329	3108	.50	30775	230935	7.14
83–84	.10334	29221	3020	.50	27711	200160	6.85
84–85	.11171	26201	2927	.50	24738	172449	6.58
85 +	1.00000	23274	23274		147711	147711	6.35

When all the values of $\hat{q}_x$ have been computed and l_0 has been selected, d_x, l_x, and L_x for successive values of x are determined from equations (2.1), (2.2), and (2.3) as shown in Table 2. For the 1970 California population we determine the number of life table infant deaths with $l_0 = 100{,}000$,

$$d_0 = l_0\hat{q}_0$$
$$= 100{,}000 \times .01801 = 1801, \qquad (2.1a)$$

the life table survivors at age one,

$$l_1 = l_0 - d_0$$
$$= 100{,}000 - 1801 = 98199, \qquad (2.2a)$$

and the number of years lived in the interval $(0, 1)$,

$$L_0 = (l_0 - d_0) + a_0'd_0$$
$$= 98199 + .09 \times 1801 = 98361. \qquad (2.3a)$$

Remark 2. The ratio d_x/L_x is known as the life-table death rate for age x. Since a life table is based entirely on the age-specific death rates of a current population, the death rates computed from the life table should be identical to the corresponding rates of the current population; symbolically

$$\frac{d_x}{L_x} = M_x = \frac{D_x}{P_x}, \qquad x = 0, 1, \ldots . \qquad (3.3)$$

To prove (3.3), we substitute (2.3) in the ratio d_x/L_x to obtain

$$\frac{d_x}{L_x} = \frac{d_x}{(l_x - d_x) + a_x'd_x}$$

or, after dividing through by l_x,

$$\frac{d_x}{L_x} = \frac{\hat{q}_x}{1 - (1 - a_x')\hat{q}_x} . \qquad (3.4)$$

Using (3.1) to substitute for $\hat{q}_x$ in (3.4) and simplifying yields M_x.

The final age interval in a life table is a half-open interval, such as age 85 and over. The values of D_w, P_w, M_w, l_w, d_w, and T_w all refer to the open interval age w and over, and $\hat{q}_w = 1$ (since there can be no survivors). The length of the interval is infinite and the necessary information for determining the average number of years lived by an individual beyond age w is unavailable. We must therefore use an approach other than equation (2.3) to determine L_w. Writing the first equation in (3.3) for $x = w$, we have

$$L_w = \frac{d_w}{M_w} . \qquad (3.5)$$

Since each one of the l_w people alive at w will eventually die, $l_w = d_w$; from (3.5) we have the required formula

$$L_w = \frac{l_w}{M_w}.$$ (3.6)

Here l_w, the number of survivors to age w, is determined in the preceding interval, or interval (x_{w-1}, x_w) and M_w is the mortality rate for age interval "w and over" in the current population. In the 1970 California life table, $w = 85$, and $l_{85} = 23274$. The death rate for ages 85 and over is $M_{85} = .157564$; therefore,

$$L_{85} = \frac{l_{85}}{M_{85}} = \frac{23274}{.157564} = 147711.$$

Using L_w and L_x, $x = 0, 1, \ldots, w-1$, we can compute column (7) in Table 2 from the formula

$$T_x = L_x + L_{x+1} + \cdots + L_w, \qquad \text{for} \quad x = 0, 1, \ldots, w-1,$$

and

$$T_w = L_w.$$

In the California 1970 life table,

$$T_w = T_{85} = L_{85} = 147711,$$

and the expectation of life at age w is

$$\hat{e}_w = \hat{e}_{85} = \frac{T_{85}}{l_{85}} = \frac{147711}{23274} = 6.35.$$

Figures 1 through 4 show graphically the probability of dying ($\hat{q}_x$), the number of survivors (l_x), the number of deaths (d_x), and the expectation of life ($\hat{e}_x$), for each age x for the total California population, 1970. Figures 5 to 8 show the corresponding four sets of quantities for the total United States population, 1970. As we see from Figure 1, the probability of dying is extremely high for the first year of life. It decreases sharply after the first year and reaches a minimum at the age of 10 years. From there on, the probability rises gradually and reaches the magnitude of $\hat{q}_0$ around age 65. Thereafter, it continues to increase monotonically and later drastically. The pattern of $\hat{q}_x$ is also reflected in l_x, d_x and $\hat{e}_x$. Since the life tables for the California population and for the United States population end at age 85, the graphs also stop at that age.

With the exception of l_0, every quantity in a life table is an estimate of the corresponding unknown theoretical value. For example, $\hat{q}_x$ is the estimate of the probability of death and $\hat{e}_x$ is the estimate of the expectation of life. When there can be no confusion, for

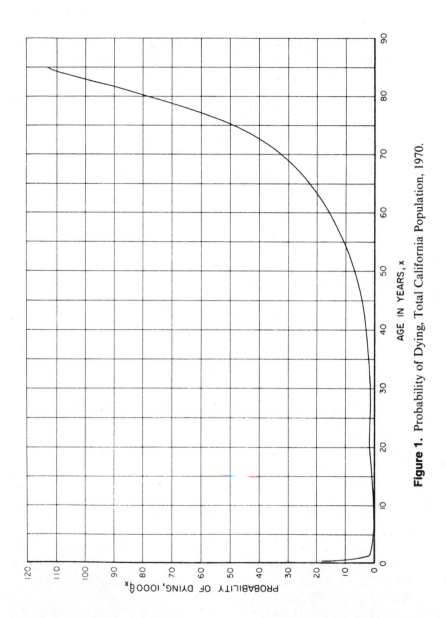

Figure 1. Probability of Dying, Total California Population, 1970.

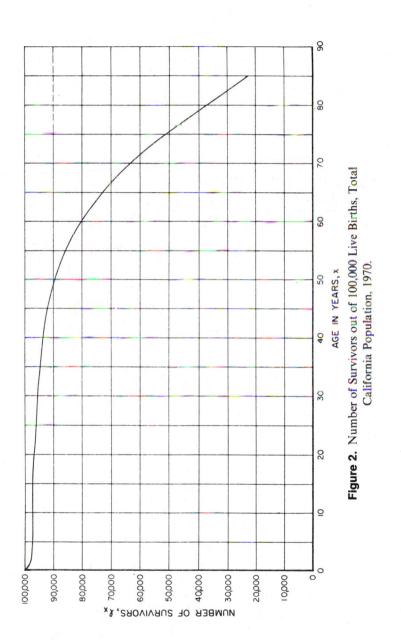

Figure 2. Number of Survivors out of 100,000 Live Births, Total California Population, 1970.

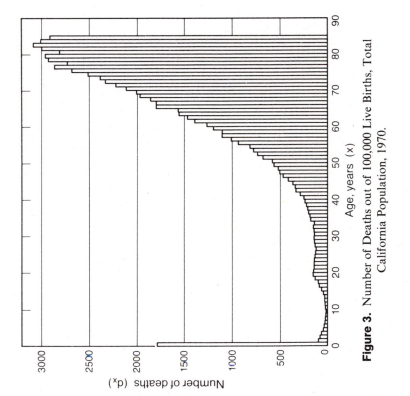

Figure 3. Number of Deaths out of 100,000 Live Births, Total California Population, 1970.

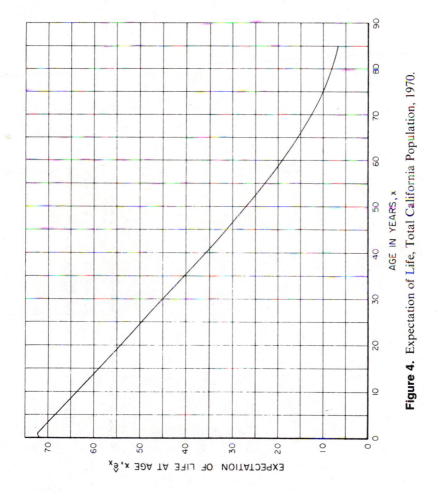

Figure 4. Expectation of Life, Total California Population, 1970.

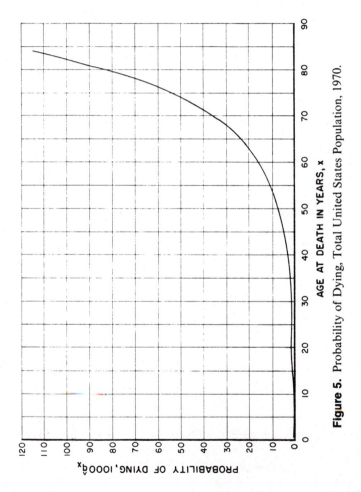

Figure 5. Probability of Dying, Total United States Population, 1970.

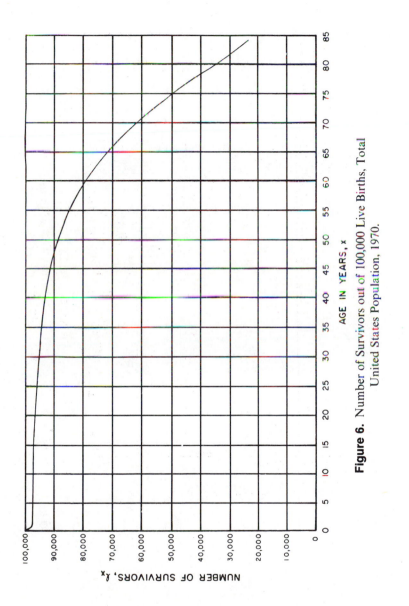

Figure 6. Number of Survivors out of 100,000 Live Births, Total United States Population, 1970.

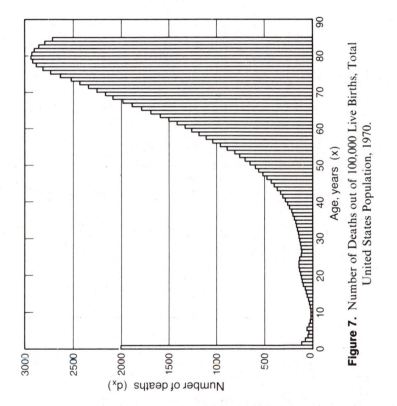

Figure 7. Number of Deaths out of 100,000 Live Births, Total United States Population, 1970.

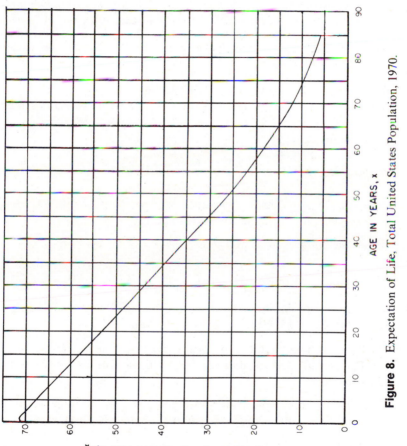

Figure 8. Expectation of Life, Total United States Population, 1970.

simplicity, we will drop the words "estimate of" and refer to $\hat{q}_x$ as the probability of death and $\hat{e}_x$ as the expectation of life, etc.

During the early development of the concept of expectation of life, a curtate expectation of life, defined as

$$e_x = \frac{l_{x+1} + l_{x+2} + \cdots}{l_x},$$

was first introduced. This expectation considers only the complete years lived by survivors, while the complete expectation of life also takes into account the fractional years lived by those who die in any year. Under the assumption that each person who dies during any year of age lives (on the average) half of that year, the complete expectation of life is given by

$$\overset{o}{e}_x = e_x + \tfrac{1}{2}.$$

Since the curtate expectation is no longer in use, in this book the symbol e_x is used to denote the true unknown expectation of life at age x.

4. Problems for Solution

1. Compute the age-specific death rate M_x and the probability of death q_x, for $x = 0, 1, \ldots, 20$ in Table 1, page 120.

2. Check the computations in Table 2, page 122 for the first 20 years of life.

3. Verify equation (3.3) on page 124.

4. Compute the probability of surviving 10 years for a person of age x, for $x = 0, 5, 10, 15, 20$ and 25 using the data in Table 2.

5. Find the average number of years lived in interval $(1,5)$, $(5,10)$, $(10,15)$, $(15,20)$, $(20,25)$ and $(25,30)$ by those who die in the respective intervals.

6. Compute the life table death rate discussed in Chapter 5 for the California population and compare it to the crude death rate.

7. Use the information in Table 2 to plot:

    (1)   the probability of dying, $\hat{q}_x$
    (2)   the number of survivors, l_x
    (3)   the number of deaths, d_x, and
    (4)   the expectation of life, $\hat{e}_x$

    for $x = 0, 1, \ldots, 85$. Discuss the difference between the two graphs for $\hat{q}_x$ and d_x.

8.   The expectation of life at any age $x, \hat{e}_x$, may be expressed as follows:

$$\hat{e}_x = \frac{\sum_{y=x} d_y(y + a'_y)}{\sum_{y=x} d_y}, \qquad x = 0, 1, \ldots \qquad \text{(A)}$$

Show that $\hat{e}_x$ in formula (A) is identically equal to $\hat{e}_x$ in formula (2.7), page 118.

9.   The mean age at death for a current population may be computed from

$$\frac{\sum_{y=x} D_y(y + a'_y)}{\sum_{y=x} D_y}, \qquad x = 1, 1, \ldots \qquad \text{(B)}$$

Is the mean age at death in formula (B) for a current population equal to the expectation of life in formula (A), problem 8 for the same current population? Explain.

10.   Use the numerical values of d_x and a'_x in Table 2 to compute the mean age at death (make appropriate assumptions for age interval 85 +) and compare it with the expectation of life at age 0, $\hat{e}_0$.

11.   Use the numerical values of D_x and a'_x in Table 1 to compute the mean age at death and compare it with the mean age at death obtained in problem 8 (make appropriate assumptions for age interval 85 +).

12.   The expectation of life $\hat{e}_x$ in column (8), Table 2 decreases as age x increases except for age 1 where $\hat{e}_1 = 72.2$ is greater than $\hat{e}_0 = 71.90$. Explain.

CHAPTER 7

The Life Table and Its Construction— the Abridged Life Table

1. Introduction

We have seen in Chapter 6 that the survival and mortality data of a population can be systematically presented in a life table and that each element in the table has its own particular significance. The entries in each column, when studied in sequence, give a dynamic picture of the survival and death processes in a population. Patterns and trends emerge. Also, the life table is the only statistical analysis that gives not one, but a sequence of sample means in ($\hat{e}_0$, $\hat{e}_1, \ldots, \hat{e}_w$). Thus, one can derive more information from a life table than from any other statistical study. It is remarkable that all this and more is accomplished with only the age-specific death rates and the fractions of the last year of life.

A table of some 85 age groups, however, does not provide a concise picture. The voluminous information in a complete life table is difficult to comprehend and too overwhelming to digest. "The power of the human mind to grasp a number of particulars is limited," Major Greenwood once fittingly remarked, " . . . in seeking to grasp everything, one tends to grasp nothing" (Yule (1934)). Furthermore, the necessary data for intervals of one year of age are usually unavailable for a population. When these data are available, misstatements of age and heapings of ages at even years or multiples of five make such information unreliable. Finally, as a random event, deaths occurring during a single year of life are subject to relatively great variation. These disadvantages can be removed by constructing an abridged rather than the complete life table.

2.   A Method of Life Table Construction

Construction of the abridged life table, like the complete life table, requires a relationship between the age-specific death rate and the estimate of probability of death. During the long history of the life table, a great variety of methods have been proposed to derive such a relationship. Section 5 gives a brief review of some of these methods. In this section, we present a simple formula based on the true meaning of the age-specific death rate and the corresponding probability.

In Chapter 4, page 72, we have given the following definition for the death rate for age interval (x_i, x_{i+1}) or interval $(x_i, x_i + n_i)$;

$$M_i = \frac{\text{No. of individuals dying in interval } (x_i, x_i + n_i)}{\text{No. of years lived in interval } (x_i, x_i + n_i) \text{ by those alive at } x_i}$$

(2.1)

and we defined the estimate of the probability as a ratio of the number of deaths in $(x_i, x_i + n_i)$ to the number of individuals living at x_i. From these we arrived at the formula

$$\hat{q}_i = \frac{n_i M_i}{1 + (1 - a_i)n_i M_i}.$$ (2.2)

The reasoning involved was intuitively obvious and needs no repetition. To reaffirm (2.2), we derive a relationship between the theoretical age-specific death rate and the corresponding probability of death. The mathematics may seem somewhat involved, but the idea is very simple.

Consider an individual alive at age x_i and an interval of interest $(x_i, x_i + n_i)$. Let $\mu(x)$ be the force of mortality (alias, mortality intensity function) at age x. It is shown in Chapter 10 that q_i, the probability that the individual will die in $(x_i, x_i + n_i)$, is

$$q_i = 1 - \exp\left\{ -\int_0^{n_i} \mu(x_i + \xi)d\xi \right\}.$$ (2.3)

This probability, q_i, is also the expected number of deaths in the interval $(x_i, x_i + n_i)$ when there is only one individual alive at x_i (cf., the expectation of a binomial random variable in Chapter 2, page 41).

The theoretical death rate for age interval $(x_i, x_i + n_i)$ is the ratio of the *expected* number of deaths, q_i, to the *expected* number of years to be lived by an individual in the interval, or

$$m_i = \frac{q_i}{\int_0^{n_i}\exp\left\{-\int_0^y \mu(x_i + \xi)d\xi\right\}dy} \, . \qquad (2.4)$$

Both the age specific death rate m_i and the probability q_i are defined for a single individual alive at age x_i.

Let a random variable τ_i be the fraction of the interval $(x_i, x_i + n_i)$ lived by an individual who dies in the interval. Clearly, τ_i is a continuous random variable and assumes values between 0 and 1. The expected value of τ_i is the fraction of the last age interval of life, denoted by a_i; that is*

$$E(\tau_i) = a_i \, . \qquad (2.5)$$

For each value t, $0 \leqslant t \leqslant 1$, the probability density function of τ_i is

$$g(t)dt = \frac{\left[\exp\left\{-\int_0^{n_it}\mu(x_i + \xi)d\xi\right\}\right]\mu(x_i + n_it)n_i\,dt}{q_i} , \qquad 0 \leqslant t \leqslant 1.$$

$$(2.6)$$

The quantity on the right-hand side of (2.6) is the probability that an individual alive at x_i will die in interval $(x_i + n_it, x_i + n_it + dn_it)$, providing that he dies in $(x_i, x_i + n_i)$. This is also the probability that τ_i will assume values in $(t, t + dt)$; that is, the density function $g(t)dt$. The expected value of τ_i may be computed as follows:

$$a_i = E(\tau_i) = \int_0^1 tg(t)\,dt$$

$$= \int_0^1 \frac{t\exp\left\{-\int_0^{n_it}\mu(x_i + \xi)d\xi\right\}}{q_i}\mu(x_i + n_it)n_i dt$$

$$= \frac{-n_i\exp\left\{-\int_0^{n_i}\mu(x_i + \xi)d\xi\right\} + \int_0^{n_i}\exp\left\{-\int_0^y\mu(x_i + \xi)d\xi\right\}dy}{n_iq_i} \, .$$

$$(2.7)$$

Substituting (2.3) and (2.4) in the last expression in (2.7) yields:

$$a_i = 1 - \frac{1}{q_i} + \frac{1}{n_im_i} \, . \qquad (2.8)$$

Solving (2.8) for q_i, we obtain the fundamental relationship between q_i

---

*For simplicity, we do not introduce a new symbol for the expectation.

and m_i:

$$q_i = \frac{n_i m_i}{1 + (1 - a_i) n_i m_i} \, . \tag{2.9}$$

Formula (2.9) is completely analogous to formula (2.2).

3. An Abridged Life Table

An abridged life table contains columns similar to those described for the complete life table; the only difference is the length of the intervals. The length of the typical interval (x_i, x_{i+1}) in the abridged life table is $n_i = x_{i+1} - x_i$, which is greater than one year (see Table 2). Thus we have

Column 1.   Age interval (x_i, x_{i+1})
Column 2.   Probability of dying in interval (x_i, x_{i+1}), $\hat{q}_i$.
Column 3.   Number alive at age x_i, l_i.
Column 4.   Number dying in the interval (x_i, x_{i+1}), d_i.
Column 5.   Fraction of last age interval of life, a_i.
Column 6.   Number of years lived in the interval (x_i, x_{i+1}), L_i.
Column 7.   Total number of years lived beyond age x_i, T_i.
Column 8.   Expectation of life at x_i, $\hat{e}_i$.

The essential element here is the average fraction of the interval lived by each person who dies at an age included in the interval. This fraction, called the fraction of last age interval of life, denoted by a_i, is a logical extension of the fraction of the last year of life, a'_x. The determination of the value of a_i and a discussion of it are presented in Section 4.

In constructing an abridged life table for a current population, two preliminary computations are necessary. The first is the computation of the age-specific death rate M_i using the formula

$$M_i = \frac{D_i}{P_i} \, , \tag{3.1}$$

where D_i and P_i are the number of deaths and the mid-year population for the age interval (x_i, x_{i+1}), respectively. The second is the computation of the estimate of probability of death q_i using the formula

$$\hat{q}_i = \frac{n_i M_i}{1 + (1 - a_i) n_i M_i} \, . \tag{2.2}$$

Starting with the values of $\hat{q}_i$, a_i, and the radix l_0, we can compute the elements in the different columns using the following formulas

$$d_i = l_i \hat{q}_i, \qquad i = 0, 1, \ldots, w - 1, \tag{3.2}$$

and

$$l_{i+1} = l_i - d_i, \qquad i = 0, 1, \ldots, w - 1, \tag{3.3}$$

respectively. The number of years lived in the interval (x_i, x_{i+1}) by the l_i survivors at age x_i is

$$L_i = n_i(l_i - d_i) + a_i n_i d_i, \qquad i = 0, 1, \ldots, w - 1. \tag{3.4}$$

The final age interval is again an open interval, and L_w is computed exactly as in the complete life table [cf. Equation (3.6) in Chapter 6, page 125]

$$L_w = \frac{l_w}{M_w}, \tag{3.5}$$

where M_w is the specific death rate for people of age x_w and over.

Table 1. Construction of an abridged life table for total California population, U.S.A., 1970

Age interval (in years)	Mid-year population in interval (x_i, x_{i+1})	Number of deaths in interval (x_i, x_{i+1})	Death Rate	Fraction of last age interval of life	Probability of dying in in interval (x_i, x_{i+1})
x_i to x_{i+1}	P_i	D_i	M_i	a_i	$\hat{q}_i$
(1)	(2)	(3)	(4)	(5)	(6)
0–1	340483	6234	.018309	.09	.01801
1–5	1302198	1049	.000806	.41	.00322
5–10	1918117	723	.000377	.44	.00188
10–15	1963681	735	.000374	.54	.00187
15–20	1817379	2054	.001130	.59	.00564
20–25	1740966	2702	.001552	.49	.00773
25–30	1457614	2071	.001421	.51	.00708
30–35	1219389	1964	.001611	.52	.00802
35–40	1149999	2588	.002250	.53	.01119
40–45	1208550	4114	.003404	.54	.01689
45–50	1245903	6722	.005395	.53	.02664
50–55	1083852	8948	.008256	.53	.04049
55–60	933244	11942	.012796	.52	.06207
60–65	770770	14309	.018565	.52	.08886
65–70	620805	17088	.027526	.51	.12893
70–75	484431	19149	.039529	.52	.18052
75–80	342097	21325	.062336	.51	.27039
80–85	210953	20129	.095419	.50	.38521
85 +	142691	22483	.157564		1.00000

Table 2. Abridged life table for total California population, U.S.A., 1970

Age interval (in years)	Probability of dying in interval (x_i, x_{i+1})	Number living at age x_i	Number dying in interval (x_i, x_{i+1})	Fraction of last age interval of life	Number of years lived in interval (x_i, x_{i+1})	Total number of years lived beyond age x_i	Expectation of life at age x_i
x_i to x_{i+1}	$\hat{q}_i$	l_i	d_i	a_i	L_i	T_i	$\hat{e}_i$
(1)	(2)	(3)	(4)	(5)	(6)	(7)	(8)
0–1	.01801	100000	1801	.09	98361	7195221	71.95
1–5	.00322	98199	316	.41	392050	7096860	72.27
5–10	.00188	97883	184	.44	488900	6704810	68.50
10–15	.00187	97699	183	.54	488074	6215910	63.62
15–20	.00564	97516	550	.59	486452	5727836	58.74
20–25	.00773	96966	750	.49	482917	5241384	54.05
25–30	.00708	96216	681	.51	479412	4758467	49.46
30–35	.00802	95535	766	.52	475837	4279055	44.79
35–40	.01119	94769	1060	.53	471354	3803218	40.13
40–45	.01689	93709	1583	.54	464904	3331864	35.56
45–50	.02664	92126	2454	.53	454863	2866960	31.12
50–55	.04049	89672	3631	.53	439827	2412097	26.90
55–60	.06207	86041	5341	.52	417387	1972270	22.92
60–65	.08886	80700	7171	.52	386290	1554883	19.27
65–70	.12893	73529	9480	.51	344419	1168593	15.89
70–75	.18052	64049	11562	.52	292496	824174	12.87
75–80	.27039	52487	14192	.51	227665	531678	10.13
80–85	.38521	38295	14752	.50	154595	304013	7.94
85 +	1.00000	23543	23543		149418	149418	6.35

The total number of years to be lived by those individuals attaining age x_i is the sum

$$T_i = L_i + L_{i+1} + \cdots + L_w, \qquad i = 0, 1, \ldots, w. \qquad (3.6)$$

The (observed) expectation of life at age x_i is the ratio

$$\hat{e}_i = \frac{T_i}{l_i}, \qquad i = 0, 1, \ldots, w. \qquad (3.7)$$

As an example, the abridged life table for the 1970 California population is given in Tables 1 and 2.

4. The Fraction of the Last Age Interval of Life, a_i

The fraction of the last age interval of life is as essential to the construction of the abridged life table as the fraction of the last year of life is to the complete life table. When a person dies at age 23, for example, he has lived in a certain fraction of the age interval $(20, 25)$. The average fraction lived in each interval (x_i, x_{i+1}) is called the fraction of the last age interval of life and depends on the probability of dying and the corresponding fraction of last year of life a'_x for each year of age within the interval. The relationship between a_i, a'_x and the probabilities $\hat{q}_x$ and $\hat{p}_x$ $(= 1 - \hat{q}_x)$ is derived as follows.

4.1. Computation of a_0. Since the first age interval in an abridged life table is one year, $a_0 = a'_0$ is the fraction of the year lived by an infant who dies during the first year of life. The computation of a_0 is shown in Table 3 using the California 1970 infant death data as an illustration. The number of deaths in column (3) tabulated by age at death is

Table 3. Computation of the fraction a_0 based on infant deaths, California total population, 1970.

Age interval at death	Average point in interval (in days)	Number of deaths in interval*	Number of days lived (2) × (3)
(1)	(2)	(3)	(4)
0–1 hour	.02	522	10
1–24 hours	.50	2110	1055
1–2 days	1.50	567	850
2–3 days	2.50	417	1042
3–4	3.50	194	679
4–5	4.50	130	585
5–6	5.50	98	539
6–7	6.50	63	409
7–14	10.00	280	2800
14–21	17.00	129	2193
21–28	24.00	107	2568
28–60	42.00	418	17556
2–3 months	73.00	338	24674
3–4	103.00	212	21836
4–5	134.00	168	22512
5–6	164.00	126	20664
6–7	195.00	91	17745
7–8	225.00	76	17100
8–9	256.00	56	14336
9–10	287.00	49	14063
10–11	318.00	54	17172
11–12	349.00	43	15007
Total		6248	215395

*Source: U.S. Department of Health, Education and Welfare, Public Health Service, National Center for Health Statistics, *Vital Statistics of the U.S.*, 1970, Vol. II, Part A, pp. 2–10, 11.

$$a_0 = \frac{215,395}{365 \times 6248} = .09.$$

usually available in vital statistics publications. The average point for each interval [Column (2)] takes into account the distribution of deaths in each interval. The product of the figures in columns (2) and (3), recorded in column (4), is the total number of days lived by individuals who died in each interval. The sum of these products, appearing in the lower right-hand corner (215,395 in this case) is the total number of days lived by the (6248) infants who die during the first year of life. This total, when divided by 365×6248, gives a_0.

WHO's formula for computing a_0. The value of a_0 varies with the infant mortality rate of a population. Generally, reduction of infant deaths occurs in the latter part of the first year of life, so that smaller the infant mortality rate, smaller is the value of a_0. For convenience, the World Health Organization has suggested the guide line in Table 4 to determine the value of a_0 based on the infant mortality rate of a population.

Table 4. Determination of a_0 based on infant mortality rate

Infant mortality rate per 1000	Value of a_0
less than 20	.09
20–40	.15
40–60	.23
greater than 60	.30

4.2.   Computation of a_1 for age interval $(1,5)$.   For a person alive at the exact age of one year [i.e., the beginning of the interval $(1,5)$], there is a probability q_1 that he will die during the year $(1,2)$, a probability $(1 - q_1)q_2 = p_1q_2$ that he will die in $(2,3)$, a probability $p_1p_2q_3$ that he will die in $(3,4)$, and a probability $p_1p_2p_3q_4$ that he will die in $(4,5)$. The corresponding periods of time that he might live are a_1', $(1 + a_2')$, $(2 + a_3')$, and $(3 + a_4')$, respectively. For example, if a person dies during the year $(2,3)$, he will have lived one complete year $(1,2)$ and a fraction a_2' of the year $(2,3)$; therefore, he will have lived a total of $(1 + a_2')$ years. The probability of dying at any time during the interval $(1,5)$ is $1 - p_1p_2p_3p_4$, and the length of the interval is $5 - 1 = 4$ years. Therefore, the formula for the fraction of the interval $(1,5)$ that a person will live if he dies between ages one and five is:

$$a_1 = \frac{q_1a_1' + p_1q_2(1 + a_2') + p_1p_2q_3(2 + a_3') + p_1p_2p_3q_4(3 + a_4')}{4(1 - p_1p_2p_3p_4)}$$

$$(4.1)$$

Using the established values of $a_1' = .43$, $a_2' = .45$, $a_3' = .47$, an $a_4' = .49$,

Table 5. Computation of the fraction a_1 for age interval $(1, 5)$ based on California mortality data, 1970.

Year of Age	Conditional probability of dying in year $(x, x + 1)$ given alive at age 1	Expected length of time lived in interval	
		Length of time lived $(1, 5)$	$(2) \times (3)$
(1)	(2)	(3)	(4)
1–2	$q_1 = .00113$	.43	.000486
2–3	$p_1 q_2 = (.99887)(.00086) = .000859$	1.45	.001246
3–4	$p_1 p_2 q_3 = (.99887)(.99914)(.00073) = .000729$	2.47	.001800
4–5	$p_1 p_2 p_3 q_4 = (.99887)(.99914)(.99927)(.00052)$ $= .000519$	3.49	.001810
Total	$1 - p_1 p_2 p_3 p_4 = .003236$		.005342

we have the estimate

$$a_1 = \frac{.43\hat{q}_1 + 1.45\hat{p}_1\hat{q}_2 + 2.47\hat{p}_1\hat{p}_2\hat{q}_3 + 3.49\hat{p}_1\hat{p}_2\hat{p}_3\hat{q}_4}{4(1 - \hat{p}_1\hat{p}_2\hat{p}_3\hat{p}_4)}$$

$$= \frac{.005342}{4 \times .003236} = .41. \tag{4.2}$$

For a given country, the probabilities, $\hat{q}_1$, $\hat{q}_2$, $\hat{q}_3$ and $\hat{q}_4$ can be determined. The fraction a_1 for the interval $(1, 5)$ may be computed from formula (4.2). The computation of a_1 for California population, 1970, is demonstrated in Table 5.

From age 5 to the last interval in the life table, the length of each age interval is 5 years and the fraction of last year of life for each single year is $a'_x = 1/2$. This simplifies the formula for the fraction a_i for interval (x_i, x_{i+5}). For age interval $(5, 10)$ for example, we have

$$a_i = \frac{\begin{aligned}.5\hat{q}_5 + (1 + .5)\hat{p}_5\hat{q}_6 + (2 + .5)\hat{p}_5\hat{p}_6\hat{q}_7 \\ + (3 + .5)\hat{p}_5\hat{p}_6\hat{p}_7\hat{q}_8 + (4 + .5)\hat{p}_5\hat{p}_6\hat{p}_7\hat{p}_8\hat{q}_9\end{aligned}}{5(1 - \hat{p}_5\hat{p}_6\hat{p}_7\hat{p}_8\hat{p}_9)}$$

$$= \frac{\hat{p}_5\hat{q}_6 + 2\hat{p}_5\hat{p}_6\hat{q}_7 + 3\hat{p}_5\hat{p}_6\hat{p}_7\hat{q}_8 + 4\hat{p}_5\hat{p}_6\hat{p}_7\hat{p}_8\hat{q}_9}{5(1 - \hat{p}_5\hat{p}_6\hat{p}_7\hat{p}_8\hat{p}_9)} + \frac{1}{10}, \tag{4.3}$$

since

$$\hat{q}_5 + \hat{p}_5\hat{q}_6 + \hat{p}_5\hat{p}_6\hat{q}_7 + \hat{p}_5\hat{p}_6\hat{p}_7\hat{q}_8 + \hat{p}_5\hat{p}_6\hat{p}_7\hat{p}_8\hat{q}_9 = 1 - \hat{p}_5\hat{p}_6\hat{p}_7\hat{p}_8\hat{p}_9.$$

$$\tag{4.4}$$

Using formulas (4.2) and (4.3), the values of the fraction a_i for the abridged life table have been computed for countries for which the required information is available, and are listed in the tables in

Appendix I. These values of a_i can be used directly in constructing life tables for the respective countries.

Remark 1.   Formulas (4.2) and (4.3) show that the fraction a_i does not depend on the absolute values of $\hat{q}_x$ or $\hat{p}_x$ but rather on the trend of mortality within the interval. For example, if $\hat{q}_5 > \hat{q}_6 > \hat{q}_7 > \hat{q}_8 > \hat{q}_9$, then the a_i value for the interval $(5, 10)$ is likely to be less than .5 regardless of the numerical values of these $\hat{q}_x$'s.

Remark 2.   The probabilities $\hat{q}_x$ and $\hat{p}_x$ are computed from the mortality data of a population in question, while the value of a_i represents the mortality pattern prevailing in the population in each interval. Since the mortality pattern hardly varies over time (although death rates do), the a_i's may be regarded as constant and used for the construction of abridged life tables of the subsequent years of the population.

The invariant property of a_i not only holds over time, but is also true for countries with similar mortality patterns. Table 6 shows a

Table 6. Fraction of last age interval of life, a_i, for sample populations.

Age	Austria 1969	California 1970	France 1969	Finland 1968	U.S.A. 1975
0–1	.12	.09	.16*	.09	.10
1–5	.37	.41	.38	.38	.42
5–10	.47	.44	.46	.49	.45
10–15	.51	.54	.54	.52	.59
15–20	.58	.59	.56	.53	.55
20–25	.48	.49	.51	.51	.51
25–30	.51	.51	.51	.51	.50
30–35	.53	.52	.53	.52	.52
35–40	.53	.53	.53	.54	.53
40–45	.52	.54	.53	.55	.54
45–50	.54	.53	.54	.53	.53
50–55	.52	.53	.52	.54	.53
55–60	.53	.52	.53	.53	.53
60–65	.54	.52	.53	.53	.52
65–70	.53	.51	.53	.52	.52
70–75	.52	.52	.52	.52	.52
75–80	.51	.51	.51	.51	.51
80–85	.48	.50	.49	.47	.49
85–90	.45		.46		
90–95	.40		.41		

*A large a_0 value for the France 1969 population is due to the fact that infants who die before 3 days old are not recorded. Age at death of these infants is not included in the calculation of a_0.

Table 7. Computation of a_i for age intervals $(5, 10)$ and $(10, 15)$ based on California population, 1970.

Age interval	Fraction of last year of life	Proportion dying in age interval	Fraction of last age interval
x to $x + 1$	a'_x	q_x	a_i
(1)	(2)	(3)	(4)
5–6	.50	.00049	
6–7	.50	.00045	
7–8	.50	.00034	.44
8–9	.50	.00031	
9–10	.50	.00030	
10–11	.50	.00031	
11–12	.50	.00033	
12–13	.50	.00035	.54
13–14	.50	.00041	
14–15	.50	.00048	

remarkable agreement of the five sets of a_i values. Thus, for countries with similar mortality patterns, the same set of a_i values may be used.

Remark 3. The assumption that $a'_x = 1/2$ for each year of age within an interval (x_i, x_{i+1}) does not necessarily imply that $a_i = 1/2$ for the entire interval. As noted above, the value of the fraction a_i depends on the mortality pattern over an entire interval and not on the mortality rate for any single year. When the mortality rate increases with age in an interval, the fraction $a_i > 1/2$; when the reverse pattern prevails, $a_i < 1/2$. The mortality data for the age intervals $(5, 10)$ and $(10, 15)$ in the 1970 California population serve to illustrate this point (see Table 7). Although $a'_x = 1/2$ for each year in the two intervals, $a_i = .44$ for interval $(5, 10)$ where mortality decreases with age, and $a_i = .54$ for interval $(10, 15)$ where mortality increases with age.

5. Significant Contributions to the Construction of Abridged Life Tables

The history of life table construction shows successive refinements of the method. The earliest tables (see *Introduction*, Chapter 6) were based solely on recorded deaths. Leonard Euler (1760) proposed formulas to compute life table survivors using the total population, total births, and age-specific number of deaths. Joshua Milne's table of 1815 took into account both population and death figures. In 1839 the English Life Tables were constructed using only registered births and deaths since, in the opinion of William Farr, census figures at that time were unreliable. Excerpts of some of the publications of life table construction have been given in Smith and Keyfitz (1977). We present a few methods of construction below.

5.1. King's Method.   This method was introduced by King (1914) in the construction of the Seventh English Life Table at the turn of the century. It was used by many English-speaking countries for about fifty years. In this method, data are arranged in five-year age groups. Population figures and the number of deaths are calculated for the central year (pivotal age) of each age group by a graduation process, yielding the values of q_x for pivotal age. Using the complement of q_x at each pivotal age and finite difference formulas, the number of survivors (l_x) is obtained. T. N. E. Greville adapted this method for the 1939–41 United States Life Tables.

5.2. Reed–Merrell Method.   In the search for a relation between the probability and the mortality rate, Lowell J. Reed and Margaret Merrell did extensive statistical studies on the thirty-three tables in J. W. Glover's 1910 series of United States Life Tables. Their findings, published in 1939, showed that the following equation satisfactorily describes the entire range of observations in Glover's tables:

$$q_i = 1 - e^{-n_i M_i - .008 n_i^3 M_i^2}.$$

They also give many formulas to determine the L_i column from the number of survivors l_i.

5.3. Greville's Method.   Greville (1940) uses a mathematical approach to derive a relation between q_i and M_i. He starts with the equation

$$M_i = -\frac{d}{dx_i} \log L_i .$$

After integrating both sides of the equation, thus yielding L_i, and applying the Euler–Maclaurin summation formula, he expresses T_i in terms of a series of exponential functions of M_i. He then uses quite skillful mathematical manipulations to arrive at the formula:

$$q_i = \frac{M_i}{(1/n_i) + M_i \left[(1/2) + (n_i/12)(M_i - \log c) \right]}$$

where the constant c is the constant in the Gompertz' law of mortality (cf. Chapter 10, Section 2.1, page 198):

$$\mu_x = Bc^x.$$

Greville also has suggested a number of formulas to compute the life table population L_i.

5.4. Weisler's Method. This method, introduced in "Une méthods simple pour la construction de tables de mortalité abrégées," *World Population Conference*, 1954, Volume IV, United Nations, essentially substitutes the specific death rate M_i for the probability of dying $\hat{q}_i$.

For an age interval $(x_i, x_i + n_i)$, let D_i be the number of deaths during a calendar year and P_i be the number of living people in the age group $(x_i, x_i + n_i)$. Then Weisler suggests that

$$\hat{p}_i = 1 - \frac{D_i}{P_i} \quad \text{or} \quad \hat{q}_i = \frac{D_i}{P_i},$$

and l_1, l_5, l_{10}, etc., are computed successively from

$$l_1 = l_0 \hat{p}_0$$
$$l_5 = l_1 (\hat{p}_{1,4})^{t_{1,4}}$$
$$l_{10} = l_5 (\hat{p}_{5,9})^{t_{5,9}}, \dots,$$

where

$$p_{x,(x+n-1)} = [l_{x+1} + \cdots + l_{x+n}] / [l_x + \cdots + l_{x+n-1}],$$

and $t_{1,4} = 4$, and $t_{x,(x+4)} = 5$ for $5 \leqslant x \leqslant 45$, $t_{x,(x+4)} > 5$ for $x \geqslant 45$. The expectation of life at x_α is computed by

$$\hat{e}_\alpha = \frac{1}{2} + \frac{l_{\alpha+1} + l_{\alpha+2} + \cdots}{l_\alpha}.$$

5.5. Sirken's Method. Sirken (1964) suggests two sets of age-specific death rates. One set is for the current population

$$M_i = \frac{D_i}{P_i}$$

and the other is for the life table quantities:

$$m_i = \frac{d_i}{L_i}.$$

Using the observed death rate M_i, he derives q_i from the equation

$$q_i = \frac{n_i M_i}{1 + \alpha_i M_i} \tag{A}$$

where the constant α_i is assumed to be the same as that in a standard table. Using q_i, he completes the columns l_i and d_i. To compute L_i, Sirken considers another equation

$$q_i = \frac{n_i m_i}{1 + a_i m_i}. \tag{B}$$

Substituting $q_i = d_i / l_i$ and $m_i = d_i / L_i$ in (B) yields

$$\frac{d_i}{l_i} = \frac{n_i d_i / L_i}{(1 + a_i) d_i / L_i} .$$

Solving the last equation for L_i gives

$$L_i = n_i l_i - a_i d_i$$

where the constant a_i is assumed to be the same as in a standard table but is different from α_i.

5.6. Keyfitz's Method. This is an iterative procedure using the basic relationship between the probability q_i and the age-specific mortality rate m_i or M_i

$$q_i = \frac{n_i M_i}{1 + (n_i - {_n}a_i) M_i} \tag{A}$$

where ${_n}a_i$ is the average number of years lived in the age interval $(x_i, x_i + n_i)$ by an individual who dies in the interval. In addition to ${_n}a_i$, Keyfitz introduces a quantity ${_n}A_i$, the average number of years already lived within the interval $(x_i, x_i + n_i)$ by a stationary population aged $(x_i, x_i + n_i)$.

Taking ${_n}a_i = n_i / 2$ on the first cycle, one obtains a first approximation to q_i by using formula (A). Then using

$$_na_i = \frac{n_i}{2} + \frac{n_i}{24} \left(\frac{d_{i+1} - d_{i-1}}{d_i} \right),$$

$$L_i = \frac{n_i}{2} (l_i + l_{i+1}) + \frac{n_i}{24} (d_{i+1} - d_{i-1})$$

and

$$_nA_i = \frac{n_i}{2} + \frac{n_i}{24} \left(\frac{L_{i+1} - L_{i-1}}{L_i} \right)$$

and other formulas one arrives at a second approximation of q_i. After each iteration, a life table is constructed and the age-specific mortality rate is compared with those observed, and an adjustment made for the next iteration. The iterative process continues until the life table age-specific rates agree with the corresponding observed rates (Keyfitz, 1966).

5.7. United Nations' and Brass' model life table systems and Coale–Demeny's regional life tables. Other interesting life tables are the model life table systems and the regional life tables. The Population Division of the United Nations has issued a set of model life tables for use by various government agencies and elsewhere. Brass (1964) has also proposed a two-parameter model of a life table system. The two systems vary in principle; Brass' system is described briefly below. Brass recognizes that if he sets $l_0 = 1$ and $l_w = 0$, then $0 \leqslant l_x \leqslant 1$ for each x and l_x is a decreasing function of x, for $0 \leqslant x \leqslant w$. He then expresses the logit of l_x as a linear function of x to determine l_x. That is, he sets $\log[l_x/(1 - l_x)] = A + BX$ and thus obtains a system of the sequence $\{l_x\}$.

Coale and Demeny (1966) published a number of regional life tables to facilitate population research. After studying a large collection of work in this area, they constructed life tables for four regions: West, North, East and South, with 24 tables for 24 levels of mortality for each region and for each sex. Thus, they provide a total of 192 life tables which are useful to demographers.

6. Problems for Solution

1. Use the density function in (2.6) to compute the expectation of the random variable τ_i.

2. Verify the computation of the age specific death rate M_i and the probability of death $\hat{q}_i$ for each age interval in Table 1, page 141.

3. Use the values of a'_x and $\hat{q}_x$ for $x = 1, \ldots, 19$, of the 1970 California population in Chapter 6, Table 2, page 122, to compute the fraction of last age interval for intervals $(1, 5)$, $(5, 10)$, $(10, 15)$, and $(15, 20)$.

4. Verify the computation in Table 2, page 142.

5. Verify the values of a_i for age interval $(5, 10)$ and $(10, 15)$ in Table 6, page 146.

6. In Table 2 replace every probability $\hat{q}_i$ by $2\hat{q}_i$ and compute the abridged life table.

7. Work out problem 6 when $\hat{q}_i$ is replaced by $1.5\hat{q}_i$ for each i.

8. Work out problem 6 when $\hat{q}_i$ is replaced by $.67\hat{q}_i$, for each i.

9. Work out problem 6 when $\hat{q}_i$ is replaced by $.50\hat{q}_i$, for each i.

10. Discuss in detail the effect of change on the value of probability $\hat{q}_i$ on the expectation of life in the life table on the basis of your computation in problems 6, 7, 8 and 9.

11. Use the number dying d_i in column (4) and the fraction a_i in column (5) in Table 2 for each age interval to compute the mean age at death for the California population, 1970 and compare it with the expectation of life at age 0, $\hat{e}_0$.

12. Give an algebraic formula for the mean age at death in problem 11 (make an appropriate assumption for age interval 85 +) and show that it is equal to the expectation of life at age 0 given in formula (3.7).

13. Use the number of deaths D_i in column (3) and the fraction a_i in column (5) in Table 1, page 141, to compute the mean age at death for the California population, 1970 and compare it with the expectation of life at age 0, $\hat{e}_0$.

14. Compute the death rate M_i and the probability $\hat{q}_i$ for each age interval when the number of deaths in Table 1 is replaced by $2D_i$.

15. Use the $\hat{q}_i$ in problem 14 to determine the expectation of life $\hat{e}_0$. Is the value of the expectation of life affected when D_i is replaced by $2D_i$? Is the mean age at death affected when D_i is replaced by $2D_i$?

16. It is often suggested that, for a small population where age specific death rates and the probabilities of death are subject to a large variation, the mean age at death may be used as a substitute for the expectation of life, $\hat{e}_0$. What is your opinion?

17. You should have found in problem 15 the expectation of life $\hat{e}_0$ = 62.09 years, which is 9.86 years less than $\hat{e}_0 = 71.95$ in Table 2. Explain the moderate reduction in the expectation of life in spite of the fact that the death rate in each age group has been doubled.

CHAPTER *8*

Statistical Inference Regarding Life Table Functions

1. Introduction

Each entry in the life table described in the preceding chapter is an estimate of the corresponding unknown true life table function. Statistical inferences about these functions may be made on the basis of the observed values. Except for L_i and T_i, every element in the table is either a sample mean or a sample proportion. Since life tables are usually based on large populations, the central limit theorem and methods of statistical inference described in Chapter 3 are directly applicable. In this chapter we derive formulas for the sample variances (and their square roots, the standard errors) of the observed life table functions and demonstrate with numerical examples the procedure of interval estimation and hypothesis testing. Specifically, we will make inference about three categories of functions: (i) q_i, the probability of death in an age interval (x_i, x_{i+1}); (ii) p_{ij}, the survival probability from age x_i to age x_j; and (iii) e_α, the expectation of life at age x_α, for $\alpha = 0, 1, \ldots, w$. The reader may wish to refer to Chapter 3 in studying this chapter.

2. The Probability of Death, q_i, and the Probability of Survival, p_i

In each age interval, the estimates of the probability of death and the probability of survival are complements of one another, $\hat{p}_i = 1 - \hat{q}_i$. Therefore, they have the same sample variance:

$$S_{\hat{q}_i}^2 = S_{\hat{p}_i}^2. \qquad (2.1)$$

For the current life table, the formulas for the variance and the standard error were given in Chapter 4, page 79; namely,

$$S_{\hat{q}_i}^2 = \frac{1}{D_i} \hat{q}_i^2 (1 - \hat{q}_i), \qquad (2.2)$$

and

$$S_{\hat{q}_i} = \hat{q}_i \sqrt{\frac{1}{D_i} (1 - \hat{q}_i)}, \qquad (2.3)$$

where D_i is the observed number of deaths in age interval (x_i, x_{i+1}) in the current population. The standardized random variable of $\hat{q}_i$ is

$$Z = \frac{\hat{q}_i - q_i}{S_{\hat{q}_i}}, \qquad (2.4)$$

which has a normal distribution with mean zero and variance one. The normal random variable in (2.4) may be used for interval estimation or for testing hypotheses concerning the probability q_i.

To find the 95% confidence interval for q_i, for example, we read from the normal distribution table on page 67 two values, -1.96 and $+1.96$, such that

$$\Pr\{ \hat{q}_i - 1.96 S_{\hat{q}_i} < q_i < \hat{q}_i + 1.96 S_{\hat{q}_i} \} = .95. \qquad (2.5)$$

From this probabilistic statement, we derive the confidence interval (cf., equation (2.5), page 54):

$$\hat{q}_i - 1.96 S_{\hat{q}_i} < q_i < \hat{q}_i + 1.96 S_{\hat{q}_i}. \qquad (2.6)$$

For a given problem, $\hat{q}_i$ and $S_{\hat{q}_i}$ can be determined, and the two limits, $\hat{q}_i - 1.96 S_{\hat{q}_i}$ and $\hat{q}_i + 1.96 S_{\hat{q}_i}$, can be found. The interval extending from the lower limit $\hat{q}_i - 1.96 S_{\hat{q}_i}$ to the upper limit $\hat{q}_i + 1.96 S_{\hat{q}_i}$ is the 95% confidence interval for the probability q_i.

As an example, consider the probability of dying in the first year of life, q_0. In the 1975 United States male population, the estimate $\hat{q}_0 = .0180$, the number of deaths $D_0 = 28,821$, and hence the standard error of $\hat{q}_0$ is:

$$S_{\hat{q}_0} = \hat{q}_0 \sqrt{\frac{1}{D_0} (1 - \hat{q}_0)}$$

$$= .0180 \sqrt{\frac{1}{28,821} (1 - .0180)}$$

$$= .000105.$$

Substituting these values in (2.6) yields the 95% confidence limits for the probability q_0:

$$\hat{q}_0 - 1.96 S_{\hat{q}_0} = .0180 - 1.96(.000105) = .0178$$

$$\hat{q}_0 + 1.96 S_{\hat{q}_0} = .0180 + 1.96(.000105) = .0182.$$

Thus we conclude with a 95% confidence that, if the 1975 United States male mortality experience prevails in a population, the probability that a newborn will not survive to the first birthday is between .0178 and .0182.

Use of formula (2.4) in testing a hypothesis about the probability of dying in an age interval follows the procedure described in Chapter 3.

Suppose we want to know if the force of mortality is higher for males than for females, or a newborn female has a better chance of surviving the first year of life than a newborn male. Here we are testing the hypothesis concerning two probabilities. The null hypothesis $H_0: q_0(\text{male}) = q_0(\text{female})$ is tested against the alternative hypothesis $H_1: q_0(\text{male}) > q_0(\text{female})$. The test statistic is the standardized normal random variable (cf. Chapter 3, Equation (1.8), page 52):

$$Z = \frac{\hat{q}_0(\text{male}) - \hat{q}_0(\text{female})}{\text{S.E.}\left[\hat{q}_0(\text{male}) - \hat{q}_0(\text{female})\right]} \tag{2.7}$$

where the standard error of the difference is given by

$$\text{S.E.}\left[\hat{q}_0(\text{male}) - \hat{q}_0(\text{female})\right]$$

$$= \sqrt{\frac{\hat{q}_0^2(\text{male})\left[1 - \hat{q}_0(\text{male})\right]}{D_0(\text{male})} + \frac{\hat{q}_0^2(\text{female})\left[1 - \hat{q}_0(\text{female})\right]}{D_0(\text{female})}}.$$

$$\tag{2.8}$$

Using the United States 1975 experience again, we have the required information given in Table 1. From Table 1 we compute the statistic

$$Z = \frac{.00375}{1.4233 \times 10^{-4}} = 26.35$$

which is significantly greater than the 99th percentile in the standard

Table 1. Estimate of probability of dying in the first year of life and the standard error for males and females, United States 1975.

	male	female	$\hat{q}_0(\text{male}) - \hat{q}_0(\text{female})$
$\hat{q}_0$	.01800	.01425	.00375
D_0	28,821	21,713	
S^2	1.10395×10^{-8}	$.92188 \times 10^{-8}$	2.0258×10^{-8}
S.E.	1.05069×10^{-4}	$.96015 \times 10^{-4}$	1.4233×10^{-4}

normal distribution, $Z_{.99} = 2.33$ on page 67. We thus conclude that in the United States 1975 population a newborn female has a better chance of surviving the first year of life than a newborn male.

3.   The Survival Probability, p_{ij}

The probability that a person of age x_i will survive to age x_j is an important quantity in survival analysis; this probability can be obtained directly from the life table. Since survival from age x_i to x_j evidently encompasses survival of every intermediate age interval, the probability p_{ij} is given by

$$p_{ij} = p_i p_{i+1} \cdots p_{j-1} \tag{3.1}$$

or

$$p_{ij} = (1 - q_i)(1 - q_{i+1}) \cdots (1 - q_{j-1}). \tag{3.2}$$

A case of particular interest is $i = 0$. Here we have p_{0j}, the probability of surviving from age 0 to a specified age x_j, given by

$$p_{0j} = p_0 p_1 \cdots p_{j-1}$$
$$= (1 - q_0)(1 - q_1) \cdots (1 - q_{j-1}). \tag{3.3}$$

To obtain the estimate of the survival probability, we need only substitute the estimates of $\hat{q}_i$ in formulas (3.2) and (3.3). When information is taken from a life table, the computation can be simplified. For example,

$$\hat{p}_{0j} = \hat{p}_0 \hat{p}_1 \cdots \hat{p}_{j-1}$$
$$= \frac{l_1}{l_0} \frac{l_2}{l_1} \cdots \frac{l_j}{l_{j-1}}$$
$$= \frac{l_j}{l_0}, \tag{3.4}$$

generally,

$$\hat{p}_{ij} = \frac{l_j}{l_i}, \qquad i < j; \quad i, j = 0, 1, \ldots, w. \tag{3.5}$$

In a current life table, the individual estimates,

$$\hat{p}_h = 1 - \hat{q}_h, \qquad h = i, \ldots, j - 1, \tag{3.6}$$

are based on the corresponding age-specific death rates so the sample variance of $\hat{p}_{ij}$ should be expressed in terms of the sample variance of the $\hat{q}_h$'s in (2.2). Since the individual estimates $\hat{q}_h$ are based on mortality information of separate age groups, they are statistically independent. Using the theorem on the variance of a product of independent random variables, we have the formula for the sample variance of $\hat{p}_{ij}$

$$S_{\hat{p}_{ij}}^2 = \hat{p}_{ij}^2 \sum_{h=i}^{j-1} \hat{p}_h^{-2} S_{\hat{p}_h}^2 \qquad (3.7)$$

where the sample variance of $\hat{p}_i$ is given in (2.2).

The abridged life tables for the 1975 United States male and female populations are given in Tables 2 and 3. For each population, the estimates of the probabilities p_{0i} and the corresponding sample variances and standard errors have been computed. The numerical results are displayed in Table 4 and Table 5, respectively. The

Table 2. Abridged life table for male population, United States, 1975.

Age Interval (in years)	Proportion Dying in Interval $(x_i, x_i + 1)$	Number Living at Age x_i	Number Dying in Interval (x_i, x_{i+1})	Fraction of Last Age Interval of Life	No. Years Lived in Interval (x_i, x_{i+1})	Total No. Years Lived Beyond Age x_i	Observed Expectation of Life at Age x_i
x_1 to x_{i+1}	$\hat{q}_i$	l_i	d_i	a_i	L_i	T_i	$\hat{e}_i$
(1)	(2)	(3)	(4)	(5)	(6)	(7)	(8)
0–1	.01800	100000	1800	.10	98380	6872524	68.73
1–5	.00311	98200	305	.42	392092	6774144	68.98
5–10	.00210	97895	206	.46	488919	6382052	65.19
10–15	.00227	97689	222	.61	488012	5893133	60.33
15–20	.00735	97467	716	.55	485724	5405121	55.46
20–25	.01043	96751	1009	.51	481283	4919397	50.85
25–30	.00995	95742	953	.49	476280	4438114	46.35
30–35	.01024	94789	971	.51	471566	3961834	41.80
35–40	.01375	93818	1290	.53	466059	3490268	37.20
40–45	.02076	92528	1921	.53	458126	3024209	32.68
45–50	.03285	90607	2976	.53	446041	2566083	28.32
50–55	.05096	87631	4466	.53	427660	2120042	24.19
55–60	.07780	83165	6470	.53	400621	1692382	20.35
60–65	.11894	76695	9122	.52	361582	1291761	16.84
65–70	.16722	67573	11300	.52	310745	930179	13.77
70–75	.24450	56273	13759	.51	247655	619434	11.01
75–80	.34209	42514	14544	.50	176210	371779	8.74
80–85	.44343	27970	12403	.47	106982	195569	6.99
85 +	1.00000	15567	15567		88587	88587	5.69

Table 3. Abridged life table for female population, United States, 1975.

Age Interval (in years)	Proportion Dying in Interval $(x_i, x_i + 1)$	Number Living at Age x_i	Number Dying in Interval (x_i, x_{i+1})	Fraction of Last Age Interval of Life	No. Years Lived in Interval (x_i, x_{i+1})	Total No. Years Lived Beyond Age x_i	Observed Expectation of Life at Age x_i
x_1 to x_{i+1}	$\hat{q}_i$	l_i	d_i	a_i	L_i	T_i	$\hat{e}_i$
(1)	(2)	(3)	(4)	(5)	(6)	(7)	(8)
0–1	.01425	100000	1425	.10	98718	7665455	76.65
1–5	.00253	98575	249	.42	393722	7566737	76.76
5–10	.00145	98326	143	.45	491237	7173015	72.95
10–15	.00128	98183	126	.56	490638	6681778	68.05
15–20	.00272	98057	267	.54	489671	6191140	63.14
20–25	.00335	97790	328	.51	488146	5701469	58.30
25–30	.00372	97462	363	.51	486421	5213323	53.49
30–35	.00488	97099	474	.53	484381	4726902	48.68
35–40	.00728	96625	703	.54	481508	4242521	43.91
40–45	.01180	95922	1132	.54	477006	3761013	39.21
45–50	.01815	94790	1720	.53	469908	3284007	34.65
50–55	.02686	93070	2500	.53	459475	2814099	30.24
55–60	.04029	90570	3649	.53	444275	2354624	26.00
60–65	.05959	86921	5180	.52	422173	1910349	21.98
65–70	.08319	81741	6800	.53	392725	1488176	18.21
70–75	.13772	74941	10321	.53	350451	1095451	14.62
75–80	.21836	64620	14110	.52	289236	745000	11.53
80–85	.32239	50510	16284	.50	211840	455764	9.02
85 +	1.00000	34226	34226		243924	243924	7.13

essential steps in the computation are the following:

(1) Record the number of deaths (D_i) occurring in each age interval in the population in Column 2, and the probability of dying $(\hat{q}_i)$ in Column 3.

(2) Use formula (2.2) to compute the sample variance of $\hat{q}_i$ and enter it in Column 4.

(3) Use formula (3.3) to compute the probability of surviving age interval $(0, x_i)$, $\hat{p}_{0i}$, and record it in Column 5. $\hat{p}_{00}$ is 1 by definition.

(4) Use formula (3.7) or

$$S_{\hat{p}_{0i}}^2 = \hat{p}_{0i}^2 \left[\hat{p}_0^{-2} S_{\hat{p}_0}^2 + \hat{p}_1^{-2} S_{\hat{p}_1}^2 + \cdots + \hat{p}_{i-1}^{-2} S_{\hat{p}_{i-1}}^2 \right]$$

to compute the variance of $\hat{p}_{0i}$ and record it in Column 6.

(5) Take the square root of the variance to obtain the standard error and record it in Column 7.

Table 4. Computation of the standard error of survival probability, male population, United States, 1975.

Age Interval	Number of Deaths in Interval (x_i, x_{i+1})	Probability of Dying in Interval (x_i, x_{i+1})	Sample Variance of $\hat{q}_i$ ($\hat{p}_i$)	Probability of Surviving Interval $(0, x_i)$	Sample Variance of $\hat{p}_{0i}$	Standard Error of $\hat{p}_{0i}$
(x_i, x_{i+1})	D_i	$\hat{q}_i$	$10^8 \times S^2_{\hat{q}_i}$	$\hat{p}_{0i}$	$10^8 \times S^2_{\hat{p}_{0i}}$	$10^4 \times S_{\hat{p}_{0i}}$
(1)	(2)	(3)	(4)	(5)	(6)	(7)
0–1	28821.	.01800	1.10395	1.00000	0.	0.
1–5	5086.	.00311	.18958	.98200	1.10395	1.05069
5–10	3717.	.00210	.11839	.97895	1.27992	1.13133
10–15	4734.	.00227	.10860	.97689	1.38800	1.17813
15–20	15637.	.00735	.34294	.97467	1.48534	1.21874
20–25	19871.	.01043	.54175	.96751	1.78938	1.33768
25–30	16678.	.00995	.58770	.95742	2.25937	1.50312
30–35	14118.	.01024	.73512	.94789	2.75333	1.65932
35–40	15567.	.01375	1.19781	.93818	3.35771	1.83240
40–45	22869.	.02076	1.84543	.92528	4.32029	2.07853
45–50	38166.	.03285	2.73456	.90607	5.72271	2.39222
50–55	60151.	.05096	4.09733	.87631	7.59795	2.75644
55–60	81142.	.07780	6.87921	.83165	9.98964	3.16064
60–65	108960.	.11894	11.43916	.76695	13.25375	3.64057
65–70	130361.	.16722	17.86319	.67573	17.01715	4.12519
70–75	135835.	.24450	33.24915	.56273	19.95799	4.46744
75–80	129830.	.34209	59.30239	.42514	21.92021	4.68190
80–85	111296.	.44343	98.33098	.27970	20.20606	4.49512
85 +	107720.	1.00000	0.	.15567	13.95140	3.73516

Statistical inference about the unknown survival probability (p_{0i}) can now be made using the computations in Table 4 and Table 5. For example, the estimate of the probability of surviving from birth to age 20 is $\hat{p}_{0,20} = .96751$ for the male population, and $\hat{p}_{0,20} = .97790$ for the female population. To test for the significance of the difference between these two probabilities, we compute the critical ratio:

$$Z = \frac{\hat{p}_{0,20}(\text{male}) - \hat{p}_{0,20}(\text{female})}{\text{S.E.}(\text{diff.})}. \qquad (3.8)$$

The standard error of the difference is given by

$$\text{S.E.}(\text{diff.}) = \sqrt{(1.78938 \times 10^{-8}) + (1.33055 \times 10^{-8})}$$

$$= 1.76633 \times 10^{-4}. \qquad (3.9)$$

Table 5. Computation of the standard error of survival probability, female population, United States, 1975.

Age Interval	Number of Deaths in Interval (x_i, x_{i+1})	Probability of Dying in Interval (x_i, x_{i+1})	Sample Variance of $\hat{q}_i$ ($\hat{p}_i$)	Probability of Surviving Interval $(0, x_i)$	Sample Variance of $\hat{p}_{0i}$	Standard Error of $\hat{p}_{0i}$
(x_i, x_{i+1})	D_i	$\hat{q}_i$	$10^8 \times S^2_{\hat{q}_i}$	$\hat{p}_{0i}$	$10^8 \times S^2_{\hat{p}_{0i}}$	$10^4 \times S_{\hat{p}_{0i}}$
(1)	(2)	(3)	(4)	(5)	(6)	(7)
0–1	21713.	.01425	.92188	1.00000	0.	0.
1–5	3974.	.00253	.16066	.98575	.92188	.96015
5–10	2468.	.00145	.08507	.98326	1.07335	1.03603
10–15	2560.	.00128	.06392	.98183	1.15247	1.07353
15–20	5630.	.00272	.13105	.98057	1.21113	1.10051
20–25	6407.	.00335	.17457	.97790	1.33055	1.15350
25–30	6332.	.00372	.21773	.97462	1.48858	1.22008
30–35	6912.	.00488	.34286	.97099	1.68434	1.29782
35–40	8698.	.00728	.60488	.96625	1.99118	1.41109
40–45	13558.	.01180	1.01488	.95922	2.52706	1.58967
45–50	22198.	.01815	1.45708	.94790	3.40156	1.84433
50–55	33830.	.02686	2.07532	.93070	4.58845	2.14207
55–60	45262.	.04029	3.44192	.90570	6.14290	2.47849
60–65	60360.	.05959	5.53242	.86921	8.48127	2.91226
65–70	78140.	.08319	8.11985	.81741	11.68037	3.41766
70–75	98160.	.13772	16.66126	.74941	15.24319	3.90425
75–80	118500.	.21836	31.45101	.64620	20.69086	4.54872
80–85	129832.	.32239	54.24518	.50510	25.77488	5.07690
85 +	177357.	1.00000	0.	.34226	25.67391	5.06694

Table 6. Statistical test for the significance of difference between survival probabilities of males and females, United States, 1975.

Age Interval (x_i, x_j)	Males		Females		Difference*	
	$\hat{p}_{ij}$	$10^4 S_{\hat{p}_{ij}}$	$\hat{p}_{ij}$	$10^4 S_{\hat{p}_{ij}}$	(2) − (4)	10^4 S.E.(diff.)
(1)	(2)	(3)	(4)	(5)	(6)	(7)
(0, 20)	.96751	1.33768	.97790	1.15350	−.01039	1.76633
(20, 40)	.95635	1.69322	.98090	1.14186	−.02455	2.04226

*Formula for the standard error of the difference, $\hat{p}_{ij}(\text{male}) - \hat{p}_{ij}(\text{female})$:

$$\text{S.E.(diff.)} = \sqrt{S^2_{\hat{p}_{ij}}(\text{male}) + S^2_{\hat{p}_{ij}}(\text{female})} .$$

Substituting the numerical values of $\hat{p}_{0,20}$ and (3.9) in (3.8) yields the value of Z,

$$Z = \frac{.96751 - .97790}{1.76633 \times 10^{-4}}$$

$$= -58.82. \tag{3.10}$$

Based on the above findings, we conclude that a newborn who is subject to the female mortality experience has a significantly greater probability of surviving to age 20 than one who is subject to the male experience.

This is also true for the survival probabilities from age 20 to age 40. Table 6 shows that

$$p_{20,40}(\text{male}) < p_{20,40}(\text{female})$$

and

$$Z = \frac{p_{20,40}(\text{male}) - p_{20,40}(\text{female})}{\text{S.E.(diff.)}}$$

$$= \frac{.95635 - .98090}{2.04226 \times 10^{-4}} = -120.2,$$

which is highly significant.

4. The Expectation of Life at Age x_α, e_α

The observed expectation of life at a given age is the sample mean lifetime of individuals living beyond this age. It is therefore an unbiased estimate of the corresponding unknown true expectation of life (cf. page 34). To avoid confusion in notation, let us consider a particular age, x_α, and denote the corresponding observed and true expectations of life by $\hat{e}_\alpha$ and e_α, respectively. Then we have $E(\hat{e}_\alpha) = e_\alpha$. The formula for the sample variance of $\hat{e}_\alpha$, however, is involved, as it must be expressed in terms of the variance of $\hat{q}_i$ in (2.2). We derive it below.

The formula for $\hat{e}_\alpha$ is

$$\hat{e}_\alpha = \frac{1}{l_\alpha} \left[L_\alpha + L_{\alpha+1} + \cdots + L_w \right]$$

$$= \frac{1}{l_\alpha} \sum_{j=\alpha}^{w} L_j, \tag{4.1}$$

where

$$L_j = n_j l_{j+1} + a_j n_j (l_j - l_{j+1})$$

$$= a_j n_j l_j + (1 - a_j) n_j l_{j+1}. \tag{4.2}$$

Substituting (4.2) in (4.1), rearranging the terms and factoring out the coefficients of the l_i's yield

$$\hat{e}_\alpha = a_\alpha n_\alpha + \sum_{j=\alpha+1}^{w} \left[(1 - a_{j-1})n_{j-1} + a_j n_j \right] \frac{l_j}{l_\alpha},$$

or

$$\hat{e}_\alpha = a_\alpha n_\alpha + \sum_{j=\alpha+1}^{w} c_j \hat{p}_{\alpha j}, \tag{4.3}$$

where

$$c_j = (1 - a_{j-1})n_{j-1} + a_j n_j \tag{4.4}$$

and

$$\frac{l_j}{l_\alpha} = \hat{p}_{\alpha j}$$

$$= \hat{p}_\alpha \hat{p}_{\alpha+1} \cdots \hat{p}_{j-1}. \tag{4.5}$$

The last product is the estimate of the probability of survival from age x_α to age x_j. The observed expectation of life $\hat{e}_\alpha$ in (4.3) is a linear function of $\hat{p}_{\alpha j}$. For every $i < j$, the probabilities $\hat{p}_{\alpha i}$ and $\hat{p}_{\alpha j}$ have $\hat{p}_\alpha, \hat{p}_{\alpha+1}, \ldots, \hat{p}_{i-1}$ in common. They are therefore *not* independent random variables. To apply the rule of variance of a linear function of independent random variables in Chapter 2, page 36, we expand the formula in (4.3) by Taylor's theorem.

First, we take the derivative of $\hat{p}_{\alpha j}$ with respect to each of the $\hat{p}_i$'s,

$$\frac{\partial}{\partial \hat{p}_i} \hat{p}_{\alpha j} = \hat{p}_{\alpha i} \hat{p}_{i+1,j}, \qquad \text{for} \quad \alpha \leqslant i < j,$$

$$= 0, \qquad \qquad \text{otherwise.} \tag{4.6}$$

Then we take the derivative of $\hat{e}_\alpha$ in (4.3) with respect to the $\hat{p}_i$'s

$$\frac{\partial}{\partial \hat{p}_i} \hat{e}_\alpha = \sum_{j=\alpha+1}^{w} c_j \frac{\partial}{\partial \hat{p}_i} \hat{p}_{\alpha j}. \tag{4.7}$$

Substituting (4.6) in (4.7), we compute the derivative

$$\frac{\partial}{\partial \hat{p}_i} \hat{e}_\alpha = \sum_{j=i+1}^{w} c_j \hat{p}_{\alpha i} \hat{p}_{i+1,j}$$

$$= \hat{p}_{\alpha i} \left[c_{i+1} + \sum_{j=i+2}^{w} c_j \hat{p}_{i+1,j} \right]$$

$$= \hat{p}_{\alpha i} \left[(1 - a_i)n_i + a_{i+1}n_{i+1} + \sum_{j=i+2}^{w} c_j \hat{p}_{i+1,j} \right]$$

$$= \hat{p}_{\alpha i} \left[(1 - a_i)n_i + \hat{e}_{i+1} \right]. \tag{4.8}$$

Because of (4.6), the derivative (4.8) vanishes when $i = w$. Now the estimates of probabilities (p_i) for two nonoverlapping age intervals are based on the mortality experiences of two distinct groups of people, and therefore are not correlated. Consequently, the variance of the expectation of life may be computed from the following formula:

$$S_{\hat{e}_\alpha}^2 = \sum_{i=\alpha}^{w-1} \left\{ \frac{\partial}{\partial \hat{p}_i} \hat{e}_\alpha \right\}^2 S_{\hat{p}_i}^2 . \tag{4.9}$$

Substituting (4.8) in (4.9) yields the desired formula for the sample variance of $\hat{e}_\alpha$:

$$S_{\hat{e}_\alpha}^2 = \sum_{i=\alpha}^{w-1} \hat{p}_{\alpha i}^2 \left[(1 - a_i)n_i + \hat{e}_{i+1} \right]^2 S_{\hat{p}_i}^2 \tag{4.10}$$

where the variance of $\hat{p}_i$ is given by

$$S_{\hat{p}_i}^2 = \frac{\hat{q}_i^2 (1 - \hat{q}_i)}{D_i} . \tag{2.2}$$

4.1. Computation of the variance of the expectation of life in a current life table.

Formula (4.10), which holds true for any age x_i in the life table, contains terms that appear repeatedly for different values of i. Therefore, the variances of $\hat{e}_i$ for all ages x_i in the life table can be calculated by a condensed computation program. Using formula (4.10) and referring to Table 7, the essential steps in the computation of the sample variance of $\hat{e}_i$ for 1975 U.S. females are the following:

(1) Record the age interval in Column 1.
(2) Record the length of the age interval n_i in Column 2, the fraction of last age interval a_i in Column 3, the number living l_i in Column 4, and the observed expectation of life $\hat{e}_i$ in Column 5.
(3) Compute the sample variance of $\hat{p}_i$ ($\hat{q}_i$) from formula (2.2) and record it in Column 6.
(4) Compute for each age interval and record in Column 7 the quantity

$$l_i^2 \left[(1 - a_i)n_i + \hat{e}_{i+1} \right]^2 S_{\hat{p}_i}^2$$

(Complete steps 1 to 4 for *all* ages. Then proceed to (5)).
(5) Sum the products in Column 7 from the bottom of the table up to x_i and enter the sum in Column 8.
(6) Divide the sum in Column 8 by l_i^2 to obtain the sample variance of the observed expectation of life and record this in Column 9.
(7) Take the square root of the variance to obtain the standard error of the expectation of life, and record this in Column 10.

Table 7. Computation of the sample variance of the observed expectation of life for females, United States, 1975.

Age interval (years) x_i to x_{i+1}	Length of interval n_i	Fraction of last age interval of life a_i	Number living at age x_i l_i	Expectation of life at age x_i $\hat{e}_i$	Sample variance of $\hat{p}_i$ $10^8 S^2_{\hat{p}_i}$	$l_i^2[(1-a_i)n_i + \hat{e}_{i+1}]^2 S^2_{\hat{p}_i}$	$\sum_{j \geq i} l_j^2[(1-a_j)n_j + \hat{e}_{j+1}]^2 S^2_{\hat{p}_j}$	Sample variance of $\hat{e}_i$ $10^4 S^2_{\hat{e}_i}$	Standard error of $\hat{e}_i$ $10^2 S_{\hat{e}_i}$
(1)	(2)	(3)	(4)	(5)	(6)	(7)	(8)	(9)	(10)
0–1	1	.10	100000	76.65	.92188	555996	2422880	2.42288	1.55656
1–5	4	.42	98575	76.76	.16066	88449	1866884	1.92125	1.38609
5–10	5	.45	98326	72.95	.08507	41225	1778435	1.83951	1.35628
10–15	5	.56	98183	68.05	.06392	26306	1737210	1.80210	1.34242
15–20	5	.54	98057	63.14	.13105	46275	1710904	1.77938	1.33393
20–25	5	.51	97790	58.30	.17457	52241	1664629	1.74072	1.31936
25–30	5	.51	97462	53.49	.21773	54069	1612388	1.69746	1.30287
30–35	5	.53	97099	48.68	.34286	69176	1558319	1.65282	1.28562
35–40	5	.54	96625	43.91	.60488	97309	1489143	1.59499	1.26293
40–45	5	.54	95922	39.21	1.01488	127491	1391834	1.51269	1.22992
45–50	5	.53	94790	34.65	1.45708	139052	1264343	1.40715	1.18623
50–55	5	.53	93070	30.24	2.07532	144481	1125291	1.29911	1.13978
55–60	5	.53	90570	26.00	3.44192	167130	980810	1.19568	1.09347
60–65	5	.52	86921	21.98	5.53242	177550	813680	1.07697	1.03777
65–70	5	.53	81741	18.21	8.11985	156240	636130	.95206	.97574
70–75	5	.53	74941	14.62	16.66126	180270	479890	.85448	.92438
75–80	5	.52	64620	11.53	31.45101	171278	299620	.71752	.84707
80–85	5	.50	50510	9.02	54.24518	128342	128342	.50305	.70926

4.2. Statistical inference about the expectation of life.

An observed expectation of life, as noted earlier in this section, is a sample mean future lifetime. We can use the normal distribution to make inference regarding expectation of life at a particular age, or in comparing expectations of life of two or more populations. In Table 8 the expectations of life for the United States 1975 female and male populations are compared. For each age the expectation of life and the standard errors are recorded in Columns 2 through 5. The difference of the expectations is given in Column 6. The standard error of the difference computed from

$$\text{S.E.(diff.)} = \sqrt{S^2_{\hat{e}_i}(\text{female}) + S^2_{\hat{e}_i}(\text{male})}$$

Table 8. Expectation of life and the standard error, females and males, United States 1975.

Age interval (years) (x_i, x_{i+1})	Females		Males		Difference $\hat{e}_i(F) - \hat{e}_i(M)$		Critical Ratio $\dfrac{\hat{e}_i(F) - \hat{e}_i(M)}{\text{S.E.(diff.)}}$
	$\hat{e}_i$	$100S_{\hat{e}_i}$	$\hat{e}_i$	$100S_{\hat{e}_i}$	(2) − (4)	S.E.(diff)	(6) ÷ (7)
(1)	(2)	(3)	(4)	(5)	(6)	(7)	(8)
0–1	76.65	1.557	68.73	1.582	7.92	2.219	356.9
1–5	76.76	1.386	68.98	1.427	7.78	1.989	391.1
5–10	72.95	1.356	65.19	1.400	7.76	1.950	398.0
10–15	68.05	1.342	60.33	1.386	7.72	1.930	400.0
15–20	63.14	1.334	55.46	1.377	7.68	1.917	400.6
20–25	58.30	1.319	50.85	1.351	7.45	1.888	394.5
25–30	53.49	1.303	46.35	1.316	7.14	1.852	385.5
30–35	48.68	1.286	41.80	1.284	6.88	1.817	378.6
35–40	43.91	1.263	37.20	1.251	6.71	1.778	377.4
40–45	39.21	1.230	32.68	1.208	6.53	1.724	378.8
45–50	34.65	1.186	28.32	1.158	6.33	1.657	382.9
50–55	30.24	1.140	24.19	1.107	6.05	1.589	380.7
55–60	26.00	1.093	20.35	1.062	5.65	1.524	370.7
60–65	21.98	1.038	16.84	1.014	5.14	1.451	354.3
65–70	18.21	.976	13.77	.969	4.44	1.375	322.9
70–75	14.62	.924	11.01	.943	3.61	1.321	273.3
75–80	11.53	.847	8.74	.911	2.79	1.244	224.3
80–85	9.02	.709	6.99	.827	2.03	1.089	186.4

is recorded in Column 7. The ratio of the difference to the corresponding standard error is recorded in Column 8.

The critical ratio for each age in Column 8 far exceeds the critical value of $Z_{.99} = 2.33$ corresponding to $\alpha = .01$ level of significance. This means that, according to the United States 1975 mortality experience, a female of any age has a greater expectation of life than a male of the same age.

5. A Life Table Based on a Sample of Deaths

When the life table of a current population is constructed from a sample of death certificates instead of all deaths, the estimate of the probability of dying ($\hat{q}_i$) for age interval (x_i, x_{i+1}) and ($\hat{q}_j$) for age interval (x_j, x_{j+1}) are no longer independent (cf., Chapter 4, Section 3.1), but are negatively correlated. Let D denote the total number of deaths occurring in a current population and f the sampling fraction, as in Chapter 4, Section 3.1. The covariance of $\hat{q}_i$ and $\hat{q}_j$ is

$$S_{\hat{q}_i,\hat{q}_j} = -\left(\frac{1}{f} - 1\right)\frac{\hat{q}_i\hat{q}_j}{D}, \tag{5.1}$$

and the variance of $\hat{q}_i$ is given in (3.19), page 81.

Since the probability of survival $\hat{p}_{ij}$ and the expectation of life $\hat{e}_\alpha$ are derived from $\hat{q}_i$, their variances contain the covariance $S_{\hat{p}_i\hat{p}_j}$. Explicitly the variance of $\hat{p}_{ij}$ is

$$S_{\hat{p}_{ij}}^2 = \hat{p}_{ij}^2\left[\sum_{h=i}^{j-1}\hat{p}_h^{-2}S_{\hat{p}_h}^2 + \sum_{h=i}^{j-1}\sum_{\substack{k=i\\h\neq k}}^{j-1}p_h^{-1}p_k^{-1}S_{\hat{p}_h\cdot\hat{p}_k}\right], \tag{5.2}$$

and the variance of $\hat{e}_\alpha$ is

$$S_{\hat{e}_\alpha}^2 = \sum_{i=\alpha}^{w-1}\hat{p}_{\alpha i}^2\left[(1-a_i)n_i + \hat{e}_{i+1}\right]^2 S_{\hat{p}_i}^2$$

$$+ \sum_{i=\alpha}^{w-1}\sum_{\substack{j=\alpha\\i\neq j}}^{w-1}\hat{p}_{\alpha i}\hat{p}_{\alpha j}\left[(1-a_i)n_i + \hat{e}_{i+1}\right]\left[(1-a_j)n_j + \hat{e}_{j+1}\right]S_{\hat{p}_i\hat{p}_j}.$$

$$\tag{5.3}$$

6.   Problems for Solution

1.   Check the computation in Table 1, page 155.

2.   Check the computation in Table 6, page 160.

3.   Explain why the variance of the survival probability

$$\hat{p}_{0j} = \frac{l_j}{l_0} \tag{3.4}$$

is not

$$S_{\hat{p}_{0j}}^2 = \frac{1}{l_0}\hat{p}_{0j}(1 - \hat{p}_{0j})$$

for a current life table.

4.   The formula for the variance of $\hat{p}_{ij}$ in (3.7) is derived from the approximate formula

$$S_{\hat{p}_{ij}}^2 = \sum_{h=i}^{j-1}\left(\frac{\partial}{\partial\hat{p}_h}\hat{p}_{ij}\right)^2 S_{\hat{p}_h}^2.$$

   (1)   Justify the above approximation.
   (2)   Derive the formula for the variance of $\hat{p}_{ij}$ based on this approximation.

5. Check the computation in Tables 4 and 5, pages 159 and 160, respectively.

6. Verify the formula for the variance of $\hat{e}_\alpha$ in (4.10), page 163.

7. Check the computation in Table 7, page 164.

8. Check the computation in Table 8, page 165.

9. Find the 95% confidence interval for the expectation of life at birth using the 1975 United States population data.

10. Compute the ratio of the probabilities $\hat{q}_i(\text{male})/\hat{q}_i(\text{female})$ for each age group in column 2, Table 2 and Table 3 pages 157, 158. Discuss the pattern of the ratio as age x_i increases.

11. Compute the ratio of the expectation of life at age 0, $\hat{e}_0(\text{female})/\hat{e}_0(\text{male})$. Would you expect the small magnitude of this ratio in view of the result in problem 10? Explain.

12. Test the hypothesis that in the U.S. 1975 population a female of age 1 year has the same probability of surviving to age 15 as a male of age 1; surviving to age 20; to age 30.

13. In a cohort life table, the survival probability p_{ij} is estimated by

$$\hat{p}_{ij} = \frac{l_j}{l_i}$$

which is an ordinary binomial proportion and has a sample variance

$$S_{\hat{p}_{ij}}^2 = \frac{1}{l_i}\,\hat{p}_{ij}(1 - \hat{p}_{ij}).$$

Show that the above formula for the sample variance of $\hat{p}_{ij}$ is the same as formula (3.7), p. 157, where $\hat{p}_h = l_{h+1}/l_h$ is a binomial proportion in l_h trials.

14. Test the hypothesis that, if the U.S. 1975 population survival experience prevails, a female of age 1 can expect to live longer than a male of the same age.

15. Test the hypothesis in problem 14 for both male and female of age 10 years.

CHAPTER *9*

The Cohort Life Table and Some Applications

1. Introduction

A cohort life table, as noted earlier, describes the mortality experience of a group of individuals from birth of the first to death of the last member of the group. Most of the theoretical aspects of the cohort life table are discussed in the following chapter. We shall briefly describe the elements of the table and their sample variances, and apply these to practical problems in Sections 4 and 6.

It is well known that for centuries actuaries have used the life table to compute premiums, annuities, and other life contingencies; and that demographers have used the same methodology in population projection, in studies of marriage and divorce, fertility, and population growth. But applications of the life table extend far beyond these two fields. In public health, the life table method has been used to study the survival of a fetus (French and Bierman, 1962; Shapiro, et al., 1962; Taylor, 1964; Dimiani, 1979), to estimate prevalence of congenital heart disease (Yerushalmy, 1969) and incidence of convulsions in young children (van den Berg and Yerushalmy, 1969), to study the duration of hospital stay of mental patients (Eaton and Whitmore, 1979), to analyze mortality data in the followup of patients, and others. Life table methodology has also been found useful in industrial management for quality control, in ecological research to determine the life cycle of animals, in biological control, and in many other fields where the concept of survival, or its connotation, can be defined. The latter part of this chapter will be devoted to some examples of applications of the life table.

2.   Elements of the Life Table

The basic variables involved in a cohort life table are l_i, the number living at age x_i and d_i, the number dying in the age interval (x_i, x_{i+1}). They satisfy the relationship

$$l_i - l_{i+1} = d_i, \qquad i = 0, 1, \ldots, w - 1. \tag{2.1}$$

The proportion of deaths in each interval is

$$\hat{q}_i = \frac{d_i}{l_i}, \qquad i = 0, 1, \ldots, w. \tag{2.2}$$

Once l_i, d_i, and $\hat{q}_i$ are determined for each interval, the remaining part of the life table can be completed in exactly the same way as in the current life table in Chapter 7. Thus we have the number of years lived in the interval (x_i, x_{i+1}),

$$L_i = n_i l_{i+1} + a_i n_i d_i, \qquad i = 0, 1, \ldots, w - 1, \tag{2.3}$$

and

$$L_w = a_w n_w d_w, \tag{2.4}$$

and the total number of years lived beyond age x_i,

$$T_i = L_i + L_{i+1} + \cdots + L_w, \qquad i = 0, 1, \ldots, w, \tag{2.5}$$

where the symbol w indicates the beginning of the last age interval. Finally, the observed expectation of life at age x_i is given by

$$\hat{e}_i = \frac{1}{l_i} T_i = \frac{1}{l_i} \sum_{j=i}^{w} L_j$$

$$= \frac{1}{l_i} \left[\sum_{j=i}^{w-1} (n_j l_{j+1} + a_j n_j d_j) + a_w n_w d_w \right], \qquad i = 0, 1, \ldots, w. \tag{2.6}$$

2.1   Observed expectation of life and sample mean future lifetime.
The observed expectation of life at age x_α,

$$\hat{e}_\alpha = \frac{L_\alpha + L_{\alpha+1} + \cdots + L_w}{l_\alpha} \tag{2.7}$$

is the sample mean lifetime of l_α individuals living beyond age x_α. If we let the l_α future lifetimes beyond x_α be denoted by $Y_{\alpha k}$, for

$k = 1, \ldots, l_\alpha$, then their mean value is

$$\overline{Y}_\alpha = \frac{1}{l_\alpha} \sum_{k=1}^{l_\alpha} Y_{\alpha k}. \qquad (2.8)$$

Obviously, the two sample means should be equal,

$$\overline{Y}_\alpha = \hat{e}_\alpha, \qquad \alpha = 0, 1, \ldots, w. \qquad (2.9)$$

We now show that equation (2.9) is indeed true.

In a life table, the l_α values of $Y_{\alpha k}$ are not individually recorded but are grouped in the form of a frequency distribution in which the ages x_i and x_{i+1} are the limits of the i-th interval and the deaths d_i are the corresponding frequencies for $i = \alpha, \alpha+1, \ldots, w$. The sum of the frequencies equals the number of individuals living at age x_α, or

$$d_\alpha + d_{\alpha+1} + \cdots + d_w = l_\alpha. \qquad (2.10)$$

The total number of years remaining to the l_α individuals depends on the exact age at which death occurs, that is, on the distribution of deaths within each age interval. Suppose that the distribution of deaths in the interval $(x_i, x_i + n_i)$ is such that, on the average, each of the d_i individuals lived a fraction a_i of the interval, or $a_i n_i$ years in the interval. Each individual then lives $x_i + a_i n_i$ years, or $x_i - x_\alpha + a_i n_i$ years beyond age x_α. The sample mean of $Y_{\alpha k}$ then is given by

$$\overline{Y}_\alpha = \frac{1}{l_\alpha} \sum_{i=\alpha}^{w} (x_i - x_\alpha + a_i n_i) d_i$$

$$= \frac{1}{l_\alpha} \left[\sum_{i=\alpha}^{w} (x_i - x_\alpha) d_i + \sum_{i=\alpha}^{w} a_i n_i d_i \right]. \qquad (2.11)$$

By definition

$$x_i - x_\alpha = n_\alpha + n_{\alpha+1} + \cdots + n_{i-1} = \sum_{j=\alpha}^{i-1} n_j, \qquad (2.12)$$

hence

$$\sum_{i=\alpha}^{w} (x_i - x_\alpha) d_i = \sum_{i=\alpha}^{w} \left(\sum_{j=\alpha}^{i-1} n_j \right) d_i$$

$$= \sum_{j=\alpha}^{w-1} n_j \left[\sum_{i=j+1}^{w} d_i \right]$$

$$= \sum_{j=\alpha}^{w-1} n_j l_{j+1}, \qquad (2.13)$$

since the number of individuals living at age x_{j+1} will all eventually die,

$$l_{j+1} = d_{j+1} + d_{j+2} + \cdots + d_w.$$

Substituting (2.13) in (2.11) gives

$$\bar{Y}_\alpha = \frac{1}{l_\alpha} \left[\sum_{j=\alpha}^{w-1} n_j l_{j+1} + \sum_{i=\alpha}^{w} a_i n_i d_i \right]$$

$$= \frac{1}{l_\alpha} \left[\sum_{j=\alpha}^{w-1} \left[n_j l_{j+1} + a_j n_j d_j \right] + a_w n_w d_w \right], \qquad (2.14)$$

which is the same as (2.6) as claimed.

3.   Sample Variance of the Life Table Functions

The procedure for statistical estimation and the testing of hypothesis about unknown true life table functions in the cohort life table is similar to that for the current life table. The only difference is in the formulas for the variances of the observed quantities. We briefly review some of these formulas in this section.

Both the estimates

$$\hat{p}_i = \frac{l_{i+1}}{l_i} \quad \text{and} \quad \hat{q}_i = 1 - \hat{p}_i \qquad (3.1)$$

are binomial proportions; their common variance is (cf., equation (2.18), page 37):

$$S_{\hat{p}_i}^2 = S_{\hat{q}_i}^2 = \frac{1}{l_i} \hat{p}_i \hat{q}_i, \qquad i = 0, 1, \ldots, w. \qquad (3.2)$$

The estimate of the survival probability for the age interval (x_i, x_j) is

$$\hat{p}_{ij} = \hat{p}_i \hat{p}_{i+1} \cdots \hat{p}_{j-1}, \qquad (3.3)$$

since to survive the interval (x_i, x_j), an individual must also survive every intermediate interval. Substituting (3.1) in (3.3) yields

$$\hat{p}_{ij} = \frac{l_{i+1}}{l_i} \times \frac{l_{i+2}}{l_{i+1}} \times \cdots \times \frac{l_j}{l_{j-1}}$$

$$= \frac{l_j}{l_i}, \qquad i < j; i, j = 0, 1, \ldots, w. \qquad (3.4)$$

This shows that $\hat{p}_{ij}$ is also a binomial proportion in l_i trials. Therefore, the sample variance of $\hat{p}_{ij}$ is simply

$$S_{\hat{p}_{ij}}^2 = \frac{1}{l_i} \hat{p}_{ij}(1 - \hat{p}_{ij}). \qquad (3.5)$$

We have seen in equation (3.7) in Chapter 8 that the sample variance of $\hat{p}_{ij}$ is

$$S_{\hat{p}_{ij}}^2 = \hat{p}_{ij}^2 \sum_{h=i}^{j-1} \hat{p}_h^{-2} S_{\hat{p}_h}^2 . \tag{3.6}$$

Substituting (3.2) in (3.6) and recognizing that

$$\hat{p}_h^{-2} S_{\hat{p}_h}^2 = \hat{p}_h^{-2} \frac{1}{l_h} \hat{p}_h \hat{q}_h$$

$$= \left(\frac{1}{l_{h+1}} - \frac{1}{l_h} \right),$$

we expand the right-hand side of (3.6),

$$\hat{p}_{ij}^2 \sum_{h=i}^{j-1} \hat{p}_h^{-2} S_{\hat{p}_h}^2 = \hat{p}_{ij}^2 \sum_{h=i}^{j-1} \left(\frac{1}{l_{h+1}} - \frac{1}{l_h} \right)$$

$$= \hat{p}_{ij}^2 \left(\frac{1}{l_j} - \frac{1}{l_i} \right)$$

$$= \frac{1}{l_i} \hat{p}_{ij} (1 - \hat{p}_{ij}), \tag{3.7}$$

and recover the formula in (3.5).

The sample variance of the observed expectation of life at age x_α, $\hat{e}_\alpha$, also has two explicit formulas. The first formula is based on the fact that $\hat{e}_\alpha$ is the sample mean of l_α future lifetimes beyond x_α; that is,

$$\hat{e}_\alpha = \overline{Y}_\alpha . \tag{2.9}$$

Using the formula for the variance of a sample mean on page 38, we find

$$S_{\hat{e}_\alpha}^2 = \frac{1}{l_\alpha^2} \sum_{i=\alpha}^{w} \left[(x_i - x_\alpha + a_i n_i) - \hat{e}_\alpha \right]^2 d_i . \tag{3.8}$$

The second formula for the sample variance of $\hat{e}_\alpha$ is deduced from (4.10) in Chapter 8:

$$S_{\hat{e}_\alpha}^2 = \sum_{i=\alpha}^{w-1} \hat{p}_{\alpha i}^2 \left[(1 - a_i) n_i + \hat{e}_{i+1} \right]^2 S_{\hat{q}_i}^2 , \tag{3.9}$$

where

$$S_{\hat{q}_i}^2 = \frac{1}{l_i} \hat{p}_i \hat{q}_i . \tag{3.2}$$

Equality of the formulas in (3.8) and (3.9) has been proven in Chiang (1960).

Using these formulas for the sample variances, we can make statistical inferences about the life table functions of two or more populations.

4. A Life Table for *Drosophila Melanogaster*

Life tables have been computed for living things other than human beings. One of the first such tables was published by Pearl and Parker (1921) for normal wild-type *Drosophila melanogaster*, the fruit fly. The present example is taken from Miller and Thomas (1958). The purpose of their study was to evaluate the effect of larval crowding and body size on the longevity of adult *Drosophila*. In the experiment, different numbers of larvae were placed in vials and observed under the same laboratory conditions. One set of data is used here for construction of a life table.

A group of $l_0 = 270$ male fruit flies were followed from the time they became adults to the death of the last member. The number of survivors at each five-day interval and the number of deaths occurring within each age interval are recorded in columns (2) and (3), respectively, in Table 1. Dividing d_x by l_x for each age interval gives the probability of dying $\hat{q}_x$ recorded in column (4). Using relations (2.3), (2.5) and (2.6) one computes the quantities L_x, T_x, and $\hat{e}_x$ for

Table 1. Life table of adult male *Drosophila melanogaster*

Age Interval (days)	Number living at age x	Number dying in (x, x + n)	Probability of dying in (x, x + n)	Days lived in (x, x + n)	Days lived beyond age x	Expectation of life at age x
$(n, x + n)$	l_x	d_x	$\hat{q}_x$	L_x	T_x	$\hat{e}_x$
(1)	(2)	(3)	(4)	(5)	(6)	(7)
0–5	270	2	.00741	1345	11660	43.2
5–10	268	4	.01493	1330	10315	38.5
10–15	264	3	.01136	1312	8985	34.0
15–20	261	7	.02682	1288	7673	29.4
20–25	254	3	.01181	1262	6385	25.1
25–30	251	3	.01195	1248	5123	20.4
30–35	248	16	.06452	1200	3875	15.6
35–40	232	66	.28448	995	2675	11.5
40–45	166	36	.21687	740	1680	10.1
45–50	130	54	.41538	515	940	7.2
50–55	76	42	.55263	275	425	5.6
55–60	34	21	.61765	118	150	4.4
60 +	13	13	1.00000	32	32	2.5

Table 2. Life table of adult female *Drosophila melanogaster*

Age Interval (days)	Number living at age x	Number dying in $(x, x+1)$	Probability of dying in $(x, x+1)$	Days lived in $(x, x+n)$	Days lived beyond age x	Expectation of life at age x
$(x, x+n)$	l_x	d_x	$\hat{q}_x$	L_x	T_x	$\hat{e}_x$
(1)	(2)	(3)	(4)	(5)	(6)	(7)
0–5	275	4	.01455	1365	10303	37.5
5–10	271	7	.02583	1338	8938	33.0
10–15	264	3	.01136	1312	7600	28.8
15–20	261	7	.02682	1288	6288	24.1
20–25	254	13	.05118	1238	5000	19.7
25–30	241	22	.09129	1150	3762	15.6
30–35	219	31	.14155	1018	2612	11.9
35–40	188	68	.36170	770	1594	8.5
40–45	120	51	.42500	472	824	6.9
45–50	69	38	.55072	250	352	5.1
50–55	31	26	.83871	90	102	3.3
55 +	5	5	1.00000	12	12	2.5

each age, and records them in columns (5), (6) and (7), respectively. The value .5 has been used for a_x for all intervals.

A similar table (Table 2) has been constructed for female adult *Drosophila*. Comparison of the two sexes with respect to the expectation of life, the survival probability, or the probability of death, can easily be made with the aid of the corresponding sample variances in Section 3.

To compare the longevity of male *Drosophila* and female *Drosophila*, we test the null hypothesis that the longevity of males is the same as females against the alternative that the male *Drosophila* live linger. The test statistic is

$$Z = \frac{\hat{e}_0(m) - \hat{e}_0(f)}{\text{S.E. (diff)}} .$$

Using the computations in Table 3, we find the value of the statistics

$$Z = \frac{43.2 - 37.5}{.9736}$$

$$= 5.85$$

which exceeds the critical value $Z_{.99} = 2.33$ at the 1% level of significance. We thus conclude that, under the laboratory conditions as described in Miller and Thomas, male *Drosophila* live longer than female *Drosophila*.

Table 3. Comparison of longevity of adult male *Drosophila* and adult female *Drosophila*

	Male	Female	Difference
Expectation of life $\hat{e}_0$ (in days)	43.2	37.5	5.7
Sample variance $S_{\hat{e}_0}^2$	.4890	.4588	.9478
Standard error $S_{\hat{e}_0}$	.6993	.6773	.9736

5. An Antenatal Life Table

Life table methodology has been applied to studies of fetal mortality. An antenatal life table, however, differs from the ordinary life table in several respects. *First*, the time at which a life begins is subject to discussion. Even if we agree that a life begins at conception, the precise moment of conception is not easily determined. Customarily, the first day of the last menstrual period (LMP) prior to beginning of pregnancy is commonly used to designate the start of gestation. But the length of the interval between the LMP and conception varies from one pregnancy to another and the determination of the LMP is subject to error. Thus the initial point of an antenatal life table is difficult to ascertain and the length of gestation cannot be accurately measured.

Second, a pregnancy is not detectable at its earliest stage. The existence of a fetus or its loss is clinically recognized during the month after the first missed menses, at the earliest. Besides, pregnancy is not as sure an event at it appears to be. In a pregnancy study, Taylor (1964) has found that

> " . . . over 90% of women who came to the clinic saying they think they are pregnant really *are* pregnant. The remaining five to ten percent resume menstruating after missing one or two periods. These may have had an early fetal death or they may not have been pregnant at all."

Due to the lack of reliable information and in order to avoid recording uncertain pregnancies, an antenatal life table often begins at a later date of gestation, such as the fourth week from LMP (French and Bierman, 1962), or the sixth week from LMP (Damiani, 1979) or the third week from LMP (Shapiro, et al., 1962).

Third, there are two possible outcomes of a pregnancy: a live birth and a fetal death. The principal objective of a pregnancy study is to estimate the risk of fetal loss as a functon of length of gestation. Therefore, the main concern of an antenatal life table is the outcome of a pregnancy, not the life expectancy of the conceptus.

Finally, a pregnancy study usually is a prospective study.

Women are admitted to a study at various stages of pregnancy and are followed until the expulsion of conceptus and beyond. For example, French and Bierman (1962) have reported that in their study "eighty percent of the pregnancies were under followup before the 20th week of gestation, 69 percent before the 16th week, and 50 percent as early as the 12th week, including 19 percent first reported between 4 and 8 weeks gestation." Using the life table method, one can combine the experience of different groups of women to establish a single integrated pregnancy history and derive significant results from it. An example follows.

This example is taken from French and Bierman (1962) and describes their findings of a prospective pregnancy study carried out on the island of Kauai, Hawaii, from 1953 to 1956. The study was designed to follow pregnancies from the time the women themselves were aware they were pregnant to the end of pregnancy. The start of followup was taken at the beginning of the fourth week from LMP. Because few pregnancies in the study were first reported during the fourth week, the actual period of observation for most cases began at a later date.

The basic data are summarized in columns (3) through (6) in Table 4. For each four-week period, column (3) shows the number of

Table 4. Calculation of antenatal life table functions, Kauai Pregnancy Study, 1953–56

Period of gestation (in weeks)	At x	Number of Pregnancies in Interval $(x, x+1)$				Probability of Outcome in Interval $(x, x+1)$ per 1000		
		First Reported	Ending in					
			Fetal Death	Live Birth	Moved Out of Area	Fetal Death	Live Birth	Still Pregnant
(1) x to $x+1$	(2) N_x	(3) r_x	(4) f_x	(5) b_x	(6) 0_x	(7) Q_{x1}	(8) Q_{x2}	(9) p_x
4–8	0	592	32	0	0	108.11	0.00	891.89
8–12	560	941	72	0	1	69.90	0.00	930.10
12–16	1428	585	77	0	2	44.78	0.00	955.22
16–20	1934	337	28	0	2	13.32	0.00	986.68
20–24	2241	248	20	1	9	8.47	0.42	991.11
24–28	2459	175	8	4	6	3.15	1.57	995.28
28–32	2616	98	8	25	4	3.00	9.39	987.61
32–36	2677	67	8	72	6	2.95	26.59	970.46
36–40	2658	40	9	1074	3	3.36	401.27	595.37
*40 +	1612	0	11	1601	0	6.82	993.18	.00

*Includes 35 live births terminating at 45–57 weeks of gestation; no fetal death occurred after 43 weeks of gestation.

women first reported to the study (r_x); column (4), the number of pregnancies ending in fetal death (f_x); column (5), the number of live births (b_x); and column (6), the number of women who moved out of the area (0_x). These figures were then used to calculate the N_x, the number of pregnancies at the beginning of each interval (column 2):

$$N_{x+1} = N_x + r_x - f_x - b_x - 0_x .$$

In columns (7), (8) and (9) are the estimated probabilities of a fetal death ($\hat{Q}_{x1}$), of a live birth ($\hat{Q}_{x2}$) during the interval ($x, x + 1$), and of women still pregnant ($\hat{p}_x$) at the end of the interval, respectively. Women first reported pregnant in a specified interval were assumed to have been under observation one-half of the interval, on the average. A similar assumption was made for those who moved out of the area. Estimated probabilities were thus calculated using the following formulas:

Fetal death: $\qquad \hat{Q}_{x1} = \dfrac{f_x}{N_x + \frac{1}{2}r_x - \frac{1}{2}0_x}$

Live birth: $\qquad \hat{Q}_{x2} = \dfrac{b_x}{N_x + \frac{1}{2}r_x - \frac{1}{2}0_x}$

Still pregnant: $\qquad \hat{p}_x = 1 - Q_{x1} - Q_{x2} .$

On the basis of these estimated probabilities, French and Bierman computed all the life table functions in Table 5 as follows:

Number still pregnant: $\quad l_{x+1} = l_x \hat{p}_x$ (Col. 2)
Number of fetal deaths: $\quad d_{x1} = l_x \hat{Q}_{x1}$ (Col. 6)
Number of live births: $\quad d_{x2} = l_x \hat{Q}_{x2}$ (Col. 7)
Probability: $\quad \hat{q}_x = \hat{Q}_{x1} + \hat{Q}_{x2}$ (Col. 5)
Pregnancies terminated: $\quad d_x = d_{x1} + d_{x2}$ (Col. 8)
Length of gestation: $\quad L_x = \frac{1}{2}(l_x + l_{x+1})$ (Col. 9)
Length of gestation beyond x: $\quad T_x = L_x + L_{x+1} + \cdots + L_{10}$ (Col. 10)
and Expected duration of gestation: $\quad \hat{e}_x = \dfrac{T_x}{l_x} .$ (Col. 11)

Table 5 differs from the ordinary life table in the additional columns (3), (4), (6) and (7). These columns have been added to accommodate the two possible outcomes of a pregnancy. The sum of the two probabilities ($\hat{Q}_{x1} + \hat{Q}_{x2}$) corresponds to $\hat{q}_x$, and the sum of

Table 5. Antenatal Life Table, Kauai Pregnancy Study, 1953–56

Period of gestation (in weeks)	Number still pregnant at gestation age x	Decrement in interval $(x, x+1)$						Number of months of followup		Average Number of lunar months of pregnancy after x
		1000 × Probability			Number			In interval $(x, x+1)$	From x on until all have delivered	
		Fetal Death	Live Birth	Total	Fetal Deaths	Live Births	Total			
(1)	(2)	(3)	(4)	(5)	(6)	(7)	(8)	(9)	(10)	(11)
x to $x+1$	l_x	$\hat{Q}_{x1}$	$\hat{Q}_{x2}$	$\hat{q}_x$	d_{x1}	d_{x2}	d_x	L_x	T_x	$\hat{e}_x$
4–8	1,000.00	108.11	0.00	108.11	108.11	0.00	108.11	945.94	7,282.80	7.28
8–12	891.89	69.90	0.00	69.90	62.34	0.00	62.34	860.72	6,336.86	7.10
12–16	829.55	44.78	0.00	44.78	37.15	0.00	37.15	810.98	5,476.14	6.60
16–20	792.40	13.32	0.00	13.32	10.55	0.00	10.55	787.12	4,665.16	5.89
20–24	781.85	8.47	0.42	8.89	6.62	0.33	6.95	778.38	3,878.04	4.96
24–28	774.90	3.15	1.57	4.72	2.44	1.22	3.66	773.07	3,099.66	4.00
28–32	771.24	3.00	9.39	12.39	2.31	7.24	9.55	766.46	2,326.59	3.02
32–36	761.69	2.95	26.59	29.54	2.25	20.25	22.50	750.44	1,560.13	2.05
36–40	739.19	3.36	401.27	404.63	2.48	296.61	299.09	589.64	809.69	1.10
*40 +	440.10	6.82	993.18	1000.00	3.00	437.10	440.10	220.05	220.05	.50

*Includes 35 live births terminating at 45–57 weeks gestation; no fetal death occurred after 43 weeks gestation.

SOURCE: Tables 4 and 5 were reproduced from: French, F. E. and Bierman, J. M. (1962). Probability of Fetal Mortality. *Public Health Reports*, 77, 835–847.

the two numbers $(d_{x1} + d_{x2})$ corresponds to d_x in the ordinary life table. The average number of lunar months of pregnancy after x in column (11) is the life expectancy of a conceptus at gestation age x. The figures in this column obviously are far less important than the expectations of life in an ordinary life table.

Column (3) in Table 5 shows the probability of fetal death at a high point of .108 during 4–8 weeks of gestation.* The probabilities continue to decline as pregnancy progresses with a slight upward swing for the last interval. On the other hand, column (4) shows that the probability of a live birth is negligible prior to the 28th week of gestation, and most of the live births take place after 36 weeks of gestation. Based on their experience, French and Bierman stated that "Results of 4 years of followup in the Kauai Pregnancy Study indicate that rates obtained from an antenatal life table more nearly reflect the true magnitude of early fetal mortality than measures previously reported." This is an encouraging testimony for the life table as a statistical method of analysis.

6.   Life Tables in Ecological Studies

An ecological study of the life cycle of a certain species usually is an observational study under a natural setting. The natural world, however, is diverse and complex; the phenomena in the natural environment are subject to constant change as a result of interactions of many confounding factors. It is far more difficult to establish a mortality pattern for an animal population in the natural environment than under a laboratory condition. In their attempt to formulate a general theory of mortality for lower organisms, Pearl and Miner (1935) had encountered so much difficulty in unraveling numerous environmental determinants that they had to abandon their effort and enter a plea for "more observational data, carefully and critically collected through the life history from birth to death of each individual of a cohort of statistically respectable magnitude." Since that time, much work has been done with the life table in ecological studies.

Three types of life tables exist in ecological sciences; their differences result from the way the basic data are collected (Hickey, 1952). *Dynamic life tables* summarize the survival experience of a given cohort over a period of years. These tables are analogous to the

---

*The highest point may really be in the 0–4 week period, since the table is (slightly) biased towards that group of women whose pregnancies have already progressed several weeks as of the time they enter the study.

cohort life tables. *Time-specific life tables*, like the current life table, are based on the data compiled from a single period of observation. This type of table is very infrequently used in ecological research, as it is difficult to compute age-specific mortality rates for a natural population. *Composite life tables*, which are most often used, are computed from miscellaneous collections of mortality data that do not agree with the criteria of either the dynamic (cohort) or the time specific (current) life tables. Some tables are computed using age at death. For example, Karl Pearson (1902) determined the life expectancies of ancient Egyptians based on the age at death recorded on 141 mummy cases. Some use information collected through a mark-release device. The life table of a herring gull (*Larus argentatus*) population by Paynter (1947) is of this type. The gulls were banded as chicks at the Bowden Scientific Station, Kent Island, Bay of Fundy, and were later recovered dead from all over North America. On the basis of the age at death, life tables were computed for the herring gull population. Data collected by the mark-release method are generally subject to bias, as not all released animals are recovered. The proportion recovered may vary with age, and those still alive are not included in the data.

Table 6. Life table for the Dall Mountain sheep (*Ovis d. dalli*) based on the known age at death of 608 sheep dying before 1937 (Murie (1944))

Age Interval (in years)	Age as % deviation from mean life length	Number dying in age interval	Number living at age x	Mortality rate in age interval	Expectation of life
x	x'	d_x	l_x	$1000\hat{q}_x$	$\hat{e}_x$
0–0.05	− 100.0	54	1000	54.0	7.1
0.5–1	− 93.0	145	946	153.0	—
1–2	− 95.9	12	801	15.0	7.7
2–3	− 71.8	13	789	16.5	6.8
3–4	− 57.7	12	776	15.5	5.9
4–5	− 43.5	30	764	39.3	5.0
5–6	− 29.5	46	734	62.6	4.2
6–7	− 15.4	48	688	69.8	3.4
7–8	− 1.1	69	640	108.0	2.6
8–9	+ 13.0	132	571	231.0	1.9
9–10	+ 27.0	187	439	426.0	1.3
10–11	+ 41.0	156	252	619.0	0.9
11–12	+ 55.0	90	96	937.0	0.6
12–13	+ 69.0	3	6	500.0	1.2
13–14	+ 84.0	3	3	1000.0	0.7

Mean length of life is 7.09 years

Table 7. Cohort life table for Dall Mountain sheep (*Ovis d. dalli*) based on the known age at death of 608 mountain sheep dying before 1937

Age interval (in years)	Number living at age x	Number dying in $(x, x + n)$	Probability of dying in $(x, x + n)$	Years lived in $(x, x + n)$	Years lived beyond x	Expectation of life at age x
$(x, x + n)$	l_x	d_x	q_x	L_x	T_x	$\hat{e}_x$
0–0.5	608	33	.054	295.8	4312.8	7.09
0.5–1	575	88	.153	265.5	4017.0	6.99
1–2	487	7	.015	483.5	3751.5	7.70
2–3	480	8	.017	476.0	3268.0	6.81
3–4	472	7	.015	468.5	2792.0	5.92
4–5	465	18	.039	456.9	2323.5	5.00
5–6	447	28	.063	433.0	1867.5	4.18
6–7	419	29	.070	404.5	1434.5	3.42
7–8	390	42	.108	369.0	1030.0	2.64
8–9	348	80	.231	308.0	661.0	1.90
9–10	268	114	.426	211.0	353.0	1.32
10–11	154	95	.619	106.5	142.0	.92
11–12	59	55	.937	31.5	35.5	.60
12–13	4	2	.500	3.0	4.0	1.00
13–14	2	2	1.000	1.0	1.0	.50

In her study of various life tables in the ecological field, Johnson (1980)* has recast several of these tables in a form consistent with the cohort life table discussed in this chapter. One of these is the life table of Dall Mountan sheep (*Ovis d. dalli*) in Mount McKinley National Park, Alaska, prepared by Murie (1944). Murie collected a total of 608 dead sheep, and estimated the age at death for each of them on the basis of the graph of its horns. Among the entire group, Murie found 121 died during their first year of life, 7 died during their second year, and so on, and only 2 were alive at the beginning of their 13th year and they died during that year. Taking the 608 sheep as a sample, Murie constructed a life table for Dall Mountain sheep (Table 6). Johnson recast in it Table 7. Both tables show that, based on this sample, the expectation of life at birth for Dall Mountain sheep is 7.1 years.

7. The Family Life Cycle

The family life cycle (FLC) is defined as the time period extending from the time of (first) marriage to the death of the

---

*L. Johnson (1980). "A comparison of life table methods used in two different fields of population research." (Personal communication)

surviving spouse. A conceptual model of the cycle contains several phases: formation, extension, completed extension, contraction, completed contraction, and dissolution. The extensions refer to the birth of children; contractions to departure of children. In a model which allows no divorces, dissolution of the FLC occurs at the death of the first spouse. The end of the dissolution phase, due to the death of the surviving spouse, is the termination of the family life cycle. In practical cases, the evolution of the family life cycle need not strictly follow the above order, and some of the phases need not be realized. For a detailed description of the model, refer to Feichtinger and Hansluwka (1976).

The family life cyle has an impact on the composition of a population, on the social well-being of the people, and on the economy of a country. The methodology developed in the family life cycle has found applications in the analysis of fertility, family health, and the effect of mortality in various countries. The World Health Organization has completed a study on "Health and the Family: Studies in the Demography of FLC and their Health Implications."

Many authors have contributed to the development of the concept and formulation of this model. They include Hiess (1931), Glick and Parke (1965), Pressat (1972), Ryder (1973), Le Bras (1973), Muhsam (1976), and Hansluwka (1977), to name a few. Myers (1959), Ryder (1976), and Feichtinger (1977) have suggested statistical measures of various indices in the family life cycle.

In this section we consider a model consisting only of formation, dissolution, and termination of the FLC; we have disregarded extension and contraction phases of the cycle. Divorce and remarriage are not considered, so that dissolution of marriage and termination of family life cycle are due to death of spouse only. In the following sections, we describe the model from a statistical perspective and are concerned with the impact of mortality on the duration of marriage, widowhood, and the family life cycle.

7.1. Probabilities of Survival and Dissolution of Marriage.

Let u be the age of the husband and v be the age of the wife at (first) marriage of a given couple. Let x be the number of *completed* years of the marriage. Following Feichtinger and Hansluwka (1976), we use the symbol $(u, v, 0)$-marriage to denote a married couple of ages u and v, respectively.

Denote the age-specific death rate for males by M_y', and for females by M_y for a single year of age $(y, y + 1)$. These are computed directly from the vital statistics of the population under consideration. The principal complete life table functions are denoted by q_y', l_y', d_y' and e_y' for males, and by q_y, l_y, d_y and e_y for females. The probability that an individual alive at age y will die in $(y, y + 1)$ is computed from

$$q_y = \frac{M_y}{1 + (1 - a_y')M_y},$$

which is given in Chapter 6, Equation (3.1). When the fraction of the last year of life is assumed to be $1/2$, i.e., $a_y' = 1/2$, for all y, the above equation becomes

$$q_y' = \frac{M_y'}{1 + (1/2)M_y'}, \qquad y = u, u + 1, \ldots, \qquad (7.1a)$$

for males, and

$$q_y = \frac{M_y}{1 + (1/2)M_y}, \qquad y = v, v + 1, \ldots \qquad (7.1b)$$

for females. Using these probabilities, the other columns in the life table can be computed in the usual manner.*

In the study of the family life cycle in a society, one is concerned with the joint probabilities of events occurring to a couple. For a $(u, v, 0)$-marriage and an age interval $(x, x + 1)$ after marriage, there are four possible composite events regarding survival and death of the husband and wife. The corresponding probabilities are

Pr{the husband dies in the year $(x, x + 1)$

and the wife survives to time $(x + 1)$}

$$= \left(\frac{d_{u+x}'}{l_u'} \right) \left(\frac{l_{v+x+1}}{l_v} \right), \qquad (7.2a)$$

Pr{the husband survives to time $(x + 1)$

and the wife dies in $(x, x + 1)$}

$$= \left(\frac{l_{u+x+1}'}{l_u'} \right) \left(\frac{d_{v+x}}{l_v} \right), \qquad (7.2b)$$

Pr{both survive to time $(x + 1)$}

$$= \left(\frac{l_{u+x+1}'}{l_u'} \right) \left(\frac{l_{v+x+1}}{l_v} \right), \qquad (7.3)$$

---

*The symbols q_y, q_y', e_y, e_y' and others in this section are estimates of the corresponding unknown probabilities and expectations. For simplicity of presentation, no distinction is made between the unknown parameters and their estimates.

and

$$\Pr\{\text{both die during the year } (x, x + 1)\}$$

$$= \left(\frac{d'_{u+x}}{l'_u} \right) \left(\frac{d_{v+x}}{l_v} \right). \tag{7.4}$$

For each x, the sum

$$\left(\frac{d'_{u+x}}{l'_u} \right) \left(\frac{l_{v+x+1}}{l_v} \right) + \left(\frac{d'_{u+x}}{l'_u} \right) \left(\frac{d_{v+x}}{l_v} \right) = \left(\frac{d'_{u+x}}{l'_u} \right) \left(\frac{l_{v+x}}{l_v} \right) \tag{7.5}$$

is the probability that the couple survives to the beginning of the year $(x, x + 1)$ and the husband dies during the year. The survival or death of the wife beyond time x is not specified. The sum

$$\sum_{x=0}^{w} \left[\left(\frac{d'_{u+x}}{l'_u} \right) \left(\frac{l_{v+x+1}}{l_v} \right) + \frac{1}{2} \left(\frac{d'_{u+x}}{l'_u} \right) \left(\frac{d_{v+x}}{l_v} \right) \right] \tag{7.6}$$

is the probability that a $(u, v, 0)$-marriage is eventually dissolved due to the death of the husband. Similarly, the sum

$$\sum_{x=0}^{w} \left[\left(\frac{l'_{u+x+1}}{l'_u} \right) \left(\frac{d_{v+x}}{l_v} \right) + \frac{1}{2} \left(\frac{d'_{u+x}}{l'_u} \right) \left(\frac{d_{v+x}}{l_v} \right) \right] \tag{7.7}$$

is the probability that a $(u, v, 0)$-marriage is eventually dissolved due to the death of the wife.

7.2. Duration of Marriage.

Death occurring in a time interval may take place at any time during the interval. Assuming that deaths are uniformly distributed over an interval, a person who dies in a time interval lives half of the interval, on the average. We shall use this assumption in all the computations in this section. Now, if the husband of a $(u, v, 0)$-marriage dies during the year $(x, x + 1)$ after marriage and the wife survives to $x + 1$, he lives half of the year and the duration of the marriage is $x + 1/2$. Similarly, if the wife dies during the year $(x, x + 1)$ and the husband survives to $x + 1$, the duration of their marriage is also $x + 1/2$. If both the husband and the wife die in the same year $(x, x + 1)$, the duration of the marriage is $x + 1/3$.

To verify this number $x + (1/3)$, we divide the year $(x, x + 1)$ into n equal subintervals with the dividing points at $x + (k/n)$, for $k = 0, 1, \ldots, n$. Suppose the first of the couple dies in the k-th subinterval $\{x + (k - 1)/n, x + (k/n)\}$, then the length of the marriage is $x + (k - 1/2)/n$. The corresponding probability is $\{2(n - k)$

$+ 1\}/n^2$. It follows that the duration of the marriage is

$$\sum_{k=1}^{n} \left[x + \frac{(k - \frac{1}{2})}{n} \right] \frac{2(n - k) + 1}{n^2} = x + \frac{2n^2 + 1}{6n^2} .$$

The last quantity tends to $x + (1/3)$ as n tends to infinity, as required to show.

The expected duration of the marriage is the weighted mean of $(x + 1/2)$ and $(x + 1/3)$, with the corresponding probabilities in (7.2a), (7.2b) and (7.4) used as weights. In other words, the expected duration of the marriage is

$$e_{uv} = \sum_{x=0}^{w} \left\{ (x + 1/2) \left[\left(\frac{d'_{u+x}}{l'_u} \right) \left(\frac{l_{v+x+1}}{l_v} \right) + \left(\frac{l'_{u+x+1}}{l'_u} \right) \left(\frac{d_{v+x}}{l_v} \right) \right] \right.$$

$$\left. + (x + 1/3) \left(\frac{d'_{u+x}}{l'_u} \right) \left(\frac{d_{v+x}}{l_v} \right) \right\}. \tag{7.8}$$

The upper limit of the summation w is the smallest positive integer for which either $l'_{u+w+1} = 0$ or $l_{v+w+1} = 0$. It is easy to show that the sum of the probabilities in (7.8) is equal to unity:

$$\frac{1}{l'_u l_v} \sum_{x=0}^{w} (d'_{u+x} l_{v+x+1} + l'_{u+x+1} d_{v+x} + d'_{u+x} d_{v+x}) = 1. \tag{7.9}$$

Since for every x

$$d'_{u+x} l_{v+x+1} + l'_{u+x+1} d_{v+x} + d'_{u+x} d_{v+x} = l'_{u+x} l_{v+x} - l'_{u+x+1} l_{v+x+1}, \tag{7.10}$$

the sum

$$\sum_{x=0}^{w} (d'_{u+x} l_{v+x+1} + l'_{u+x+1} d_{v+x} + d'_{u+x} d_{v+x})$$

$$= \sum_{x=0}^{w} (l'_{u+x} l_{v+x} - l'_{u+x+1} l_{v+x+1}) = l'_u l_v ,$$

equation (7.9) follows.

Formula (7.8) may be simplified. We first write e_{uv} in three separate summations:

$$e_{uv} = \frac{1}{l'_u l_v} \left\{ \sum_{x=0}^{w} x [d'_{u+x} l_{v+x+1} + l'_{u+x+1} d_{v+x} + d'_{u+x} d_{v+x}] \right.$$

$$+ \left(\frac{1}{2} \right) \sum_{x=0}^{w} [d'_{u+x} l_{v+x+1} + l'_{u+x+1} d_{v+x} + d'_{u+x} d_{v+x}]$$

$$\left. - \left(\frac{1}{6} \right) \sum_{x=0}^{w} d'_{u+x} d_{v+x} \right\}. \tag{7.11}$$

The first sum is

$$\sum_{x=0}^{w} x\left[d'_{u+x} l_{v+x+1} + l'_{u+x+1} d_{v+x} + d'_{u+x} d_{v+x} \right]$$

$$= \sum_{x=0}^{w} x\left[l'_{u+x} l_{v+x} - l'_{u+x+1} l_{v+x+1} \right]$$

$$= \sum_{x=0}^{w-1} l'_{u+x+1} l_{v+x+1}, \qquad (7.12)$$

while the second sum is equal to $l'_u l_v$. The expected duration of marriage in (7.8) reduces to

$$e_{uv} = \frac{1}{2} + \frac{1}{l'_u l_v}\left[\sum_{x=0}^{w} l'_{u+x+1} l_{v+x+1} - \frac{1}{6} \sum_{x=0}^{w} d'_{u+x} d_{v+x} \right]. \qquad (7.13)$$

The last formula is suitable for a computer program.

7.3.   Duration of Widowhood.   The wife of a $(u, v, 0)$-marriage becomes a widow when her husband dies during the year $(x, x + 1)$. The duration of widowhood depends on whether she survives the year. If she survives to time $x + 1$, she becomes a widow at the age $v + x + 1/2$, and the duration of widowhood is $(1/2) + e_{v+x+1}$, where e_{v+x+1} is the expectation of life at age $v + x + 1$.

If she also dies in the year $(x, x + 1)$, the duration of her widowhood is $1/6$ of the year. To show this, we divide the year $(x, x + 1)$ into n equal subintervals. The possible length of her widowhood is from zero to $(n - 1)/n$ of the year. Suppose the duration of her widowhood is k/n of the year. The corresponding probability is $(n - k)/n^2$. Therefore, the duration of her widowhood is

$$\sum_{k=1}^{n-1} \frac{(n-k)}{n^2}\left(\frac{k}{n} \right) = \frac{n^2 - 1}{6n^2}.$$

The last quantity tends to $1/6$ as n tends to infinity.

The probabilities of the survival and death events are given in (7.2a) and (7.4), respectively. When these events are considered for every year since marriage, we have the duration of widowhood for the wife,

$$W = \sum_{x=0}^{w} \left[\left(\frac{d'_{u+x}}{l'_u} \right)\left(\frac{l_{v+x+1}}{l_v} \right)\left\{ \frac{1}{2} + e_{v+x+1} \right\} \right.$$

$$\left. + \frac{1}{6}\left(\frac{d'_{u+x}}{l'_u} \right)\left(\frac{d_{v+x}}{l_v} \right) \right]. \qquad (7.14)$$

Using similar reasoning, we find the duration of widowerhood for the husband,

$$W' = \sum_{x=0}^{w} \left[\left(\frac{l'_{u+x+1}}{l'_u} \right) \left(\frac{d_{v+x}}{l_v} \right) \left\{ \frac{1}{2} + e'_{u+x+1} \right\} \right.$$

$$\left. + \frac{1}{6} \left(\frac{d'_{u+x}}{l'_u} \right) \left(\frac{d_{v+x}}{l_v} \right) \right] \tag{7.15}$$

It should be noted that neither the sum of the probabilities in (7.14) nor the sum of the probabilities in (7.15) is equal to unity. Thus neither W nor W' is a bona fide mean of the durations of widowhood enumerated. They have, however, an intuitively appealing relationship with the duration of marriage and the life expectancies at the time of marriage.

The wife of a $(u, v, 0)$-marriage will remain married for an expected duration of e_{uv}, or endure widowhood for the duration of W. Since she is either married or widowed after the time of marriage, the sum of these two periods must be equal to her expectation of life at the time of the marriage. A similar statement holds for the husband. In other words, the expectation of life of the wife (or the husband) at the time of the marriage is equal to the duration of marriage plus the duration of widowhood. That is,

$$e_v = e_{uv} + W \tag{7.16}$$

for the wife, and

$$e'_u = e_{uv} + W' \tag{7.17}$$

for the husband.

To prove equation (7.16) we recall the expectation of life

$$e_v = \frac{1}{2} + \frac{1}{l_v} \sum_{x=0}^{w} l_{v+x+1} \tag{7.18}$$

and use formulas (7.13) and (7.14) to write the sum on the right-hand side of (7.16),

$$e_{uv} + W = \left[\frac{1}{2} + \frac{1}{l'_u l_v} \sum_{x=0}^{w} l'_{u+x+1} l_{v+x+1} - \frac{1}{6} \sum_{x=0}^{w} \left(\frac{d'_{u+x}}{l'_u} \right) \left(\frac{d_{v+x}}{l_v} \right) \right]$$

$$+ \left[\frac{1}{l'_u l_v} \sum_{x=0}^{w} d'_{u+x} l_{v+x+1} \left\{ \frac{1}{2} + e_{v+x+1} \right\} \right.$$

$$\left. + \frac{1}{6} \sum_{x=0}^{w} \left(\frac{d'_{u+x}}{l'_u} \right) \left(\frac{d_{v+x}}{l_v} \right) \right], \tag{7.19}$$

where

$$\frac{1}{2} + e_{v+x+1} = \frac{1}{2} + \left[\frac{1}{2} + \frac{1}{l_{v+x+1}} \sum_{y=x+1}^{w} l_{v+y+1} \right],$$

so that

$$l_{v+x+1}\left\{ \frac{1}{2} + e_{v+x+1} \right\} = \sum_{y=x}^{w} l_{v+y+1}. \tag{7.20}$$

Substituting (7.20) in the third sum in (7.19) gives

$$\sum_{x=0}^{w} d'_{u+x}l_{v+x+1}\left\{ \frac{1}{2} + e_{v+x+1} \right\} = \sum_{x=0}^{w} d'_{u+x} \sum_{y=x}^{w} l_{v+y+1}$$

$$= \sum_{y=0}^{w} l_{v+y+1} \sum_{x=0}^{y} d'_{u+x}, \tag{7.21}$$

where the sum of the numbers of deaths is

$$\sum_{x=0}^{y} d'_{u+x} = l'_u - l'_{u+y+1} \tag{7.22}$$

and (7.21) becomes

$$\sum_{x=0}^{w} d'_{u+x}l_{v+x+1}\left\{ \frac{1}{2} + e_{v+x+1} \right\} = \sum_{y=0}^{w} l_{v+y+1}(l'_u - l'_{u+y+1})$$

$$= l'_u \sum_{y=0}^{w} l_{v+y+1} - \sum_{y=0}^{w} l'_{u+y+1}l_{v+y+1}. \tag{7.23}$$

When (7.23) is introduced in (7.19) and simplified, we find

$$e_{uv} + W = \frac{1}{2} + \frac{1}{l_v} \sum_{y=0}^{w} l_{v+y+1}, \tag{7.24}$$

which is equal to e_v, the expectation of life for the wife at the time of marriage. Equation (7.17) can be verified in the same manner.

7.4. Duration of the Family Life Cycle.   It is conceptually clear that the duration of the family life cycle is equal to the duration of marriage plus the duration of widowhood. However, it cannot be determined at the time of marriage which one of the couple will die first. Further, the period of widowhood for the wife is not the same as that for the husband. A simple combination of the two periods of widowhood is not obvious. Therefore, we need to address the problem of widowhood afresh.

Consider again the year $(x, x + 1)$ since marriage. There are four mutually exclusive events that may occur during the year leading to widowhood: (1) The husband dies during the year and the wife survives the year. In this case, the duration of widowhood for the wife is $\{(1/2) + e_{v+x+1}\}$. (2) The husband survives the year and the wife dies during the year. In this case, the duration of widowerhood for the husband is $\{(1/2) + e'_{u+x+1}\}$. (3) Both die during the year. In this case, either the husband or the wife will endure widowhood during the year. The duration of widowerhood for the husband is $1/6$ of the year and the duration of widowhood for the wife is also $1/6$ of the year. For each x these four events are mutually exclusive events. The expected duration of widowhood (or aloneness) is defined as the weighted mean of the four sequences of periods of widowhood with the corresponding probabilities used as weights. In formula,

$$E[\text{widowhood}] = \frac{1}{l'_u l_v} \sum_{x=0}^{w} \left[d'_{u+x} l_{v+x+1} \left\{ \frac{1}{2} + e_{v+x+1} \right\} \right.$$

$$+ l'_{u+x+1} d_{v+x} \left\{ \frac{1}{2} + e'_{u+x+1} \right\}$$

$$\left. + \left\{ \frac{1}{6} + \frac{1}{6} \right\} d'_{u+x} d_{v+x} \right]. \qquad (7.25)$$

The sum of the probabilities in (7.25) is equal to one [cf. equation (7.9)].

Comparing formula (7.25) with formulas (7.14) and (7.15), we find

$$E(\text{widowhood}) = W + W'. \qquad (7.26)$$

While algebraically the expected duration of widowhood is the sum of the two durations of widowhood, formula (7.25) is a much more meaningful measure of widowhood of a married couple than either W or W' or their combinations. It is the arithmetic mean of all possible periods of widowhood that either the husband or the wife of a married couple may experience during their life time, with the corresponding probabilities used as weights. Thus $E[\text{widowhood}]$ complies with the definition of the mathematical expectation of a random variable.

With the expected duration of widowhood well defined, we are now in a position to define the expected duration of the family life cycle, $E(FLC)$. Namely,

$$E(FLC) = E(\text{duration of marriage}) + E(\text{widowhood}). \quad (7.27)$$

In view of the relationships in equations (7.16), (7.17) and (7.26) above, we have

$$E(\text{widowhood}) = e'_u + e_v - 2e_{uv} \qquad (7.28)$$

and

$$E(FLC) = e'_u + e_v - e_{uv}. \tag{7.29}$$

The above findings may be summarized as follows.

The expected duration of widowhood of a $(u, v, 0)$-married couple is the mathematical expectation of the period of widowhood of the couple. The expected duration of the family life cycle is the sum of the expected duration of marriage and the expected duration of widowhood. It is related with the expectations of life of the couple at marriage and the duration of marriage as in formula (7.29).

8. Problems for Solution

1. Show that the sample mean length of life at age 0 ($\overline{Y}_0$) is equal to the expectation of life at age 0 ($\hat{e}_0$).

2. Show that the formulas for the sample variances of the observed expectation of life at age x_α in (3.8) and (3.9) are equal.

3. Compute the probability $\hat{p}_x$ and its sample variance for each x based on the data in Tables 1 and 2, pages 174 and 175, respectively.

4. Compute the survival probability $\hat{p}_{0x}$ and its standard error for each x for the male and female *Drosophila* in Tables 1 and 2.

5. *Continuation.* Test the hypothesis $p_{0x}(m) = p_{0x}(f)$ for $x = 5$, 10 and 15.

6. Use formula (3.9) to compute the sample variance of the expectation of life $\hat{e}_x$ for each x for the male and female *Drosophila* in Tables 1 and 2.

7. Test the hypothesis $e_x(m) = e_x(f)$ for $x = 0, 5, 10, 15$ and 20.

8. Check the computation of antenatal life table functions in Table 4, page 177.

9. Check the computation of antenatal life table functions in Table 5, page 179.

10. Prepare a report on the findings of the Kauai Pregnancy Study, 1953–56 based on the information given in Tables 4 and 5.

11. Compute the survival probability $\hat{p}_{0x}$ and its standard error based on the cohort life table for Dall Mountain sheep in Table 7, page 182.

12. Compute the standard error for the expectation of life $\hat{e}_x$ for each x in Table 7.

13. Find the 95% confidence interval for the expectation of life for the Dall Mountain sheep at age $x = 0$ and at age $x = 1$.

14. Derive formula (7.13) for the duration of marriage e_{uv} from formula (7.8).

15. Verify the equation

$$e'_u = e_{uv} + W' \tag{7.17}$$

for the husband.

16. Let a random variable $x + t$ be the time at death in the interval $(x, x + 1)$ so that t assumes values between 0 and 1. Suppose that t is uniformly distributed in $(0, 1)$. Find the expectation and variance of t.

17. Let random variables $x + t_1$ and $x + t_2$ be the time at death in the interval $(x, x + 1)$ for the husband and the wife of a $(u, v, 0)$-marriage, respectively. Suppose they are independent and uniformly distributed in the interval $(0, 1)$. Let $x + t_{(1)}$ be the time at death of the one who dies first. Show that the expectation of $t_{(1)}$ is $E(t_{(1)}) = \frac{1}{3}$ and the variance of $t_{(1)}$ is $\mathrm{var}(t_{(1)}) = \frac{1}{6}$.

18. *Continuation.* Let $x + t_{(2)}$ be the time at death in $(x, x + 1)$ of the second (surviving) spouse. Find the expectation and variance of $t_{(2)}$.

19. *Continuation.* Let $t_{(2)} - t_{(1)}$ be the difference between the time at death of the husband and wife. This is the length of widowhood of the surviving spouse in the interval $(x, x + 1)$. Find the expected value and variance of $t_{(2)} - t_{(1)}$. Compare this approach with that in Section 7.3.

20. Compute the duration of marriage e_{uv} for a couple of age at marriage $u = 25$ years and $v = 20$ years, respectively, if they are subject to the 1975 U.S. population survival experience in Tables 2 and 3, Chapter 8.

21. *Continuation.* Compute the duration of widowhood for the husband W' and for the wife W. Do they satisfy the equations $e'_u = e_{wv} + W'$ and $e_v = e_{uv} + W$? What is the duration of the family life cycle for this couple?

22. Work problems 20 and 21 for $u = v = 20$ years. For $u = 30$ years and $v = 25$ years.

CHAPTER *10*

*Statistical Theory of the Life Table**

1. Introduction

The concept of the life table originated in the study of human longevity. It was presented as a subject peculiar to actuarial science, demography, and public health, and, as a result, the development of the life table has not received sufficient attention in the field of statistics. In fact, the life table is a statistical tool for the study of problems of mortality and is similar to reliability theory. From a statistical viewpoint, human life is a random experiment; its outcomes, survival and death, are subject to chance. A life table systematically records the outcomes for a number of individuals in a certain population. Thus, the elements in the life table are random variables. They can be subjected to purely statistical analysis. The purpose of this chapter is to derive the probability distributions for the observed life table functions and to discuss some optimality properties of these functions when they are regarded as estimates of the corresponding unknown parameters. The presentation will focus on the cohort life table but, whenever necessary, clarification will be made for the current life table. A typical abridged life table appears in Table 1.

---

*A knowledge of statistical theory is required for a thorough understanding of the material in this chapter. The reader whose interest is primarily in the application of the life table may skip this chapter at the first reading.

Table 1. Abridged life table

Age interval (in years)	Number living at age x_i	Proportion dying in interval (x_i, x_{i+1})	Fraction of last age interval of life	Number dying in interval (x_i, x_{i+1})	Number of years lived in interval (x_i, x_{i+1})	Total number of years lived beyond age x_i	Observed expectation of life at age x_i
x_i to x_{i+1}	l_i	$\hat{q}_i$	a_i	d_i	L_i	T_i	$\hat{e}_i$
x_0 to x_1	l_0	$\hat{q}_0$	a_0	d_0	L_0	T_0	$\hat{e}_0$
$\cdots$	$\cdots$	$\cdots$	$\cdots$	$\cdots$	$\cdots$	$\cdots$	$\cdots$
x_w & over	l_w	$\hat{q}_w$		d_w	L_w	T_w	$\hat{e}_w$

The following symbols are also used in the text:

$$p_{ij} = \text{Pr}\{\text{an individual alive at age } x_i \text{ will survive to age } x_j\},$$

$$i \leqslant j; i, j = 0, 1, \ldots , \quad (1.1)$$

and

$$1 - p_{ij} = \text{Pr}\{\text{an individual alive at age } x_i \text{ will die before age } x_j\},$$

$$i \leqslant j; i, j = 0, 1, \ldots . \quad (1.2)$$

When $x_j = x_{i+1}$, we drop the second subscript and write p_i for $p_{i,i+1}$. No particular symbol is introduced for the probability $1 - p_{ij}$ except when $x_j = x_{i+1}$, in which case we write $1 - p_i = q_i$. Finally, the symbol e_i is used to denote the true (unknown) expectation of life at age x_i, estimated by the observed expectation of life, $\hat{e}_i$. (This is used more generally. A "hat" over a symbol indicates the *observed* value, which is an estimate of the true (un"hatted") value.)

All the quantities in the life table, except l_0 and a_i are treated as random variables in this chapter. The radix, l_0, is usually set equal to a convenient number, such as $l_0 = 100,000$, so that the value of l_i clearly indicates the proportion of survivors to age x_i. We therefore consider l_0 a constant in deriving the probability distributions of the other life table functions. The distributions of the quantities in columns L_i and T_i are not discussed because of their limited use. One remark should be made regarding the final age interval (x_w and over): In a conventional table the last interval is usually an open interval, e.g., 85 and over; statistically speaking, x_w is a random variable and is treated accordingly. Discussion of this point is given in Section 3.1. Throughout this chapter we shall assume a homogeneous population in which all individuals are subjected to the same force of mortality, and in which one individual's survival is independent of the survival of any other individual in the group.

2. The Probability Distribution of the Number of Survivors at Age x, l_x

The various elements in a life table are usually given for integral ages or for other discrete intervals. In the derivation of the distribution of survivors, however, age is more conveniently treated as a continuous variable so that the distribution of l_x, the number of individuals surviving to age x, is derived for all x.

The probability distribution of l_x depends on the force of mortality, or intensity of risk of death, $\mu(x)$, defined as follows:

$$\mu(x)\Delta + o(\Delta) = \text{Pr}\{\text{an individual alive at age } x \text{ will die}$$

$$\text{in interval } (x, x + \Delta)\}, \quad (2.1)$$

where $o(\Delta)$ refers to some function such that $\Delta \to 0$, the ratio $o(\Delta)/\Delta$ $\to 0$. Let the continuous random variable X be the life span of a person so that the distribution function

$$F_X(x) = \Pr\{X \leqslant x\}, \qquad x \geqslant 0, \tag{2.2}$$

is the probability that the individual will die prior to (or at) age x. Consider now the interval $(0, x + \Delta)$ and the corresponding distribution function $F_X(x + \Delta) = \Pr\{X \leqslant x + \Delta\}$. For an individual to die prior to $x + \Delta$ he must die prior to x or else he must survive to x and die during the interval $(x, x + \Delta)$. Therefore, we get the relation

$$F_X(x + \Delta) = F_X(x) + [1 - F_X(x)][\mu(x)\Delta + o(\Delta)] \tag{2.3}$$

or

$$\frac{F_X(x + \Delta) - F_X(x)}{\Delta} = [1 - F_X(x)]\left[\mu(x) + \frac{o(\Delta)}{\Delta}\right]. \tag{2.4}$$

Taking the limits of both sides of (2.4) as $\Delta \to 0$, we arrive at the differential equation

$$\frac{d}{dt} F_X(x) = [1 - F_X(x)]\mu(x) \quad \text{or} \quad \frac{F_X'(x)}{1 - F_x(x)} = \mu(x) \tag{2.5}$$

with the initial condition

$$F_X(0) = 0. \tag{2.6}$$

Integrating (2.5) and using (2.6) yield the solution

$$1 - F_X(x) = \exp\left(-\int_0^x \mu(t)\,dt\right) = p_{0x}, \qquad x \geqslant 0. \tag{2.7}$$

Equation (2.7) gives the probability that one individual alive at age 0 will survive to age x.

   If there are l_0 individuals alive at age 0 who are subject to the same force of mortality, the number l_x of survivors at age x is clearly a binomial random variable with the probability p_{0x} of surviving to x. The probability distribution of l_x is therefore

$$\Pr\{l_x = k\} = \frac{l_0!}{k!\,(l_0 - k)!}\, p_{0x}^k (1 - p_{0x})^{l_0 - k}, \qquad k = 0, 1, \ldots, l_0. \tag{2.8}$$

   For $x = x_i$, the probability that an individual will survive the age interval $(0, x_i)$ is

$$p_{0i} = \exp\left\{-\int_0^{x_i} \mu(\tau)\,d\tau\right\} \tag{2.9}$$

and the probability distribution of the number of survivors, l_i, is

$$\Pr\{l_i = k_i \mid l_0\} = \frac{l_0!}{k_i!\,(l_0 - k_i)!}\, p_{0i}^{k_i}(1 - p_{0i})^{l_0 - k_i},$$

$$k_i = 0, 1, \ldots, l_0. \quad (2.10)$$

The expected value and variance of l_i given l_0 are

$$E(l_i \mid l_0) = l_0 p_{0i} \qquad (2.11)$$

and

$$\mathrm{Var}(l_i \mid l_0) = l_0 p_{0i}(1 - p_{0i}), \qquad (2.12)$$

respectively [cf., pp. 39–41, Chapter 2, Section 3, on the binomial distribution].

In general, the probability of surviving the age interval (x_i, x_j) is

$$p_{ij} = \exp\left\{ -\int_{x_i}^{x_j} \mu(\tau)\,d\tau \right\}, \qquad \text{for} \quad i \leqslant j, \qquad (2.13)$$

with the obvious relation

$$p_{\alpha j} = p_{\alpha i} p_{ij}, \qquad \text{for} \quad \alpha \leqslant i \leqslant j. \qquad (2.14)$$

If we start with l_i individuals at x_i, the number of survivors l_j at x_j, for $i \leqslant j$, is also a binomial random variable with probability p_{ij} and probability distribution

$$\Pr\{l_j = k_j \mid l_i\} = \frac{l_i!}{k_j!\,(l_i - k_j)!}\, p_{ij}^{k_j}(1 - p_{ij})^{l_i - k_j}, \qquad k_j = 0, \ldots, l_i.$$

$$(2.15)$$

The expected value and the variance are given by

$$E(l_j \mid l_i) = l_i p_{ij} \qquad (2.16)$$

and

$$\mathrm{Var}(l_j \mid l_i) = l_i p_{ij}(1 - p_{ij}). \qquad (2.17)$$

When $j = i + 1$, (2.15) becomes

$$\Pr\{l_{i+1} = k_{i+1} \mid l_i\} = \frac{l_i!}{k_{i+1}!\,(l_i - k_{i+1})!}\, p_i^{k_{i+1}}(1 - p_i)^{l_i - k_{i+1}}. \quad (2.18)$$

It is intuitively clear (and follows from (2.13) and (2.14)) that given l_i people alive at age x_i, the probability distribution of the number of people alive at x_j, for $x_j > x_i$, is independent of l_0, $l_1, \ldots, l_{i-1}$. This means that for each k_j

$$\Pr\{l_j = k_j \mid l_0, l_1, \ldots, l_i\} = \Pr\{l_j = k_j \mid l_i\}. \qquad (2.19)$$

Consequently,

$$E(l_j | l_0, \ldots, l_i) = E(l_j | l_i),$$

and

$$\text{Var}(l_j | l_0, \ldots, l_i) = \text{Var}(l_j | l_i).$$

In other words, for each u, the sequence $l_0, l_1, \ldots, l_u$ is a Markov process.

2.1. Mortality laws. The survival probability in (2.7) has been known to students of the life table for more than two hundred years. Unfortunately, it has not received much recognition from investigators in statistics, although various forms of this function have appeared in diverse areas of research. We shall mention a few such forms below in terms of the probability density function of X,

$$f_X(x) = \frac{dF_X(x)}{dx} = \mu(x)\exp\left(-\int_0^x \mu(t)\,dt\right), \qquad x \geqslant 0. \quad (2.20)$$

(i) *Gompertz Distribution.* In a celebrated paper of the law of human mortality, Benjamin Gompertz [1825] attributed death to two causes: chance and the deterioration of the power to withstand destruction. In deriving his law of mortality, however, he considered only deterioration and assumed that an individual's resistance to death decreases at a rate proportional to the force of resistance itself. Since the force of mortality $\mu(t)$ is a measure of an individual's susceptibility to death, Gompertz used the reciprocal $1/\mu(t)$ as a measure of the resistance to death and thus arrived at the formula

$$\frac{d}{dt}\left(\frac{1}{\mu(t)}\right) = -h\frac{1}{\mu(t)}, \qquad (2.21)$$

or

$$\frac{d}{dt}\mu(t) = h\mu(t), \qquad (2.21a)$$

where h is a positive constant. Integrating (2.21a) gives

$$\log \mu(t) = ht + k, \qquad (2.22)$$

where "log" denotes the natural logarithm. Equation (2.22) when rearranged becomes the Gompertz law of mortality

$$\mu(t) = Bc^t, \qquad B > 0, \quad c > 0. \qquad (2.23)$$

The corresponding density function and distribution function are given, respectively, by

$$f(x) = Bc^x e^{-B[c^x - 1]/\log c} \qquad (2.24)$$

and

$$F_X(x) = 1 - \exp\left\{-\frac{B}{\log c}(c^x - 1)\right\}. \qquad (2.25)$$

(ii) *Makeham's distribution.* In 1860 W. M. Makeham suggested the modification

$$\mu(t) = A + Bc^t \qquad (2.26)$$

which restores the missing "chance" component to the Gompertz formula. In this case, we have

$$f(x) = [A + Bc^x]\exp\{-[Ax + B(c^x - 1)/\log c]\} \qquad (2.27)$$

and

$$F_X(x) = 1 - \exp\{-[Ax + B(c^x - 1)/\log c]\}. \qquad (2.28)$$

(iii) *Weibull distribution.* When the force of mortality is assumed to be a power function of t, $\mu(t) = \mu a t^{a-1}$, we have

$$f(x) = \mu a x^{a-1} e^{-\mu x^a} \qquad (2.29)$$

and

$$F_X(x) = 1 - e^{-\mu x^a}. \qquad (2.30)$$

This distribution, recommended by W. Weibull (1939) for studies of the life span of materials, is used extensively in reliability theory.

(iv) *Exponential distribution.* If $\mu(t) = \mu$ is a constant, then

$$f(x) = \mu e^{-\mu x} \qquad (2.31)$$

and

$$F_X(x) = 1 - e^{-\mu x} \qquad (2.32)$$

a formula that plays a central role in the problem of life testing (Epstein and Sobel (1953)).

3.   Joint Probability Distribution of the Numbers of Survivors

Let us consider, for a given u, the joint probability distribution of $l_1, l_2, \ldots, l_u$ given l_0,

$$\Pr\{l_1 = k_1, \ldots, l_u = k_u \mid l_0\}. \qquad (3.1)$$

It follows from the multiplication formula in page 8 and the Markovian property in equation (2.19) that

$$\Pr\{l_1 = k_1, l_2 = k_2, \ldots, l_u = k_u \mid l_0\}$$
$$= \Pr\{l_1 = k_1 \mid l_0\}\Pr\{l_2 = k_2 \mid k_1\} \ldots \Pr\{l_u = k_u \mid k_{u-1}\}. \quad (3.2)$$

Substituting (2.18) in (3.2) yields a chain of binomial distributions:

$$\Pr\{l_1 = k_1, l_2 = k_2, \ldots, l_u = k_u \mid l_0\}$$
$$= \prod_{i=0}^{u-1} \frac{k_i!}{k_{i+1}!\,(k_i - k_{i+1})!}\, p_i^{k_{i+1}}(1 - p_i)^{k_i - k_{i+1}},$$

$$\text{for} \quad k_{i+1} = 0, 1, \ldots, k_i, \quad \text{with} \quad k_0 = l_0. \quad (3.3)$$

Formula (3.3) shows that when a cohort of people is observed at regular points in time, x_i, the number of survivors to the end of the interval (x_i, x_{i+1}), l_{i+1}, has a binomial distribution depending solely on the number of individuals alive at the beginning of the interval $l_i = k_i$.

The covariance between l_i and l_j may be obtained directly from (3.3); a somewhat simpler approach is the following. By definition the covariance is

$$\mathrm{Cov}(l_i, l_j) = E(l_i l_j) - E(l_i)E(l_j) = E(l_i l_j) - (l_0 p_{0i})(l_0 p_{0j}) . \quad (3.4)$$

where

$$E(l_i l_j) = E\big[\, l_i E(l_j \mid l_i)\big] = E\big[\, l_i^2 p_{ij}\big] = E\big[\, l_i^2\big] p_{ij} . \quad (3.5)$$

Since l_i is a binomial random variable in l_0 trials with the probability p_{0i},

$$E\big[\, l_i^2\big] = l_0 p_{0i}(1 - p_{0i}) + \big[\, l_0 p_{0i}\big]^2. \quad (3.6)$$

Substituting (3.5) and (3.6) successively in (3.4) and using the relationship $p_{0i}p_{ij} = p_{0j}$, we have the formula for the covariance

$$\mathrm{Cov}(l_i, l_j) = l_0 p_{0j}(1 - p_{0i}), \qquad i \leqslant j; \quad i, j = 0, 1, \ldots, u. \quad (3.7)$$

When $j = i$, (3.7) is the variance of l_i in equation (2.12).

The correlation coefficient ρ_{l_i, l_j} for l_i and l_j is given by

$$\rho_{l_i, l_j} = \frac{p_{0j}(1 - p_{0i})}{\sqrt{p_{0i}(1 - p_{0i})p_{0j}(1 - p_{0j})}} = \sqrt{\frac{p_{0j}(1 - p_{0i})}{p_{0i}(1 - p_{0j})}} \quad (3.8)$$

which is always positive for $0 < i < j$. This means that the larger the number of individuals alive at x_i, the more survivors there are likely to be at x_j. For a given i, the correlation coefficient decreases as x_j

increases. Thus the effect of the former on the latter decreases when x_j becomes farther away from x_i. The above findings are summarized in the following theorem.

Theorem 1: *For a given u, the number of survivors $l_1, \ldots, l_u$ in the life table forms a chain of binomial distributions; the joint probability distribution, the expected values, covariances and correlation coefficients are given in (3.3), (2.11) (3.7), and (3.8) respectively.*

3.1.   An urn scheme. The life table functions can be generated from an entirely different approach. As an example, consider an experiment in which balls are drawn with replacement from an infinite sequence of urns, numbered $0, 1, \ldots$. In the i-th urn there is a proportion p_i of white balls and a proportion q_i of black balls with $0 < p_i < 1$ and $p_i + q_i = 1$. Beginning with the 0-th urn, a number l_0 of balls is drawn of which l_1 are white; then a total of l_1 balls are drawn from the first urn of which l_2 are white; l_2 balls are then drawn from the second urn of which l_3 are white, and so. In general, the number l_{i+1} of white balls from the i-th urn is the number of balls to be drawn from the next or the $(i+1)$-th urn. The experiment terminates as soon as no white balls are drawn. Let the last urn from which balls are drawn be the W-th urn, so that $l_i > 0$ for $i \leqslant W$ and $l_i = 0$ for $i > W$.

The correspondence between the urn scheme and the life table is evident. For example, l_0 is the initial size of the cohort, p_i (or q_i) is the probability of surviving (or dying in) an age interval, and l_i is the number of survivors at age x_i, $i = 0, 1, \ldots$. The number W corresponding to the beginning of the last age interval is also a random variable, which we shall now discuss.

To derive the probability distribution of W, we note that for $W = w$ there must be $l_w = k_w$ drawings from the w-th urn for $1 \leqslant k_w \leqslant l_0$ and all k_w balls drawn must be black balls. Therefore, we have the probability

$$\Pr\{ W = w \} = \sum_{k_w = 1}^{l_0} \frac{l_0!}{k_w! (l_0 - k_w)!} \, p_{0w}^{k_w} (1 - p_{0w})^{l_0 - k_w} (1 - p_w)^{k_w},$$

$$w = 0, 1, \ldots, \quad (3.9)$$

where, for convenience,

$$p_{0w} = p_0 p_1 \cdots p_{w-1}. \quad (3.10)$$

The expectation of W is more conveniently obtained if the probability in (3.9) is rewritten as

$$\Pr\{ W = w \} = (1 - p_{0,w+1})^{l_0} - (1 - p_{0w})^{l_0}, \quad (3.11)$$

which can be verified by direct computation. The expectation of W is now given by

$$E(W) = \sum_{w=0}^{\infty} w\left[(1 - p_{0,w+1})^{l_0} - (1 - p_{0w})^{l_0}\right]. \qquad (3.12)$$

For a given v, we write the partial sum

$$\sum_{w=0}^{v} w\left[(1 - p_{0,w+1})^{l_0} - (1 - p_{0w})^{l_0}\right]$$

$$= \sum_{w=1}^{v}\left[(1 - p_{0,v+1})^{l_0} - (1 - p_{0w})^{l_0}\right]. \qquad (3.13)$$

Letting $v \to \infty$ and $p_{0,v+1} \to 0$, we have from (3.13)

$$E(W) = \sum_{w=1}^{\infty}\left[1 - (1 - p_{0w})^{l_0}\right]. \qquad (3.14)$$

For $l_0 = 1$,

$$E(W) = p_{01} + p_{02} + p_{03} + \cdots \qquad (3.15)$$

which is closely related to the expectation of life e_0 (cf., equation (6.18) page 213).

If the force of mortality were independent of age, i.e., if $\mu(\tau) = \mu$ for $0 \leqslant \tau < \infty$, then the proportion of white balls in each urn would be constant with $p_i = p$. In this case $p_{0i} = p^i$,

$$\Pr\{W = w\} = (1 - p^{w+1})^{l_0} - (1 - p^w)^{l_0}$$

$$= \sum_{k=1}^{l_0} (-1)^{k+1} \frac{l_0!}{k!(l_0 - k)!}(1 - p^k)p^{wk}, \qquad (3.16)$$

and the expectation and the variance all have closed forms. Using (3.16) we compute the expectation

$$E(W) = \sum_{k=1}^{l_0} (-1)^{k+1} \frac{l_0!}{k!(l_0 - k)!}(1 - p^k)^{-1}p^k \qquad (3.17)$$

and variance

$$\text{Var}(W) = \sum_{k=1}^{l_0} (-1)^{k+1} \frac{l_0!}{k!(l_0 - k)!}(1 + p^k)(1 - p^k)^{-2}p^k$$

$$- [E(W)]^2. \qquad (3.18)$$

When $l_0 = 1$, W has the geometric distribution with

$$E(W) = \frac{p}{1 - p} \qquad (3.17a)$$

and

$$\text{Var}(W) = \frac{p}{(1-p)^2}. \qquad (3.18a)$$

4. Joint Probability Distribution of the Numbers of Deaths

In a life table covering the entire life span of each individual in a given population, the sum of the deaths at all ages is equal to the size of the original cohort. Symbolically,

$$d_0 + d_1 + \cdots + d_w = l_0, \qquad (4.1)$$

where d_w is the number of deaths in the age interval "x_w and over". Each individual in the original cohort has a probability $p_{0i}q_i$ of dying in the interval (x_i, x_{i+1}), $i = 0, 1, \ldots, w$. Since an individual dies once and only once in the span covered by the life table,

$$p_{00}q_0 + \cdots + p_{0w}q_w = 1, \qquad (4.2)$$

where $p_{00} = 1$ and $q_w = 1$. Equations (4.1) and (4.2) define a multinomial distribution. *Thus, the numbers of deaths, $d_0, \ldots, d_w$, in a life table have a joint probability distribution*

$$\Pr\{d_0 = \delta_0, \ldots, d_w = \delta_w\} = \frac{l_0!}{\delta_0! \ldots \delta_w!} (p_{00}q_0)^{\delta_0} \cdots (p_{0w}q_w)^{\delta_w};$$

$$(4.3)$$

the expectation, variance, and covariance are given, respectively, by

$$E(d_i \mid l_0) = l_0 p_{0i} q_i, \qquad (4.4)$$

$$\text{Var}(d_i) = l_0 p_{0i} q_i (1 - p_{0i} q_i), \qquad (4.5)$$

and

$$\text{Cov}(d_i, d_j) = -l_0 p_{0i} q_i p_{0j} q_j, \qquad (4.6)$$

for $i \neq j$; $i, j = 0, 1, \ldots, w$.

In the discussion above, age 0 was chosen only for simplicity. For any given age, say x_α, the probability that an individual alive at age x_α will die in a subsequent interval (x_i, x_{i+1}) is $p_{\alpha i}q_i$ and the sum

$$\sum_{i=\alpha}^{w} p_{\alpha i} q_i = 1, \qquad (4.7)$$

and thus the numbers of deaths in intervals beyond x_α also have a multinomial distribution.

5. Optimality Properties of $\hat{p}_j$ and $\hat{q}_j$*

The estimators $\hat{p}_j$ and $\hat{q}_j$ are complementary to one another,

$$\hat{p}_j + \hat{q}_j = 1, \qquad i = 0, 1, \ldots . \tag{5.1}$$

Therefore, they have the same optimality properties. We consider $\hat{p}_j$ in the following discussion.

5.1. Maximum likelihood estimator of p_j.

Let us introduce, for each individual in the cohort l_0, a sequence of random variables $\{\epsilon_i\}$ defined as follows:

$$\epsilon_i = 1 \qquad \text{if the individual dies in } (x_i, x_{i+1})$$
$$= 0 \qquad \text{otherwise} \tag{5.2}$$

with the corresponding probabilities

$$\Pr\{\epsilon_i = 1\} = p_{0i}q_i = p_{0i}(1 - p_i)$$
$$\Pr\{\epsilon_i = 0\} = 1 - p_{0i}(1 - p_i). \tag{5.3}$$

Clearly,

$$\sum_{i=0}^{\infty} \epsilon_i = 1$$

and

$$\Pr\{\epsilon_0 = 1\} + \Pr\{\epsilon_i = 1\} + \cdots = q_0 + p_0 q_1 + \cdots = 1. \tag{5.4}$$

This simply states that the probability is one that an individual alive at age x_0 will eventually die. The joint probability of the random variables in the sequence is

$$\prod_{i=0}^{\infty} \left[p_{0i}(1 - p_i) \right]^{\epsilon_i}. \tag{5.5}$$

For the entire cohort, there are l_0 sequences of random variables $\{\epsilon_{i\alpha}\}$, $\alpha = 1, \ldots, l_0$. For each α, let $f_\alpha(\epsilon_{i\alpha}; p_i)$ be the corresponding probability function,

$$f_\alpha(\epsilon_{i\alpha}; p_i) = \prod_{i=0}^{\infty} \left[p_{0i}(1 - p_i) \right]^{\epsilon_{i\alpha}} \qquad \text{for } \sum_{i=0}^{\infty} \epsilon_{i\alpha} = 1$$
$$= 0 \qquad\qquad\qquad \text{otherwise.} \tag{5.6}$$

Assuming that the survival of an individual is independent of other individuals, the l_0 sequences are stochastically independent; therefore,

---

*For a discussion on optimality properties of an estimate and on maximum likelihood estimators, see Section 7.

the joint probability distribution of the l_0 sequences is given by

$$f(\epsilon_{i\alpha}; p_i) = \prod_{\alpha=1}^{l_0} f_\alpha(\epsilon_{i\alpha}; p_i)$$

$$= \prod_{\alpha=1}^{l_0} \prod_{i=0}^{\infty} \left[p_{0i}(1 - p_i) \right]^{\epsilon_{i\alpha}}, \tag{5.7}$$

which is known as the likelihood function of the random variables $\epsilon_{i\alpha}$ for $i = 0, \ldots$ and $\alpha = 1, \ldots, l_0$. Making the substitution of

$$\sum_{\alpha=1}^{l_0} \epsilon_{i\alpha} = d_i, \tag{5.8}$$

we rewrite (5.7) as

$$L = f(\epsilon_{i\alpha}; p_i) = \prod_{i=0}^{\infty} \left[p_{0i}(1 - p_i) \right]^{d_i}. \tag{5.9}$$

Now the maximum-likelihood estimator is the collection of values $\hat{p}_0, \hat{p}_1, \ldots,$ for which the likelihood function (5.9) attains a maximum. In this case, the maximizing values can be obtained by differentiation. Writing the logarithm of (5.9) as

$$\log L = \log f(\epsilon_{i\alpha}; p_i) = \sum_{i=0}^{\infty} d_i \log\left[p_{0i}(1 - p_i) \right] \tag{5.10}$$

and setting the derivative of $\log L$ equal to zero, we have the equation

$$\frac{\partial}{\partial p_j} \log L = \frac{-d_j}{1 - p_j} + \frac{\sum_{i=j+1}^{\infty} d_i}{p_j} = 0, \qquad j = 0, 1, \ldots, \tag{5.11}$$

and the maximum-likelihood estimators

$$\hat{p}_j = \frac{\sum_{i=j+1}^{\infty} d_i}{\sum_{i=j}^{\infty} d_i} = \frac{l_{j+1}}{l_j}, \tag{5.12}$$

where

$$l_j = \sum_{i=j}^{\infty} d_i \tag{5.13}$$

is the number of survivors at age x_j. It should be noted that if all the l_w individuals alive at x_w die within the interval (x_w, x_{w+1}), then $\epsilon_{i\alpha} = 0$, $d_i = 0$, and $l_i = 0$ for all $i > w$, so that there is no contribution to the likelihood function beyond the w-th factor. Consequently, the maximum-likelihood estimator in (5.12) is defined only for $l_j > 0$, i.e., for $j \leqslant w$. With this understanding, let us compute the first two moments.

We have shown in Section 2 that, given $l_j > 0$, the number l_{j+1} has a binomial distribution; therefore

$$E[\hat{p}_j] = E\left(\frac{l_{j+1}}{l_j}\right) = E\left[\frac{1}{l_j}E(l_{j+1}\,|\,l_j)\right] = p_j. \qquad (5.14)$$

Thus $\hat{p}_j$ (and $\hat{q}_j$) are unbiased estimators of the corresponding probabilities. Direct computation gives also

$$E[\hat{p}_j^2] = E\left(\frac{1}{l_j}\right)p_j(1-p_j) + p_j^2 \qquad (5.15)$$

and the variance

$$\mathrm{Var}(\hat{p}_j) = E\left(\frac{1}{l_j}\right)p_j(1-p_j) = \mathrm{Var}(\hat{q}_j). \qquad (5.16)$$

When l_0 is large, (5.16) may be approximated by

$$\mathrm{Var}(\hat{p}_j) = \frac{1}{E(l_j)}\,p_j(1-p_j). \qquad (5.17)$$

Justification of (5.17) is left to the reader.

For the covariance between $\hat{p}_j$ and $\hat{p}_k$ for $j < k$, we require that l_k (and hence l_j and l_{j+1}) be positive and compute the conditional expectation

$$E[\hat{p}_k\,|\,\hat{p}_j] = E\left[\frac{l_{k+1}}{l_k}\,\Big|\,\hat{p}_j\right] = E\left[\frac{1}{l_k}E(l_{k+1}\,|\,l_k)\,|\,\hat{p}_j\right] = p_k = E(\hat{p}_k).$$

$$(5.18)$$

Hence it follows that

$$E[\hat{p}_j\hat{p}_k] = E[\hat{p}_jE(\hat{p}_k\,|\,\hat{p}_j)] = E[\hat{p}_j]E[\hat{p}_k]$$

and

$$\mathrm{Cov}(\hat{p}_j,\hat{p}_k) = 0. \qquad (5.19)$$

Therefore $\hat{p}_j$ and $\hat{p}_k$ have a zero correlation coefficient.

Observe that the formula (5.19) giving zero covariance holds only for non-overlapping age intervals. If both of the two intervals considered begin with age x_α but extend to the ages x_j and x_k, respectively, the covariance between the proportions $\hat{p}_{\alpha j}$ and $\hat{p}_{\alpha k}$ is not zero. An easy computation shows that

$$\mathrm{Cov}(\hat{p}_{\alpha j},\hat{p}_{\alpha k}) = E\left(\frac{1}{l_\alpha}\right)p_{\alpha k}(1-p_{\alpha j}), \qquad \alpha < j \leqslant k. \qquad (5.20)$$

This becomes the variance of $\hat{p}_{\alpha j}$, when $k = j$.

Although $\hat{p}_j$ and $\hat{p}_k$ have zero covariance, they are not independently distributed. The following proof is for the case where $j = 0$ and

$k = 1$. To prove that $\hat{p}_0$ and $\hat{p}_1$ are not independently distributed, it is sufficient to prove the inequality

$$E(\hat{p}_0^2)E(\hat{p}_1^2) > E(\hat{p}_0^2\hat{p}_1^2).\qquad(5.21)$$

In view of (5.15), the left hand side of (5.21) is

$$E\left(\frac{l_1^2}{l_0^2}\right)\left[E\left(\frac{1}{l_1}\right)p_1q_1 + p_1^2\right]\qquad(5.22)$$

and the right hand side of (5.21) can be written

$$E\left(\frac{l_1^2}{l_0^2}\left[\frac{1}{l_1}\,p_1q_1 + p_1^2\right]\right);\qquad(5.23)$$

therefore inequality (5.21) holds if, and only if,

$$E(l_1^2)E\left(\frac{1}{l_1}\right) > E(l_1).\qquad(5.24)$$

It can be shown that

$$E\left(\frac{1}{l_1}\right) > \frac{1}{E(l_1)}\;;$$

hence (5.21) holds if

$$E(l_1^2)\frac{1}{E(l_1)} > E(l_1)\qquad(5.25)$$

or if

$$E(l_1^2) - [E(l_1)]^2 > 0,\qquad(5.26)$$

which is always true since the left hand side is the variance of l_1, proving (5.21) and the assertion that $\hat{p}_0$ and $\hat{p}_1$ are not independently distributed.

5.2. Cramér–Rao lower bound for the variance of an unbiased estimator of p_j.

In (5.16) we have the exact formula for the variance of $\hat{p}_j$. We now determine the lower limit for the variance of an unbiased estimator. Let $\tilde{p}_j$ be any unbiased estimator of p_j. According to the theorem by Cramér and Rao, the variance of $\tilde{p}_j$ satisfies the inequality*

$$\mathrm{Var}(\tilde{p}_j) \geqslant \frac{1}{-E\left((\partial^2/\partial p_j^2)\log L\right)}\qquad(5.27)$$

---

*It should be pointed out that when the parameters p_j, $j = 0, 1, \ldots$, are estimated jointly, the lower bound is a function of the expectations $E(\partial^2\log L/\partial p_j^2)$ and $E(\partial^2\log L/\partial p_j\partial p_k)$, $j, k = 0, 1, \ldots$. Formula (5.27), however, is correct, because in the present case the expectations of the "mixed" partial derivatives vanish whenever $j \neq k$.

where $\log L$ is the logarithm of the likelihood function defined in (5.10). First let us sketch the proof of (5.27).

The derivative $\partial \log L / \partial p_j$ is obviously a random variable; we compute the expectations

$$E\left[\frac{\partial}{\partial p_j} \log L\right] = E\left[\frac{1}{L} \frac{\partial}{\partial p_j} L\right] = \frac{\partial}{\partial p_j} E[1] = 0 \qquad (5.28)$$

and

$$E\left[\frac{\partial^2}{\partial p_j^2} \log L\right] = E\left[\frac{1}{L} \frac{\partial^2}{\partial p_j^2} L - \left(\frac{1}{L} \frac{\partial}{\partial p_j} L\right)^2\right]$$

$$= \frac{\partial^2}{\partial p_j^2} E[1] - E\left[\left(\frac{\partial}{\partial p_j} \log L\right)^2\right]$$

$$= - E\left[\left(\frac{\partial}{\partial p_j} \log L\right)^2\right], \qquad (5.29)$$

from which we have the variance of $\partial \log L / \partial p_j$

$$\mathrm{Var}\left(\frac{\partial}{\partial p_j} \log L\right) = E\left[\left(\frac{\partial}{\partial p_j} \log L\right)^2\right] = - E\left[\frac{\partial^2}{\partial p_j^2} \log L\right]. \quad (5.30)$$

Since $\tilde{p}_j$ is an unbiased estimator of p_j, the covariance between $\tilde{p}_j$ and $\partial \log L / \partial p_j$ is unity, as shown by the following computation

$$\mathrm{Cov}\left(\tilde{p}_j, \frac{\partial}{\partial p_j} \log L\right) = E\left[\tilde{p}_j \frac{\partial}{\partial p_j} \log L\right] = E\left[\tilde{p}_j \frac{1}{L} \frac{\partial}{\partial p_j} L\right]$$

$$= \frac{\partial}{\partial p_j} E[\tilde{p}_j] = \frac{\partial}{\partial p_j} p_j = 1. \qquad (5.31)$$

Since the square of the covariance between two random variables cannot exceed the product of the two variances, we have

$$\mathrm{Var}(\tilde{p}_j)\mathrm{Var}\left(\frac{\partial}{\partial p_j} \log L\right) \geqslant 1. \qquad (5.32)$$

Substituting (5.30) in (5.32) gives (5.27) and the proof is complete.

In the present case

$$- E\left[\frac{\partial^2}{\partial p_j^2} \log L\right] = \frac{l_0 p_{0j}}{p_j(1 - p_j)} \qquad (5.33)$$

and the lower bound is

$$\frac{1}{l_0 p_{0j}} p_j(1 - p_j). \qquad (5.34)$$

The difference between the lower bound in (5.34) and the exact formula (5.16) lies in the difference between $1/l_0 p_{0j}$ and $E(1/l_j)$.

Therefore, relative to the lower bound, the efficiency of $\hat{p}_j$ is $[l_0 p_{0j} E(1/l_j)]^{-1}$. However, we shall show in the next section that the maximum-likelihood estimator $\hat{p}_j$ given in (5.12) has the minimum variance of all the unbiased estimators of p_j; thus the lower bound cannot be attained in this case.

5.3. Sufficiency and efficiency of $\hat{p}_j$. We first define *sufficient statistic* in general terms. Let $X_1, \ldots, X_n$ be a sample of random variables with the joint probability (density) function $f(x_1, \ldots, x_n; \theta_1, \ldots, \theta_r)$ depending upon unknown parameters $\theta_1, \ldots, \theta_r$. Functions $T_k = T_k(X_1, \ldots, X_n)$, $k = 1, \ldots, r$, are called joint sufficient statistics for $\theta_1, \ldots, \theta_r$ if and only if the joint probability (density) function $f(x_1, \ldots, x_n; \theta_1, \ldots, \theta_r)$ can be factored as follows:

$$f(x_1, \ldots, x_n; \theta_1, \ldots, \theta_r)$$
$$= g(T_1, \ldots, T_r; \theta_1, \ldots, \theta_r) h(x_1, \ldots, x_n; T_1, \ldots, T_r) \quad (5.35)$$

where g is a function of both the sufficient statistics and the parameters, whereas h is independent of the parameters. This factorization shows that, given the sufficient statistics $T_1, \ldots, T_r$, any function of $x_1, \ldots, x_n$ adds no further information about the parameters $\theta_1, \ldots, \theta_r$. In other words, sufficient statistics exhaust all the information about the parameters contained in the sample. The concept of sufficient statistic was introduced by Fisher (1922) and the above factorization was developed by Neyman (1935). For a detailed discussion on sufficiency and other optimality properties of estimators, the reader should consult Lehmann (1959), Hogg and Craig (1965), Kendall and Stuart (1961), and other standard textbooks in statistics.

In the present case, the random variables are $\epsilon_{i\alpha}$ and the parameters are $p_0, p_1, \ldots$; the joint probability of $\epsilon_{i\alpha}$ is given in (5.7) or (5.9),

$$f(\epsilon_{i\alpha}; p_i) = \prod_{i=0}^{\infty} \left[p_{0i}(1 - p_i) \right]^{d_i}. \quad (5.9)$$

Using the relation $l_i = d_i + d_{i+1} + \cdots$, we rewrite (5.9) as

$$f(\epsilon_{i\alpha}; p_i) = \prod_{i=0}^{\infty} (1 - p_i)^{d_i} p_i^{l_{i+1}} \quad (5.36)$$

which is easily factored:

$$f(\epsilon_{i\alpha}; p_i) = g(l_i; p_i) h(\epsilon_{i\alpha}; l_i) \quad (5.37)$$

where

$$g(l_i; p_i) = \prod_{i=0}^{\infty} \frac{l_i!}{(l_i - l_{i+1})! \, l_{i+1}!} (1 - p_i)^{l_i - l_{i+1}} p_i^{l_{i+1}} \quad (5.38)$$

and

$$h(\epsilon_{i\alpha}, l_i) = \prod_{i=0}^{\infty} \frac{(\sum_{\alpha=1}^{l_0} \epsilon_{i\alpha})! \, (l_i - \sum_{\alpha=1}^{l_0} \epsilon_{i\alpha})!}{l_i!} . \quad (5.39)$$

According to the Fisher–Neyman factorization criterion, the statistics l_i are jointly sufficient for p_i, $i = 0, 1, \ldots$.

We want to show that, for any unbiased estimator $\tilde{p}_j$ of p_j,

$$\mathrm{Var}(\tilde{p}_j) \geqslant \mathrm{Var}(\hat{p}_j), \quad (5.40)$$

and the equality sign holds if and only if $\tilde{p}_j = \hat{p}_j$. To prove (5.40) we note that, since l_j and l_{j+1} are sufficient statistics for p_j, the conditional expectation

$$E(\tilde{p}_j \mid l_j, l_{j+1}) = \theta(l_j, l_{j+1}) \quad (5.41)$$

is independent of p_j. Since $\tilde{p}_j$ is unbiased, we have

$$p_j = E(\tilde{p}_j) = E\big[E(\tilde{p}_j \mid l_j, l_{j+1})\big] = E\big[\theta(l_j, l_{j+1})\big] \quad (5.42)$$

for any value $0 \leqslant p_j \leqslant 1$. Now if we restrict l_j to positive values only, then the joint probability distribution of l_j and l_{j+1} is

$$\frac{1}{1 - (1 - p_{0j})^{l_0}} \left[\binom{l_0}{l_j} p_{0j}^{l_j} (1 - p_{0j})^{l_0 - l_j} \right] \left[\binom{l_j}{l_{j+1}} p_j^{l_{j+1}} (1 - p_j)^{l_j - l_{j+1}} \right],$$

$$(5.43)$$

for $l_j = 1, 2, \ldots, l_0$ and $l_{j+1} = 0, 1, \ldots, l_j$. Substituting (5.43) in (5.42) yields the identity

$$p_j \equiv \sum_{l_j=1}^{l_0} \sum_{l_{j+1}=0}^{l_j} \frac{\theta(l_j, l_{j+1})}{1 - (1 - p_{0j})^{l_0}} \left[\binom{l_0}{l_j} p_{0j}^{l_j} (1 - p_{0j})^{l_0 - l_j} \right]$$

$$\times \left[\binom{l_j}{l_{j+1}} p_j^{l_{j+1}} (1 - p_j)^{l_j - l_{j+1}} \right]. \quad (5.44)$$

Since (5.44) is an identity in p_j, it has the unique solution

$$\theta(l_j, l_{j+1}) = \frac{l_{j+1}}{l_j} \quad (5.45)$$

meaning that

$$E\big[\tilde{p}_j \mid l_j, l_{j+1}\big] = \hat{p}_j . \quad (5.46)$$

The variance of $\tilde{p}_j$ can now be computed:

$$\mathrm{Var}(\tilde{p}_j) = E(\tilde{p}_j - p_j)^2 = E\big[(\tilde{p}_j - \hat{p}_j) + (\hat{p}_j - p_j)\big]^2$$

$$= E(\tilde{p}_j - \hat{p}_j)^2 + E(\hat{p}_j - p_j)^2 + 2E(\tilde{p}_j - \hat{p}_j)(\hat{p}_j - p_j), \quad (5.47)$$

where the expectation of the cross product

$$E(\tilde{p}_j - \hat{p}_j)(\hat{p}_j - p_j) = E\left[E(\tilde{p}_j - \hat{p}_j)(\hat{p}_j - p_j) | l_j, l_{j+1}\right]$$
$$= E\left[E\{(\tilde{p}_j - \hat{p}_j) | l_j, l_{j+1}\}(\hat{p}_j - p_j)\right] = 0. \quad (5.48)$$

Therefore,

$$\mathrm{Var}(\tilde{p}_j) = E(\tilde{p}_j - \hat{p}_j)^2 + \mathrm{Var}(\hat{p}_j) \qquad (5.49)$$

and

$$\mathrm{Var}(\tilde{p}_j) > \mathrm{Var}(\hat{p}_j), \qquad (5.50)$$

which was to be shown. The two variances are equal only in the case when $\tilde{p}_j = \hat{p}_j$. Thus we have the following theorem.

Theorem 2. *The estimators $\hat{p}_j$ and $\hat{q}_j$ in the life table are the unique, unbiased, efficient maximum likelihood estimators of the corresponding probabilities p_j and q_j.*

6. Distribution of the Observed Expectation of Life at Age x_α, $\hat{e}_\alpha$

The observed expectation of life summarizes the mortality experience of a population from a given age to the end of the life span. At age x_i the expectation expresses the average number of years remaining to an individual living at that age if all individuals are subjected to the estimated probabilities of death $\hat{q}_j$ for $j \geq i$. This is certainly the most useful column in the life table.

Consider a given age x_α, and the corresponding observed expectation of life at age x_α, $\hat{e}_\alpha$. Let Y_α denote the future lifetime beyond age x_α of a particular individual. We have shown in equation (2.9), Chapter 9, that $\hat{e}_\alpha$ is the sample mean of future lifetime beyond x_α of the l_α individuals. That is,

$$\hat{e}_\alpha = \bar{Y}_\alpha. \qquad (6.1)$$

According to the central limit theorem in Chapter 3, the observed expectation of life $\hat{e}_\alpha$ has a normal distribution with the expectation

$$E(\hat{e}_\alpha) = E(Y_\alpha) \qquad (6.2)$$

and the variance (cf., equation (5.16) in Section 5)

$$\mathrm{Var}(\hat{e}_\alpha) = E\left(\frac{1}{l_\alpha}\right)\mathrm{Var}(Y_\alpha). \qquad (6.3)$$

It is therefore sufficient to discuss the distribution of Y_α instead of the distribution of $\hat{e}_\alpha$.

Clearly, Y_α is a continuous random variable that may take on any non-negative real number. For a given individual, let y_α be the value that the random variable Y_α assumes; then $x_\alpha + y_\alpha$ is the entire life span of the individual. Let $f(Y_\alpha)$ be the probability density function of the random variable Y_α, and let dy_α be an infinitesimal time interval. Since Y_α can assume values between y_α and $y_\alpha + dy_\alpha$ if and only if the individual survives the age interval $(x_\alpha, x_\alpha + y_\alpha)$ and dies in the interval $(x_\alpha + y_\alpha, x_\alpha + y_\alpha + dy_\alpha)$, we have

$$f(y_\alpha)\,dy_\alpha = \exp\left(-\int_{x_\alpha}^{x_\alpha + y_\alpha} \mu(\tau)\,d\tau\right)\mu(x_\alpha + y_\alpha)\,dy_\alpha, \qquad y_\alpha \geqslant 0. \quad (6.4)$$

The function $f(y_\alpha)$ in (6.4) is a proper probability density function since it is never negative and since the integral of the function from $y_\alpha = 0$ to $y_\alpha = \infty$ is equal to unity. To check this, we evaluate the integral

$$\int_0^\infty f(y_\alpha)\,dy_\alpha = \int_0^\infty \exp\left(-\int_{x_\alpha}^{x_\alpha + y_\alpha} \mu(\tau)\,d\tau\right)\mu(x_\alpha + y_\alpha)\,dy_\alpha. \quad (6.5)$$

We define a quantity Φ

$$\Phi = \int_{x_\alpha}^{x_\alpha + y_\alpha} \mu(\tau)\,d\tau = \int_0^{y_\alpha} \mu(x_\alpha + t)\,dt \quad (6.6)$$

and substitute the differential

$$d\Phi = \mu(x_\alpha + y_\alpha)\,dy_\alpha \quad (6.7)$$

in the integral to give the solution

$$\int_0^\infty f(y_\alpha)\,dy_\alpha = \int_0^\infty e^{-\Phi}\,d\Phi = 1. \quad (6.8)$$

The mathematical expectation of the random variable Y_α is the expected length of life beyond age x_α, and thus is the true expectation of life at age x_α. In accordance with the definition given the symbol e_α, we may write

$$e_\alpha = \int_0^\infty y_\alpha f(y_\alpha)\,dy_\alpha = \int_0^\infty y_\alpha \exp\left(-\int_{x_\alpha}^{x_\alpha + y_\alpha} \mu(\tau)\,d\tau\right)\mu(x_\alpha + y_\alpha)\,dy_\alpha.$$

$$(6.9)$$

Thus the expectation e_α and the variance

$$\sigma_{Y_\alpha}^2 = \int_0^\infty (y_\alpha - e_\alpha)^2 f(y_\alpha)\,dy_\alpha \quad (6.10)$$

both depend on the force of mortality $\mu(\tau)$.

The expectation of life at age x_α is conventionally defined as

$$e_\alpha = \int_0^\infty \exp\left(-\int_{x_\alpha}^{x_\alpha + y_\alpha} \mu(\tau)\,d\tau\right)dy_\alpha. \quad (6.11)$$

It is instructive to prove that the two definitions (6.9) and (6.11) are identical. To integrate (6.9) by parts, let $u = y_\alpha$, $du = dy_\alpha$,

$$v = -\exp\left(-\int_{x_\alpha}^{x_\alpha + y_\alpha} \mu(\tau)\, d\tau\right) \tag{6.12}$$

and

$$dv = \exp\left(-\int_{x_\alpha}^{x_\alpha + y_\alpha} \mu(\tau)\, d\tau\right) \mu(x_\alpha + y_\alpha)\, dy_\alpha. \tag{6.13}$$

The integration then yields:

$$\int_0^\infty y_\alpha \exp\left(-\int_{x_\alpha}^{x_\alpha + y_\alpha} \mu(\tau)\, d\tau\right) \mu(x_\alpha + y_\alpha)\, dy_\alpha$$

$$= -y_\alpha \exp\left(-\int_{x_\alpha}^{x_\alpha + y_\alpha} \mu(\tau)\, d\tau\right) \Big|_0^\infty$$

$$+ \int_0^\infty \exp\left(-\int_{x_\alpha}^{x_\alpha + y_\alpha} \mu(\tau)\, d\tau\right) dy_\alpha. \tag{6.14}$$

The first term on the right vanishes and the second term is the same as (6.11) proving that the two formulas of e_α in (6.9) and (6.11) are identical.

The formula for $\hat{e}_\alpha$ in a life table is

$$\hat{e}_\alpha = \frac{L_\alpha + L_{\alpha+1} + \cdots + L_w}{l_\alpha} \tag{6.15}$$

or, as shown on page 162,

$$\hat{e}_\alpha = a_\alpha n_\alpha + \sum_{j=\alpha+1}^{w} c_j \hat{p}_{\alpha j} \tag{6.16}$$

where

$$c_j = (1 - a_{j-1})n_{j-1} + a_j n_j \tag{6.17}$$

and a_j is the fraction of the last age interval of life for interval (x_j, x_{j+1}) and n_j is the length of the interval. Since $\hat{p}_{\alpha j}$ is an unbiased estimate of the probability $p_{\alpha j}$, the expectation of $\hat{e}_\alpha$ is also given by

$$e_\alpha = a_\alpha n_\alpha + \sum_{j=\alpha+1}^{w} c_j p_{\alpha j}, \tag{6.18}$$

which is equivalent to the expectation in (6.9).

The formula for the variance of $\hat{e}_\alpha$ is given in (6.3), or using (6.10),

$$\mathrm{Var}(\hat{e}_\alpha) = E\left(\frac{1}{l_\alpha}\right) \int_0^\infty (y_\alpha - e_\alpha)^2 f(y_\alpha)\, dy_\alpha. \tag{6.19}$$

Since $\hat{e}_\alpha$ is a linear function of $\hat{p}_{\alpha j}$, we can derive another expression for the variance of $\hat{e}_\alpha$ by following the derivation of the sample variance of $\hat{e}_\alpha$ for the current life table in Chapter 8, pages 162 to 163. The final formula is similar. Taking the derivative of $\hat{e}_\alpha$ in (6.16) with respect to $\hat{p}_i$ and simplifying yield the formula:

$$\text{Var}(\hat{e}_\alpha) = \sum_{i=\alpha}^{w-1} p_{\alpha i}^2 \left[(1 - a_i)n_i + e_{i+1}\right]^2 \text{Var}(\hat{p}_i), \qquad (6.20)$$

where

$$\text{Var}(\hat{p}_i) = E\left(\frac{1}{l_i}\right) p_i q_i. \qquad (6.21)$$

Thus we have:

Theorem 3. *If the distribution of deaths in the age interval (x_i, x_{i+1}) is such that, on the average, each of the d_i individuals lives $a_i n_i$ years in the interval, for $i = \alpha, \alpha + 1, \ldots, w$, then for large l_α the probability distribution of $\hat{e}_\alpha$, the observed expectation of life at age x_α, as given by (6.15), is asymptotically normal and has mean and variance given by (6.18) and (6.20), respectively.*

7. Maximum Likelihood Estimation—An Appendix

To help the reader better understand the material in this Chapter, a brief review of the method of maximum-likelihood estimation and the concept of optimality properties of an estimator is presented. For simplicity, our discussion will be confined to independent and identically distributed (i.i.d.) random variables, but argument holds equally well when the random variables are dependent.

Let $X_1, \ldots, X_n$ be a sample of random variables from the same distribution having the density function $f(x; \theta)$, where θ is the parameter to be estimated. The joint density function of $X_1, \ldots, X_n$ is called the likelihood function, or

$$L(\theta; x) = f(x_1; \theta) \cdots f(x_n; \theta), \qquad (7.1)$$

where L is a function of θ. For discrete distributions, $f(x; \theta)$ is a probability function.

A statistic $\hat{\theta}(x_1, \ldots, x_n)$ is called a maximum-likelihood estimator of θ if the function $L(\hat{\theta}; x)$ is a maximum. Thus, the principle of maximum-likelihood is to find a function $\hat{\theta}$ of $(x_1, \ldots, x_n)$ for which the likelihood function L attains a maximum. Since a maximizing value of L also maximizes the logarithm of L, for convenience, we usually determine a maximum likelihood estimator from the equation

$$\frac{d}{d\theta} \log L(\theta; x) = 0, \qquad (7.2)$$

which is known as the maximum-likelihood equation. If a distribution involves two parameters, $f(x; \theta_1, \theta_2)$, then the likelihood function (7.1) will contain two parameters, and there will be two simultaneous equations in (7.2).

A maximum-likelihood estimator, however, does not always exist and equation (7.2) may have more than one solution. But, a unique maximum likelihood estimator does exist in many well-known distributions to render this method of estimation practical. A few examples will help to illustrate the procedure of finding estimators.

Example 1. Let $X_1, \ldots, X_n$ be a sample of i.i.d. dichotomous variables with the probability function

$$\Pr\{X_i = 1\} = p \quad \text{and} \quad \Pr\{X_i = 0\} = 1 - p, \qquad i = 1, \ldots, n.$$
$$(7.3)$$

For the purpose of estimation, this probability function is rewritten as

$$f(x_i; p) = p^{x_i}(1 - p)^{1 - x_i}, \qquad i = 1, \ldots, n, \qquad (7.4)$$

so that the likelihood function has the simple form,

$$L(p; \mathbf{x}) = \prod_{i=1}^{n} f(x_i; p) = p^{\Sigma x_i}(1 - p)^{\Sigma(1 - x_i)}. \qquad (7.5)$$

The sum Σx_i, the total number of 1's in the sample, is a binomial random variable. The logarithm of the likelihood function is

$$\log L(p, x) = \sum_{i=1}^{n} x_i \log p + \sum_{i=1}^{n} (1 - x_i) \log(1 - p). \qquad (7.6)$$

Taking the derivative of the log likelihood function as in (7.6) gives the likelihood equation

$$\frac{1}{\hat{p}} \sum_{i=1}^{n} x_i - \frac{1}{1 - \hat{p}} \sum_{i=1}^{n} (1 - x_i) = 0, \qquad (7.7)$$

and the maximum-likelihood estimator of p,

$$\hat{p} = \frac{1}{n} \sum_{i=1}^{n} x_i. \qquad (7.8)$$

Therefore, the sample proportion is the maximum likelihood estimator of the probability, p.

Example 2. Let $X_1, \ldots, X_n$ be a sample of n i.i.d. random variables from a normal distribution with the density function

$$f(x; \theta) = \frac{1}{\sqrt{2\pi}} e^{-(x - \theta)^2/2}. \qquad (7.9)$$

The likelihood function is

$$L(\theta; \mathbf{x}) = \left(\frac{1}{\sqrt{2\pi}}\right)^n \exp\left(-\sum_{i=1}^{n} (x_i - \theta)^2/2\right) \qquad (7.10)$$

and its logarithm is

$$\log L(\theta; \mathbf{x}) = -n \log\sqrt{2\pi} - \frac{1}{2} \sum_{i=1}^{n} (x_i - \theta)^2. \qquad (7.11)$$

The maximum-likelihood equation

$$\frac{d}{d\theta} \log L(\theta; \mathbf{x}) = 0$$

has the unique solution:

$$\hat{\theta} = \frac{1}{n} \sum_{i=1}^{n} x_i = \overline{X}. \qquad (7.12)$$

Thus the sample mean is the maximum likelihood estimator of the population mean in the normal distribution.

Example 3. If the density function in Example 2 is replaced by

$$f(x; \theta_1, \theta_2) = \frac{1}{\sqrt{2\pi\theta_2}} e^{-(x-\theta_1)^2/2\theta_2}, \qquad (7.13)$$

then the logarithm of the likelihood function contains two parameters, the mean θ_1 and the variance θ_2;

$$\log L(\theta_1, \theta_2; \mathbf{x}) = -n \log\sqrt{2\pi} - \frac{n}{2} \log\theta_2 - \sum_{i=1}^{n} (x_i - \theta_1)^2/2\theta_2. \qquad (7.14)$$

Differentiating (7.14) with respect to θ_1 and θ_2, respectively, yields two simultaneous equations:

$$\frac{\partial}{\partial\theta_1} \log L = 0: \qquad \sum_{i=1}^{n} (x_i - \hat{\theta}_1) = 0$$

$$\frac{\partial}{\partial\theta_2} \log L = 0: \qquad n\hat{\theta}_2 - \sum_{i=1}^{n} (x_i - \hat{\theta}_1)^2 = 0. \qquad (7.15)$$

The solutions are

$$\hat{\theta}_1 = \overline{X}, \qquad (7.16)$$

and

$$\hat{\theta}_2 = \frac{1}{n} \sum_{i=1}^{n} (x_i - \overline{X})^2. \qquad (7.17)$$

Example 4. Let $X_1, \ldots, X_n$ be a sample from the exponential distribution:

$$f(x; \theta) = \theta e^{-\theta x}. \qquad (7.18)$$

The log likelihood function is

$$\log L(\theta; \mathbf{x}) = n \log \theta - \theta \sum_{i=1}^{n} x_i, \qquad (7.19)$$

and the derivative is

$$\frac{d}{d\theta} \log L(\theta; \mathbf{x}) = \frac{n}{\theta} - \sum_{i=1}^{n} x_i.$$

Setting the derivative equal to zero yields the maximum likelihood estimator

$$\hat{\theta} = \frac{1}{\bar{X}}. \qquad (7.20)$$

7.1. Optimality properties of an estimator.

Unbiasedness. An estimator $\hat{\theta}(X_1, \ldots, X_n)$ is said to be unbiased if the expectation $E[\hat{\theta}(X_1, \ldots, X_n)] = \theta$. In example 2, the sample mean is an unbiased estimator of the population mean, but the estimator of the variance in (7.17) is a biased estimator, since

$$E\left[\frac{1}{n} \sum_{i=1}^{n} (X_i - \bar{X})^2 \right] = \frac{n-1}{n} \theta_2.$$

An unbiased estimator of the variance is

$$S^2 = \frac{1}{n-1} \sum_{i=1}^{n} (X_i - \bar{X})^2.$$

Since the factor $(n-1)/n \to 1$, as $n \to \infty$, the bias of (7.17) is negligible for large n. Generally, a maximum likelihood estimator is unbiased, at least asymptotically.

Consistency. An estimator $\hat{\theta}_n$ is said to be consistent if it converges in probability to the true value θ_0 of the parameter; symbolically, if, for any $\epsilon > 0$,

$$\lim_{n \to \infty} \Pr\{|\hat{\theta}_n - \theta_0| < \epsilon\} = 1.$$

The maximum-likelihood estimator is consistent.

Efficiency (minimum-variance). A maximum likelihood estimator is efficient in the sense that it has a variance as small or smaller than the variance of any other estimator. If $\hat{\theta}$ is a maximum likelihood (unbiased) estimator and $\tilde{\theta}$ is any other (unbiased) estimator, then

$$V(\hat{\theta}) \leqslant V(\tilde{\theta}).$$

Asymptotic normality.   When the sample size n is sufficiently large, the distribution of the maximum likelihood estimator $\hat{\theta}_n$ is approximately normal with mean θ and variance

$$V(\hat{\theta}_n) = \frac{1}{-E\left[(d^2/d\theta^2)\log L(\theta;X)\right]} . \tag{7.21}$$

Example 5.   In Example 1 on dichotomous variables, we take the second derivative of the log likelihood function of (7.6) to find

$$E\left[\frac{d^2}{d\theta^2}\log L(\theta:X)\right] = -\frac{n}{p(1-p)} .$$

Therefore, the asymptotic variance of the estimator $\hat{p}$ is

$$\sigma^2 = \frac{p(1-p)}{n} . \tag{7.22}$$

8. Problems for Solution

1.   Find the expected value and the variance of the Weibull distribution in (2.29), page 199.

2.   Find the expected value and the variance of the exponential distribution in (2.31), page 199.

3.   Derive the formulas for the expectation of l_j in (2.16) and the variance of l_j in (2.17) directly from the probability distribution (2.15), page 197.

4.   Derive the formula for the covariance of l_i and l_j in (3.4) directly from the joint probability distribution in (3.3), page 200.

5.   Derive the formulas for the expected value in (4.4), the variance in (4.5), and the covariance in (4.6) from the probability distribution in (4.3), page 203.

6.   Find the maximum-likelihood estimator of p_i from the likelihood function in (5.9), page 205.

7.   Derive the formula for the covariance of $\hat{p}_{\alpha j}$ and $\hat{p}_{\alpha k}$ in (5.20), page 206.

8.   Prove that $\theta(l_j, l_{j+1}) = l_{j+1}/l_j$ in (5.45), page 210, is a solution of the identity (5.44) and that it is the only solution of (5.44).

9.   Let L be the likelihood function of the number of deaths

$$L = \frac{l_0!}{d_0!d_1!d_2!l_3!}(p_{00}q_0)^{d_0}(p_{01}q_1)^{d_1}(p_{02}q_2)^{d_2}P_{03}^{l_3}.$$

Find the maximum-likelihood estimator $\hat{p}_1$ of p_1 and the asymptotic variance of $\hat{p}_1$.

10. Show that $\hat{p}_i$ and $\hat{p}_{i+1}$ are not linearly correlated.

11. Verify the formula for the variance of the expectation of life $\hat{e}_\alpha$ in (6.20), page 214.

12. Derive the formula for the covariance of $\hat{e}_1$ and $\hat{e}_2$.

13. In arriving at inequality (5.25), we used the fact that if X (or l_1) is a positive random variable, then

$$E\left(\frac{1}{X}\right) > \frac{1}{E(X)}.$$

Prove the above inequality.

14. Show that the sample variance

$$S^2 = \frac{1}{n-1} \sum_{i=1}^{n} (X_i - \bar{X})^2$$

in Section 7.1 is an unbiased estimate of the variance of X.

15. Find the asymptotic variance of the estimate $\hat{\theta} = 1/\bar{X}$ in (7.20) for the exponential distribution in (7.18).

16. Find the asymptotic variance of the estimate $\hat{\theta}_1 = \bar{X}$ in (7.16) for the normal distribution in (7.13) if the variance θ_2 is known.

CHAPTER *11*

Medical Follow-up Studies

1. Introduction

Medical follow-up studies and life testing have as their common immediate objective the estimation of life expectancy and survival rates for a defined population at risk. Such studies usually must be terminated before all survival information is complete and therefore are said to be truncated. The nature of the problem in an investigation concerned with the follow-up of patients is the same as in the life testing of such items as light bulbs, although differences in sample size may prefer different approaches. For illustration, we will look at some cancer survival data of a large sample and will use terminology consistent with that of a typical medical follow-up study.

In a typical follow-up study, a group of individuals with some common morbidity experience is followed from a well-defined initial point, such as the date of hospital admission. The purpose of such a study is typically to evaluate a certain therapeutic measure by comparing the expectation of life and survival rates of treated patients with those of untreated patients, or by comparing the expectation of life of treated and presumably cured patients with that of the general population. When the period of observation ends, there will usually remain a number of individuals for whom the mortality data are incomplete. Some patients will withdraw from the study due to termination of observation (e.g., the study ends); some patients will be lost to the study because of follow-up failure; some patients will have died from causes other than those under study so that the chance of dying from the specific cause cannot be determined directly. The difference between withdrawals and lost cases is obvious. Every patient is subject to the risk of being lost at any time during the study period, but withdrawal can occur only in a particular interval determined by the time of entrance to the study and the time of termination of observation.

In any event, the above three sources of incomplete information create interesting statistical problems in the estimation of survival probability and the expectation of life. Many contributions have been made to methods of analysis of follow-up data. They include the studies of Greenwood (1925), Frost (1933), Berkson and Gage (1952), Fix and Neyman (1951), Boag (1949), Elveback (1958), Armitage (1959), Kaplan and Meier (1958), Dorn (1950), Littell (1952), Cutler and Ederer (1958), Kuzma (1967), and Drolette (1975). Chiang (1961a) is a good reference for most of the material presented in this chapter.

Proper analysis of incomplete information due to deaths from other causes and lost cases requires the concept of competing risks. Reference is made to Birnbaum (1978), Chiang (1968), and David and Moeschberger (1978) for a detailed treatment of the topic of competing risks. The purpose of this chapter is to adapt the life table methodology presented in Chapter 10 to the special conditions of follow-up studies where there are patients withdrawing from the study due to termination of observation. Section 2 is devoted to the estimation of the probability of survival for the time interval $(x, x + 1)$. A brief review of the formulas for the estimators is presented. Section 3 is devoted to the estimation of the x year survival probability p_{0x}. In Section 4, we introduce a method of computing the expectation of life $\hat{e}_x$ based on the incomplete information of follow-up studies. An application of the theoretical material will be given in Section 5 where a life table for cervical cancer patients will be presented.

2. Estimation of the Probability of Survival for Interval $(x, x + 1)$, p_x

Consider a follow-up study conducted over a period of y years. A total of N_0 patients are admitted to the study at various times during the study period and observed until their deaths or until the end of the observation period (such as termination of the study), whichever comes first. The time of admission is taken as the common point of origin for all N_0 patients. For a given patient, time zero is the date of admission. Thus if Patient A is admitted to the study on January 1, 1975 and Patient B is admitted on July 1, 1978, their points of origin are January 1, 1975 and July 1, 1978, respectively. The first anniversary of follow-up for Patient A is January 1, 1976, while for Patient B it is July 1, 1979. It is customary in medical follow-up studies to use the anniversary year (the number of years since admission) as the time scale. The typical interval will be denoted by $(x, x + 1)$, for $x = 0, 1, \ldots, y - 1$, so that x is the exact number of years of follow-up. The symbol p_x will be used to denote the probability that a patient alive at time x will survive to the end of the interval $(x, x + 1)$, and q_x the probability that he will die during the interval, so that $p_x + q_x = 1$.

2.1. Basic random variables and likelihood functions. For each interval $(x, x + 1)$ let N_x be the number of patients alive at the beginning of the interval. Clearly, N_x is also the number of survivors of those who entered the study at least x years before the closing date.[†] The number N_x will decrease as x increases because of death and withdrawal of patients due to termination of observation. The decrease in N_x is systematically described in Table 1.

The N_x individuals who begin the interval $(x, x + 1)$ may be divided into two mutually exclusive groups according to their date of entrance into the study. A group of m_x patients who entered the study more than $x + 1$ years before the closing date will be observed for the entire interval; a second group of n_x patients who entered the study less than $x + 1$ years before its termination is composed of patients due to withdraw in the interval because the termination date precedes their $(x + 1)$th anniversary date. Of the m_x patients, d_x will die in the interval and s_x will survive to the end of the interval and become N_{x+1}; of the n_x patients, d'_x will die before the termination date and

Table 1. Distribution of N_x patients according to withdrawal status and survival status in the interval $(x, x + 1)$

Survival status	Total number of patients	Withdrawal status in the interval	
		Number to be observed for the entire interval*	Number due to withdraw during the interval**
Total	N_x	m_x	n_x
Survivors	$s_x + w_x$	s_x	w_x
Deaths	D_x	d_x	d'_x

*Survivors among those admitted to the study more than $(x + 1)$ years before closing date for individual patients.
**Survivors among those admitted to the study less than $(x + 1)$ years but more than x years before closing data for individual patients.

[†]The methods presented in this Chapter are equally applicable to data based on either the date of last observation for individual patients or on the common closing date of a study.

w_x will survive to the termination date of observation. The sum $d_x + d'_x = D_{\dot{x}}$ is the total number of deaths in the interval. Thus s_x, d_x, w_x, and d'_x are the basic random variables under investigation and they will be used to estimate the probability p_x and its complement.

Consider first the group of m_x individuals, each of whom has a probability p_x of surviving and $q_x = 1 - p_x$ of dying in the interval $(x, x + 1)$. The random variable s_x, the number of survivors to the end of the interval, has a binomial distribution:

$$C_1 p_x^{s_x}(1 - p_x)^{d_x} \tag{2.1}$$

where the binomial coefficient C_1 plays no role in the estimation of p_x. The expected number of survivors and the expected number of deaths are given by [cf. Equation (2.6), Chapter 2, page 41]

$$E(s_x \mid m_x) = m_x p_x \quad \text{and} \quad E(d_x \mid m_x) = m_x(1 - p_x), \tag{2.2}$$

respectively.

The random variable w_x, the number of patients surviving to the end of the observation period, also has a binomial distribution. Suppose we let

$$p_x\left(\tfrac{1}{2}\right) = \Pr\{\text{a patient will survive to the time}$$

$$\text{of withdrawal in } (x, x + 1)\}. \tag{2.3}$$

Then the probability distribution of w_x is

$$C_2\left[p_x\left(\tfrac{1}{2}\right)\right]^{w_x}\left[1 - p_x\left(\tfrac{1}{2}\right)\right]^{d'_x} \tag{2.4}$$

where the binomial coefficient C_2 again plays no role in the estimation of p_x.

For the entire group of N_x patients, there are two independent binomial distributions with the likelihood function

$$L(x; p_x) = p_x^{s_x}(1 - p_x)^{d_x}\left[p_x\left(\tfrac{1}{2}\right)\right]^{w_x}\left[1 - p_x\left(\tfrac{1}{2}\right)\right]^{d'_x}. \tag{2.5}$$

The maximum likelihood estimator of p_x can be obtained from (2.5) when there is an explicit formula for $p_x\left(\tfrac{1}{2}\right)$.

2.2.   Formulas for the estimators of p_x.   Several formulas have been suggested in the literature for the estimator of the probability of surviving the interval $(x, x + 1)$. For a review of these formulas, refer to Kuzma (1967) and Drolette (1975).

2.2.1.   The Actuarial Method.   The actuarial method is the most commonly used method in medical follow-up studies. It was first proposed by Frost (1933) in a follow-up study of tuberculosis patients, and later described by Berkson and Gage (1950), Merrell and Shulman (1955),

Cutler and Ederer (1958), and others. The method does not distinguish between the two separate groups of patients (m_x and n_x). The formula for the estimate is

$$\overset{\circ}{p}_x = 1 - \frac{D_x}{N_x - \frac{1}{2}w_x}, \qquad (2.6)$$

based on the assumption that each withdrawal is observed for half of the interval. If the ratio in (2.6) is regarded as a binomial proportion in ($N_x - \frac{1}{2}w_x$) trials, then the sample variance $\overset{\circ}{p}_x$ is

$$\mathrm{Var}(\overset{\circ}{p}_x) = \frac{1}{N_x - \frac{1}{2}w_x} \overset{\circ}{p}_x \overset{\circ}{q}_x. \qquad (2.7)$$

Formula (2.6) is derived entirely on an intuitive and heuristic basis. But its simplicity makes this method well accepted in epidemiological and medical research.

2.2.2. Estimator A. An explicit formula for the probability $p_x(\frac{1}{2})$ defined in (2.3) depends on the time of withdrawal. Generally, patients' entrances into a study and their deaths occur at random. A plausible assumption, therefore, is that a withdrawal takes place at random during the interval ($x, x + 1$). Under this assumption, the probability $p_x(\frac{1}{2})$ is

$$p_x(\tfrac{1}{2}) = \int_x^{x+1} \exp\left(- \int_x^t \mu(\tau)\,d\tau \right) dt. \qquad (2.8)$$

If the force of mortality is constant within the interval ($x, x + 1$) with $\mu(\tau) = \mu_x$, then

$$p_x(\tfrac{1}{2}) = \int_x^{x+1} \exp(-(t-x)\mu_x)\,dt = \frac{1}{\mu_x}(1 - e^{-\mu_x})$$

$$= -\frac{1}{\log p_x}(1 - p_x). \qquad (2.9)$$

Substituting (2.9) in (2.5), we find the likelihood function,

$$L_A(x; p_x) = p_x^{s_x}(1 - p_x)^{d_x + w_x}(\log p_x)^{-n_x}\left[(1 - p_x) + \log p_x\right]^{d'_x}. \qquad (2.10)$$

Taking the derivative of the logarithm of $L_A(x; p_x)$ with respect to p_x and setting the derivative equal to zero yields the maximum-likelihood equation

$$\frac{s_x}{p_x} - \frac{d_x + w_x}{1 - p_x} - \frac{n_x}{p_x \log p_x} + \frac{d'_x(1 - p_x)}{\left[(1 - p_x) + \log p_x\right] p_x} = 0. \qquad (2.11)$$

The solution of this equation is the maximum-likelihood estimator of p_x. This estimator is known as Estimator A (see, e.g., Drolette (1975)).

While equation (2.11) admits no simple analytic solution, the numerical value of the estimator can be easily obtained by means of a computer program.

2.2.3. Estimator B.

When a patient's withdrawal takes place at random in the interval $(x, x + 1)$, the average length of time that he is under observation is half of the interval $(x, x + 1)$, or the interval $(x, x + \frac{1}{2})$. The probability of surviving the half interval $(x, x + \frac{1}{2})$ is

$$p_x(\tfrac{1}{2}) = \exp(-\tfrac{1}{2}\,\mu_x) = p_x^{1/2}. \tag{2.12}$$

Since the probability of surviving an interval $(x, x + 1)$ usually is close to one, $p_x^{1/2}$ is also a good approximation to the probability in (2.9), or

$$p_x^{1/2} \doteq -(1 - p_x)/\log p_x. \tag{2.13}$$

The quantities on both sides of (2.13) have been computed for selected values of p_x, and the results shown in Table 2 justify the approximation.

Taking $p_x^{1/2}$ as the probability of surviving to the time of withdrawal and $(1 - p_x^{1/2})$ as the probability of dying before the time of withdrawal, the random variable w_x has the probability distribution

$$C_2\, p_x^{w_x/2}\left(1 - p_x^{1/2}\right)^{d_x'}. \tag{2.14}$$

The expected number of survivors and the expected number of deaths are given by

$$E(w_x \mid n_x) = n_x p_x^{1/2} \quad \text{and} \quad E(d_x' \mid n_x) = n_x(1 - p_x^{1/2}), \tag{2.15}$$

respectively. The corresponding likelihood function is

$$L_B(x; p_x) = p_x^{s_x + (1/2)w_x}(1 - p_x)^{d_x}\left(1 - p_x^{1/2}\right)^{d_x'}. \tag{2.16}$$

Taking the derivative of $\log L_B(x; p_x)$ and setting the derivative equal to zero yields a quadratic equation in $p_x^{1/2}$:

$$(N_x - \tfrac{1}{2}n_x)\hat{p}_x + \tfrac{1}{2}d_x'\hat{p}_x^{1/2} - (s_x + \tfrac{1}{2}w_x) = 0. \tag{2.17}$$

Table 2. Comparison between $p_x^{1/2}$ and $-(1 - p_x)/\log p_x$

p_x	$p_x^{1/2}$	$-(1 - p_x)/\log p_x$
.70	.837	.841
.75	.866	.869
.80	.894	.896
.85	.922	.923
.90	.949	.949
.95	.975	.975

The solution of (2.17) is the maximum-likelihood estimator,

$$\hat{p}_x = \left[\frac{-\frac{1}{2}d_x' + \sqrt{\frac{1}{4}d_x'^2 + 4(N_x - \frac{1}{2}n_x)(s_x + \frac{1}{2}w_x)}}{2(N_x - \frac{1}{2}n_x)} \right]^2. \qquad (2.18)$$

The probability of dying in $(x, x + 1)$ is

$$\hat{q}_x = 1 - \hat{p}_x. \qquad (2.19)$$

The asymptotic variance of $\hat{p}_x$ is

$$\text{Var}(\hat{p}_x) = \frac{\hat{p}_x \hat{q}_x}{M_x}, \qquad \text{where} \quad M_x = m_x + n_x(1 + \hat{p}_x^{1/2})^{-1} \qquad (2.20)$$

The estimator $\hat{p}_x$ in (2.18) is known as Estimator B (see Drolette (1975)).

2.2.4. Elvebeck's Estimator.

When the interval is sufficiently short, a linear approximation is adequate and

$$p_x(\tfrac{1}{2}) = 1 - \tfrac{1}{2}q_x = \tfrac{1}{2}(1 + p_x). \qquad (2.21)$$

The likelihood function is

$$L_E(x; p_x) = p_x^{s_x}(1 - p_x)^{D_x}(1 + p_x)^{w_x}, \qquad (2.22)$$

which leads to the estimator

$$p_x^* = \frac{w_x - D_x + \sqrt{(w_x - D_x)^2 + 4N_x s_x}}{2N_x} \qquad (2.23)$$

The asymptotic variance is

$$\text{Var}(p_x^*) = \frac{p_x^*(1 - p_x^{*2})}{(N_x + n_x)[1 + p_x^* - n_x/(N_x + n_x)]} \qquad (2.24)$$

2.2.5. Drolette's Estimator.

Estimator A, Estimator B, and Elvebeck's estimator are all based on the assumption of random distribution of withdrawals. When a study uses an anniversary method of follow-up in which patients are called in once a year on the anniversary of their entry into the study, the information on survival and death of patients all relates to the end of an interval $(x, x + 1)$. There are no patients who withdraw during the interval. In this type of follow-up study, $n_x = 0$, $m_x = N_x$; the likelihood function is simply

$$L_D(x; p_x) = p_x^{s_x}(1 - p_x)^{d_x}, \qquad (2.25)$$

and the estimator is

$$p_x^{**} = \frac{S_x}{m_x}, \qquad (2.26)$$

with the variance

$$\text{Var}(p_x^{**}) = \frac{1}{m_x} p_x^{**} q_x^{**}. \qquad (2.27)$$

2.2.6. Kaplan–Meier's Estimator.

In this method, a patient is dropped from consideration in the estimation of p_x immediately upon his withdrawal from the study. Application of this method requires knowledge of the order of the withdrawals and deaths. For illustration, suppose there is $w_x = 1$ withdrawal at time τ and $D_x = 1$ death at time t. The formula for the estimator p_x' depends on the relative positions of τ and t on the time axis.

Case 1. $x \leqslant \tau < t \leqslant x + 1$. The withdrawal takes place before death occurs. We divide the time interval $(x, x + 1)$ into three consecutive subintervals (x, τ), (τ, t), and $(t, x + 1)$. The probability of surviving the interval $(x, x + 1)$ is equal to the product of the probabilities of surviving the three consecutive subintervals:

$$p_x = \Pr\{x, x + 1\}$$
$$= \Pr\{x, \tau\} \times \Pr\{\tau, t\} \times \Pr\{t, x + 1\}.$$

The estimates of the three probabilities are

$$\Pr(x, \tau) = \frac{N_x}{N_x} = 1, \text{ as there are no deaths occuring in } (x, \tau),$$

$$\Pr(\tau, t) = \frac{N_x - 2}{N_x - 1},$$

since, with the withdrawal occurring at τ, the interval (τ, t) starts with $N_x - 1$ patients and, due to death at t, ends with $N_x - 2$ patients. Also

$$\Pr(t, x + 1) = \frac{N_x - 2}{N_x - 2} = 1, \text{ as there are no deaths in } (t, x + 1).$$

Therefore the estimate is

$$p_x' = \frac{N_x - 2}{N_x - 1}. \qquad (2.28)$$

Case 2. $x \leqslant t < \tau \leqslant x + 1$. Death occurs before withdrawal takes place. The probability of surviving the interval $(x, x + 1)$ is now

$$p_x = \Pr\{x, t\} \Pr\{t, \tau\} \Pr\{\tau, x + 1\}.$$

Since death occurs in the first subinterval but not in the second and third subintervals, the estimate is

$$p'_x = \left(\frac{N_x - 1}{N_x}\right)\left(\frac{N_x - 1}{N_x - 1}\right)\left(\frac{N_x - 2}{N_x - 2}\right)$$

$$= \frac{N_x - 1}{N_x} . \tag{2.29}$$

While the estimators in (2.28) and (2.29) differ, the numerator in each expression is the number of patients under observation after the (first) death, and the denominator is one greater than the numerator. Generally, the withdrawal time is denoted by τ_i, for $i = 1, \ldots, w_x$, and the time at death by t_j, $0 \leqslant t_j \leqslant 1$, $j = 1, \ldots, D_x$. The $w_x + D_x$ values are merged in a single sequence in order of increasing magnitude. Let N'_j be the number of patients who are still under observation after the j-th death, for $j = 1, \ldots, D_x$. Then the formula for the estimator of the probability of surviving the interval $(x, x + 1)$ is

$$p'_x = \prod_{j=1}^{D_x} \frac{N'_j}{N'_j + 1} . \tag{2.30}$$

The approximate formula for the variance of p'_x is

$$\mathrm{Var}(p'_x) = p'^2_x \sum_{j=1}^{D_x} \left[N'_j(N'_j + 1)\right]^{-1}. \tag{2.31}$$

2.2.7. Estimator C. If the time of death of each of the D_x patients and the time of withdrawal of each of the w_x patients are known, there will be N_x individual observations. The corresponding estimator is the most efficient (has the smallest variance) among all the estimators discussed in this section. Again we let t_j be the time of death in $(x, x + 1)$ of the j-th patient, $j = 1, \ldots, D_x$. It is a continuous random variable, takes on values between zero and one, and has the density function

$$f(t_j; x) = e^{-t_j \mu_x}\mu_x = -p'^{t_j}_x \log p_x ,$$

$$0 \leqslant t_j \leqslant 1; \quad j = 1, \ldots, D_x . \tag{2.32}$$

Let τ_i be the time of withdrawal in the interval $(x, x + 1)$ of the i-th patient in the group w_x, for $i = 1, \ldots, w_x$. The variable τ_i also is a continuous random variable assuming values between zero and one with the density function

$$g(\tau_i; x) = e^{-\tau_i \mu_x} = p^{\tau_i}_x,$$

$$0 \leqslant \tau_i \leqslant 1; \quad i = 1, \ldots, w_x . \tag{2.33}$$

Finally, each of the s_x patients survives the interval $(x, x + 1)$ with the probability p_x. Therefore, the likelihood function for the entire group of N_x random variables is

$$L_C(x; p_x) = p_x^{s_x} \left(\prod_{i=1}^{w_x} p_x^{\tau_i} \right) \prod_{j=1}^{D_x} \left(p_x^{t_j} \log p_x \right)$$

$$= p_x^{T_x} (\log p_x)^{D_x}. \tag{2.34}$$

where

$$T_x = s_x + \sum_{i=1}^{w_x} \tau_i + \sum_{j=1}^{D_x} t_j \tag{2.35}$$

is the total length of observation of the N_x patients in the interval $(x, x + 1)$. Maximizing the likelihood function in (2.34) yields Estimator C,

$$\tilde{p}_x = e^{-D_x/T_x} = e^{-\tilde{\mu}_x}. \tag{2.36}$$

The exponent,

$$\tilde{\mu}_x = \frac{D_x}{T_x}, \tag{2.37}$$

an estimator of the force of mortality μ_x, is the number of deaths occurring in the interval $(x, x + 1)$ divided by the total length of observation in the interval of the N_x individuals (alive at time x). Thus $\tilde{\mu}_x$ in (2.37) is exactly the specific death rate for interval $(x, x + 1)$ as defined in equation (2.1), Chapter 4, page 72. The logarithm of $\tilde{p}_x$ is the death rate multiplied by -1, or

$$\log \tilde{p}_x = -\left(\frac{D_x}{T_x} \right),$$

a well-known relationship in mortality analysis.

The asymptotic variance of the estimator is

$$\mathrm{Var}(\tilde{p}_x) = \tilde{p}_x^2 \left(\frac{D_x}{T_x^2} \right). \tag{2.38}$$

The formulas for both the estimator $\tilde{p}_x$ in (2.36) and the variance in (2.38) are simple for practical computations.

2.3. A summary of the estimators. Statistical estimation of a parameter, such as the probability of survival p_x, depends upon the amount of information available for analysis. The more information there is, the fewer assumptions are needed, and the better the estimate will be. The criterion of "goodness" of an estimator varies considerably from a theoretical viewpoint to a practical perception of a problem. Theoretical assessment of an estimator emphasizes the asymptotic proper-

Table 3. Summary of the estimators of the survival probability for interval $(x, x + 1)$

Estimator (formula no.)	Theoretical Basis	Method of Estimation	Required Information	Reference
Actuarial Estimator (2.6)	Heuristic	Intuitive	N_x, D_x, w_x	Berkson & Gage (1952) Cutler & Ederer (1958) Merrell & Shulman (1955)
Estimator A (2.11)	Parametric, Exact	Maximum-likelihood	N_x, n_x, s_x, d_x'	Chiang (1961a)
Estimator B (2.18)	Parametric, Approximate	Maximum-likelihood	N_x, n_x, s_x, d_x'	Chiang (1961a)
Elvebeck's Estimator (2.23)	Parametric, Approximate	Maximum-likelihood	N_x, w_x, s_x, D_x	Elvebeck (1958)
Drolette's Estimator (2.26)	Non-parametric	Maximum-likelihood	m_x, s_x	Drolette (1975)
Kaplan–Meier Estimator (2.30)	Non-parametric	Non-parametric	Relative values of τ_j and t_j	Kaplan & Meier (1958)
Estimator C (2.36)	Parametric, Exact	Maximum-likelihood	D_x and sums of τ_j and of t_j	Chiang (1961a)

ties of the estimator as the sample size (N_x in the present case) tends to infinity. For practical purposes, simplicity in formula and intuitive appeal of an estimator are more important. A careful practitioner can achieve both by collecting more information for the problem at hand.

The estimators of p_x are summarized in Table 3. The choice of an estimator is partly dictated by the information available. Estimator C requires the most information and the Drolette estimator requires the least. While all the estimators are consistent and asymptotically normal, Estimator C is preferred over the others because it has a simple formula and the smallest variance. Generally, a follow-up study is an extensive undertaking involving a tremendous amount of expense, effort and time, even for a project of moderate size. But it requires only a minimal amount of bookkeeping to record the time of withdrawal and the time at death, and to compute a specific death rate in equation (2.37) for each interval $(x, x + 1)$. Therefore, in a practical problem extra effort should be made to record such information and use Estimator C to estimate the probability p_x.

2.4. Consistency of the estimators. The estimators presented above are all consistent estimators in the sense that they all approach the unknown probability p_x when N_x is large. In addition, Estimator A, Estimator B, Estimator C, Elvebeck's estimator and Drolette's estimator are all Fisher consistent. When the random variables (d_x, d'_x, w_x, s_x) are replaced with the corresponding expected values, the estimators become identical with the probability p_x.

Consider for example, Estimator B. Substituting the expectations

$$E(s_x) = m_x p_x, \qquad E(w_x) = n_x p_x^{1/2}, \qquad E(d'_x) = n_x(1 - p_x^{1/2})$$

in (2.18) we find

$$p_x = \left[\frac{-\tfrac{1}{2}n_x(1 - p_x^{1/2}) + \sqrt{\tfrac{1}{4}n_x^2(1 - p_x^{1/2})^2 + 4(N_x - \tfrac{1}{2}n_x)[m_x p_x + \tfrac{1}{2}n_x p_x^{1/2}]}}{2(N_x - \tfrac{1}{2}n_x)} \right]^2 \tag{2.27}$$

The identity in (2.27) is easily verified. Since $m_x = (N_x - \tfrac{1}{2}n_x) - \tfrac{1}{2}n_x$, the second term under the square root may be written as

$$4(N_x - \tfrac{1}{2}n_x)\left[\{(N_x - \tfrac{1}{2}n_x) - \tfrac{1}{2}n_x\}p_x + \tfrac{1}{2}n_x p_x^{1/2}\right]$$

$$= 4(N_x - \tfrac{1}{2}n_x)^2 p_x + 4(N_x - \tfrac{1}{2}n_x)p_x^{1/2}\left[\tfrac{1}{2}n_x(1 - p_x^{1/2})\right], \tag{2.28}$$

and the quantity under the square root becomes a complete square:

$$\left(\sqrt{}\right)^2 = \left[\tfrac{1}{2}n_x\left(1 - p_x^{1/2}\right) + 2\left(N_x - \tfrac{1}{2}n_x\right)p_x^{1/2}\right]^2. \qquad (2.29)$$

Substituting (2.29) in the right hand side of (2.27) yields

$$\left[\frac{-\tfrac{1}{2}n_x\left(1 - p_x^{1/2}\right) + \left[\tfrac{1}{2}n_x\left(1 - p_x^{1/2}\right) + 2\left(N_x - \tfrac{1}{2}n_x\right)p_x^{1/2}\right]}{2\left(N_x - \tfrac{1}{2}n_x\right)}\right]^2 = p_x,$$

proving Fisher consistency for Estimator B, $\hat{p}_x$.

3. Estimation of the Survival Probability, p_{ij}

A life table for follow-up patients can be readily constructed once the estimates $\hat{p}_x$ and $\hat{q}_x$ have been determined for each interval of the study (Section 2). The procedure is the same as that for the current life table. Because of their practical importance, the survival probability and the expectation of life are discussed below.

The probability that a patient alive at time $x = i$ will survive to time $x = j$ is estimated from the formula

$$\hat{p}_{ij} = \hat{p}_i\hat{p}_{i+1}\cdots\hat{p}_{j-1}, \qquad i < j; \qquad i, j = 1, 2, \ldots, y, \qquad (3.1)$$

where $\hat{p}_x$ may be any one of the estimators discussed in Section 2. Since the estimators $\hat{p}_x$ for $x = 1, 2, \ldots, y$, are uncorrelated, the sample variance of $\hat{p}_{ij}$ has the same form as that given in equation (3.7), Chapter 8:

$$S_{\hat{p}_{ij}}^2 = \hat{p}_{ij}^2 \sum_{h=i}^{j-1} \hat{p}_h^{-2}S_{\hat{p}_h}^2. \qquad (3.2)$$

The sample variance $S_{\hat{p}_h}^2$ is given in Section 2.

When $i = 0$ and $j = x$, the formula in (3.1) becomes the estimate of the x year survival probability:

$$\hat{p}_{0x} = \hat{p}_0\hat{p}_1\cdots\hat{p}_{x-1}. \qquad (3.3)$$

4. Estimation of the Expectation of Life, e_α

The observed expectation of life at time α is computed from the following formula:*

$$\hat{e}_\alpha = \tfrac{1}{2} + \hat{p}_\alpha + \hat{p}_\alpha\hat{p}_{\alpha+1} + \cdots + \hat{p}_\alpha\hat{p}_{\alpha+1}\cdots\hat{p}_{y-1}$$

$$+ \hat{p}_\alpha\hat{p}_{\alpha+1}\cdots\hat{p}_y + \cdots . \qquad (4.1)$$

---

*For simplicity, we assume that $n_x = 1$, $a_x = \tfrac{1}{2}$ and $c_x = 1$ for all x in the formula for $\hat{e}_\alpha$.

Consider a study covering a period of y years. If no survivors remain from the patients who entered the program in its first year, $\hat{p}_{y-1}$ will be zero, and $\hat{e}_\alpha$ can be computed from (4.1). Normally there would be w_{y-1} survivors who were admitted in the first year of the program that are still living at the closing date. In this case, the estimate $\hat{p}_{y-1}$ is greater than zero, and the values of $\hat{p}_y, \hat{p}_{y+1}, \ldots$ cannot be observed within the time limits of the study. Consequently, $\hat{e}_\alpha$ cannot be obtained from equation (4.1).

Usually w_{y-1} is small and we can estimate $\hat{e}_\alpha$ with a certain degree of accuracy. Suppose we rewrite equation (4.1) in the form

$$\hat{e}_\alpha = \tfrac{1}{2} + \hat{p}_\alpha + \hat{p}_\alpha \hat{p}_{\alpha+1} + \cdots + \hat{p}_\alpha \hat{p}_{\alpha+1} \cdots \hat{p}_{y-1}$$
$$+ \hat{p}_{\alpha y}(\hat{p}_y + \hat{p}_y \hat{p}_{y+1} + \cdots), \tag{4.2}$$

where $\hat{p}_{\alpha y}$ is written for $\hat{p}_\alpha \hat{p}_{\alpha+1} \cdots \hat{p}_{y-1}$. The problem is to determine $\hat{p}_y, \hat{p}_{y+1}, \ldots$ in the last term, since the preceding terms can be computed from the data available.

Consider a typical interval $(z, z+1)$ beyond time y with the survival probability of p_z. If the force of mortality is constant beyond y, the probability of surviving the interval $(z, z+1)$ is independent of z, i.e.,

$$p_z = p, \qquad z = y, y+1, \ldots . \tag{4.3}$$

Under this assumption, we may replace the last term of (4.2) with $\hat{p}_{\alpha y}(\hat{p} + \hat{p}^2 + \cdots)$, which is just $\hat{p}_{\alpha y}\hat{p}/(1 - \hat{p})$, or

$$\hat{p}_{\alpha y}(\hat{p} + \hat{p}^2 + \cdots) = \hat{p}_{\alpha y}\frac{\hat{p}}{1 - \hat{p}}. \tag{4.4}$$

As a result, we have

$$\hat{e}_\alpha = \tfrac{1}{2} + \hat{p}_\alpha + \hat{p}_\alpha \hat{p}_{\alpha+1} + \cdots + \hat{p}_\alpha \hat{p}_{\alpha+1} \cdots \hat{p}_{y-1} + \hat{p}_{\alpha y}\left(\frac{\hat{p}}{1 - \hat{p}}\right). \tag{4.5}$$

If the force of mortality is assumed to be constant beginning with time $(y - 1)$ instead of time y, $\hat{p}$ may be set equal to $\hat{p}_{y-1}$. In order to have small sample variation, however, the estimate of $\hat{p}$ should be based on as large a sample as possible. Suppose there exists a time t, for $t < y$, such that probabilities $\hat{p}_t, \hat{p}_{t+1}, \ldots$, are approximately equal, thus indicating a constant force of mortality after time t. Then, $\hat{p}$ should be set equal to $\hat{p}_t$, and the formula for the observed expectation of life becomes

$$\hat{e}_\alpha = \tfrac{1}{2} + \hat{p}_\alpha + \hat{p}_\alpha \hat{p}_{\alpha+1} + \cdots + \hat{p}_\alpha \hat{p}_{\alpha+1} \cdots \hat{p}_{y-1} + \hat{p}_{\alpha y}\left(\frac{\hat{p}_t}{1 - \hat{p}_t}\right), \tag{4.6}$$

for $\alpha = 0, \ldots, y - 1$.

The error introduced by assuming a constant force of mortality beyond y and choosing $\hat{p}_t$ for $\hat{p}$ appears only in the last terms of (4.6). When α is small, $\hat{p}_{\alpha y}$ is small, and the error introduced by this method will have little effect on the value of $\hat{e}_\alpha$.

4.1. Sample variance of the observed expectation of life.

In Chapter 10 we proved that the covariance of the estimated probabilities of surviving any two non-overlapping intervals is zero; hence, the sample variance of the observed expectation of life may be computed from

$$s_{\hat{e}_\alpha}^2 = \sum_{x \geqslant \alpha} \left\{ \frac{\partial}{\partial \hat{p}_x} \hat{e}_\alpha \right\}^2 s_{\hat{p}_x}^2 . \tag{4.7}$$

The derivatives, taken at the observed point $\hat{p}_x$, $x \geqslant \alpha$, are given by

$$\left\{ \frac{\partial}{\partial \hat{p}_x} \hat{e}_\alpha \right\} = \hat{p}_{\alpha x} \left[\hat{e}_{x+1} + \tfrac{1}{2} \right], \qquad x \neq t \tag{4.8}$$

where

$$\hat{p}_{\alpha x} = \hat{p}_\alpha \hat{p}_{\alpha+1} \cdots \hat{p}_{x-1},$$

and

$$\left\{ \frac{\partial}{\partial \hat{p}_t} \hat{e}_\alpha \right\} = \hat{p}_{\alpha t} \left[\hat{e}_{t+1} + \frac{1}{2} + \frac{\hat{p}_{ty}}{(1-\hat{p}_t)^2} \right], \qquad \alpha \leqslant t. \tag{4.9}$$

For $t < \alpha$, the factors $\hat{p}_\alpha$, $\hat{p}_{\alpha+1}, \ldots, \hat{p}_{y-1}$ and $\hat{p}_{\alpha y}$ in (4.6) do not contain $\hat{p}_t$, hence the derivative,

$$\frac{\partial}{\partial \hat{p}_t} \hat{e}_\alpha = \frac{\partial}{\partial \hat{p}_t} \hat{p}_{\alpha y} \left(\frac{p_t}{1-\hat{p}_t} \right) = \hat{p}_{\alpha y} \frac{1}{(1-\hat{p}_t)^2} , \qquad \alpha > t. \tag{4.10}$$

Substituting (4.8), (4.9) and (4.10) in (4.7) gives the sample variance of $\hat{e}_\alpha$,

$$S_{\hat{e}_\alpha}^2 = \sum_{\substack{x=\alpha \\ x \neq t}}^{y-1} \hat{p}_{\alpha x}^2 \left[\hat{e}_{x+1} + \frac{1}{2} \right]^2 S_{\hat{p}_x}^2 + \hat{p}_{\alpha t}^2 \left[\hat{e}_{t+1} + \frac{1}{2} + \frac{\hat{p}_{ty}}{(1-\hat{p}_t)^2} \right]^2 S_{\hat{p}_t}^2 ,$$
$$\alpha \leqslant t, \tag{4.11}$$

and

$$S_{\hat{e}_\alpha}^2 = \sum_{x=\alpha}^{y-1} \hat{p}_{\alpha x}^2 \left[\hat{e}_{x+1} + \frac{1}{2} \right]^2 S_{\hat{p}_x}^2 + \frac{\hat{p}_{\alpha y}^2}{(1-\hat{p}_t)^4} S_{\hat{p}_t}^2 , \qquad \alpha > t. \tag{4.12}$$

The values of $\hat{p}_x$ and the sample variance of $\hat{p}_x$ are given in Section 2.

In formula (4.11) or (4.12), when the first term (for $x = \alpha$) is taken out of the summation, we have a recursive equation

$$S_{\hat{e}_\alpha}^2 = \left[\hat{e}_{\alpha+1} + \tfrac{1}{2} \right]^2 S_{\hat{p}_\alpha}^2 + \hat{p}_\alpha^2 S_{\hat{e}_{\alpha+1}}^2 , \qquad \text{for} \quad \alpha \neq t. \tag{4.13}$$

Therefore, the variance of $\hat{e}_\alpha$ may be computed recursively starting with the largest value of α.

5. An Example of Life Table Construction for a Follow-up Population

Application of the methods developed in this section is illustrated with data collected by the Tumor Registry of the California State Department of Health Services. The material selected consists of 5,982 white female patients with a diagnosis of cervical cancer who were admitted to certain California hospitals and clinics between January 1, 1942 and December 31, 1954. For the purpose of this illustration, the closing date is December 31, 1954, and the date of entrance to follow-up for each patient is the date of hospital admission. Each patient was observed until death or until the closing date, whichever came first. Because of lack of information regarding the time of death and the time of withdrawal, Estimator B from Section 2 is used in this illustration.

The first step is to construct a table similar to Table 4 showing the survival experience of the patients which are grouped according to their withdrawal status during each time period of follow-up. The interval length selected (column 1) depends upon the nature of the investigation; generally a fixed length of one year is used. The total number of patients admitted to the study is entered as N_0 in the first line of column 2, which is 5,982. Among them there were $m_0 = 5,317$ patients (column 3) admitted to the study prior to January 1, 1954, and observed for the entire interval $(0, 1)$. Of the m_0 patients, s_0 (4,030, column 4) survived to their first anniversary and d_0 (1,287, column 5) died during the first year of follow-up. In addition, there were n_0 (665, column 6) patients due to withdraw in the interval $(0, 1)$, of which w_0 (576, column 7) survived to the closing date and d_0' (89, column 8) died before the closing date. The second interval began with the $s_0 = 4,030$ survivors from the first interval, which is entered as N_1 in column 2 of line 2. The N_1 patients were again divided successively by withdrawal and survival status. Of the N_1 patients, m_1 (3,489, column 3) were the survivors of those admitted prior to January 1, 1953, and hence were observed for the entire interval $(1, 2)$; n_1 (541, column 8) were the survivors of those admitted during the year 1953 and hence were due to withdraw during the interval $(1, 2)$. At the beginning of the final interval $(12, 13)$ there were $N_{12} = 72$ survivors of the patients admitted in 1942; all were due to withdraw during the last interval, or $n_{12} = 72$ (last line, column 6). Of the 72 patients, $w_{12} = 72$ (column 7) were alive at the closing date.

This means that $\hat{p}_{12}$ is greater than zero, and $\hat{p}_z$ for $z \geqslant 12$ cannot be observed.

This material has been used to construct a life table for the cervical cancer patients. The steps involved are similar to those described in the construction of current life tables in Chapter 6. At the expense of repetition but to allow easy reference, they are stated below:

(1) $\hat{p}_x$ and $\hat{q}_x$.   For each interval $(x, x + 1)$, use formulas (2.18) and (2.19) to compute $\hat{p}_x$ and $\hat{q}_x$.

(2) d_x and l_x.   Assume $l_0 = 100{,}000$; use $\hat{q}_0, \hat{q}_1, \ldots,$ to obtain d_x and l_x from

$$d_x = l_x \hat{q}_x \quad \text{and} \quad l_{x+1} = l_x - d_x, \quad \text{for} \quad x = 0, 1, \ldots, 12.$$

(3) a_x and L_x.   The fraction of last year of life is assumed to be $a_x = .5$, which is quite appropriate for studies as this one. The quantity L_x is computed from

$$L_x = l_{x+1} + a_x d_x;$$

plugging in $a_x = .5$ and $d_x = l_x - l_{x+1}$, we get a more convenient formula

$$L_x = \tfrac{1}{2}(l_x + l_{x+1}), \quad x = 0, 1, \ldots, 12.$$

(4) T_x and $\hat{e}_x$ beyond the observation period.   Information derived from a follow-up study is inadequate for the construction of a life table inasmuch as it is limited to the study period (13 years in this example). Therefore, we use

$$\hat{e}_\alpha = \tfrac{1}{2} + \hat{p}_\alpha + \hat{p}_\alpha \hat{p}_{\alpha+1} + \cdots + \hat{p}_\alpha \hat{p}_{\alpha+1} \cdots \hat{p}_{y-1}$$

$$+ \hat{p}_{\alpha y}\left(\frac{\hat{p}_t}{1 - \hat{p}_t} \right) \tag{4.6}$$

and

$$\hat{e}_{13} = \frac{1}{2} + \frac{\hat{p}_t}{1 - \hat{p}_t}. \tag{2.19a}$$

Estimating p_t with $\hat{p}_{11}$,

$$\hat{p}_t = \hat{p}_{11} = 1 - \hat{q}_{11} = 1 - .05106 = .94894$$

gives the required value

$$\hat{e}_{13} = \frac{1}{2} + \frac{.94894}{1 - .94894} = 19.0848.$$

Table 4. Survival experience following diagnosis of cancer of the cervix uteri, cases initially diagnosed 1942–1954, California, U.S.A.

Interval since diagnosis (in years)	Number living at beginning of interval $(x, x+1)$	Number to be observed for entire interval $(x, x+1)$*			Number due for withdrawal in interval $(x, x+1)$**		
		Total number	Number surviving the interval	Number dying in the interval	Total due for withdrawal	Number living at time of withdrawal	Number dying before withdrawal
$(x, x+1)$	N_x	m_x	s_x	d_x	n_x	w_x	d'_x
(1)	(2)	(3)	(4)	(5)	(6)	(7)	(8)
0–1	5982	5317	4030	1287	665	576	89
1–2	4030	3489	2845	644	541	501	40
2–3	2845	2367	2117	250	478	459	19
3–4	2117	1724	1573	151	393	379	14
4–5	1573	1263	1176	87	310	306	4
5–6	1176	918	861	57	258	254	4
6–7	861	692	660	32	169	167	2
7–8	660	496	474	22	164	161	3
8–9	474	356	344	12	118	116	2
9–10	344	256	245	11	88	85	3
10–11	245	164	158	6	81	78	3
11–12	158	76	72	4	82	80	2
12–13	72	0	0	0	72	72	0

*Survivors of those admitted more than $x + 1$ years prior to closing date.
**Survivors of those admitted between x and $x + 1$ years prior to closing date.
SOURCE: Tumor Registry, Department of Health Services, State of California.

Table 5. Life table of patients diagnosed as having cancer of the cervix uteri, cases initially diagnosed 1942–1954, California, U.S.A.

Interval since diagnosis (in years) $(x, x+1)$	Number living at time x l_x	Probability of dying in interval $(x, x+1)$ q_x	Number dying in interval $(x, x+1)$ d_x	Fraction of last year of life a_x	Number of years lived in interval $(x, x+1)$ L_x	Number of years lived beyond x T_x	Observed expectation of life at x $\hat{e}_x$
(1)	(2)	(3)	(4)	(5)	(6)	(7)	(8)
0–1	100,000	.24254	24,254	.5	87,873	1,289,575	12.90
1–2	75,746	.18143	13,743	.5	68,875	1,201,702	15.86
2–3	62,003	.10303	6,388	.5	58,809	1,132,827	18.27
3–4	55,615	.08576	4,770	.5	53,230	1,074,018	19.31
4–5	50,845	.06413	3,261	.5	49,215	1,020,788	20.08
5–6	47,584	.05820	2,769	.5	46,200	971,573	20.42
6–7	44,815	.04376	1,961	.5	43,835	925,373	20.65
7–8	42,854	.04320	1,851	.5	41,929	881,538	20.57
8–9	41,003	.03369	1,381	.5	40,313	839,609	20.48
9–10	39,622	.04655	1,844	.5	38,700	799,296	20.17
10–11	37,778	.04385	1,657	.5	36,950	760,596	20.13
11–12	36,121	.05106	1,844	.5	35,199	723,646	20.03
12–13	34,277	.00000	0	.5	34,277	688,447	20.08
13	34,277					654,170	19.08*

*For computation of $\hat{e}_{13}$ and T_{13} (see 2.19a)

Using this figure

$$T_{13} = l_{13}\hat{e}_{13} = 34,277 \times 19.0848 = 654,170.$$

(5) T_x *and* $\hat{e}_x$. The quantities T_x and $\hat{e}_x$ for other intervals now can be obtained by simple computations. For example,

$$T_{12} = L_{12} + T_{13}.$$

In general

$$T_x = L_x + T_{x+1}, \qquad x = 0, 1, \ldots, 12,$$

and $\hat{e}_x$ (except for $\hat{e}_{13}$) is computed from

$$\hat{e}_x = \frac{T_x}{l_x}, \qquad x = 0, 1, \ldots, 12.$$

The results of the computations are given in Table 5.

To compare the survival experience of different study groups and to make other statistical inferences, we computed the standard

Table 6. Survival experience after diagnosis of cancer of the cervix uteri, cases initially diagnosed, 1942–1954, California, U.S.A. The main life table functions and their standard errors.

Interval since diagnosis (in years)	x-year survival rate $\hat{p}_{0x}$		Estimated probability of death in interval $(x, x+1)$		Observed expectation of life at x*	
$(x, x+1)$	$1000\,\hat{p}_{0x}$	$1000\,S_{\hat{p}_{0x}}$	$1000\,\hat{q}_x$	$1000\,S_{\hat{q}_x}$	$\hat{e}_x$	$S_{\hat{e}_x}$
(1)	(2)	(3)	(4)	(5)	(6)	(7)
0–1	1000.00	0.00	242.54	5.69	12.90	2.83
1–2	757.46	5.69	181.43	6.26	15.86	3.74
2–3	620.03	6.65	103.03	5.95	18.27	4.57
3–4	556.15	6.84	85.76	6.38	19.31	5.09
4–5	508.45	7.33	64.13	6.50	20.08	5.56
5–6	475.84	7.61	58.20	7.23	20.42	5.94
6–7	448.15	7.95	43.76	7.34	20.65	6.31
7–8	428.54	8.29	43.20	8.45	20.57	6.60
8–9	410.03	8.71	33.69	8.85	20.48	6.89
9–10	396.22	9.17	46.55	12.15	20.17	7.13
10–11	377.78	9.98	43.85	14.30	20.13	7.47
11–12	361.21	10.97	51.06	20.30	20.03	7.81
12–13	342.77	12.73	00.00	00.00	20.08	7.79
13	342.77	12.73	——	——	19.08	7.79

*$t = 11$
SOURCE: Tumor Registry, Department of Health Services, State of California

error of the survival rate [equation (3.2)], of probability of death [equation (2.20)], and of the expectation of life [equations (4.11), (4.12), and (4.13)] for each x. Numerical values of the standard errors and the main life table functions are shown in Table 6.

For example, at $x = 2$, the calculations for $S_{\hat{q}_2}$ were as follows: Using the formula

$$S_{\hat{q}_x}^2 = \frac{\hat{q}_x(1 - \hat{q}_x)}{M_x} \qquad \text{where} \quad M_x = m_x + n_x(1 + \hat{p}_x^{1/2})^{-1},$$

$$M_2 = m_2 + n_2(1 + \hat{p}_2^{1/2})^{-1} = 2367 + 478(1 + .8967^{1/2})^{-1}$$

$$= 2,612.495$$

$$S_{\hat{q}_2}^2 = \frac{\hat{q}_2(1 - \hat{q}_2)}{M_2} = \frac{.10303(.89697)}{2612.495} = .00003537$$

$$S_{\hat{q}_2} = \sqrt{.00003537} = .00595 = S_{\hat{p}_2}$$

To calculate $S_{\hat{p}_{03}}$ from $S_{\hat{p}_{0x}}^2 = \hat{p}_{0x}^2 \sum_{u=0}^{x-1} \hat{p}_u^{-2} S_{\hat{p}_u}^2$:

$$S_{\hat{p}_{03}}^2 = \hat{p}_{03}^2 \sum_{u=0}^{2} \hat{p}_u^{-2} S_{\hat{p}_u}^2$$

$$= (.55615)^2 \left[\frac{(.00569)^2}{(.75746)^2} + \frac{(.00626)^2}{(.81857)^2} + \frac{(.00595)^2}{(.98697)^2} \right]$$

$$= (.30930)[.0001513] = .00004680$$

$$S_{\hat{p}_{03}} = \sqrt{.00004680} = .00684$$

To calculate $S_{\hat{e}_2}$ from $S_{\hat{e}_\alpha}^2 = \hat{p}_\alpha^2 S_{\hat{e}_{\alpha+1}}^2 + [\hat{e}_{\alpha+1} + \tfrac{1}{2}]^2 S_{\hat{p}_\alpha}^2$:

$$S_{\hat{e}_2}^2 = \hat{p}_2^2 S_{\hat{e}_3}^2 + [\hat{e}_3 + .5]^2 S_{\hat{p}_2}^2$$

$$= (1 - .10303)^2 5.09^2 + [19.31 + .5]^2(.00595)^2$$

$$= 20.84450 + .01389 = 20.8584$$

$$S_{\hat{e}_2} = \sqrt{20.8584} = 4.57.$$

6. Problems for Solution

1. Find Estimator B in (2.18) from the likelihood function $L_B(x; p_x)$ in (2.16), page 227.

2. Find Elvebeck's Estimator in (2.23) from the likelihood function $L_E(x; p_x)$ in (2.22), page 227.

3. Justify the likelihood function $L_C(x; p_x)$ in (2.34), page 230, and derive from it Estimator C in (2.36), and the asymptotic variance in (2.38).

4. In reference to Table 1, page 223, suppose that $N_x = 100$, $m_x = 95$, $s_x = 91$, $n_x = 5$, and $w_x = 4$. Use this information to complete the following estimates of p_x, the probability of surviving the year $(x, x + 1)$, and the corresponding asymptotic variances: (1) The Actuarial Method; (2) Estimator A; (3) Estimator B; and (4) Elbeveck's Estimator.

5. *Continuation.* Suppose the mean withdrawal time of the $w_x = 4$ patients is $\bar{\tau} = .55$ and the mean time at death of the $D_x = 5$ patients is $\bar{t} = .45$. Compute Estimator C and the corresponding asymptotic variance.

6. *Continuation.* In problem 4, suppose that when the withdrawal time, $\tau_1, \ldots, \tau_4$, and the times at death, $t_1, \ldots, t_5$, are merged, the merged sequence is $\tau_1 < t_1 < \tau_2 < \tau_3 < t_2 < t_3 < \tau_4 < t_4 < t_5$. Find the Kaplan–Meier Estimator and the corresponding variance of the estimator.

7. Check the computations in Table 5, page 239.

8. Check the computations in Table 6, page 240.

9. Compute the life table of patients diagnosed as having cancer of the cervix uteri based on the data in Table 4 using the actuarial method.

10. Compute the life table using the data in Table 4 and Elvebeck's Estimator.

11. Find the 95% confidence interval for the true five-year survival rate for patients with a diagnosis of cancer of the cervix uteri (based on the 1942–54 California experience in Tables 4, 5, and 6).

12. *Continuation.* Test the hypothesis that, for a patient with a diagnosis of cancer of the cervix uteri, the probability of surviving the first three years since diagnosis (p_{03}) is smaller than the probability of surviving the next three (p_{36}).

13. *Continuation.* Test the hypothesis $q_0 = q_1$.

14. Plot the survival curve of cervical cancer patients (p_{0x}) in Table 6 and discuss the pattern.

15. *Continuation.* Plot the probability of dying in time interval $(x, x + 1)$ since diagnosis for cervical cancer patients $\hat{q}_x$ in Table 5 and discuss the pattern.

16. *Continuation.* Plot the probability of surviving time interval $(x, x + 1)$ since diagnosis for cervical cancer patients $\hat{p}_x (= 1 - \hat{q}_x)$ and discuss the pattern. Which of the three curves $(\hat{p}_{0x}, \hat{q}_x, \hat{p}_x)$ more accurately describes the change in survival and death of the patients? Explain.

17. *Continuation.* Find the 95% confidence interval for expectation of life of a patient at time of diagnosis, e_0. At first anniversary, e_1.

CHAPTER *12*

*A New Life Table—For Survival and Stages of Disease**

1. Introduction

Since the pioneering work of Graunt (1662) and Halley (1693) nearly three centuries ago, date of birth has been used as the point of origin and age of individuals as the reference scale for almost every life table constructed. The force of mortality is generally considered to be dependent on the age of a person and the expectation of life is computed for each age: $0, 1, 5, \ldots$. This convention was interrupted when the life table method was introduced for the analysis of survival data in medical follow-up studies of patients afflicted with cancer or other diseases. In these studies, the time of admission to a follow-up study is used as the starting point of a life table and the time interval since admission replaces the age interval in the ordinary life table. This change was based on the fact that a person who is afflicted with cancer, for example, is subject to a greater chance of dying than a normal person of the same age, and that the force of mortality is a function of time since contracting the disease. However, the life table methodology is essentially unaltered in such studies (cf., Chapter 11).

The change from the birth of an individual to the "birth of a case" as the point of departure is plausible in medical follow-up studies, but is inadequate for studies where the development of a

---

*Those readers whose interest is in application may skip Sections 3 and 4 at the first reading.

disease is by stages. In the natural evolution of cancer, for example, there are stages of the disease determined by the growth and size of tumors and metastasis of the disease. The development of diabetes also occurs in stages—from chemical diabetes to clinical diabetes to diabetes with complications. Generally, chronic diseases advance with time from mild through intermediate stages to severe stages to death. Often, the process is irreversible but a patient may die while being in any one of the stages. Patients in a given stage of a disease not only are subject to different forces of mortality than those in another stage, but may also advance to the next stage and experience a greater chance of dying. The process is dynamic, and the stages of the disease are a dominating factor in the survival or death of a patient. Therefore, the length of life of a patient must be considered as a function of both the age of the patient and the stage of the disease. A stochastic model to describe survival and stages of a disease has been proposed in Chiang (1980); the density function, distribution function, and the maximum likelihood estimators of the parameters involved have been derived. The purpose of this chapter is to propose a new life table methodology to accommodate the information derived from such studies.

The life table presented in this chapter has applications to most areas where the concept of "stage" can be defined, the end result need not be death. For example, this life table methodology can be applied to analyses of human fertility and child spacing, where the term "stage" refers to birth order while the end result is the completion of the family. A fertility table is presented in Section 6 which includes an example of a current United States population.

2. Description of the Life Table

Consider a chronic disease which is characterized by s stages. The disease advances in succession from stage i to stage $i + 1$, $i = 1, \ldots, s - 1$, and from each stage a patient may enter the death state R. The length of stay in stage i by a patient who advances to stage $i + 1$ is denoted by τ_i and by a patient who dies while in stage i is denoted by t_i. For distinction, we call τ_i the waiting time, and t_i the life time in stage i. Suppose that a group of l_1 individuals who have contracted the disease (i.e., entering stage 1) at an average age of x_1 are followed throughout their life time. Among the group, a number of d_1 individuals died during the first stage with an average life time $\bar{t}_1$ and l_2 individuals advanced to stage 2 with an average waiting time $\bar{\tau}_1$ in stage 1. The average age of the l_2 individuals at the time of entrance to stage 2 is x_2. The l_2 individuals are followed until death or until they advance to stage 3, and so on. Finally, there are l_s individuals who enter the last stage at an average age of x_s. The mean life time beyond x_s is $\bar{t}_s$. The process is shown in the following diagram.

Age at
entrance
to a stage

No. advancing
to a stage

Waiting time
in a stage

The information derived from the experience of a cohort l_1 is recorded in Table 1. The first four columns of Table 1 show the stage (i), the mean age at entrance to stage i (x_i), the number advancing to stage i (l_i), and the number dying in stage i (d_i). From these we compute the proportion of patients advancing from stage i to stage $i + 1$,

$$\hat{p}_i = \frac{l_{i+1}}{l_i}, \qquad i = 1, \ldots, s - 1, \qquad (2.1)$$

with $\hat{p}_s = 0$, recorded in column (5), and the proportion dying in stage i,

$$\hat{q}_i = \frac{d_i}{l_i}, \qquad i = 1, \ldots, s - 1, \qquad (2.2)$$

with $\hat{q}_s = 1$, recorded in column (6). In columns (7) and (8) we record the mean waiting time $\bar{\tau}_i$ and the mean life time $\bar{t}_i$, respectively.

Beginning with x_i, the d_i patients who died while in stage i have lived $d_i \bar{t}_i$ years before death occurs and the l_{i+1} patients who advanced to stage $i + 1$ have lived $l_{i+1} \bar{\tau}_i = l_{i+1}(x_{i+1} - x_i)$ years in stage i. Therefore, the total number of years lived in stage i is

$$L_i = l_{i+1}(x_{i+1} - x_i) + d_i \bar{t}_i, \qquad i = 1, \ldots, s. \qquad (2.3)$$

These are recorded in column (9). Summing over L_j, for $j = 1, \ldots, s$, gives the total number of years lived beyond x_i by the entire cohort. That is,

$$T_i = L_i + \cdots + L_s, \qquad i = 1, \ldots, s, \qquad (2.4)$$

with $T_s = L_s$, recorded in column (10).

Table 1. Life Table for Survival and Stages of Disease

Stage of Disease i	Mean Age at Entrance to Stage i x_i	Number Advancing to Stage i l_i	Number Dying in Stage i d_i	Proportion Advancing from Stage i to Stage $i+1$ $\hat{p}_i$	Proportion Dying in Stage i $\hat{q}_i$	Mean Waiting Time in Stage i $\bar{\tau}_i$	Mean Life Time in Stage i $\bar{t}_i$	Number of Years Lived in Stage i L_i	Total Number of Years Lived Beyond x_i T_i	Expectation of Life at Age x_i $\hat{e}_i$
(1)	(2)	(3)	(4)	(5)	(6)	(7)	(8)	(9)	(10)	(11)
1	x_1	l_1	d_1	$\hat{p}_1$	$\hat{q}_1$	$\bar{\tau}_1$	$\bar{t}_1$	L_1	T_1	$\hat{e}_1$
2	x_2	l_2	d_2	$\hat{p}_2$	$\hat{q}_2$	$\bar{\tau}_2$	$\bar{t}_2$	L_2	T_2	$\hat{e}_2$
$\cdots$	$\cdots$	$\cdots$	$\cdots$	$\cdots$	$\cdots$	$\cdots$	$\cdots$	$\cdots$	$\cdots$	$\cdots$
i	x_i	l_i	d_i	$\hat{p}_i$	$\hat{q}_i$	$\bar{\tau}_i$	$\bar{t}_i$	L_i	T_i	$\hat{e}_i$
$\cdots$	$\cdots$	$\cdots$	$\cdots$	$\cdots$	$\cdots$	$\cdots$	$\cdots$	$\cdots$	$\cdots$	$\cdots$
s	x_s	l_s	d_s	0	1	0	$\bar{t}_s$	L_s	T_s	$\hat{e}_s$

The expectation of life at x_i in column (11) is obtained from

$$\hat{e}_i = \frac{T_i}{l_i}, \qquad i = 1, \ldots, s, \tag{2.5}$$

as in the ordinary life table.

3. Biometric Functions of the Life Table

We can describe the illness and death process schematically in the following diagram:

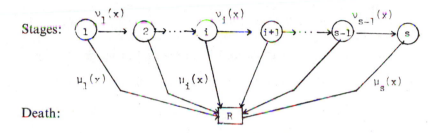

The arrows indicate the directions transitions take place, either from one stage to the next ($i \rightarrow i + 1$), or from a stage to the state of death ($i \rightarrow R$). For an individual of age x in stage i, we define the force of morbidity:

$$\nu_i(x)\Delta + o(\Delta) = \Pr\{\text{the individual will advance to stage } i + 1$$

$$\text{in time element } (x, x + \Delta)\} \tag{3.1}$$

for $i = 1, \ldots, s - 1$, and the force of mortality:

$$\mu_i(x)\Delta + o(\Delta) = \Pr\{\text{the individual will enter death state } R$$

$$\text{in time element } (x, x + \Delta)\} \tag{3.2}$$

for $i = 1, \ldots, s$. Let

$$\nu_{ii}(x) = -\left[\nu_i(x) + \mu_i(x)\right] \tag{3.3}$$

for $i = 1, \ldots, s - 1$, and

$$\nu_{ss}(x) = -\mu_s(x) \tag{3.4}$$

so that

$$1 + \nu_{ii}(x)\Delta + o(\Delta) = \Pr\{\text{the individual will remain in stage } i$$

$$\text{during time element } (x, x + \Delta)\} \tag{3.5}$$

for $i = 1, \ldots, s$.

The force of morbidity $\nu_i(x)$ and the force of mortality $\mu_i(x)$ (alias incidence rates and intensity functions) that are measures of the intensity of transitions are functions of stage (i) and age (x). In order to derive explicit formulas for the biometric functions in the life table, we assume that each of the intensity functions is a product of two factors:

$$\nu_i(x) = \nu_i \theta(x), \quad \mu_i(x) = \mu_i \theta(x) \quad \text{and} \quad \nu_{ii}(x) = \nu_{ii}\theta(x), \quad (3.6)$$

with

$$\nu_{ii} = -(\nu_i + \mu_i). \quad (3.7)$$

The first factor (ν_i or μ_i) depends on the stage (i) from which an individual exits while the second factor $\theta(x)$ is a function of the age x at which a transition takes place.

3.1. Probability of advancement from stage i to stage $i + 1$, p_i.

$p_i = \Pr\{\text{an individual of age } x_i \text{ in stage } i \text{ will advance to stage } i + 1\}$

$$= \int_0^\infty \left[\exp\left\{ \int_{x_i}^{x_i + \tau} \nu_{ii}\theta(\xi)\, d\xi \right\} \right] \nu_i \theta(x_i + \tau)\, d\tau \quad (3.8)$$

where the exponential function is the probability of remaining in stage i from time (age) x_i to $x_i + \tau$, while the sum $\nu_i \theta(x + \tau)\, d\tau + o(d\tau)$ is the probability of advancing from stage i to stage $i + 1$ in the time element $(x_i + \tau, x_i + \tau + d\tau)$. Since for different values of τ, the corresponding transitions $i \to i + 1$ are mutually exclusive, the addition theorem implies that the integral from $\tau = 0$ to $\tau = \infty$ is the probability of advancing from i to $i + 1$. When the integration is effected, the result is

$$p_i = \frac{\nu_i}{-\nu_{ii}} = \frac{\nu_i}{\nu_i + \mu_i}. \quad (3.9)$$

3.2. Probability of dying in stage i, q_i.   Using similar reasoning, we compute

$q_i = \Pr\{\text{an individual of age } x_i \text{ will die while in stage } i\}$

$$= \int_0^\infty \left[\exp\left\{ \int_{x_i}^{x_i + t} \nu_{ii}\theta(\xi)\, d\xi \right\} \right] \mu_i \theta(x_i + t)\, dt$$

$$= \frac{\mu_i}{-\nu_{ii}} = \frac{\mu_i}{\nu_i + \mu_i}. \quad (3.10)$$

Since an individual in stage i will eventually move on to stage $i + 1$ or die,

$$p_i + q_i = 1. \quad (3.11)$$

This is also evident from (3.9) and (3.10).

3.3.   Waiting time in stage i, τ_i.   For an individual of age x_i in stage i, let τ_i be the length of time that he will remain in stage i until he advances to stage $i + 1$. The density function of τ_i is

$$h_i(\tau) = \exp\left\{ \int_{x_i}^{x_i + \tau} v_{ii}\theta(\xi)\,d\xi \right\} v_i\theta(x_i + \tau), \qquad (3.12)$$

and the distribution function of τ_i is

$$H_i(\tau) = \int_0^\tau h_i(\xi)\,d\xi$$

$$= \frac{-v_i}{v_{ii}}\left[1 - \exp\left\{ \int_{x_i}^{x_i + \tau} v_{ii}\theta(\xi)\,d\xi \right\} \right]. \qquad (3.13)$$

As $\tau \to \infty$,

$$H_i(\infty) = \frac{-v_i}{v_{ii}} < 1. \qquad (3.14)$$

This means that the waiting time τ_i is an improper random variable. The difference

$$1 - \frac{-v_i}{v_{ii}} = \frac{\mu_i}{v_i + \mu_i} = q_i \qquad (3.15)$$

is the probability that the individual will not advance to stage $i + 1$ but will enter the death state R.

3.4.   Life time in stage i, t_i.   For an individual of age x_i in stage i, let t_i be the length of time that he will remain in stage i until he dies. The density function of t_i is

$$g_i(t) = \exp\left\{ \int_{x_i}^{x_i + t} v_{ii}\theta(\xi)\,d\xi \right\} \mu_i\theta(x_i + t), \qquad (3.16)$$

and the distribution function of t_i is

$$G_i(t) = \int_0^t g_i(\xi)\,d\xi$$

$$= \frac{-\mu_i}{v_{ii}}\left[1 - \exp\left\{ \int_{x_i}^{x_i + t} v_{ii}\theta(\xi)\,d\xi \right\} \right]. \qquad (3.17)$$

As $t \to \infty$,

$$G_i(\infty) = \frac{-\mu_i}{v_{ii}} < 1. \qquad (3.18)$$

This means that the life time t_i is an improper random variable. The difference

$$1 - \frac{-\mu_i}{v_{ii}} = \frac{v_i}{v_i + \mu_i} = p_i$$

is the probability that the individual will not enter the death state R from stage i but will advance to stage $i + 1$.

3.5.   Life time beyond x_i, Y_i.   For an individual of age x_i in stage i, let Y_i be his future life time beyond x_i. The density function $f_{Y_i}(t)$ and the distribution function $F_{Y_i}(t)$ of Y_i may be derived as follows. By definition

$$f_{Y_i}(t)\,dt = \Pr\{t \leqslant Y_i < t + dt\} \tag{3.19}$$

is the probability that an individual who is in i at x_i will die in the time element $(x_i + t, x_i + t + dt)$. Since the individual may be in any one of the stages $i, i + 1, \ldots, s$, immediately before death, the density function $f_{Y_i}(t)$ is the sum of $s - i + 1$ terms:

$$f_{Y_i}(t)\,dt = f_i(t)\,dt + f_{i+1}(t)\,dt + \cdots$$
$$+ f_j(t)\,dt + \cdots + f_s(t)\,dt. \tag{3.20}$$

Each $f_j(t)\,dt$ in equation (3.20) corresponds to the sequence of transitions $i \to i + 1 \to \cdots \to j \to R$. The first term $f_i(t)\,dt + o(dt)$, for example, is the probability of transition $i \to R$ occurring in the time element $(x_i + t, x_i + t + dt)$, so that

$$f_i(t)\,dt = \exp\left(v_{ii}\int_{x_i}^{x_i+t}\theta(\xi)\,d\xi\right)\mu_i\theta(x_i + t)\,dt. \tag{3.21}$$

The exponential function in (3.21) is the probability of remaining in stage i throughout the interval $(x_i, x_i + t)$ while the sum $\mu_i\theta(x_i + t)\,dt + o(dt)$ is the probability of entering death state R from stage i during the interval $(x_i + t, x_i + t + dt)$.

The function $f_{i+1}(t)\,dt$ represents the sequence of transitions $i \to i + 1 \to R$. For each τ, if the transition $i \to i + 1$ occurs in $(x_i + \tau, x_i + \tau + d\tau)$, the probability of the event $i \to i + 1 \to R$ occurring is

$$\exp\left\{v_{ii}\int_{x_i}^{x_i+\tau}\theta(\xi)\,d\xi\right\}v_i\theta(x_i + \tau)\,d\tau$$

$$\times \exp\left\{v_{i+1,i+1}\int_{x_i+\tau}^{x_i+t}\theta(\xi)\,d\xi\right\}\mu_{i+1}\theta(x_i + t)\,dt. \tag{3.22}$$

Integrating (3.22) from $\tau = 0$ to $\tau = t$ yields

$$f_{i+1}(t) = v_i\mu_{i+1}\theta(x_i + t)\left[\sum_{l=i}^{i+1}\frac{1}{(v_{ll} - v_{\alpha\alpha})}\exp\left\{v_{ll}\int_{x_i}^{x_i+t}\theta(\xi)\,d\xi\right\}\right], \tag{3.23}$$

$\alpha = i, i + 1; \ \alpha \neq l.$

In general, $f_j(t)$ corresponds to the sequence $i \to i+1 \to \cdots \to j \to R$, and is given by

$$f_j(t) = v_i \ldots v_{j-1} \mu_j \theta(x_i + t)$$

$$\times \sum_{l=i}^{j} \frac{1}{\prod_{\substack{\alpha=i \\ \alpha \neq l}}^{j}(v_{ll} - v_{\alpha\alpha})} \exp\left\{ v_{ll} \int_{x_i}^{x_i+t} \theta(\xi)\, d\xi \right\}, \quad (3.24)$$

$j = i, \ldots, s$.

Substituting (3.24) for $j = i, \ldots, s$ in (3.20) gives the desired formula for the density function of the life time beyond x_i:

$$f_{Y_i}(t) = \sum_{j=i}^{s} v_i \ldots v_{j-1} \mu_j \theta(x_i + t)$$

$$\times \sum_{l=i}^{j} \frac{1}{\prod_{\substack{\alpha=i \\ \alpha \neq l}}^{j}(v_{ll} - v_{\alpha\alpha})} \exp\left\{ v_{ll} \int_{x_i}^{x_i+t} \theta(\xi)\, d\xi \right\} \quad (3.25)$$

$i = 1, \ldots, s$.

The distribution function of Y_i is derived directly from the density function:

$$F_{Y_i}(t) = \int_0^t f_{Y_i}(\xi)\, d\xi$$

$$= -\sum_{j=i}^{s} v_i \ldots v_{j-1} \mu_j \sum_{l=i}^{j} \frac{1}{\prod_{\substack{\alpha=i \\ \alpha \neq l}}^{j}(v_{ll} - v_{\alpha\alpha})v_{ll}}$$

$$\times \left[1 - \exp\left\{ v_{ll} \int_{x_i}^{x_i+t} \theta(\xi)\, d\xi \right\} \right] \quad (3.26)$$

for $i = 1, \ldots, s$.

As $t \to \infty$, the exponential functions vanish, and (3.26) reduces to

$$F_{Y_i}(\infty) = -\sum_{j=i}^{s} v_i \ldots v_{j-1} \mu_j \sum_{l=i}^{j} \frac{1}{\prod_{\substack{\alpha=i \\ \alpha \neq l}}^{j}(v_{ll} - v_{\alpha\alpha})v_{ll}}, \quad (3.27)$$

$i = 1, \ldots, s$.

Since an individual in stage i eventually dies, we expect

$$F_{Y_i}(\infty) = 1, \quad i = 1, \ldots, s, \quad (3.28)$$

for each i. An algebraic proof of (3.28) may be found in Chiang (1980). Therefore, Y_i is a proper random variable for every i, $i = 1, \ldots, s$.

3.6.   Expectation of life at x_i, e_i.   The mathematical expectation of Y_i is the expectation of life at age x_i, or

$$E[Y_i] = e_i, \qquad i = 1, \ldots, s. \tag{3.29}$$

Computing this by using the density function $f_{Y_i}(t)$, we get

$$e_i = \int_0^\infty t f_{Y_i}(t)\, dt$$

which upon substitution and integration yields the expectation

$$e_i = - \sum_{j=i}^s \nu_i \cdots \nu_{j-1} \mu_j \sum_{l=i}^j \frac{1}{\prod_{\substack{\alpha=i \\ \alpha \neq l}}^j (\nu_{ll} - \nu_{\alpha\alpha}) \nu_{ll}}$$

$$\times \int_0^\infty \exp\left\{ \nu_{ll} \int_{x_i}^{x_i+t} \theta(\xi)\, d\xi \right\} dt, \tag{3.30}$$

$i = 1, \ldots, s$. Thus the expectation of life is dependent upon the specific functions $\theta(x)$.

When the transitions $j \to j+1$ and $j \to R$ are independent of age, $\theta(\xi) = 1$, and the integration in (3.30) becomes

$$\int_0^\infty e^{\nu_{ll} t}\, dt = \frac{-1}{\nu_{ll}}$$

and the expectation of life at x_i in (3.30) reduces to

$$e_i = \sum_{j=i}^s \nu_i \cdots \nu_{j-1} \mu_j \sum_{l=i}^j \frac{1}{\prod_{\substack{\alpha=i \\ \alpha \neq l}}^j (\nu_{ll} - \nu_{\alpha\alpha}) \nu_{ll}^2}. \tag{3.31}$$

It is instructive to derive the expectation e_i from a different perspective. Let the random variable Z_j be the length of stay in stage j, which has an exponential distribution with parameter $-\nu_{jj}$ so that[†]

$$E[Z_j] = \frac{1}{-\nu_{jj}}, \qquad E[Z_j^2] = \frac{2}{\nu_{jj}^2}. \tag{3.32}$$

Clearly, $Z_1, \ldots, Z_s$ are independently distributed random variables. Now we introduce an indicator function ϵ_{ij},

$$\epsilon_{ij} = 1 \qquad \text{if a patient advances from state } i \text{ to stage } j,$$
$$= 0 \qquad \text{otherwise.}$$

Its expectations are

$$E[\epsilon_{ij}] = P_{ij}, \qquad E[\epsilon_{ij}^2] = P_{ij} \tag{3.33}$$

[†]$z_j = \tau_j$ if $j \to j+1$ occurs, $z_j = t_j$ if $j \to R$ occurs.

where

$$p_{ij} = p_i p_{i+1} \cdots p_{j-1} = \prod_{\alpha=i}^{j-1} \frac{\nu_\alpha}{-\nu_{\alpha\alpha}}, \qquad (3.34)$$

and its variance is

$$\mathrm{Var}[\epsilon_{ij}] = (1 - p_{ij})p_{ij}, \qquad i < j; \quad i,j = 1, \ldots, s. \qquad (3.35)$$

Since a patient's advancement from stage i to stage j is dependent upon his advancement to each intermediate stage α, for $i < \alpha < j$, the indicators $\epsilon_{i\alpha}$ and ϵ_{ij} are dependent random variables, and their covariance is given by

$$\mathrm{Cov}(\epsilon_{i\alpha}, \epsilon_{ij}) = \mathrm{Var}[\epsilon_{i\alpha}] p_{\alpha j}$$

$$= (1 - p_{i\alpha})p_{ij}, \qquad i < \alpha \leqslant j; \quad i,j = 1, \ldots, s. \qquad (3.36)$$

Now an individual in stage i at age x_i may advance to succeeding stages (j) and stay in each stage (j) for a period of time (Z_j). The life time of an individual beyond x_i is the sum of the lengths of stay Z_j for $j = i, i+1, \ldots, s$, provided the individual makes the advancement $i \to i+1 \to \cdots \to j$, for $i \leqslant j \leqslant s$. Therefore,

$$Y_i = Z_i + \sum_{j=i+1}^{s} \epsilon_{ij} Z_j, \qquad i = 1, \ldots, s, \qquad (3.37)$$

and the expectation of Y_i is simply

$$e_i = E[Y_i] = \frac{1}{-\nu_{ii}} + \sum_{j=i+1}^{s} p_{ij} \frac{1}{-\nu_{jj}}, \qquad i = 1, \ldots, s. \qquad (3.38)$$

The two expressions for e_i in (3.31) and (3.38) are of course equal. A proof of their equality is given in Chiang (1980).

From formula (3.37), we also have the variance of Y_i

$$\mathrm{Var}[Y_i] = \sum_{j=i}^{s} \mathrm{Var}[\epsilon_{ij} Z_j] + 2 \sum_{\alpha=i+1}^{s-1} \sum_{j=\alpha+1}^{s} \mathrm{Cov}[\epsilon_{i\alpha} Z_\alpha, \epsilon_{ij} Z_j], \qquad (3.39)$$

where the variance of the product $\epsilon_{ij} Z_j$ is given by

$$\mathrm{Var}[\epsilon_{ij} Z_j] = (2 - p_{ij})p_{ij} \frac{1}{\nu_{jj}^2}, \qquad (3.40)$$

and the covariance between $\epsilon_{i\alpha} Z_\alpha$ and $\epsilon_{ij} Z_j$ is

$$\mathrm{Cov}[\epsilon_{i\alpha} Z_\alpha, \epsilon_{ij} Z_j] = \mathrm{Cov}[\epsilon_{i\alpha}, \epsilon_{ij}] E[Z_\alpha] E[Z_j]$$

$$= (1 - p_{i\alpha})p_{ij} \frac{1}{\nu_{\alpha\alpha}\nu_{jj}}. \qquad (3.41)$$

Substituting (3.40) and (3.41) in (3.39) yields the desired formula for the variance of Y_i,

$$\text{Var}[Y_i] = \sum_{j=i}^{s} (2 - p_{ij})p_{ij}\frac{1}{v_{jj}^2} + 2 \sum_{\alpha=i+1}^{s-1} (1 - p_{i\alpha}) \sum_{j=\alpha+1}^{s} p_{ij} \frac{1}{v_{\alpha\alpha}v_{jj}}$$

(3.42)

$i \leqslant \alpha < j; \ \alpha, i, j = 1, \ldots, s.$

4. Probability Distribution of the Life Table Functions

The probability distributions of the observed quantities in this life table are similar to those for entries in the ordinary life table. Having resolved the theoretical problems of the biometric functions in Section 3, we can now state some of the probability distributions of the observed quantities. The reader may refer to Chapter 10 for a detailed discussion of related theoretical matters.

4.1. Joint distribution of $l_2, \ldots, l_s$.   Given the original cohort l_1, the number of patients advancing from stage 1 to stage i has a binomial distribution with

$$\Pr\{l_i = k_i \mid l_1\} = \binom{l_1}{k_i} p_{1i}^{k_i}(1 - p_{1i})^{l_1 - k_i}, \qquad k_i = 0, 1, \ldots, l_1, \quad (4.1)$$

where p_{1i}, the probability of the advancement $1 \to 2 \to \cdots \to i$, is given in (3.34). The numbers $l_2, \ldots, l_s$ of patients advancing to stages $2, \ldots, s$, have a chain binomial distribution

$$\Pr\{l_2 = k_2, \ldots, l_s = k_s \mid l_1\} = \prod_{i=1}^{s-1} \binom{k_i}{k_{i+1}} p_i^{k_{i+1}} q_i^{k_i - k_{i+1}},$$

$$k_{i+1} = 0, \ldots, k_i, \quad (4.2)$$

with $k_1 = l_1$. It is easy to show that the covariance,

$$\text{Cov}(l_i, l_j \mid l_1) = l_1(1 - p_{1i})p_{1j}, \qquad 1 \leqslant i < j \leqslant s, \qquad (4.3)$$

is greater than zero as might be expected (cf., equation (3.36)), so that the numbers l_i and l_j are positively correlated. However, for fixed i, the covariance decreases as j increases.

4.2. The probability distribution of $d_1, \ldots, d_s$.   The sequence of numbers $d_1, \ldots, d_s$ has a multinomial distribution as in the ordinary life table

$$\Pr\{d_1 = \delta_1, \ldots, d_s = \delta_s \mid l_1\} = \frac{l_1!}{\delta_1! \ldots \delta_s!} \prod_{i=1}^{s} (p_{1i}q_i)^{\delta_i}, \quad (4.4)$$

where δ_i are non-negative integers satisfying the condition $\delta_1 + \cdots + \delta_s = l_1$. The expectations, variances, and covariance are respectively given by

$$E[d_i | l_1] = l_1 p_{1i} q_i,\tag{4.5}$$

$$\text{Var}[d_i | l_1] = l_1 p_{1i} q_i (1 - p_{1i} q_i),\tag{4.6}$$

and

$$\text{Cov}[d_i, d_j | l_1] = -l_1 p_{1i} q_i p_{1j} q_j, \qquad i \neq j; \quad i, j = 2, \ldots, s.\tag{4.7}$$

4.3. Expectations and variances of L_i and T_i. These observed quantities are directly related to the random variables Y_i and Z_i from section 3.5. Namely,

$$L_i = l_i Z_i\tag{4.8}$$

and

$$T_i = l_i Y_i.$$

We use the relations in (4.8) to find the expectation of L_i

$$E[L_i | l_1] = -l_1 p_{1i} \frac{1}{v_{ii}}, \qquad i = 1, \ldots, s,\tag{4.9}$$

and the variance of L_i

$$\text{Var}[L_i | l_1] = [l_1 p_{1i} + 2(1 - p_{1i})] l_1 p_{1i} \frac{1}{v_{ii}^2}, \qquad i = 1, \ldots, s.\tag{4.10}$$

Similarly, we can use the expectation of Y_i in (3.38) and the variance of Y_i in (3.42) to obtain the expectation of T_i

$$E[T_i | l_1] = -l_1 p_{1i} \left[\sum_{j=i}^{s} p_{ij} \frac{1}{v_{jj}} \right]\tag{4.11}$$

and compute the variance of T_i from

$$\text{Var}[T_i | l_1] = l_1 p_{1i} [l_1 p_{1i} + (1 - p_{1i})] \text{Var}[Y_i]$$
$$+ l_1 p_{1i} (1 - p_{1i}) [E(Y_i)]^2.\tag{4.12}$$

4.4. Expectation and variance of $\hat{e}_i$. The observed expectation of life at age x_i ($\hat{e}_i$) is the sample mean life time beyond x_i, or

$$\hat{e}_i = \bar{Y}_i,\tag{4.13}$$

with the sample size being l_i. It follows that the expectation of $\hat{e}_i$ is

$$E[\hat{e}_i] = E[Y_i]$$
$$= -\sum_{j=i}^{s} p_{ij} \frac{1}{v_{jj}}\tag{4.14}$$

and the variance of $\hat{e}_i$ is

$$\text{Var}[\hat{e}_i] = E\left[\frac{1}{l_i}\right]\text{Var}[Y_i] \tag{4.15}$$

When l_i is large, $E[1/l_i]$ may be approximated by

$$E\left[\frac{1}{l_i}\right] \doteq \frac{1}{E(l_i)} = \frac{1}{l_1 p_{1i}}$$

and the variance has the form

$$\text{Var}[\hat{e}_i] = \frac{1}{l_1 p_{1i}}\text{Var}[Y_i] \tag{4.16}$$

where $\text{Var}[Y_i]$ is given in (3.42).

5.   Life Tables for Subpopulations and Their Relationship with the Life Table for the Entire Population

A life table may be constructed for an entire patient population whose members are of various ages, races, sexes, etc., or for each specific subgroup of patients. The resulting tables are closely related. Each element in the life table for the entire study population is either the sum or a weighted mean of corresponding elements in the individual life tables for the subgroups. Suppose that a patient population is divided into several groups according to age at the beginning of stage 1. For each age group, we affix a subindex to each of the life table quantity. Then, with reference to Table 1, we have for the ath age group, x_{ia}, l_{ia}, d_{ia}, $\hat{p}_{ia}$, $\hat{q}_{ia}$, $\bar{\tau}_{ia}$, $\bar{t}_{ia}$, L_{ia}, T_{ia} and $\hat{e}_{ia}$. Obviously, the numbers l_i and d_i are the sums of l_{ia} and d_{ia}; respectively,

$$l_i = \sum_a l_{ia} \quad \text{and} \quad d_i = \sum_a d_{ia}, \qquad i = 1, \ldots, s, \tag{5.1}$$

where the summations are taken over all age groups. The age at stage i (x_i), the waiting time ($\bar{\tau}_i$), and the life time ($\bar{t}_i$) are the weighted means of the corresponding quantities, x_{ia}, $\bar{\tau}_{ia}$, and $\bar{t}_{ia}$,

$$x_i = \sum_a \frac{l_{ia}}{l_i} x_{ia}, \tag{5.2}$$

$$\bar{\tau}_i = \sum_a \frac{l_{i+1,a}}{l_{i+1}} \bar{\tau}_{ia}, \tag{5.3}$$

and

$$\bar{t}_i = \sum_a \frac{d_{ia}}{d_i} \bar{t}_{ia}, \qquad i = 1, \ldots, s. \tag{5.4}$$

Easy computations give the relationship between the proportions

$$\hat{p}_i = \sum_a \frac{l_{ia}}{l_i} \hat{p}_{ia}, \qquad i = 1, \ldots, s, \qquad (5.5)$$

and

$$\hat{q}_i = \sum_a \frac{l_{ia}}{l_i} \hat{q}_{ia}, \qquad i = 1, \ldots, s, \qquad (5.6)$$

and between the total number of years lived beyond x_i,

$$T_i = \sum_a T_{ia}, \qquad i = 1, \ldots, s. \qquad (5.7)$$

It follows that the expectation of life at x_i, e_i, is the weighted mean of the corresponding expectations $\hat{e}_{ia}$,

$$\hat{e}_i = \sum_a \frac{l_{ia}}{l_i} \hat{e}_{ia}, \qquad i = 1, \ldots, s. \qquad (5.8)$$

6. A Fertility Table for Studies of Human Reproduction

Human reproduction has been studied nearly always in reference to a woman's age for the reason that a woman's fertility is age dependent. Fertility rates are determined for each age of women; birth rates are expressed specifically for a woman's age. Even in mathematical modeling of human fertility, a woman's age has been considered the underlying variable. Since the introduction of effective contraceptive measures in the early 1950's, the decision to reproduce is more often a prerogative of a couple than a function of the fecundability of a woman. As a result, a woman's age no longer plays the exclusive role in determining reproduction, and birth order or parity of women has emerged as an important factor in the formation of reproductive patterns of the human population.

In view of this new development, in this section we consider birth order, instead of women's age, as the basic variable to study human reproduction, and propose a fertility table using parity of women as the criterion to summarize the reproductive experience of a study population. Life table methodology has been adopted in the construction of the table. Each interval in the table corresponds to the parity of women, occurrence of a birth defines the beginning of an interval, and the age of women serves as the measuring scale along the time axis. A woman's exposure time to childbirth is treated as a random variable. In section 6.1, we present the definition of the parity specific fertility rate, parity progression ratio and their relationships, and we derive maximum likelihood estimators of these quantities and other elements in the table. In section 6.2 we give a description of the table and in section 6.3 some preliminary computations needed for the current fertility table. The data from the United States 1978 white population are used for illustration.

Many interesting studies of human fertility and reproduction have been reported in the literature. A. J. Lotka (1925) devised the intrinsic rate to measure natural increase in human populations; C. Gini (1924) suggested that birth intervals be treated as waiting times; L. Henry (1972) proposed several mathematical formulations for the measurement of human fertility using the assumption that the interval between births is independent of birth order. K. Srinivasan (1966) applied a probability model to the study of interlive birth intervals; J. A. Menken and M. C. Sheps (1972) discussed the distribution of birth intervals from a sampling frame viewpoint. Life table methodology also has been applied to fertility studies. J. M. Hoem (1970) discussed fertility models of the life table type; F. W. Oechsli (1975) considered both age and parity of women in his description of a population model. C. M. Suchindran and N. K. Namboodir and K. West (1979) used life table methods to study increment and decrement in human reproduction. M. C. Sheps and J. A. Menken (1973) discussed several models in their investigation of conception and birth. G. Rodriguez and J. Hobcroft (1980) analyzed birth intervals of a Columbia population in the form of the life table. However, in all the above investigations, age of women has been treated either as the chief variable or in conjunction with birth order. Such consideration has made the fertility problem more complex and analysis of human reproduction more difficult. The fertility table proposed here is a more realistic description of the changed reproductive behavior of the human population; it also has alleviated much complexity inherent in the traditional approach to the problem.

6.1.   Maximum-likelihood Estimation of the Elements in the Fertility Table.   From a stochastic viewpoint human reproduction is a staging process; each stage is defined by birth of a child. The process advances from one stage to the next until a family is completed. A woman of parity 0 (with no children) may live through her reproductive years without producing any child or she may have a baby and then stop reproducing, or she may continue to give birth to a second child and then stop, etc. Once a woman has given birth, the reproductive mechanism starts anew. The process may stop at any stage (parity). The parameters that govern human reproduction are a set of fertility rates $[r_0(x), r_1(x), \dots]$ prevailing in a study population over the reproductive period. Each $r_i(x)$ is a function of a woman's age x and parity i. These rates determine the expected number of children that a woman will have, exposure time between successive births, and the fertility pattern of the population under study as a whole. For convenience, we let $r_i(x) = r_i\theta(x)$ so that

$$r_i\theta(x)\Delta x + o(\Delta x) = \Pr\{\text{a woman of age } x \text{ and parity } i \text{ will give birth}$$

$$\text{to an infant in } (x, x + \Delta x)\},$$

$$i = 0, 1, 2, \ldots, \quad (6.1)$$

for any age x within the reproductive period of women. Here r_i is the fertility rate specific for parity i, or parity specific fertility rate, while $\theta(x)$ is a function of age x of the woman at which a birth takes place. However, age of a woman at the birth of a child may be related to her future reproduction. For example, a woman who has her first child at an older age is less likely to have many more children than a younger mother.

For a woman of parity i at age x_i, the exponential function

$$\exp\left(-r_i \int_{x_i}^{x}\theta(\tau)\,d\tau\right) \quad (6.2)$$

is the probability that she will not have another child in age interval (x_i, x). If $x = x_w$, the age at the end of reproductive period, the quantity

$$\exp\left(-r_i \int_{x_i}^{x_w}\theta(\tau)\,d\tau\right) = q_i \quad (6.2a)$$

is the probability that she will stop reproducing after ith birth, and

$$p_i = 1 - \exp\left(-r_i \int_{x_i}^{x_w}\theta(\tau)\,d\tau\right) \quad (6.3)$$

is the probability that she will have another child. The probability p_i is known as the parity progression ratio.

Consider a sample of l_0 women of parity 0 and of an average age x_0 who are to be observed throughout their reproductive years. For the αth woman in the sample, we introduce a vector

$$(\epsilon_{0\alpha}, \epsilon_{1\alpha}, \epsilon_{2\alpha}, \ldots)' \quad (6.4)$$

such that

$$\epsilon_{i\alpha} = 1 \quad \text{if she has } i \text{ children in her life,}$$

$$= 0 \quad \text{otherwise,} \quad (6.5)$$

for $i = 0, 1, \ldots$; $\alpha = 1, 2, \ldots, l_0$. The sum

$$\sum_{\alpha=1}^{l_0} \epsilon_{i\alpha} = d_i \quad (6.6)$$

is the number of women in the sample who have i children in their life, or the number of women whose final family size is i, and the sum

$$\sum_{i=j}\sum_{\alpha=1}^{l_0}\epsilon_{i\alpha}=\sum_{i=j}d_i=l_j \qquad (6.7)$$

is the number of women who have j or more children in their life. The number l_j is also equal to the number of children of birth order j produced by the cohort of l_0 women.

Let $x_{i\alpha}$ be the age of the αth women at birth of the ith child and $x_{w\alpha}$ her age at the end of her reproductive period. Then the likelihood function of the vector $(\epsilon_{0\alpha},\epsilon_{1\alpha},\dots)'$ is

$$f_\alpha=\prod_{j=0}\left[\prod_{i=0}^{j-1}\exp(-r_i w_{i\alpha})r_i\theta(x_{i+1,\alpha})\right]^{\epsilon_{j\alpha}}\exp(-r_j w_{j\alpha}^*\epsilon_{j\alpha}) \qquad (6.8)$$

where the upper limit of j is the highest parity of women in the sample, the quantity

$$w_{i\alpha}=\int_{x_{i\alpha}}^{x_{i+1,\alpha}}\theta(\tau)\,d\tau \qquad (6.9)$$

is the exposure time of αth women during parity i, and

$$w_{j\alpha}^*=\int_{x_{j\alpha}}^{x_{w\alpha}}\theta(\tau)\,d\tau \qquad (6.10)$$

is her reproductive span remaining after the jth birth. The likelihood function for the sample of l_0 vectors is the product of f_α in (6.8),

$$L=\prod_{\alpha=1}^{l_0}f_\alpha; \qquad (6.11)$$

its logarithm is

$$\log L=\sum_{\alpha=1}^{l_0}\sum_{j=0}\left\{\sum_{i=0}^{j-1}\left[-\epsilon_{j\alpha}r_i w_{i\alpha}+\epsilon_{j\alpha}\log r_i+\epsilon_{j\alpha}\log\theta(x_{i+1,\alpha})\right]\right.$$

$$\left.-\epsilon_{j\alpha}r_j w_{j\alpha}^*\right\}. \qquad (6.12)$$

From which we find the likelihood equation

$$-\sum_{\alpha=1}^{l_0}\epsilon_{i\alpha}w_{i\alpha}^*-\sum_{\alpha=1}^{l_0}\sum_{j=i+1}\epsilon_{j\alpha}w_{i\alpha}+\sum_{\alpha=1}^{l_0}\sum_{j=i+1}\epsilon_{j\alpha}\frac{1}{r_i}=0, \qquad (6.13)$$

and the maximum likelihood estimator

$$r_i=\frac{l_{i+1}}{\sum_{\alpha=1}^{l_0}\epsilon_{i\alpha}w_{i\alpha}^*+\sum_{\alpha=1}^{l_0}\sum_{j=i+1}\epsilon_{j\alpha}w_{i\alpha}}. \qquad (6.14)$$

The first sum in the denominator in (6.14),

$$\sum_{\alpha=1}^{l_0} \epsilon_{i\alpha} w_{i\alpha}^* = \sum_{\alpha=1}^{l_0} \epsilon_{i\alpha} \int_{x_{i\alpha}}^{x_{w\alpha}} \theta(\tau)\,d\tau, \qquad (6.15)$$

is the reproductive span remaining of the d_i women who stop reproducing after the ith birth, while each sum in the second term,

$$\sum_{\alpha=1}^{l_0} \epsilon_{j\alpha} w_{i\alpha} = \sum_{\alpha=1}^{l_0} \epsilon_{j\alpha} \int_{x_{i\alpha}}^{x_{i+1,\alpha}} \theta(\tau)\,d\tau, \qquad (6.16)$$

is the exposure time during parity i of the d_j women who go on to have j children in their life. Since the total number of children a woman has in her life may be related to the age and exposure time at early births, the quantity $w_{i\alpha}$ in formula (6.16) may be different for different values of j. In other words, the exposure time is a function of age (x), parity (i) and future reproduction (j). From formula (6.14) we see that *a fertility rate for parity i is the ratio of the number of children born to women of parity i to the total time of exposure to risk of childbearing of these women during parity i.*

Let the denominator of (6.14) be denoted by L_i,

$$L_i = \sum_{\alpha=1}^{l_0} \epsilon_{i\alpha} w_{i\alpha}^* + \sum_{\alpha=1}^{l_0} \sum_{j=i+1} \epsilon_{j\alpha} w_{i\alpha}, \qquad (6.17)$$

so that formula (6.14) may be rewritten as

$$r_i = \frac{l_{i+1}}{L_i}. \qquad (6.18)$$

If $\theta(x)$ is constant for x in the interval $(x_{i\alpha}, x_{i+1,\alpha})$, the constant may be set equal to one. Then the exposure times in (6.15), (6.16) and (6.17) become

$$\sum_{\alpha=1}^{l_0} \epsilon_{i\alpha} w_{i\alpha}^* = \sum_{\alpha=1}^{l_0} \epsilon_{i\alpha}(x_{w\alpha} - x_{i\alpha}), \qquad (6.15a)$$

$$\sum_{\alpha=1}^{l_0} \epsilon_{j\alpha} w_{i\alpha} = \sum_{\alpha=1}^{l_0} \epsilon_{j\alpha}(x_{i+1,\alpha} - x_{i\alpha}), \qquad j = i+1, \ldots, \quad (6.16a)$$

and

$$L_i = \sum_{\alpha=1}^{l_0} \epsilon_{i\alpha}(x_{w\alpha} - x_{i\alpha}) + \sum_{\alpha=1}^{l_0} \sum_{j=i+1} \epsilon_{j\alpha}(x_{i+1,\alpha} - x_{i\alpha}), \qquad (6.17a)$$

respectively. Let $x_{i \cdot j}$ be the mean age at birth of the ith child of the d_j women, for $j = i, i+1, \ldots,$ x_i be the mean age at birth of the ith child of the l_i women, and $x_{w\cdot i}$ be the mean age at the end of the reproductive period of the d_i women so that

$$x_{i\cdot j} = \frac{\sum_{\alpha=1}^{l_0} \epsilon_{j\alpha} x_{i\alpha}}{d_j}, \qquad j = i, i+1, \ldots, \tag{6.19}$$

$$x_i = \sum_{j=i}^{l_0} \sum_{\alpha=1}^{l_0} \frac{\epsilon_{j\alpha} x_{i\alpha}}{l_i} = \sum_{j=i} \frac{d_j x_{i\cdot j}}{l_i}, \qquad i = 0, 1, \ldots, \tag{6.20}$$

and

$$x_{w\cdot i} = \sum_{\alpha=1}^{l_0} \frac{\epsilon_{i\alpha} x_{w\alpha}}{d_i}, \qquad i = 0, 1, \ldots .$$

The total exposure time in (6.17a) may be written as

$$L_i = d_i(x_{w\cdot i} - x_{i\cdot i}) + \sum_{j=i+1} d_j(x_{i+1\cdot j} - x_{i\cdot j}), \tag{6.21}$$

or as

$$L_i = d_i(x_{w\cdot i} - x_i) + l_{i+1}(x_{i+1} - x_i), \qquad i = 0, 1, \ldots . \tag{6.22}$$

While the mean ages $x_{i\cdot j}$ usually are not recorded, the mean ages x_i are available in vital statistics of most study populations. Substituting (6.22) in (6.14) yields a simple formula for the fertility rate,

$$r_i = \frac{l_{i+1}}{d_i(x_{w\cdot i} - x_i) + l_{i+1}(x_{i+1} - x_i)}, \qquad i = 0, 1, \ldots . \tag{6.23}$$

The probability that a woman of parity i will reproduce is estimated by the proportion

$$\hat{p}_i = \frac{l_{i+1}}{l_i}, \qquad i = 0, 1, \ldots . \tag{6.24}$$

Equations (6.23) and (6.24) imply an important relationship between the parity progression ratio $\hat{p}_i$ and the parity specific fertility rate r_i,

$$\hat{p}_i = \frac{(x_{w\cdot i} - x_i)r_i}{1 + (x_{w\cdot i} - x_{i+1})r_i}, \qquad i = 0, 1, \ldots \tag{6.25}$$

which can be used to compute $\hat{p}_i$ from r_i for a current study population. Often $x_{w\cdot i}$ is set to be x_w for all women.

Taking the second derivative of $\log L$ in (6.12), we find also the sample variance of the parity specific fertility rate,

$$S_{r_i}^2 = \frac{l_{i+1}}{L_i^2}. \tag{6.26}$$

6.2.   Description of the Fertility Table.   The reproductive experience of a cohort of l_0 women as described in the preceding section can be summarized in a table. The resulting table is a cohort fertility table. When the reproductive experience of all the women of a population during a current year is summarized in a table, the resulting table is a current fertility table. The two types of tables are similar in appearance. The description presented in this section applies to both tables; references will be made to the current fertility table.

The fertility table proposed here has the appearance of an ordinary life table but differs in context, meaning and functional utility of the columns. Elements in the table are in reference to specific parities, but implicitly they are functions of a woman's age. All relations between elements of the table are derived in the absence of mortality and assume a closed population. Reference is made to Table 2.

Column 1. Parity (or birth order) i.   Birth order refers to the infant, while parity refers to the mother. A woman is of parity i if she has had i (live) births, so that the duration of parity i extends from the birth of the ith child to the birth of the $(i + 1)$th child or to the end of her reproductive period if the woman stops reproducing after her ith child. The last birth order in the table varies with the fertility pattern of a study population.

Column 2. Mean age of women at the ith birth, x_i.   In a current fertility table, this is the mean age of women at the ith (live) birth during the study year.

Unlike the ordinary life table where age interval is fixed in advance, the mean age of women for each parity is determined from the study population or from annual vital statistics data. It is an exact age, is not predetermined, and is subject to variation. The age at the end of the reproductive years of a woman is denoted by $x_{w\alpha}$. Usually, it is taken as 45 or 50 years for all women.

Column 3. Parity progression ratio for parity i, $\hat{p}_i$.   Each $\hat{p}_i$ is an estimate of the probability that a woman who has i live births will go on to have an $(i + 1)$th child. The time interval associated with the probability is from $x_{i\alpha}$ to $x_{w\alpha}$ for the α-th woman. For a current fertility table, the sequence of values $(\hat{p}_0, \hat{p}_1, \dots)$ is determined from the census and vital statistics records of the current population. A formula that relates $\hat{p}_i$ to the fertility rate r_i has been given in section 6.1, equation (6.25).

Column 4. Proportion of women who stop reproducing after the ith (live) birth, $\hat{q}_i$.   For each i, the proportion $\hat{q}_i$ is an estimate of the probability that a woman of parity i will stop reproducing. Clearly,

$$\hat{p}_i + \hat{q}_i = 1. \tag{6.27}$$

Column 5. Number of women who have i or more live births, l_i. For a current fertility table, the first figure in this column, l_0, is an arbitrary radix defining a theoretical population engaged in human reproduction. Each number that follows (l_i) represents the number of women out of the original theoretical cohort l_0 who have i or more live births. Equivalently it is the number of women of parity i eligible to have an $(i + 1)$th child. The figures $(l_1, l_2, \ldots)$ are meaningful only in relation to the radix l_0. The radix is set equal to some convenient number, such as $l_0 = 10000$ and the remaining figures in the column can be successively computed from the equation

$$l_{i+1} = l_i \hat{p}_i, \qquad i = 0, 1, \ldots . \tag{6.28}$$

The sequence $\{l_0, l_1, l_2, \ldots \}$ plotted against the parities $\{0, 1, 2, \ldots \}$ provides a "survival curve" illustrating the proportion of women still "in the running" after having a number of live births. For each i, l_i is also the number of live births of birth order i of the l_0 women.

Column 6. Number of women who stop reproducing after the ith live birth, d_i. Each d_i is also the number of women in the original population who have a final family size of i live births. Numerically, d_i is computed from

$$d_i = l_i - l_{i+1}, \qquad i = 0, 1, \ldots \tag{6.29}$$

or from

$$d_i = l_i \hat{q}_i, \qquad i = 0, 1, \ldots . \tag{6.30}$$

The numbers $(d_0, d_1, \ldots)$ taken together form a frequency distribution of women in the population according to completed family size.

Column 7. Total exposure time to childbearing of women of parity i, L_i. The number of women of parity i (l_i) and the numbers of women who stop reproducing at higher parities j (d_j) have an obvious relationship,

$$l_i = \sum_{j=i} d_j . \tag{6.31}$$

Exposure time during a given parity is related to future reproduction of a woman. Let $x_{i \cdot j}$ be the mean age at the ith birth of d_j women and $x_{w \cdot i}$ be the mean age at the end of reproductive period of the d_i women. Then the exposure time of d_j women is

$$d_j(x_{i+1 \cdot j} - x_{i \cdot j}), \qquad j = i + 1 \ldots \tag{6.32}$$

and the total exposure time of l_i women is

$$L_i = d_i(x_{w \cdot i} - x_{i \cdot i}) + \sum_{j=i+1} d_j(x_{i+1 \cdot j} - x_{i \cdot j}). \tag{6.21}$$

Because the mean age x_i in column 2 is the weighted mean of $x_{i \cdot j}$ [cf. Equation (6.20)], formula (6.21) may be rewritten as

$$L_i = d_i(x_{w \cdot i} - x_i) + l_{i+1}(x_{i+1} - x_i), \qquad (6.22)$$

which is the basic formula for computing L_i.

Column 8. Total reproductive span remaining for women after the ith birth, T_i. This is the number of reproductive years remaining to the members of the population who have attained parity i. Each T_i is computed from

$$T_i = L_i + L_{i+1} + \cdots . \qquad (6.33)$$

Column 9. Fertility rate for women of parity i, r_i. Each r_i is the mean number of births per woman per year of exposure for women of parity i, or

$$r_i = \frac{l_{i+1}}{L_i} . \qquad (6.34)$$

This column describes the change in fertility over parity. The reciprocal of r_i,

$$\frac{1}{r_i} = \frac{L_i}{l_{i+1}} , \qquad (6.35)$$

is the average number of years that a woman of parity i waits until the birth of an $(i + 1)$th child.

Column 10. Fertility rate beyond the ith live birth, R_i. For each i, R_i is the cumulative fertility rate from parity i on. Specifically, it is the number of live births beyond the ith birth order per woman per year of exposure produced by women of parity i and beyond. In formula

$$R_i = (l_{i+1} + l_{i+2} + \cdots)/T_i . \qquad (6.36)$$

Note that each R_i is also a weighted mean of the parity specific fertility rate r_j, namely

$$R_i = \sum_{j=i} \frac{L_j}{T_i} r_j . \qquad (6.37)$$

The reciprocal of R_i is the average number of years that a woman of parity i or beyond waits for the birth of a child,

$$\frac{1}{R_i} = \frac{T_i}{l_{i+1} + l_{i+2} + \cdots} , \qquad i = 0, 1, \ldots \qquad (6.38)$$

Column 11. Expected length of waiting time from age at ith birth to the completion of family, $\hat{e}_i$. This is the mean waiting time in years between the ith birth and completion of family. It is computed from the equation

$$\hat{e}_i = \frac{1}{l_i} \sum_{j=i} d_j(x_j - x_i) \qquad i = 0, 1, \ldots . \qquad (6.39)$$

Although the number of children a woman will have is uncertain and the time interval between successive births is subject to variation, the life table approach to fertility analysis provides a means to estimate the needed time for a woman to complete her family.

6.3. Computation of parity progression ratio for a current population. Construction of a fertility table from the vital statistics and census data of a current population requires a prior computation of the parity progression ratio for each parity. Table 3 records the necessary information for the computation of $\hat{p}_i$. The data from the United States 1978 white population are used for illustration.

Column (1). Parity i.

Column (2). Number of women in the reproductive period who are of parity i, P_i. This number is also an estimate of the total length of time that women of parity i are exposed to the risk of childbearing.

Column (3). Number of live births of birth order i during the current year, b_i.

Column (5). Fertility rate for women of parity i, r_i. By definition

$$r_i = \frac{\text{No. of births of order } (i + 1)}{\text{Total exposure time of women of parity } i} . \qquad (6.40)$$

Using the information in column (2) and (3), we compute r_i from

$$r_i = \frac{b_{i+1}}{P_i} . \qquad (6.41)$$

Column (6). Parity progression ratio, $\hat{p}_i$. The relationship between the parity progression ratio $\hat{p}_i$ and the parity specific fertility rate r_i is basic to the construction of a fertility table for a current population. According to the discussion in section 6.1, the relationship is

$$\hat{p}_i = \frac{(x_{w \cdot i} - x_i) r_i}{1 + (x_{w \cdot i} - x_{i+1}) r_i} , \qquad (6.25)$$

Using $r_i = b_{i+1} / P_i$ given in column (5), $\hat{p}_i$ can be computed for each parity i.

In Table 3, the number of births b_i, the number of women P_i and the mean age x_i for every parity i were taken from the census and vital statistics publications of the United States, while fertility rates r_i in column (5) and parity progression ratios in column (6) were computed using formulas (6.41) and (6.25), respectively.

Remark 1.   The end of reproductive period of women in a population is often assumed to be at the same age, such as $x_w = 45$ or 50 years, for all women. This assumption is plausible in general and is valid when the women of parity i in a current population (P_i in Column 2, Table 3) are women of all ages up to x_w. Under this assumption, $x_{w \cdot i}$ may be replaced by x_w in formula (6.25) and in other formulas.

Remark 2.   A fertility table for a current population describes the reproductive experience of the population. Every element in the table is an estimate of the corresponding measure in the population. In particular, the parity specific fertility rate r_i in column (9) of Table 2 is equal to the corresponding parity specific rate r_i in column (5) of Table 3, or

$$\frac{l_{i+1}}{L_i} = r_i = \frac{b_{i+1}}{P_i} . \tag{6.42}$$

Proof of the equality is straightforward. Using formula (6.22) for L_i,

$$\frac{l_{i+1}}{L_i} = \frac{l_{i+1}}{d_i(x_{w \cdot i} - x_i) + l_{i+1}(x_{i+1} - x_i)} . \tag{6.43}$$

Dividing the numerator and the denominator on the right-hand side of (6.43) by l_i and using the definition of $\hat{p}_i$ in (6.24), we find

$$\frac{l_{i+1}}{L_i} = \frac{\hat{p}_i}{(x_{w \cdot i} - x_i) - \hat{p}_i(x_{w \cdot i} - x_{i+1})} . \tag{6.44}$$

The right-hand side reduces to b_{i+1}/P_i when (6.25) is introduced for $\hat{p}_i$ and (6.41) for r_i. The assertion in (6.42) is proven.
We also have

$$R_i = (b_{i+1} + \cdots)/(P_i + \cdots). \tag{6.45}$$

6.4.   Summary and Discussion.   The human reproductive process is governed by a set of fertility rates $[r_0\theta(x), r_1\theta(x), \dots]$ prevailing over the childbearing years of women in a study population. Each r_i is a function of parity i while $\theta(x)$ is a function of women's age x at which time birth occurs. Due to effective contraceptive methods and the wide acceptance of modern family planning practices, birth order has replaced the age of women as the chief determinant in the reproduction of children.

Table 2. Fertility Table, U.S. White Population, 1978.

| Parity or birth order | Mean age of women at the ith birth (in years) | Parity progression ratio for parity i (c.f. Table 2) | Proportion of women who stop reproducing after the ith live birth | Number of women who have i or more live births | Number of women who stop reproducing after the ith live birth | Total exposure time to childbearing of women of parity i | Total reproductive span remaining for women after the ith birth[1] | Fertility rate for women of parity i | Fertility rate beyond the ith live birth | Expected length of waiting time from age at ith birth to completion of family[2] |
| i | x_i | $\hat{p}_i$ | $\hat{q}_i$ | l_i | d_i | L_i | T_i | $1000r_i$ | $10000R_i$ | $\hat{e}_i$ |
(1)	(2)	(3)	(4)	(5)	(6)	(7)	(8)	(9)	(10)	(11)
0	22.15	.5979	.4021	10000	4021	98517	228501	60.7	63.7	2.71
1	23.26	.8203	.1797	5979	1074	36249	129984	135.3	66.0	3.41
2	25.89	.5095	.4905	4905	2406	51327	93735	48.7	39.2	1.54
3	28.03	.3402	.6598	2499	1649	29624	42408	28.7	27.6	.89
4	29.96	.2820	.7180	850	610	9621	12784	24.9	25.2	.67
5	31.82	.2441	.7559	240	181	2477	3163	23.8	25.9	.52
6	33.37	.2888	.7112	59	42	511	686	33.3	33.5	.57
7	34.67	.3247	.6753	17	11	125	175	48.0	34.3	.68
8 +	36.61			6	6	50	50		0	0

[1] Age at end of reproductive period is assumed to be $x_w = 45$ years for all women.
[2] The author benefited from a discussion with A. Golbeck on the value of $\hat{e}_i$.

Table 3. Calculation of parity progression ratio, U.S. White population, 1978

Parity	Number of[1] women of parity i in study year (in 1000)	Number of[2] live births of order i during study year	Mean age of[2] women at ith live birth during study year	Fertility rate for women of parity i (per 1000)	Parity progression ratio for women of parity i
i	P_i	b_i	x_i	$1000r_i$	$\hat{p}_i$
(1)	(2)	(3)	(4)	(5)	(6)
0	18,923		22.15*	60.7	.5979
1	6,497	1,148,966	23.26	135.3	.8203
2	8,166	878,834	25.89	48.7	.5095
3	5,028	397,777	28.03	28.7	.3402
4	2,231	144,158	29.96	24.9	.2820
5	1,032	55,472	31.82	23.6	.2441
6	362	24,322	33.37	33.4	.2888
7	249	12,095	34.67	42.7**	.3247
8 +	80	14,039	36.61		
Total	42,568	2,675,633		62.9	

Source: [1] Bureau of the Census, U.S. Department of Commerce, Current Population Reports, Population Characteristics, Series P-230, No. 341, October, 1978, Table 7, pp. 34–35.
[2] National Center for Health Statistics, U.S. Department of Health and Human Services, Vital Statistics of the United States, 1978, Vol. 1—Natality, Table 1–57.
*Mean age of women of parity 0 during study year.
**42.7 = 14,039/(249 + 80).

In view of this new development, a fertility table for the analysis of human reproduction is proposed, where the occurrence of a birth defines the beginning of an interval, and the age of women serves as a measuring scale along the time axis. The table contains a number of measures including the probability of reproduction, the exposure time, and fertility rate, etc. These measures are all for specific parities, but implicitly they are functions of the age of women.

A fertility table may be for a "cohort" of women in a prospective study or for a current population. In either case, the table gives a comprehensive description of the reproductive experience of a female population but it requires only a minimum amount of information and simple computation. The basic data needed for the table are the number of births of each birth order, the mean age of women at each birth, and the number of women of each parity. The fertility table presented in Table 2 contains a total of eleven columns. In an application, one may retain only those columns that will serve the particular purpose of the study.

7. Problems for Solution

1. Use the definitions of $v_i\theta(x)$ and $v_{ii}\theta(x)$ in (3.6) and (3.7) to show the probability that an individual of age x_i in stage i will advance to stage $i + 1$, p_i, as given in formula (3.8). And show that when the integration is effected, the probability reduces to that in formula (3.9).

2. Derive the formula for the distribution function of the waiting time in stage i, $H_i(\tau)$, from the density function $h_i(\tau)$ in (3.12).

3. Justify the formula in (3.22) and derive from it the density function $f_{i+1}(t)$ in (3.23).

4. Derive the density function $f_{i+2}(t)$.

5. Show for distinct numbers $\lambda_1, \ldots, \lambda_s$,

$$(1) \qquad \sum_{i=1}^{s} \frac{1}{\displaystyle\prod_{\substack{j=1 \\ j \neq i}}^{s} (\lambda_i - \lambda_j)} = 0,$$

$$(2) \qquad \sum_{i=1}^{s} \frac{1}{\displaystyle\prod_{\substack{j=1 \\ j \neq i}}^{s} (\lambda_i - \lambda_j)\lambda_i} = (-1)^{s-1} \frac{1}{\displaystyle\prod_{i=1}^{s} \lambda_i},$$

$$(3) \qquad \sum_{i=1}^{s} \frac{1}{\displaystyle\prod_{\substack{j=1 \\ j \neq i}}^{s} (\lambda_i - \lambda_j)\lambda_i^2} = (-1)^{s-1} \frac{1}{\displaystyle\prod_{i=1}^{s} \lambda_i} \left(\sum_{i=1}^{s} \frac{1}{\lambda_i} \right).$$

6. Verify the density function $f_j(\tau)$ in (3.24).

7. Derive the distribution function $F_{Y_i}(t)$ in (3.26).

8. Show that $F_{Y_i}(\infty) = 1$ in (3.27).

9. The length of stay in stage j, Z_j, has an exponential distribution. State the density function and justify it. From the density function, find the expectations $E[Z_j]$ and $E[Z_j^2]$. Compare your result with (3.32).

10. Justify the relation between the covariance $\text{Cov}(\epsilon_{i\alpha}, \epsilon_{ij})$ and the variance $\text{Var}[\epsilon_{i\alpha}]$, and verify the formula (3.36).

11. Use the last equation in problem 5 to show that the expectation e_i in (3.31) is equal to the expectation e_i in (3.38).

12. Verify the formula for the variance of Y_i in (3.42).

13. Verify the formulas for the expectation and the variance $E[L_i \mid l_1]$ and $\text{Var}[L_i \mid l_1]$ in (4.9) and (4.10), respectively.

14. Justify the likelihood function for $(\epsilon_{0\alpha}, \epsilon_{1\alpha}, \ldots)$, f_α, in (6.8).

15. Derive the estimate of the i-th parity fertility rate r_i in (6.14) from the likelihood function (6.11).

16. Obtain the formula for L_i in (6.22) from (6.17a).

17. Derive the relationship in (6.25) between the parity progression ratio ($\hat{p}_i$) and the parity specific fertility rate (r_i) from (6.23) and (6.24).

18. Check the assertion in (6.42) that the fertility rate in the fertility table is equal to the fertility rate derived from the census and natality data of the current population.

19. Show that the fertility rate R_i in column (10), Table 2 can be determined also from the number of births and the number of women in a current population as follows:

$$R_i = (b_{i+1} + b_{i+2} + \cdots)/(P_i + P_{i+1} + \cdots). \qquad (6.45)$$

20. Check the computations in Tables 2 and 3 for the fertility table in section 6.

21. Obtain the number of births b_i, the mean age of women at i-th birth x_i, and the number of women of parity i for $i = 0, 1, \ldots$ from the census and natality statistics of a current population of your choice. Use these data to compute the fertility rate r_i and parity progression ratio $\hat{p}_i$ as in Table 3 and construct a fertility table for the population as in Table 2. Discuss your findings.

Appendix I

Fraction of Last Age Interval of Life a_i For Selected Countries

Table 1
Austria, 1969

Age Interval $x_i - x_{i+1}$	Fraction of Last Age Interval of Life a_i		
	Both Sexes	Male	Female
0–1	.12	.12	.12
1–5	.37	.37	.37
5–10	.47	.47	.47
10–15	.51	.51	.49
15–20	.58	.58	.55
20–25	.48	.49	.48
25–30	.51	.50	.54
30–35	.53	.53	.53
35–40	.53	.52	.53
40–45	.52	.51	.54
45–50	.54	.54	.53
50–55	.52	.53	.52
55–60	.53	.54	.53
60–65	.54	.53	.54
65–70	.53	.52	.54
70–75	.52	.50	.53
75–80	.51	.50	.51
80–85	.48	.47	.49
85–90	.45	.44	.45
90–95	.40	.40	.40

Table 2
California, 1970

Age Interval $x_i - x_{i+1}$	Fraction of Last Age Interval of Life a_i
0–1	.09
1–5	.41
5–10	.44
10–15	.54
15–20	.59
20–25	.49
25–30	.51
30–35	.52
35–40	.53
40–45	.54
45–50	.53
50–55	.53
55–60	.52
60–65	.52
65–70	.51
70–75	.52
75–80	.51
80–85	.50

Table 3
Canada, 1968

Age Interval $x_i - x_{i+1}$	Fraction of Last Age Interval of Life a_i		
	Both Sexes	Male	Female
0–1	.11	.11	.12
1–5	.41	.42	.40
5–10	.45	.45	.44
10–15	.54	.54	.53
15–20	.57	.59	.53
20–25	.48	.47	.51
25–30	.50	.49	.53
30–35	.52	.52	.52
35–40	.53	.53	.53
40–45	.54	.54	.54
45–50	.53	.53	.53
50–55	.54	.54	.54
55–60	.54	.53	.54
60–65	.53	.53	.53
65–70	.53	.52	.53
70–75	.52	.51	.53
75–80	.52	.51	.53
80–85	.50	.49	.51
85–90	.47	.46	.48

Table 4
Costa Rica, 1963

Age Interval $x_i - x_{i+1}$	Fraction of Last Age Interval of Life a_i		
	Both Sexes	Male	Female
0–1	.28	.27	.28
1–5	.29	.29	.28
5–10	.40	.42	.38
10–15	.49	.50	.50
15–20	.55	.55	.55
20–25	.53	.53	.54
25–30	.53	.51	.55
30–35	.51	.51	.51
35–40	.49	.51	.48
40–45	.53	.54	.52
45–50	.53	.51	.55
50–55	.53	.53	.52
55–60	.54	.55	.53
60–65	.53	.55	.51
65–70	.54	.56	.52
70–75	.53	.52	.54
75–80	.51	.52	.51
80–85	.50	.50	.50

Table 5
Finland, 1968

Age Interval $x_i - x_{i+1}$	Fraction of Last Age Interval of Life a_i		
	Both Sexes	Male	Female
0–1	.09	.08	.09
1–5	.38	.41	.34
5–10	.49	.48	.49
10–15	.52	.53	.50
15–20	.53	.53	.54
20–25	.51	.52	.51
25–30	.51	.52	.48
30–35	.52	.51	.52
35–40	.54	.54	.53
40–45	.55	.54	.55
45–50	.53	.52	.54
50–55	.54	.54	.53
55–60	.53	.53	.54
60–65	.53	.53	.54
65–70	.52	.51	.53
70–75	.52	.51	.53
75–80	.51	.49	.52
80–85	.47	.47	.48

Table 6
France, 1969

Age Interval $x_i - x_{i+1}$	Fraction of Last Age Interval of Life a_i		
	Both Sexes	Male	Female
0–1	.16*	.15*	.17*
1–5	.38	.39	.36
5–10	.46	.47	.45
10–15	.54	.55	.52
15–20	.56	.56	.55
20–25	.51	.50	.51
25–30	.51	.51	.52
30–35	.53	.53	.54
35–40	.53	.53	.52
40–45	.53	.53	.53
45–50	.54	.54	.54
50–55	.52	.52	.52
55–60	.53	.53	.53
60–65	.53	.52	.53
65–70	.53	.52	.54
70–75	.52	.51	.53
75–80	.51	.50	.52
80–85	.49	.48	.50
85–90	.46	.45	.47
90–95	.41	.39	.42

*The large values of a_0 for the France 1969 population are due to the fact that infants who die before 3 days old are not recorded. Age at death of these infants is not included in the calculation of a_0.

Table 7
East Germany, 1967

Age Interval $x_i - x_{i+1}$	Fraction of Last Age Interval of Life a_i		
	Both Sexes	Male	Female
0–1	.38	.38	.38
1–5	.46	.46	.46
5–10	.52	.53	.51
10–15	.56	.58	.54
15–20	.50	.50	.51
20–25	.52	.51	.53
25–30	.52	.52	.53
30–35	.52	.52	.52
35–40	.54	.54	.54
40–45	.54	.55	.54
45–50	.52	.53	.52
50–55	.54	.54	.54
55–60	.54	.53	.54
60–65	.53	.53	.53
65–70	.53	.53	.53
70–75	.52	.51	.52
75–80	.51	.49	.49
80–85	.48	.47	.49
85–90	.43	.43	.43
90–95	.39	.39	.39

Table 8
West Germany, 1969

Age Interval $x_i - x_{i+1}$	Fraction of Last Age Interval of Life a_i		
	Both Sexes	Male	Female
0–1	.10	.10	.11
1–5	.39	.39	.38
5–10	.46	.46	.46
10–15	.52	.51	.52
15–20	.57	.58	.54
20–25	.52	.51	.53
25–30	.51	.51	.51
30–35	.52	.52	.53
35–40	.54	.54	.55
40–45	.53	.53	.53
45–50	.51	.51	.51
50–55	.58	.58	.57
55–60	.54	.54	.54
60–65	.54	.53	.54
65–70	.52	.52	.53
70–75	.52	.51	.53
75–80	.51	.49	.52
80–85	.49	.47	.49
85–90	.44	.43	.45
90–95	.39	.38	.40

Table 9
Hungary, 1967

Age Interval $x_i - x_{i+1}$	Fraction of Last Age Interval of Life a_i		
	Both Sexes	Male	Female
0–1	.10	.10	.11
1–5	.35	.35	.33
5–10	.45	.47	.42
10–15	.52	.51	.54
15–20	.55	.57	.52
20–25	.51	.52	.50
25–30	.52	.52	.53
30–35	.52	.51	.52
35–40	.53	.52	.55
40–45	.53	.52	.53
45–50	.54	.54	.53
50–55	.53	.53	.52
55–60	.54	.54	.54
60–65	.53	.53	.54
65–70	.53	.52	.54
70–75	.52	.51	.53
75–80	.50	.50	.51
80–85	.48	.47	.48

Table 10
Ireland, 1966

Age Interval $x_i - x_{i+1}$	Fraction of Last Age Interval of Life a_i		
	Both Sexes	Male	Female
0–1	.13	.12	.13
1–5	.38	.39	.37
5–10	.47	.47	.46
10–15	.48	.48	.46
15–20	.55	.56	.54
20–25	.51	.50	.53
25–30	.51	.50	.53
30–35	.52	.52	.51
35–40	.55	.56	.54
40–45	.54	.55	.54
45–50	.50	.50	.50
50–55	.53	.53	.52
55–60	.52	.53	.52
60–65	.52	.52	.53
65–70	.52	.51	.53
70–75	.52	.52	.53
75–80	.49	.49	.50
80–85	.48	.48	.48
85–90	.45	.44	.46
90–95	.39	.38	.40

Table 11
North Ireland, 1966

Age Interval $x_i - x_{i+1}$	Fraction of Last Age Interval of Life a_i		
	Both Sexes	Male	Female
0–1	.13	.13	.14
1–5	.36	.38	.35
5–10	.45	.47	.41
10–15	.50	.49	.52
15–20	.58	.59	.56
20–25	.52	.54	.48
25–30	.51	.53	.49
30–35	.52	.50	.56
35–40	.53	.51	.55
40–45	.53	.54	.53
45–50	.56	.57	.55
50–55	.54	.54	.54
55–60	.55	.54	.55
60–65	.54	.53	.55
65–70	.52	.52	.53
70–75	.52	.51	.53
75–80	.50	.49	.51
80–85	.50	.49	.51

Table 12
Italy, 1966

Age Interval $x_i - x_{i+1}$	Fraction of Last Age Interval of Life a_i		
	Both Sexes	Male	Female
0–1	.16	.15	.17
1–5	.35	.36	.35
5–10	.46	.47	.45
10–15	.53	.54	.53
15–20	.53	.53	.52
20–25	.51	.51	.50
25–30	.52	.51	.53
30–35	.53	.52	.54
35–40	.53	.53	.53
40–45	.53	.53	.53
45–50	.54	.54	.54
50–55	.54	.54	.53
55–60	.54	.54	.54
60–65	.53	.53	.54
65–70	.52	.52	.53
70–75	.52	.51	.53

Table 13
The Netherlands, 1968

Age Interval $x_i - x_{i+1}$	Fraction of Last Age Interval of Life a_i		
	Both Sexes	Male	Female
0–1	.11	.11	.11
1–5	.41	.43	.39
5–10	.47	.47	.45
10–15	.51	.50	.53
15–20	.54	.55	.52
20–25	.49	.48	.51
25–30	.51	.50	.53
30–35	.51	.51	.51
35–40	.54	.54	.54
40–45	.53	.53	.53
45–50	.55	.55	.54
50–55	.54	.54	.53
55–60	.54	.54	.53
60–65	.53	.52	.54
65–70	.53	.52	.54
70–75	.52	.51	.53
75–80	.51	.50	.52
80–85	.49	.49	.50
85–90	.46	.46	.47
90–95	.42	.42	.42

Table 14
Norway, 1968

Age Interval $x_i - x_{i+1}$	Fraction of Last Age Interval of Life a_i		
	Both Sexes	Male	Female
0–1	.12	.10	.14
1–5	.44	.46	.42
5–10	.45	.46	.42
10–15	.56	.55	.60
15–20	.55	.56	.52
20–25	.51	.50	.52
25–30	.48	.48	.50
30–35	.54	.55	.55
35–40	.54	.55	.54
40–45	.56	.56	.56
45–50	.54	.53	.54
50–55	.53	.54	.53
55–60	.53	.53	.54
60–65	.54	.54	.53
65–70	.54	.53	.55
70–75	.53	.52	.54
75–80	.51	.50	.52
80–85	.50	.49	.50
85–90	.47	.46	.47
90–95	.42	.41	.43

Table 15
Okinawa, 1960

Age Interval $x_i - x_{i+1}$	Fraction of Last Age Interval of Life a_i		
	Both Sexes	Male	Female
0–1	.32	.32	.31
1–5	.38	.37	.40
5–10	.45	.47	.45
10–15	.50	.51	.48
15–20	.50	.51	.49
20–25	.51	.53	.49
25–30	.52	.51	.53
30–35	.51	.52	.50
35–40	.50	.48	.52
40–45	.52	.51	.52
45–50	.53	.53	.54
50–55	.52	.52	.52
55–60	.52	.52	.52
60–65	.53	.52	.54
65–70	.53	.53	.53
70–75	.52	.52	.53
75–80	.52	.52	.52
80–85	.50	.50	.50

Table 16
Panama, 1968

Age Interval $x_i - x_{i+1}$	Fraction of Last Age Interval of Life a_i		
	Both Sexes	Male	Female
0–1	.23	.23	.24
1–5	.33	.33	.33
5–10	.44	.44	.44
10–15	.49	.49	.50
15–20	.54	.53	.56
20–25	.53	.52	.54
25–30	.49	.49	.49
30–35	.48	.48	.49
35–40	.48	.47	.50
40–45	.49	.49	.50
45–50	.51	.51	.52
50–55	.53	.53	.53
55–60	.52	.52	.52
60–65	.52	.52	.52
65–70	.52	.53	.52
70–75	.44	.44	.45

Table 17
Portugal, 1960

Age Interval $x_i - x_{i+1}$	Fraction of Last Age Interval of Life a_i		
	Both Sexes	Male	Female
0–1	.26	.25	.27
1–5	.27	.27	.27
5–10	.42	.44	.41
10–15	.50	.50	.50
15–20	.53	.54	.52
20–25	.53	.52	.54
25–30	.52	.52	.52
30–35	.52	.52	.52
35–40	.52	.53	.52
40–45	.53	.53	.53
45–50	.53	.53	.53
50–55	.53	.54	.53
55–60	.54	.53	.54
60–65	.54	.53	.54
65–70	.54	.53	.55
70–75	.53	.52	.54
75–80	.52	.51	.53
80–85	.48	.47	.49
85–90	.45	.44	.46
90–95	.39	.38	.40

Table 18
Romania, 1965

Age Interval $x_i - x_{i+1}$	Fraction of Last Age Interval of Life a_i		
	Both Sexes	Male	Female
0–1	.23	.22	.24
1–5	.33	.34	.32
5–10	.46	.47	.43
10–15	.51	.51	.51
15–20	.56	.56	.54
20–25	.51	.51	.51
25–30	.51	.51	.52
30–35	.51	.51	.50
35–40	.53	.52	.53
40–45	.52	.52	.53
45–50	.54	.55	.53
50–55	.53	.53	.53
55–60	.54	.54	.54
60–65	.53	.53	.53
65–70	.54	.52	.55
70–75	.51	.51	.52

Table 19
Scotland, 1968

Age Interval $x_i - x_{i+1}$	Fraction of Last Age Interval of Life a_i		
	Both Sexes	Male	Female
0–1	.13	.13	.23
1–5	.40	.42	.38
5–10	.44	.44	.43
10–15	.53	.53	.53
15–20	.56	.57	.55
20–25	.49	.48	.52
25–30	.51	.51	.52
30–35	.53	.53	.53
35–40	.54	.53	.54
40–45	.54	.54	.54
45–50	.54	.55	.54
50–55	.53	.54	.52
55–60	.54	.54	.53
60–65	.53	.53	.54
65–70	.52	.52	.53
70–75	.51	.50	.52
75–80	.50	.49	.51
80–85	.49	.47	.50

Table 20
Spain, 1965

Age Interval $x_i - x_{i+1}$	Fraction of Last Age Interval of Life a_i		
	Both Sexes	Male	Female
0–1	.38	.39	.37
1–5	.46	.47	.46
5–10	.53	.53	.52
10–15	.55	.56	.52
15–20	.54	.53	.53
20–25	.54	.53	.55
25–30	.51	.50	.52
30–35	.52	.52	.52
35–40	.53	.53	.53
40–45	.54	.53	.54
45–50	.54	.54	.54
50–55	.54	.54	.54
55–60	.54	.54	.55
60–65	.54	.53	.55
65–70	.54	.53	.55
70–75	.53	.52	.54
75–80	.52	.51	.53

Table 21
Sri Lanka, 1952

Age Interval $x_i - x_{i+1}$	Fraction of Last Age Interval of Life a_i	
	Male	Female
0–1*	.28	.35
1–5	.46	.45
5–10	.53	.53
10–15	.55	.42
15–20	.49	.55
20–25	.51	.54
25–30	.52	.53
30–35	.53	.53
35–40	.53	.54
40–45	.54	.53
45–50	.54	.53
50–55	.53	.53
55–60	.53	.53
60–65	.53	.53
65–70	.53	.53
70–75	.52	.52
75–80	.50	.52
80–85	.42	.45
85–90	.35	.35

* a_0 values are estimated from the experience of the India 1941–50 populations

Table 22
Sweden, 1966

Age Interval $x_i - x_{i+1}$	Fraction of Last Age Interval of Life a_i		
	Both Sexes	Male	Female
0–1	.08	.08	.08
1–5	.44	.44	.45
5–10	.45	.44	.48
10–15	.53	.52	.55
15–20	.56	.57	.53
20–25	.51	.50	.53
25–30	.52	.53	.51
30–35	.53	.52	.55
35–40	.52	.53	.51
40–45	.53	.53	.54
45–50	.54	.55	.53
50–55	.54	.55	.53
55–60	.54	.54	.53
60–65	.53	.53	.54
65–70	.54	.53	.55
70–75	.53	.52	.54
75–80	.52	.51	.53
80–85	.50	.49	.50
85–90	.46	.45	.47
90–95	.42	.41	.42

Table 23
Switzerland, 1968

Age Interval $x_i - x_{i+1}$	Fraction of Last Age Interval of Life a_i		
	Both Sexes	Male	Female
0–1	.10	.10	.11
1–5	.36	.37	.36
5–10	.45	.45	.45
10–15	.52	.54	.47
15–20	.57	.58	.52
20–25	.49	.48	.49
25–30	.49	.50	.48
30–35	.51	.53	.49
35–40	.54	.54	.53
40–45	.53	.53	.54
45–50	.55	.55	.55
50–55	.54	.54	.53
55–60	.54	.55	.53
60–65	.54	.53	.54
65–70	.53	.53	.54
70–75	.52	.52	.53
75–80	.51	.50	.52
80–85	.50	.49	.51
85–90	.47	.45	.48
90–95	.41	.39	.42

Table 24
United States, 1970

Age Interval $x_i - x_{i+1}$	Fraction of Last Age Interval of Life a_i		
	Both Sexes	Male	Female
0–1	.09	.09	.09
1–5	.40	.40	.39
5–10	.46	.47	.45
10–15	.55	.56	.53
15–20	.54	.55	.53
20–25	.51	.51	.52
25–30	.51	.50	.52
30–35	.52	.52	.53
35–40	.53	.53	.53
40–45	.54	.54	.53
45–50	.54	.54	.53
50–55	.53	.53	.53
55–60	.53	.53	.53
60–65	.52	.52	.53
65–70	.52	.51	.53
70–75	.51	.51	.53
75–80	.51	.50	.52
80–85	.49	.48	.50

Table 25
Yugoslavia, 1968

Age Interval $x_i - x_{i+1}$	Fraction of Last Age Interval of Life a_i		
	Both Sexes	Male	Female
0–1	.23	.22	.24
1–5	.29	.31	.28
5–10	.45	.46	.43
10–15	.51	.51	.52
15–20	.53	.54	.53
20–25	.51	.52	.50
25–30	.51	.52	.50
30–35	.52	.53	.52
35–40	.53	.53	.53
40–45	.53	.52	.53
45–50	.54	.54	.54
50–55	.52	.52	.52
55–60	.54	.54	.55
60–65	.53	.53	.54
65–70	.54	.53	.55
70–75	.52	.51	.53
75–80	.49	.49	.50
80–85	.49	.48	.49
85–90	.45	.45	.46
90–95	.38	.38	.38

Table 26
Japan, 1975

Age Interval $x_i - x_{i+1}$	Fraction of last age interval of life, a_i		
	Both Sexes	Male	Female
0–1	.14	.14	.15
1–5	.39	.40	.38
5–10	.44	.44	.44
10–15	.52	.52	.52
15–20	.56	.56	.55
20–25	.51	.50	.51
25–30	.50	.50	.51
30–35	.52	.52	.51
35–40	.54	.54	.53
40–45	.53	.54	.53
45–50	.53	.52	.54
50–55	.53	.53	.54
55–60	.54	.54	.54
60–65	.54	.54	.54
65–70	.57	.53	.54
70–75	.53	.52	.54
75–80	.52	.51	.53
80–85	.50	.48	.50

Computed by E. Miyaoka

Appendix II-1

Computer Program for Construction of Complete Life Tables

This is a complete life table computer program, written and debugged by Robert Chiang, in November, 1978. The program is written in the Fortran IV language, and is designed for use with most IBM computers, particularly the 360/370 model. The first three cards of the program are "job control language" cards, and may vary from one installation to another.

The input data must conform to the usual 86 single year age groupings. The input data is as follows:

TITLE denotes the title of the table (not to exceed 80 characters)

P(I) denotes the midyear population of each year of age
D(I) denotes the number of deaths in each year of age
A(I) denotes the fraction of the last year of life

P(I) and D(I) must appear in the input for each of the 86 single years of age. A(I) must appear in the input only for the first 5 single years of age. A(I) is assumed to be 0.50 for the other age groupings.

The proper formats for TITLE, P(I), D(I) and A(I) are specified in lines 22 through 28 (statement numbers 5, 11 and 15) in the program, with an example of the actual input data appearing in lines 224 through 243.

```
1.      //COMPLETE JOB
2.      // EXEC FORTCG
3.      //FORT.SYSIN DD *
4.      C
5.      C  THIS IS A FORTRAN IV PROGRAM DESIGNED FOR MOST IBM COMPUTERS,
6.      C  WRITTEN AND DEBUGGED BY ROBERT CHIANG IN NOV., 1978
7.      C  THE FIRST THREE CARDS ARE JCL CARDS AND WILL VARY FROM ONE
8.      C INSTALLATION TO ANOTHER.
9.      C
10.            DIMENSION TITLE(20)
11.            DOUBLE PRECISION     P(86),D(86),A(85),Z,SEE,SEQ,SES
12.            DOUBLE PRECISION RM(86),Q(86),DD(86),SL(86),YL(86),E(86),T(86)
13.            DOUBLE PRECISION VQ(86),F(85),C(85),VE(85),VS(86),B,W,R
14.      C THIS PROGRAM WILL CONSTRUCT A COMPLETE LIFETABLE
15.      C ALL INPUT DATA MUST CONFORM TO THE USUAL 86 SINGLE YEAR AGE GROUPINGS
16.      C THE USER MUST INPUT A TITLE WHICH DOESN'T EXCEED  A LENGTH OF 20A4
17.      C THE TITLE INPUTTED WILL FOLLOW THE HEADING IN STATEMENT #90
18.      C THE INPUT DATA IS AS FOLLOWS:
19.      C P(I) DENOTES THE MIDYEAR POPULATION OF THE AGE INTERVAL
20.      C D(I) DENOTES THE NUMBER OF DEATHS IN THE AGE INTERVAL
21.      C A(I) DENOTES THE FRACTION OF THE LAST AGE INTERVAL OF LIFE
22.            READ (5,5) (TITLE(I), I=1,20)
23.          5 FORMAT (20A4)
24.            READ (5,11) (P(I),I=1,86)
25.            READ (5,11) (D(I),I=1,86)
26.         11 FORMAT (10F8.0)
27.            READ (5,15) (A(I), I=1,85)
28.         15 FORMAT (10F3.2)
29.            DO 20 I=11,85
30.         20 A(I)=0.50
31.            SL(1)=100000.0
32.      C SL(I) DENOTES THE NUMBER  LIVING AT THE AGE I-1 IN THE COHORT
33.      C SL(I) IS THE SAME AS LITTLE L, AS USED IN TEXTBOOKS
34.      C RM(I) DENOTES THE DEATH RATE IN THE INTERVAL (IT REPRESENTS M OF X)
35.      C Q(I) REPRESENTS THE PROBABILITY OF DYING IN THE INTERVAL
36.      C DD(I) DENOTES THE NUMBER DYING IN THE INTERVAL OF THE COHORT
37.      C DD(I) REPRESENTS LITTLE L AS USED IN THE TEXTBOOK
38.      C YL(I) REPRESENTS THE NUMBER OF YEARS LIVED IN THE INTERVAL.  (BIG L)
39.            DO 40 I=1,86
40.            RM(I)=D(I)/P(I)
41.            IF (I-86) 30,35,30
42.         30 Q(I)=RM(I)/(1.0+(1.0-A(I))*RM(I))
43.            DD(I)=SL(I)*Q(I)
44.            SL(I+1)=SL(I)-DD(I)
45.            YL(I)=(SL(I)-DD(I))+(A(I)*DD(I))
46.            GO TO 40
47.      C NEXT FOLLOW THE SPECIAL CALCULATIONS FOR THE LAST AGE INTERVAL
48.         35 DD(I)=SL(I)
49.            Q(I)=1.000000
50.            YL(I)=SL(I)/RM(I)
51.      C T(I) REPRESENTS THE TOTAL NUMBER OF YEARS LIVED BEYOND AGE I
52.      C E(I) REPRESENTS THE OBSERVED EXPECTATION OF LIFE AT AGE I
53.            T(I)=YL(I)
54.            E(I)=T(I)/SL(I)
55.         40 CONTINUE
56.            DO 45 I=1,85
57.            T(86-I)=T(87-I)+YL(86-I)
58.            E(86-I)=T(86-I)/SL(86-I)
59.         45 CONTINUE
60.      C NEXT FOLLOW THE CALCULATIONS FOR VARIANCES AND STANDARD ERRORS
61.      C VQ(I) DENOTES THE VARIANCE OF Q(I)
62.      C C(I) AND F(I) ARE ARRAYS NEEDED FOR COMPUTING VE(I), THE VARIANCE OF E(I)
63.      C BOTH VQ(I) AND VE(I) ARE MULTIPLIED BY A BASE FACTIOR OF 10**8
64.            DO 50 I=1,86
65.            VQ(I)=(Q(I)*Q(I)*(1.0-Q(I)))/D(I)
66.            IF (I-86) 46,49,46
67.         46 B=1.0-A(I)+E(I+1)
68.            C(I)=SL(I)*SL(I)*B*B*VQ(I)
69.         49 VQ(I)=VQ(I)*(10.0**8.0)
70.         50 CONTINUE
71.            F(85)=C(85)
72.            DO 55 I=1,84
```

```
 73.          55 F(85-I)=F(86-I)+C(85-I)
 74.             DO 60 I=1,85
 75.             VE(I)=F(I)/(SL(I)*SL(I))
 76.             VE(I)=VE(I)*(10.0**4.0)
 77.          60 CONTINUE
 78.       C  NEXT FOLLOW THE COMPUTATIONS FOR THE MODE E(I)
 79.             J=1
 80.             EMO=DD(1)
 81.             DO 70 I=2,86
 82.             IF (EMO-DD(I)) 65,65,70
 83.          65 J=I
 84.             EMO=DD(I)
 85.          70 CONTINUE
 86.             IMO=J-1
 87.       C  NEXT FOLLOW COMPUTATIONS FOR THE MEDIAN OF E(I)
 88.             EMD=1.0
 89.             DO 80 I=2,86
 90.             IF (SL(I)-50000.) 73,73,75
 91.          73 EMD=(SL(I-1)-50000.)/(SL(I-1)-SL(I)) +EMD
 92.             GO TO 85
 93.          75 EMD=EMD+1.0
 94.          80 CONTINUE
 95.             EMD=85.0
 96.          85 WRITE (6,90) (TITLE(I), I=1,20)
 97.          90 FORMAT (1H1,7X,'CONSTRUCTION OF COMPLETE LIFETABLE FOR ', 20A4)
 98.       C  THE VARIABLE MM IS AN INDICATOR VARIABLE FOR THE THREE TABLES GIVEN
 99.             MM=1
100.             WRITE (6,95) MM
101.          95 FORMAT (/55X, 'TABLE', I2//)
102.             WRITE (6,100)
103.         100 FORMAT(/3X, 'AGE', 13X, 'MIDYEAR', 8X 'NUMBER OF', 6X,'DEATH',10X,
104.            1'FRACTION', 7X, 'PROPORTION'   /    3X,'INTERVAL', 8X, 'POPULATION'
105.            2,5X, 'DEATHS',9X,'RATE',11X,'OF LAST',8X, 'DYING IN',  /   3X,
106.            2'(IN YEARS)', 6X,'IN INTERVAL',4X,'IN INTERVAL',4X, 'IN INTERVAL',
107.            44X,'YEAR',11X,'INTERVAL'/ 3X,'X TO X+1', 8X, '(X,X+1)',8X,'(X,X+1)
108.            5',8X,'(X,X+1)',8X,'OF LIFE',8X,'(X,X+1)'/ 19X, 'P(I)', 11X,'D(I)',
109.            611X, 'M(I) ',10X,'A(I)', 11X,'Q(I)'/)
110.             DO 110  I=1,85
111.       C  COMPUTATIONS TO DETERMINE WHEN TO TURN THE PAGE AND RERUN THE HEADING
112.       C  SIMILAR COMPUTATIONS FOLLOW AROUND STATEMENTS 126 AND 146
113.             IF (I-26) 104,103,101
114.         101 IF (I-52) 104,103,102
115.         102 IF (I-78) 104,103,104
116.         103 WRITE (6,90) (TITLE(L), L=1,20)
117.             WRITE (6,95) MM
118.             WRITE (6,100)
119.         104 IH=I-1
120.             WRITE (6,105) IH  ,I,      P(I), D(I), RM(I), A(I),Q(I)
121.         105 FORMAT (/8X,I2, '-', I2,    7X, F9.0,5X, F7.0,8X, F7.6,9X,F3.2,
122.            112X, F7.5)
123.         110 CONTINUE
124.             I=86
125.             IH=I-1
126.             WRITE (6,115) IH,           P(I), D(I), RM(I),      Q(I)
127.         115 FORMAT (/8X, I2, '+',   9X, F9.0, 5X, F7.0,8X, F7.6,24X, F7.5///)
128.             WRITE (6,90) (TITLE(I), I=1,20)
129.             MM=2
130.             WRITE (6,95) MM
131.             WRITE (6,125)
132.         125 FORMAT (/3X, 'AGE', 12X, 'PROPORTION', 4X, 'NUMBER',2X, 'NUMBER',8
133.            1X, 'FRACTION',5X,'NUMBER OF',6X, 'TOTAL',11X, 'OBSERVED' / 3X,
134.            2 'INTERVAL', 7X, 'DYING IN', 6X, 'LIVING' ,2X, 'DYING IN', 6X,
135.            3'OF LAST',6X,'YEARS LIVED',4X, 'NUMBER OF', 7X, 'EXPECTATION' /
136.            43X, '(IN YEARS)', 5X, 'INTERVAL', 6X, 'AT AGE', 2X, 'INTERVAL',6X
137.            5'YEAR', 9X,        'IN INTERVAL',4X,'YEARS LIVED',5X, 'OF LIFE AT' /
138.            63X,'X TO X+1',7X,'(X,X+1)',7X,'X',7X,'(X,X+1)',7X,'OF LIFE',6X,
139.            7'(X,X+1)',8X, 'BEYOND AGE X', 4X, 'AGE X' /18X,'Q(I)',10X,'SL(I)'
140.            8,3X,'DD(I)',9X, 'A(I)',9X, 'L(I) ',10X,'T(I)',12X,'E(I)'/)
141.             DO 135 I=1,85
142.             IF (I-26) 129,128,126
143.         126 IF (I-52) 129,128,127
144.         127 IF (I-78) 129,128,129
```

```
145.          128 WRITE (6,90) (TITLE(L), L=1,20)
146.              WRITE (6,95) MM
147.              WRITE (6,125)
148.          129 IH=I-1
149.              WRITE (6,130) IH,I,        Q(I),SL(I),DD(I),A(I),YL(I),T(I),E(I)
150.          130 FORMAT (/8X, I2, '-', I2,      8X, F6.5,4X, F7.0,5X, F7.0,6X, F3.2,
151.              18X, F9.0,7X, F9.0,7X, F6.2)
152.          135 CONTINUE
153.              I=86
154.              IH=85
155.              WRITE (6,140) IH,        Q(I),SL(I),DD(I),      YL(I),T(I),E(I)
156.          140 FORMAT (/8X, I2, '+',      9X, F7.5,4X, F7.0,5X, F7.0,9X,
157.              18X, F9.0,7X, F9.0,7X, F6.2///)
158.              WRITE (6,90) (TITLE(I), I=1,20)
159.              MM=3
160.              WRITE (6,95) MM
161.              WRITE (6,145)
162.          145 FORMAT  (/3X, 'AGE', 13X, 'PROPORTION', 4X, 'SAMPLE', 4X, 'SAMPLE'
163.              1,6X, 'NUMBER',      26X,                  'OBS. EXP.',' SAMPLE
164.              2',4X, 'SAMPLE'/ 3X, 'INTERVAL', 8X, 'DYING IN', 6X, 'VARIANCE', 2X
165.              3, 'STD.ERROR', 3X, 'LIVING AT', 2X, 'VARIANCE', 2X, 'STD.ERROR',
166.              32X, 'LIFE FOR', 2X, 'VARIANCE', 2X, 'STD.ERROR'/ 3X, '(IN YEARS)',
167.              46X, 'AGE INTERVAL', 2X, 'OF Q(I)', 3X, 'OF Q(I)', 5X, 'AGE X(I)',
168.              53X, 'OF SL(I)', 2X, 'OF SL(I)', 3X, 'INTERVAL',2X, 'OF E(I)', 3X,
169.              6'OF E(I)'/3X, 'X TO X+1',8X            'Q(I)', 10X, 'VQ(I)', 5X,
170.              7'SEQ', 9X, 'SL(I)', 6X, 'VS(I)', 5X, 'SES', 8X, 'E(I)', 6X, 'VE(I)
171.              8', 5X, 'SEE'/)
172.      C   SEQ DENOTES THE STANDARD ERROR OF Q(I)
173.      C   SEE DENOTES THE STANDARD ERROR OF E(I)
174.      C   SES DENOTES THE STANDARD ERROR OF SL(I)
175.      C   VS(I) DENOTES THE VARIANCE OF SL(I)
176.              DO 155 I=1,85
177.              SEQ=DSQRT(VQ(I))
178.              SEE=DSQRT(VE(I))
179.              W=SL(I)/SL(1)
180.              VS(I)=SL(1)*W*(1.0-W)
181.              SES=DSQRT(VS(I))
182.              IF (I-26) 149,148,146
183.          146 IF (I-52) 149,148,147
184.          147 IF (I-78) 149,148,149
185.          148 WRITE (6,90) (TITLE(L), L=1,20)
186.              WRITE (6,95) MM
187.              WRITE (6,145)
188.          149 IH=I-1
189.              WRITE (6,150) IH, I,        Q(I),VQ(I),SEQ,SL(I),VS(I),SES,E(I),
190.              1VE(I),SEE
191.          150 FORMAT(/5X, I2, '-', I2,      9X, F6.5,8X, F8.4,2X, F7.4,4X, F7.0,4X
192.              1, F7.1, 3X, F7.2, 4X, F5.2,5X, F7.4,3X, F6.4)
193.          155 CONTINUE
194.              I=86
195.              SEQ=DSQRT(VQ(I))
196.              W=SL(86)/SL(1)
197.              VS(86)=SL(1)*W*(1.0-W)
198.              SES=DSQRT(VS(I))
199.              IH=85
200.              WRITE (6,160) IH,        Q(I),VQ(I),SEQ,SL(I),VS(I),SES,E(I)
201.          160 FORMAT(/5X, I2,   '+', 10X,      F7.5,7X, F9.4,      F9.4,4X, F7.0,4X
202.              1, F7.1, 3X, F7.2, 4X, F5.2)
203.              WRITE (6,165)
204.          165 FORMAT (//1X, 'VARIANCE OF Q(I) IS MULTIPLIED BY A FACTOR OF 100,0
205.              100,000.')
206.              WRITE (6,166)
207.          166 FORMAT (/1X,'STANDARD ERROR OF Q(I) IS MULTIPLIED BY A BASE FACTOR
208.              1 OF 10,000.')
209.              WRITE (6,167)
210.          167 FORMAT (/1X, 'VARIANCE OF E(I) IS MULTIPLIED BY A BASE FACTOR OF
211.              110,000.')
212.              WRITE (6,168)
213.          168 FORMAT (/1X, 'STD. ERROR OF E(I) IS MULTIPLIED BY A FACTOR OF 100.
214.              1')
215.              WRITE (6,170) EMD
216.          170 FORMAT (/1X, 'THE MEDIAN EXPECTATION OF LIFE (THE AGE AT WHICH EXA
217.              1CTLY ONE HALF OF THE ORIGINAL COHORT SURVIVES) IS EQUAL TO ',F5.2)
218.              WRITE (6,175)  IMO
```

```
219.      175 FORMAT (/1X, 'THE MODE EXP. OF LIFE -TO THE NEAREST LOWER AGE INTE
220.          1RVAL LIMIT- IS EQUAL TO  ', I2)
221.          RETURN
222.          END
223.   //GO.SYSIN DD *
224.   TOTAL CALIFORNIA POPULATION, USA, 1970
225.     340483. 326154. 313699. 323441. 338904. 362161. 379642. 386980. 391610. 397724.
226.     406118. 388927. 395025. 388526. 385085. 377127.368156. 366198. 354932. 350966.
227.     359833. 349557. 365839. 370548. 295189. 304013. 305558. 310554. 275897. 261592.
228.     264083. 247777. 241726. 232025. 233778. 234338. 224302. 228652. 226727. 235980.
229.     249027. 232893. 239747. 238783. 248100. 253828. 244857. 247955. 252137. 242126.
230.     243799. 220599. 213448. 203618. 202388. 201750. 193828. 187257. 178602. 171807.
231.     174613. 157734. 154174. 144149. 140100. 135857. 129386. 123925. 112574. 119063.
232.     114066. 100781.  93031.  89992.  86561.  81003.  73552.  70516.  60616.  56410.
233.      57646.  48299.  39560.  34439.  31009. 142691.
234.       6234.    368.    269.    237.    175.    179.    171.    131.    121.    121.
235.        126.    127.    138.    158.    186.    235.    344.    385.    506.    584.
236.        583.    562.    572.    564.    421.    416.    391.    461.    411.    392.
237.        399.    378.    388.    365.    434.    439.    475.    519.    549.    606.
238.        665.    719.    863.    874.    993.   1140.   1268.   1362.   1422.   1530.
239.       1594.   1710.   1793.   1870.   1981.   2217.   2333.   2483.   2392.   2517.
240.       2733.   2743.   2911.   2968.   2954.   3391.   3278.   3352.   3331.   3736.
241.       3846.   3704.   3706.   3830.   4063.   4275.   4383.   4259.   4181.   4227.
242.       4424.   4288.   3995.   3753.   3669.  22483.
243.   .09.43.45.47.49
244.   //
```

Appendix II-2

Computer Program for Construction of Abridged Life Tables

This is an abridged life table computer program, written and debugged by Robert Chiang in November 1978. The program is written in the Fortran IV language and is designed for use with most IBM computers, particularly the 360/370 model. The first three cards of the program are "job control language" cards, and may vary from one installation to another.

The input data must conform to the usual 19 age quinquennial age groups: 0–1, 1–5, 5–10, 10–15, 15–20, . . . , 80–85, 85 +. The input data is as follows:

TITLE denotes the title of the table (not to exceed 80 characters)

P(I) denotes the midyear population of the age interval
D(I) denotes the number of deaths in the age interval
A(I) denotes the fraction of the last age interval of life

The proper formats for TITLE, P(I), D(I), and A(I) are specified in lines 22 through 28 (statement numbers 5, 11 and 15) in the program, with an example of actual input data appearing in lines 213 through 218.

```
 1.      //ABRIDGED JOB
 2.      // EXEC FORTCG
 3.      //FORT.SYSIN DD *
 4.      C
 5.      C  THIS IS A FORTRAN IV LANGUAGE PROGRAM DESIGNED FOR MOST IBM COMPUTERS,
 6.      C  WRITTEN AND DEBUGGED BY ROBERT CHIANG IN NOV., 1978.
 7.      C  THE FIRST THREE CARDS ABOVE ARE JCL CARDS AND WILL VARY FROM ONE
 8.      C  INSTALLATION TO ANOTHER.
 9.      C
10.            DIMENSION TITLE(20)
11.            DOUBLE PRECISION     P(19),D(19),A(18),Z,SEE,SEQ,SES
12.            DOUBLE PRECISION X(19),RM(19),Q(19),DD(19),SL(19),YL(19),E(19)
13.            DOUBLE PRECISION T(19),VQ(19),F(18),C(18),VE(18),VS(19),B,W,R
14.      C  THIS PROGRAM WILL CONSTRUCT AN ABRIDGED LIFETABLE
15.      C  ALL INPUT DATA MUST CONFORM TO THE USUAL 19 QUINQUENNIAL  AGE GROUPS.
16.      C  THE USER MUST INPUT A TITLE WHICH DOESN'T EXCEED  A LENGTH OF 20A4
17.      C  THE TITLE INPUTTED WILL FOLLOW THE HEADING IN STATEMENT #90
18.      C  THE INPUT DATA IS AS FOLLOWS:
19.      C  P(I) DENOTES THE MIDYEAR POPULATION OF THE AGE INTERVAL
20.      C  D(I) DENOTES THE NUMBER OF DEATHS IN THE AGE INTERVAL
21.      C  A(I) DENOTES THE FRACTION OF THE LAST AGE INTERVAL OF LIFE
22.            READ (5,5) (TITLE(I), I=1,20)
23.          5 FORMAT (20A4)
24.            READ (5,11) (P(I),I=1,19)
25.            READ (5,11) (D(I),I=1,19)
26.         11 FORMAT (10F8.0 / 9F8.0)
27.            READ (5,15) (A(I), I=1,18)
28.         15 FORMAT (18F3.2)
29.      C  Z IS SIMPLY AN INDICATOR VARIABLE FOR SETTING UP THE AGE INTERVALS
30.      C  X(I) DENOTES THE LOWER BOUNDS OF THE I TH AGE INTERVAL
31.            Z=0.0
32.            DO 20 I=1,2
33.            X(I)=Z
34.            Z=Z+1.0
35.         20 CONTINUE
36.            DO 25 I=3,19
37.            Z=Z+1.0
38.            X(I)=(Z*5.0)-10.0
39.         25 CONTINUE
40.            SL(1)=100000.0
41.      C  SL(I) DENOTES THE NUMBER  LIVING AT THE AGE X(I) IN THE COHORT
42.      C  SL(I) IS THE SAME AS SMALL L, AS USED IN LIFETABLE MANUALS
43.      C  RM(I) DENOTES THE DEATH RATE IN THE INTERVAL (IT REPRESENTS M OF I)
44.            DO 40 I=1,19
45.            RM(I)=D(I)/P(I)
46.            IF (I-19) 30,35,30
47.      C  THE VARIABLE R REPRESENTS THE RANGE OR LENGTH OF THE INTERVAL.
48.      C  THE VARIABLE R REPRESENTS LITTLE N, AS USED IN THE LIFETABLE MANUALS
49.      C  Q(I) REPRESENTS THE PROBABILITY OF DYING IN THE INTERVAL
50.      C  DD(I) DENOTES THE NUMBER DYING IN THE INTERVAL OF THE COHORT
51.      C  DD(I) REPRESENTS LITTLE L AS USED IN THE LIFETABLE MANUALS
52.      C  YL(I) REPRESENTS THE NUMBER OF YEARS LIVED IN THE INTERVAL.  (BIG L)
53.         30 R=X(I+1)-X(I)
54.            Q(I)=(R*RM(I))/(1.0+(1.0-A(I))*R*RM(I))
55.            DD(I)=SL(I)*Q(I)
56.            SL(I+1)=SL(I)-DD(I)
57.            YL(I)=R*(SL(I)-DD(I))+(A(I)*R*DD(I))
58.            GO TO 40
59.      C  T(I) REPRESENTS THE TOTAL NUMBER OF YEARS LIVED BEYOND AGE X(I)
60.      C  E(I) REPRESENTS THE OBSERVED EXPECTATION OF LIFE AT AGE X(I)
61.      C  NEXT FOLLOW THE SPECIAL CALCULATIONS FOR THE LAST AGE INTERVAL
62.         35 DD(19)=SL(19)
63.            Q(19)=1.0
64.            YL(19)=SL(19)/RM(19)
65.            T(19)=YL(19)
66.            E(19)=T(19)/SL(19)
67.         40 CONTINUE
68.            DO 45 I=1,18
69.            T(19-I)=T(20-I)+YL(19-I)
70.            E(19-I)=T(19-I)/SL(19-I)
71.         45 CONTINUE
72.            DO 50 I=1,19
73.      C  NEXT FOLLOW THE CALCULATIONS FOR VARIANCES AND STANDARD ERRORS
74.      C  VQ(I) DENOTES THE VARIANCE OF Q(I)
```

```
 75.              VQ(I)=(Q(I)*Q(I)*(1.0-Q(I)))/D(I)
 76.              IF (I-19) 46,49,46
 77.           46 R=X(I+1)-X(I)
 78.              B=((1.0-A(I))*R)+E(I+1)
 79.        C  C(I) AND F(I) ARE ARRAYS NEEDED FOR COMPUTING VE(I), THE VARIANCE OF E(I)
 80.        C  VQ(I) AND VE(I) ARE MULTIPLIED BY BASE FACTORS OF  10,000
 81.              C(I)=SL(I)*SL(I)*B*B*VQ(I)
 82.           49 VQ(I)=VQ(I)*(10.0**4.0)
 83.           50 CONTINUE
 84.              F(18)=C(18)
 85.              DO 55 I=1,17
 86.           55 F(18-I)=F(19-I)+C(18-I)
 87.              DO 60 I=1,18
 88.              VE(I)=F(I)/(SL(I)*SL(I))
 89.              VE(I)=VE(I)*(10.0**4.0)
 90.           60 CONTINUE
 91.        C  NEXT FOLLOW THE COMPUTATIONS FOR THE MODE E(I)
 92.              J=1
 93.              EMO=DD(1)
 94.              DO 70 I=2,19
 95.              IF (EMO-DD(I)) 65,65,70
 96.           65 J=I
 97.              EMO=DD(I)
 98.           70 CONTINUE
 99.              EMO=X(J)
100.        C  NEXT FOLLOW COMPUTATIONS FOR THE MEDIAN OF E(I)
101.              DO 80 I=2,19
102.              IF (SL(I)-50000.0) 75,75,80
103.           75 EMD=(50000.0-SL(I))/(SL(I-1)-SL(I))
104.              EMD=EMD*(X(I-1)-X(I))+X(I)
105.              GO TO 85
106.           80 CONTINUE
107.              EMD=X(19)
108.           85 WRITE (6,90) (TITLE(I), I=1,20)
109.           90 FORMAT (1H1,7X,'CONSTRUCTION OF ABRIDGED LIFETABLE FOR ', 20A4)
110.        C  THE VARIABLE MM IS AN INDICATOR VARIABLE FOR THE THREE TABLES GIVEN
111.              MM=1
112.              WRITE (6,95) MM
113.           95 FORMAT (/55X, 'TABLE', I2//)
114.              WRITE (6,100)
115.          100 FORMAT(/3X, 'AGE', 13X, 'MIDYEAR', 8X 'NUMBER OF', 6X,'DEATH',10X,
116.             1'FRACTION', 7X, 'PROPORTION'  /  3X,'INTERVAL', 8X, 'POPULATION'
117.             2,5X, 'DEATHS',9X,'RATE',11X,'OF LAST',8X, 'DYING IN',  /  3X,
118.             2'(IN YEARS)', 6X,'IN INTERVAL',4X,'IN INTERVAL',4X, 'IN INTERVAL',
119.             44X,'AGE INTERVAL', 3X, 'INTERVAL' / 3X, 'X(I) TO X(I+1)', 2X,
120.             5'(X(I),X(I+1))', 2X, '(X(I),X(I+1))', 2X, '(X(I),X(I+1))', 2X
121.             6'OF LIFE', 8X, '(X(I),X(I+1))' / 19X, 'P(I)', 11X, 'D(I)', 11X,
122.             7'M(I) ',10X, 'A(I)', 11X, 'Q(I)'/)
123.              DO 110 I=1,18
124.              WRITE (6,105) X(I), X(I+1), P(I), D(I), RM(I), A(I),Q(I)
125.          105 FORMAT (/6X, F3.0, '-', F3.0,7X, F9.0,5X, F7.0,9X, F7.6,9X,F3.2,
126.             112X, F7.5)
127.          110 CONTINUE
128.              I=19
129.              WRITE (6,115) X(I),        P(I), D(I), RM(I),      Q(I)
130.          115 FORMAT (/6X, F3.0, '+', 10X, F9.0, 5X, F7.0,9X, F7.6,24X, F7.5///)
131.              WRITE (6,90) (TITLE(I), I=1,20)
132.          117 FORMAT (1H1)
133.              MM=2
134.              WRITE (6,95) MM
135.              WRITE (6,125)
136.          125 FORMAT (/3X, 'AGE', 12X, 'PROPORTION', 4X, 'NUMBER',2X, 'NUMBER',8
137.             1X, 'FRACTION',5X,'NUMBER OF',6X, 'TOTAL',11X, 'OBSERVED' / 3X,
138.             2 'INTERVAL', 7X, 'DYING IN', 6X, 'LIVING' ,2X, 'DYING IN', 6X,
139.             3'OF LAST',6X,'YEARS LIVED',4X, 'NUMBER OF', 7X, 'EXPECTATION' /
140.             43X, '(IN YEARS)', 5X, 'INTERVAL', 6X,  'AT AGE', 2X, 'INTERVAL',6X
141.             5,'AGE INTERVAL ','IN INTERVAL',4X,'YEARS LIVED',5X, 'OF LIFE AT' /
142.             63X, 'X(I) TO X(I+1)', 1X, '(X(I),X(I+1))',1X, 'X(I)',4X,'(X(I),X(I
143.             7+1)) ','OF LIFE',6X,'(X(I),X(I+1))',2X , 'BEYOND AGE X(I)', 1X,
144.             8'AGE X(I)'                        / 19X, 'Q(I)',9X, 'SL(I)',3X
145.             9,'DD(I)', 9X, 'A(I)', 9X, 'L(I) ', 10X, 'T(I)',12X, 'E(I)'/)
146.              DO 135 I=1,18
147.              WRITE (6,130) X(I),X(I+1),Q(I),SL(I),DD(I),A(I),YL(I),T(I),E(I)
148.          130 FORMAT (/6X, F3.0, '-', F3.0,7X, F7.5,4X, F7.0,5X, F7.0,6X, F3.2,
```

```
149.            18X, F9.0,7X, F9.0,7X, F6.2)
150.       135 CONTINUE
151.           I=19
152.           WRITE (6,140) X(I),          Q(I),SL(I),DD(I),       YL(I),T(I),E(I)
153.       140 FORMAT (/6X, F3.0, '+',      10X, F7.5,4X, F7.0,5X, F7.0,9X,
154.           18X, F9.0,7X, F9.0,7X, F6.2///)
155.           WRITE (6,90) (TITLE(I), I=1,20)
156.           MM=3
157.           WRITE (6,95) MM
158.           WRITE (6,145)
159.       145 FORMAT   (/3X, 'AGE', 13X, 'PROPORTION', 4X, 'SAMPLE', 4X, 'SAMPLE'
160.           1,6X, 'NUMBER',         26X,            'OBS. EXP.',' SAMPLE
161.           2',4X, 'SAMPLE'/ 3X, 'INTERVAL', 8X, 'DYING IN', 6X, 'VARIANCE', 2X
162.           3, 'STD.ERROR', 3X, 'LIVING AT', 2X, 'VARIANCE', 2X, 'STD.ERROR',
163.           32X, 'LIFE FOR', 2X, 'VARIANCE', 2X, 'STD.ERROR'/ 3X, '(IN YEARS)',
164.           46X, 'AGE INTERVAL', 2X, 'OF Q(I)', 3X, 'OF Q(I)', 5X, 'AGE X(I)',
165.           53X, 'OF SL(I)', 2X, 'OF SL(I)', 3X, 'INTERVAL',2X, 'OF E(I)', 3X,
166.           6'OF E(I)'/ 3X, 'X(I) TO X(I+1)', 2X, 'Q(I)', 10X, 'VQ(I)', 5X,
167.           7'SEQ', 9X, 'SL(I)', 6X, 'VS(I)', 5X, 'SES', 8X, 'E(I)', 6X, 'VE(I)
168.           8', 5X, 'SEE'/)
169.     C  SEQ DENOTES THE STANDARD ERROR OF Q(I)
170.     C  SEE DENOTES THE STANDARD ERROR OF E(I)
171.     C  SES DENOTES THE STANDARD ERROR OF SL(I)
172.     C  VS(I) DENOTES THE VARIANCE OF SL(I)
173.           DO 155 I=1,18
174.           SEQ=DSQRT(VQ(I))
175.           SEE=DSQRT(VE(I))
176.           W=SL(I)/SL(1)
177.           VS(I)=SL(1)*W*(1.0-W)
178.           SES=DSQRT(VS(I))
179.           WRITE (6,150) X(I), X(I+1),Q(I),VQ(I),SEQ,SL(I),VS(I),SES,E(I),
180.           1VE(I),SEE
181.       150 FORMAT(/3X, F3.0, '-', F3.0,8X, F7.5,8X, F8.4,2X, F7.4,4X, F7.0,4X
182.           1, F7.1, 3X, F7.2, 4X, F5.2,5X, F7.4,3X, F6.4)
183.       155 CONTINUE
184.           I=19
185.           SEQ=DSQRT(VQ(I))
186.           W=SL(19)/SL(1)
187.           VS(19)=SL(1)*W*(1.0-W)
188.           SES=DSQRT(VS(I))
189.           WRITE (6,160) X(I),          Q(I),VQ(I),SEQ,SL(I),VS(I),SES,E(I)
190.       160 FORMAT(/3X, F3.0, '+', 11X,      F7.5,10X, F6.4,3X,F6.4,4X, F7.0,4X
191.           1, F7.1, 3X, F7.2, 4X, F5.2)
192.           WRITE (6,165)
193.       165 FORMAT (//1X, 'VARIANCE OF Q(I) IS MULTIPLIED BY A FACTOR OF 100,0
194.           100,000.')
195.           WRITE (6,166)
196.       166 FORMAT (/1X,'STANDARD ERROR OF Q(I) IS MULTIPLIED BY A BASE FACTOR
197.           1 OF 10,000.')
198.           WRITE (6,167)
199.       167 FORMAT (/1X, 'VARIANCE OF E(I) IS MULTIPLIED BY A BASE FACTOR OF
200.           110,000.')
201.           WRITE (6,168)
202.       168 FORMAT (/1X, 'STD. ERROR OF E(I) IS MULTIPLIED BY A FACTOR OF 100.
203.           1')
204.           WRITE (6,170) EMD
205.       170 FORMAT (/1X, 'THE MEDIAN EXPECTATION OF LIFE (THE AGE AT WHICH EXA
206.           1CTLY ONE HALF OF THE ORIGINAL COHORT SURVIVES) IS EQUAL TO ',F5.2)
207.           WRITE (6,175)  EMO
208.       175 FORMAT (/1X, 'THE MODE EXP. OF LIFE -TO THE NEAREST LOWER AGE INTE
209.           1RVAL LIMIT- IS EQUAL TO ', F5.2)
210.           RETURN
211.           END
212.     //GO.SYSIN DD *
213.      TOTAL CALIFORNIA POPULATION, USA, 1970
214.       340483.1302198.1918117.1963681.1817379.1740966.1457614.1219389.1149999.1208550
215.      1245903.1083852. 933244. 770770. 620805. 484431. 342097. 210953. 142691.
216.        6234.   1049.    723.    735.   2054.   2702.   2071.   1964.   2588.   4114.
217.        6722.   8948.  11942.  14309.  17088.  19149.  21325.  20129.  22483.
218.      .09.41.44.54.59.49.51.52.53.54.53.53.52.52.51.52.51.50
219.     //
```

References

Adlakha, A. [1972]. Model life tables: An empirical test of their applicability to less developed countries. *Demography, 9*, 589–601.

Armitage, P. [1959]. The comparison of survival curves. *J. Royal Statist. Soc., A122*, 279–300.

Arriaga, E. E. [1968]. New Life Tables for Latin American Populations in the Nineteenth and Twentieth Centuries. *Monograph Series No. 3*, Institute of International Studies, University of California, Berkeley.

Bailar, B. A. [1976]. Some sources of error and their effect on census statistics. *Demography, 13*, 273–286.

Barclay, G. W. [1958]. *Techniques of Population Analysis*. Wiley, New York.

Barlow, R. E. and F. Proschan [1965]. *Mathematical Theory of Reliability*. Wiley, New York.

Bartholomew, D. J. [1963]. The sampling distribution of an estimate arising in life testing. *Technometrics, 5*, 361–74.

Berkson, J. and L. Elvebeck [1960]. Competing exponential risks, with particular reference to smoking and lung cancer. *J. Amer. Statist. Assoc., 55*, 415–428.

Berkson, J. and R. P. Gage [1950]. Calculation of survival rates for cancer. *Proc., Staff Meetings, Mayo Clinic, 25*, 270–86.

Berkson, J. and R. P. Gage [1932]. Survival curve for cancer patients following treatment. *J. Amer. Statistic. Assoc., 47*, 501–515.

Birnbaum, Z. W. [1979]. On the mathematics of competing risks," *Vital and Health Statistics, Series 2*, No. 77, pp. 1–58, National Center for Health Statistics.

Boag, J. W. [1949]. Maximum likelihood estimates of the proportion of patients cured by cancer therapy. *J. Royal Statist. Soc., 11*, 15–53.

Borel, E. [1934]. *Les Probabilités et la Vie*. Presses Universitaires de France.

Braun, H. I. [1980]. Regression-like analysis of birth interval sequence. *Demography, 17*, 207–223.

Breslow, N. [1974]. Covariance analysis of censored survival data. *Biometrics, 30*, 89–99.

Brownlee, J. [1913]. The relationship between 'corrected' death rates and life table death rates. *Journal of Hygiene, XIII*, 178–190.

Brownlee, J. [1922]. The use of death rates as a measure of hygienic conditions, *Medical Research Council Special Report Series, 670*, H. M. Stationery Office, London.

Campbell, H. [1965]. Changes in mortality trends in England and Wales, 1931–1961. *Vital and Health Statistics, Series 3*, No. 3.

Canadian Department of National Health and Welfare and the Dominion Bureau of Statistics [1960]. *Illness and Health Care in Canada, Canadian Sickness Survey*, 1950–1951. The Queen's Printer and Controller of Stationery, Ottawa.

Chase, C. C. [1967]. International comparison of perinatal and infant mortality. *Vital and Health Statistics*, Series 3, No. 6, 1–97. U.S. Dept. of Health, Education and Welfare, Public Health Service.

Chiang, C. L. [1960a]. A stochastic study of the life table and its applications: I. Probability distributions of the biometric functions. *Biometrics, 16*, 618–635.

Chiang, C. L. [1960b]. A stochastic study of the life table and its applications: II. Sample variance of the observed expectation of life and other biometric functions. *Human Biol., 32*, 221–238.

Chiang, C. L. [1961a]. A stochastic study of the life table and its applications: III. The follow-up study with the consideration of competing risks. *Biometrics, 17*, 57–78.

Chiang, C. L. [1961b]. Standard error of the age-adjusted death ratio. *Vital Statistics, Special Reports Selected Studies, 47*, 275–285. National Center for Health Statistics.

Chiang, C. L. [1967]. Variance and covariance of life table functions estimated from a sample of deaths. *Vital and Health Statistics*, Ser. 2, No. 20, 1–8. National Center for Health Statistics.

Chiang, C. L. [1968]. *Introduction to Stochastic Processes in Biostatistics*. Wiley, New York.

Chiang, C. L. [1972]. On constructing current life tables. *J. Am. Statist. Assoc., 67*, 538–541.

Chiang, C. L. [1978]. *The Life Table and Mortality Analysis*, World Health Organization, Geneva.

Chiang, C. L. [1979]. Survival and stages of disease. *Math. Biosci., 43*, 159–171.

Chiang, C. L. [1980]. *An Introduction to Stochastic Processes and their Applications*. R. E. Krieger, Huntington, New York.

Chiang, C. L. and R. Chiang [1982]. The family life cycle revisited. *Proceedings, World Health Organization Conference on Family Life Cycle Methodology*.

Chiang, C. L. and B. J. van den Berg [1982]. A fertility table for the analysis of human reproduction. *Mathematical Biosciences, 62*, 237–251.

Chu, G., C. Langhauser, J. Fortman, P. Schoenfeld, and F. Belzer [1973]. A survival analysis of patients undergoing dialysis or renal transplantation. *Trans. Amer. Soc. Artificial Internal Organs, 10*, 126–129.

Coale, A. J. and P. Demeny [1966]. *Regional Life Tables and Stable Populations*. Princeton University Press, Princeton, New Jersey.

Coale, A. and T. J. Trussel [1974]. Model fertility tables: Variations in age structure of childbearing in human populations. *Population Index, 40*, 186–192.

Cohen, J. [1965]. Routine morbidity statistics as a tool for defining public health priorities. *Isr. J. Med. Sci., 1*, 457.

Cornfield, J. [1951]. A method of estimating comparative rates from clinical data. Applications to cancer of the lung, breast and cervix. *J. Natl. Cancer Inst., 11*, 1269–1275.

Cutler, S. J. and F. Ederer [1958]. Maximum utilization of the life table method in analyzing survival. *J. Chron. Dis., 8*, 699–712.

Das Gupta, A. S. [1954]. Accuracy index of census age distributions. *Proc., World Population Conference, 4*, United Nations, New York.

Das Gupta, A. S., et al. [1965]. Population Perspective of Thailand. *Sankhya*, Series B, *27*, 1–46.

David, H. A., and M. L. Moeschberger [1978]. *The Theory of Competing Risks*. C. Griffin, London.

Demeny, P. [1965]. Estimation of vital rates for populations in the process of destabilization. *Demography*, *2*, 516–530.

Densen, P. M. [1950]. Long-time follow-up in morbidity studies: the definition of the group to be followed. *Human Biol.*, *22*, 233.

Derksen, J. B. D. [1948]. The calculation of mortality rates in the construction of life tables. A mathematical statistical study. *Population Studies*, *1*, 457.

Devroede, G. and W. F. Taylor [1976]. On calculating cancer risk and survival of ulcerative colitis patients with the life table method. *Gastroenterology*, *71*, 505–509.

Doering, C. R. and A. L. Forbes [1939]. Adjusted death rates. *Proceedings of the National Academy of Science*, *25*, 461–467.

Doll, R. and P. Cook [1967]. Summarizing indices for comparison of cancer incidence data. *Internat. J. Cancer*, *2*, 269–279.

Doll, R. and A. B. Hill [1952]. A study of the etiology of carcinoma of the lung. *Brit. J. Med.*, *2*, 1271.

Dorn, H. [1950]. Methods of analysis for follow-up studies. *Human Biol.*, *22*, 238–248.

Drolette, M. E. [1975]. The effect of incomplete follow-up. *Biometrics*, *31*, 135–144.

Dublin, L. I. and A. J. Lotka [1925]. On the true rate of natural increase. *Journal American Statistical Association*, *20*, 205–339.

Dublin, L. I. and A. J. Lotka [1937]. Uses of the life table in vital statistics. *J. Amer. Publ. Hlth. Assoc.*

Dublin, L. I. and A. J. Lotka, and M. Spiegelman [1949]. *Length of Life: A Study of the Life Table*. Ronald Press, New York.

Duda, R. and G. Duda [1967]. Life tables of the population of the city of Jassy. *Rev. Med. Chir. Soc. Med. Nat. Iasi.*, *73*, 673–80.

Eaton, W. W. [1974]. Mental hospitalization as a reinforcement process. *Amer. Sociol. Rev.*, *39*, 252–260.

Elandt-Johnson, R. C. [1973]. Age-at-onset distribution in chronic diseases. A life table approach to analysis of family data. *J. Chronic Dis.*, *26*, 529–45.

El-Badry, M. A. [1969]. Higher female than male mortality in some countries of South Asia: A digest. *J. Amer. Statist. Assoc.*, *64*, 1234–1244.

Elvebeck, L. [1958]. Estimation of survivorship in chronic disease: The actuarial method. *J. Amer. Statist. Assoc.*, *53*, 420–440.

Elvebeck, L. [1966]. Discussion of 'indices of mortality and tests of their statistical significance'. *Hum. Biol.* *38*, 322–324.

Epstein, B. and M. Sobel [1953]. Life testing. *J. Amer. Statist. Assoc.*, *48*, 486–502.

Fabia, J. and M. Drolette [1970]. Life tables up to age 10 for mongols with and without congenital heart defect. *J. Ment. Defic. Res.*, *14*, 235–42.

Feichtinger, G. and H. Hansluwka [1976]. The impact of mortality on the life cycle and the family in Austria. *WHO Technical Report Series* No. 587, 51–78. World Health Organization, Geneva.

Feichtinger, G. [1977]. Methodische problems der familienlebenszyklus-statistik. *Festschrift* zum 60. Geburtstag W. Krelles. Mohr, Tubingen.

Fisher, L. and P. Kanarek [1974]. Presenting censored survival data when censoring and survival times may not be independent. *Reliability and Biometry* (Proschan and Serfling, eds.) *SIAM*, 291–320, Philadelphia.

Fleiss, J. L. [1973]. *Statistical Methods for Rates and Proportions*. Wiley, New York.

Fleiss, J. L., D. L. Dunner, F. Stallone, and R. R. Fieve [1976]. The life table. A method for analyzing longitudinal studies. *Arch. Gen. Psychiatry*, *33*, 107–12.

Flinn, M. W. [1970]. *British Population Growth, 1700–1850*. Macmillan, London.

Frechet, M. [1947]. Sur les expressions analytique de la mortalite variables pour la vie entiere. *J. Societe de Statistique de Paris*, *88*, 261–285.

French, F. E. and J. M. Bierman [1962]. Probability of fetal mortality. *Public Health Reports, 77*, 835–847.

Frost, W. H. [1933]. Risk of persons in familiar contact with pulmonary tuberculosis. *Amer. J. Publ. Hlth., 23*, 426–432.

Frumkin, G. [1954]. Estimation de la qualite des statistiques demographiques. *Proceedings of the World Population Conference, 4*, United Nations, New York.

Fukushima, N. Z. [1974]. A study on the method of constructing abridged life tables and the interpolation for individual years of life. *J. Med. Sci., 20*, 11–48.

Gehan, E. A. [1969]. Estimating survival functions from the life table. *J. Chron. Dis., 21*, 629–44.

George, L. and A. P. Norman [1971]. Life tables for cystic fibrosis. *Arch. Dis. Child, 46*, 139–43.

Gershenson, H. [1961]. *Measurement of Mortality*. Society of Actuaries, Chicago.

Gille, H. [1949]. The demographic history of the Northern European countries in the eighteenth century. *Population Studies, 3*, 3–65.

Gini, C. [1924]. Premieres recherches sur la fecundabilite de la femme. *Proceedings of the International Mathematics Congress*, 889–892, Toronto.

Glick, P. C. and R. Parke [1965]. New approach in studying the life cycle of the family. *Demography, 2*, 187–202.

Glover, J. W. [1921]. *United States Life Tables, 1890, 1901, 1910 and 1901–1910*. Bureau of the Census, Washington.

Gompertz, B. [1825]. On the nature of the function expressive of the law of human mortality. *Phil. Trans. Royal Soc., 155*, 513–593.

Graunt, J. [1662]. *Natural and Political Observations Made upon the Bills of Mortality*. Reprinted by the Johns Hopkins Press, Baltimore, 1939.

Greenwood, M., et al. [1922]. Discussion on the value of life-tables in statistical research. *J. Royal Statist. Soc., 85*, 537–560.

Greenwood, M. [1926]. A report on the natural duration of cancer. *Reports on Public Health and Medical Subjects, 33*, 1–26. H. M. Stationery Office.

Greenwood, M. [1942]. Medical statistics from Graunt to Farr. *Biometrika, 32*, 101–127, 203–225.

Grenander, U. [1956]. On the theory of mortality measurement. *Skandinavisk Aktuarietidskrift, 39*, 1–55.

Greville, T. N. E. [1943]. Short methods of constructing abridged life tables. *Record Amer. Inst. Actuaries, 32*, 29–43.

Greville, T. N. E. [1946]. *United States Life Tables and Actuarial Tables, 1939–41*. National Office of Vital Statistics.

Gurunanjappa, B. S. [1969]. Life tables for Alaska natives. *Public Health Rep., 84*, 65–69.

Haenszel, W. [1950]. A standardized rate for mortality defined in units of lost years of life. *J. Amer. Publ. Hlth. Assoc., 40*, 17–26.

Haenszel, W. (ed.) [1966]. Epidemiological approaches to the study of cancer and other chronic diseases. *Nat. Cancer Instit., Monograph No. 19*.

Hajnal, J. [1950]. Rates of dissolution of marriages in England and Wales, 1938–39. *Papers of the Royal Commission on Population, 2*, 178–187. H. M. Stationery Office, London.

Hakama, M. [1970]. Age adjustment of incidence rates in cancer epidemiology. *Acta Path. Microb. Scand., Suppl. 213*.

Halley, E. [1693]. An estimate of the degrees of the mortality of mankind, drawn from curious tables of the births and funerals at the city of Breslau. *Philos. Trans. Royal Soc., 17*, 596–610, London.

Hanse, M. H., W. N. Hurwitz, and M. A. Bershad [1961]. Measurement errors in censuses and surveys. *Bulletin of the Int. Statist. Inst.*, *38*, Part 2, 359–374, Tokyo.

Hansluwka, H. [1976]. Mortality and the life cycle of the family. Some implications of recent research. *World Health Statistics Report*, *29*, 220–227.

Harris, T. E., P. Meier, and J. W. Tukey [1950]. Timing of the distribution of events between observations. *Human Biol.*, *22*, 249–270.

Heiss, F. [1933]. Die familienstatistik im fragenprogramm der volkzahlungen. *Jahrbucher fur Nationalokonomie und Statistik*, 138 Band–II Folge, Band 83.

Henry, L. [1972]. *On the Measurement of Human Fertility*. Selected Writings. Translated and edited by M. C. Sheps and E. Lapierre-Adamcyk. New York: Elsevier.

Hickey, J. J. [1952]. Survival studies of banded birds. *U.S. Fish Wildlife Ser. Spec. Sci. Reports Wildlife*, *15*, 1–177.

Hill, A. B. [1966]. *Principles of Medical Statistics*. Oxford Univ. Press, New York.

Hoem, J. M. [1970]. Probabilistic fertility models of the life table type. *Theor. Popul. Biol.*, *1*, 12–38.

Hoem, J. M. [1971]. On the interpretation of certain vital rates as averages of underlying forces of transition. *Theor. Popul. Biol.*, *2*, 454–458.

Hoem, J. M. [1975]. The construction of increment-decrement life tables: A comment on articles by R. Schoen and V. Nelson. *Demography*, *12*, 661–4.

Hogg, R. V. and A. T. Craig [1965]. *Introduction to Mathematical Statistics* (2nd ed). Macmillan, New York.

Holford, T. R. [1976]. Life tables with concomitant information. *Biometrics*, *32*, 587–97.

Hyrenius, H. and J. Quist [1970]. Life table technique for the working ages. *Demography*, *7*, 393–9.

Irwin, A. C. [1976]. Life tables as 'predictors' of average longevity. *Can. Med. Assoc.*, *114*, 539–41.

Irwin, J. O. [1949]. The standard error of an estimate of expectation of life. *J. Hygiene*, *47*, 188–189.

Jacobson, P. H. [1964]. Cohort survival for generations since 1840. *Milbank Memorial Fund Quarterly*.

Jordan, C. W., Jr. [1967]. *Life Contingencies* (2nd ed.). Society of Actuaries, Chicago.

Kalton, G. [1968]. Standardization: A technique to control for extraneous variables. *Appl. Statist.*, *17*, 118–136.

Kaplan, E. L. and P. Meier [1958]. Nonparametric estimation from incomplete observations. *J. Amer. Statist. Assoc.*, *53*, 457–481.

Kendall, M. C. and A. Stuart [1961]. *The Advanced Theory of Statistics*, Vol. 2, Griffin, London.

Keyfitz, N. [1966]. A life table that agrees with the data. *J. Amer. Statist. Assoc.*, *61*, 305–312.

Keyfitz, N. [1968]. *Introduction of the Mathematics of Population*. Addison-Wesley, Reading, Massachusetts.

Keyfitz, N. [1970]. Finding probabilities from observed rates, or how to make a life table. *The American Statistician*, *24*, 28–33.

Keyfitz, N. and W. Flieger [1968]. *World Population: An Analysis of Vital Data*. Univ. of Chicago Press, Chicago, Illinois.

Kilpatrick, S. J. [1963]. Mortality comparisons in socio-economic groups. *Appl. Statist.*, *12*, 65–86.

King, G. [1914]. On a short method of constructing an abridged mortality table. *J. Inst. Actuaries*, *48*, 294–303.

Kitagawa, E. M. [1964]. Standardized comparisons in population research. *Demography*, *1*, 296–315.

Kitagawa, E. M. [1966]. Theoretical considerations in the selection of a mortality index, and some empirical comparisons. *Hum. Biol.*, *38*, 293–308.

Kloetzel, K. and J. C. Dias [1968]. Mortality in Chagas' disease: Life-table for the period 1949–1967 in an unselected population. *Rev. Inst. Med. Trop. Sao Paulo*, *10*, 5–8.

Krall, J. M., V. A. Uthoff and J. B. Harley [1975]. A step-up procedure for selecting variables associated with survival. *Biometrics*, *31*, 49–57.

Krieger, G. [1967]. Suicides in San Mateo County. *California Medicine*, *107*, 153–155.

Krishnan, P. [1971]. Divorce tables for females in the United States: 1960. *J. of Marriage and the Family*, *33*, 318–320.

Kruegel, D. L. and J. M. Peck [1974]. Maryland abridged life tables by color and sex: 1969–1971. *Md. State Med. J.*, *23*, 49–55.

Kuzma, J. W. [1967]. A comparison of two life table methods. *Biometrics*, *23*, 51–64.

La Bras, H. [1973]. Parents, grand-parents, bisaieux. *Population*, *28*, 9–38.

Lew, E. A. and F. Seltzer [1970]. Uses of the life table in public health. *Milbank Memorial Fund Quarterly*, *48*, Suppl., 15–37.

Linder, F. E. and R. D. Grove [1959]. Techniques of vital statistics. Reprint of Chapter I-IV. *Vital Statistics Rates in the United States, 1900–1940*. U.S. Government Printing Office, Washington, D.C.

Littell, A. S. [1952]. Estimation of the T-year survival rate from follow-up studies over a limited period of time. *Human Biol.*, *24*, 87–116.

Lopez, A. [1961]. *Problems in Stable Population Theory*. Office of Population Research, Princeton University, Princeton, New Jersey.

Makeham, W. M. [1860]. On the law of mortality and the construction of annuity tables. *J. Inst. Actuaries*, *8*.

Mantel, N. [1974]. Branching experiments: A generalized application of the life-table method. *Proceedings of SIMS Conference on Epidemiology* (D. Ludwig, K. L. Cooke, ed.), 69–74. Society for Industrial and Applied Mathematics, Philadelphia.

Mantel, N. and C. R. Stark [1968]. Computation of indirect-adjusted rates in the presence of confounding. *Biometrics*, *24*, 997–1005.

Mattila, A. and K. Rosendahl [1969]. Factors affecting life expectancy. *Acta. Socio-Med. Scand. 1*, Suppl. 1, 51.

McCann, J. C. [1976]. A technique for estimating life expectancy with crude vital rates. *Demography*, *13*, 259–72.

Medsger, T. A., Jr., A. T. Masi, G. P. Rodnan, T. G. Benedek, and H. Robinson [1971]. Survival with systemic sclerosis (scleroderma). A life-table analysis of clinical and demographic factors in 309 patients. *Ann. Intern. Med.*, *75*, 369–76.

Medsger, T. A., Jr. and A. T. Masi [1973]. Survival with scleroderma. II. A life-table analysis of clinical and demographic factors in 358 male U.S. veteran patients. *J. Chronic Dis.*, *26*, 647–60.

Medsger, T. A., Jr., H. Robinson, and A. T. Masi [1971]. Factors affecting survivorship in polymyositis. A life-table study of 124 patients. *Arthritis Rheum.*, *14*, 249–58.

Menken, J. A. and M. C. Sheps [1972]. The sampling frame as a determinant of observed distributions of duration variables. *Population Dynamics*, T. N. E. Greville, ed. New York: Academic Press, 57–87.

Merrell, M. and L. E. Shulman [1955]. Determination of prognosis in chronic disease, illustrated by systemic lupus erythematosus. *J. Chron. Dis.*, *1*, 12–32.

Miller, R. S. and J. L. Thomas [1958]. The effect of larval crowding and body size on the longevity of adult Drosophila Melanogaster. *Ecology*, *39*, 118–125.

Mitra, S. [1973]. On the efficiency of the estimates of life table functions. *Demography*, *10*, 421–426.

Mould, R. F. [1976]. Calculation of survival rates by the life table and other methods. *Clin. Radiol.*, *27*, 33–8.

Muhsam, H. V. [1976]. Family and demography. *J. Comparative Family Studies*, *VII*, No. 2.

Mukherjee, S. P. and S. K. Das [1975]. Abridged life tables for rural West Bengal, 1969. *Indian J. Public Health*, *19*, 3–9.

Myers, R. J. [1964]. Analysis of mortality in the Soviet Union according to 1958–59 life tables. *Transactions, Society of Actuaries*.

Murie, A. [1944]. The wolves of Mount McKinley. *Fauna of the National Parks of the U.S. Fauna Series*, *5*, U.S. Dept. of Interior, National Park Service, Washington, D.C.

Myers, R. J. [1959]. Statistical measures in the marital life cycles of men and women. *Internationaler Bevolkerungskongres*, 229–233. Union Internationale pur l'etude Scientific de la Population, Wien.

Nanjo, Z. [1974]. A study on the method of constructing abridged life tables and the interpolation for individual years of life. *Tukushima J. Med. Sci.*, *20*, 11–48.

National Center for Health Statistics [1974]. *Vital Statistics of the United States*, 1970, Volume 2, Mortality. U.S. Government Printing Office, Washington, D.C.

National Office of Vital Statistics [1959]. Method of constructing the 1949–51 national, divisional, and state life tables. *Vital Statistics—Special Reports*, *41*, 1959.

Neidhardt, F. O. [1971]. Estimation of survival in life table methods, applied to a sample of prostatectomies. *Nord. Med.*, *85*, 129–30.

Neumann, H. G. [1970]. Evaluation of the results of intrauterine contraception. Two year analysis of the Rostock studies by means of the life table method of Tietze and Potter. *Geburtshilfe Frauenheilkd*, *30*, 537–47.

Oechsli, F. W. [1975]. A population model based on a life table that includes marriage and parity. *Theor. Popul. Biol.*, *2*, 229–45.

Oleinick, A. and N. Mantel [1970]. Family studies in systemic lupus erythematosus. II. Mortality among siblings and offspring of index cases with a statistical appendix concerning life table analysis. *J. Chronic Dis.*, *22*, 617–24.

Oster, J., M. Mikkelsen, and A. Nielsen [1975]. Mortality and life-table in Down's syndrome. *Acta. Paediatr. Scand.*, *64*, 322–6.

Oficina Sanitaria Panamericana [1940]. Consultas. *Boletin de la Oficina Sanitaria Panamericana*, *19*, 283–285.

Pachal, T. K. [1975]. A note on the relation between expectation of life at birth and life table mortality rate for the age group 0–4 years. *Indian J. Public Health*, *19*, 9–10.

Padley, R. [1959]. Cause of death statements in Ceylon: A study in levels of diagnostic reporting. *Bulletin of the World Health Organization*, *20*, 677–695.

Park, C. B. [1955]. Statistical observations on death rates and causes of death in Korea. *Bulletin of the World Health Organization*, *13*, 69–108.

Pascua, M. [1952]. Evolution of mortality in Europe during the twentieth century. *Epidemiological and Vital Statistics Report* (World Health Organization), *5*, 4–8.

Paynter, R. A. [1947]. The fate of banded Kent Island Herring Gulls. *Bird Banding*, *18*, 156–170.

Pearl, R. [1940]. *Introduction to Medical Biometry and Statistics*, W. B. Saundners, Philadelphia and London.

Pearl, R. and J. R. Miner [1935]. Experimental studies of the duration of life XIV. The comparative mortality of certain lower organisms. *Rev. Biol.*, *10*, 60–79.

Pearson, K. [1902]. On the change in expectation of life in man during a period of circa 2000 years. *Biometrika*, *1*, 261–264.

Pressat, R. [1972]. *Demographic Analysis*. Translated by J. Matras. Aldine-Atherton, New York.

Rao, C. R. [1945]. Information and accuracy attainable in the estimation of statistical parameters. *Bull. Calcutta Math. Soc.*, *37*, 81–91.

Reed, L. H. and M. Merrill [1939]. A short method for constructing an abridged life table. *Amer. J. Hygiene*, *30*, 33–62.

Reid, D. D. and G. A. Rose [1964]. Assessing the comparability of mortality statistics. *Brit. Med. J.*, *2*, 1437–1439.

The Registrar-General's Decennial Supplement, England and Wales, 1921 [1933]. Part III, *Estimates of Population, Statistics of Marriages, Births, and Deaths, 1911–1920*, xxxiii–lxix. H. M. Stationery Office, London.

Registrar-General's Statistical Review of England and Wales for the year 1934 [1936]. *New Annual Series*, No. 14, H. M. Stationery Office, London.

Registrar-General's Statistical Review of England and Wales for the year 1937 [1940]. *New Annual Series*, No. 17, H. M. Stationery Office, London.

Robinson, M. J. and A. P. Norman [1975]. Life tables for cystic fibrosis. *Arch. Dis. Child.*, *50*, 962–5.

Rodriquez, G. and J. Hobcraft [1980]. Illustrative analysis: Life table analysis of birth intervals in Columbia. *World Fertility Survey Reports* #16.

Ryder, N. B. [1973]. Influence of changes in the family cycle upon family life— Reproductive behavior and the family life cycle. *Symposium on Population and the Family*, Honolulu.

Ryder, N. B. [1976]. Methods in measuring the family life cycle. Session 2.2 of the Mexico Conference of the IUSSP. *IUSSP Newsletter* No. 5, 25–26.

Sadie, J. L. [1970]. An evaluation of demographic data pertaining to the non-white population of South Africa. *South African J. Econ.*, *38*, 1–34.

Santas, J. L. [1972]. Evaluation of the mortality ratio and life expectancy levels in the State of Sao Paulo, Brazil in 1970. *Rev. Saude Publica*, *6*, 269–72.

Schwartz, D. and P. Lazar [1963]. Taux de mortalite par une cause donnee de deces en tenant compte des autres causes de deces ou de disparition. Unite de Recherches Statistiques de l'Institut National d'Hygiene, Ministere de la Sante Publique, France.

Saveland, W. and P. C. Glick [1969]. First marriage decrement tables by color and sex for the United States in 1958–60. *Demography*, *6*, 243–260.

Schoen, R. [1975]. Constructing increment-decrement life tables. *Demography*, *12*, 313, 324.

Schoen, R. and V. E. Nelson [1974]. Marriage, divorce and mortality: A life table analysis. *Demography*, *11*, 267–290.

Seigel, D. G. [1975]. Life table rates and person month ratios as summary statistics for contraceptive trials. *J. Steroid Biochem.*, *6*, 933–6.

Sewell, W. E. [1972]. Life table analysis of the results of coronary surgery. *Chest*, *61*, 481.

Shapiro, S., E. W. Jones and P. M. Densen [1962]. A life table of pregnancy terminations and correlated fetal loss. *Milbank Memorial Fund Quarterly*, *40*, 7–45.

Shapiro, S., E. R. Schlesinger, and R. E. I. Nesbitt [1968]. *Infant, Perinatal, Maternal and Childhood Mortality in the United States*. American Public Health Association, Vital and Health Statistics Monographs, Harvard University Press, Cambridge, Mass.

Sheps, M. C. [1958]. Shall we count the living or the dead? *New Eng. J. Med.*, *259*, 1210–14.

Sheps, M. C. [1959]. An examination of some methods of comparing several rates or proportions. *Biometrics*, *15*, 87–97.

Sheps, M. C. [1961]. Marriage and mortality. *Amer. J. Publ. Hlth.*, *51*, 547–55.

Sheps, M. C. and J. A. Menken [1973]. *Mathematical Models of Conception and Birth*. Chicago: University of Chicago Press.

Sirken, M. G. [1964]. Comparisons of two methods of constructing abridged life tables by reference to a 'standard' table. *Vital and Health Statistics*, Series 2, No. 4, 1–11. National Center for Health Statistics, U.S. Dept. of Health, Education and Welfare.

Smith, D. and N. Keyfitz [1977]. *Mathematical Demography*—Selected papers. Springer-Verlag, New York.

Snow, F. C. [1920]. An elementary rapid method of constructing an abridged life table. Supplement to the 75th Annual Report of the Registrar General of Births, Deaths, and Marriages in England and Wales. Part II. Abridged Life Tables.

Spiegelman, M. [1968]. *Introduction to Demography* (revised edition). Cambridge, Harvard University Press.

Spiegelman, M. and H. H. Marks [1966]. Empirical testing of standards for the age adjustment of death rates by the direct method. *Hum. Biol.*, *38*, 280–92.

Srinivasan, K. [1966]. An application of a probability model to the study of interlive birth intervals. *Sankhya*, 28B: 175–192.

Stark, C. R. and N. Mantel [1966]. Effects of maternal age and birth order on the risk of mongolism and leukemia. *J. Natl. Cancer Inst.*, *37*, 687–693.

Stolnitz, G. J. [1956]. *Life Tables from Limited Data: A Demographic Approach*. Office of Population Research, Princeton University, Princeton, New Jersey.

Suchindran, C. M., N. K. Namboodir, and K. West [1979]. Increment-decrement tables for human reproduction. *J. Biosocial Sci.*, *11* (4), 443–456.

Sullivan, J. M. [1971]. A review of Taiwanese infant and child mortality statistics 1961–1968. *Taiwan Population Studies Working Paper No. 10*. Ann Arbor, University of Michigan Population Studies Center.

Swartout, H. O. and R. G. Webster [1940]. To what degree are mortality statistics dependable? *Amer. J. Publ. Hlth.*, *30*, 811–815.

Taylor, W. F. [1964]. On the methodology of measuring the probability of fetal death in a prospective study. *Hum. Biol.*, *36*, 86–103.

Thylstrup, A. and I. Rolling [1975]. The life table method in clinical dental research. *Community Dent. Oral Epidemiol.*, *3*, 5–10.

United Nations, Department of Economic and Social Affairs [1955]. *Manuals on methods of estimating population*, ST/SOA/Ser. A. Population Studies No. 23, Manual II. *Methods of appraisal of quality of basic data for population estimates*. United Nations, New York.

United Nations, Department of Economic and Social Affairs [1958]. *Handbook of population census methods*. Ser. E, No. 5, Rev. 1, Vol. I. *General aspects of a population census*. United Nations, New York.

United Nations, Department of Economic and Social Affairs [1967]. *Manuals on methods of estimating population*, ST/SOA/Ser. A. Manual IV. Methods of estimating basic demographic measures from incomplete data.

United Nations Statistical Office, Department of Economic and Social Affairs

[1955]. *Handbook of Vital Statistics Methods*. Ser. F., No. 7, United Nations, New York.

United Nations Statistical Office, Department of Economic and Social Affairs [1971]. *Demographic Yearbook*, 1970, 22nd edition, United Nations, New York.

van den Berg, B. J. and J. Yerushalmy [1969]. Studies on convulsions in young children. I. Incidence of febrile and nonfebrile convulsions by age and other factors. *Pediatric Research*, *3*, 298–304.

Walker, A. E., H. K. Leuchs, H. Lechtape-Gruter, W. F. Caveness and C. Kretschmann [1971]. The life expectancy of head injured men with and without epilepsy. *Zentralb. Neurochir.*, *32*, 3–9.

Weibull, W. [1939]. A statistical theory of the strength of material. *Ing. Vetenskaps Akad. Handl.*, *151*.

Weiss, K. M. [1973]. A method for approximating age-specific fertility in the construction of life tables for anthropological populations. *Human Biology*, *45*, 195–210.

Westergaard, H. [1916]. Scope and methods of statistics. *J. Amer. Statist. Assoc.*, *15*, 260–264.

Wiesler, H. [1954]. Une methods simple pour la construction de table de mortalite abredees. *World Population Conference*, Vol. IV, United Nations, New York.

Wilson, E. G. [1938]. The standard deviation for sampling for life expectancy. *J. Amer. Statist. Assoc.*, *33*, 705–708.

World Health Organization [1967]. The accuracy and comparability of death statistics. *Chronicle*, *21*, 11–17.

World Health Organization [1965]. *World Health Statistics Annual*. Geneva, Switzerland.

World Health Organization [1977]. *World Health Statistics Annual*. Geneva, Switzerland.

Yerushalmy, J. [1951]. A mortality index for use in place of the age-adjusted death rate. *Amer. J. Publ. Hlth.*, *41*, 907–922.

Yerushalmy, J. [1969]. The California Child Health and Development Studies. Study design, and some illustrative findings on congenital heart disease. *Excerpta Medica International Congress Series No. 204, Congenital Malformations. Proc., Third International Conference*, The Hague, the Netherlands, 299–306.

Yule, G. U. [1924]. A mathematical theory of evolution based on the conclusion of Dr. J. C. Willis, F.R.S. *Phil. Trans. Royal Soc.* (London), *B213*, 21–87.

Yule, G. U. [1934]. On some points relating to vital statistics, more especially statistics of occupational mortality. *J. Royal Statist. Soc.*, *97*, 1–84.

Zahl, S. [1955]. A Markov process model for follow-up studies. *Hum. Biol.*, *27*, 90–120.

Author Index

Subject Index